PUDGE

ALSO BY DOUG WILSON

Brooks: The Biography of Brooks Robinson

The Bird: The Life and Legacy of Mark Fidrych

Fred Hutchinson and the 1964 Cincinnati Reds

Doug Wilson

PUDGE

THE BIOGRAPHY *of* CARLTON FISK

THOMAS DUNNE BOOKS
ST. MARTIN'S PRESS ♨ NEW YORK

THOMAS DUNNE BOOKS.
An imprint of St. Martin's Press.

PUDGE. Copyright © 2015 by Doug Wilson. All rights reserved. Printed in the United States of America. For information, address St. Martin's Press, 175 Fifth Avenue, New York, N.Y. 10010.

www.thomasdunnebooks.com
www.stmartins.com

The Library of Congress Cataloging-in-Publication Data
is available upon request.

ISBN 978-1-250-06543-8 (hardcover)
ISBN 978-1-4668-7234-9 (e-book)

Our books may be purchased in bulk for promotional, educational, or business use. Please contact your local bookseller or the Macmillan Corporate and Premium Sales Department at (800) 221-7945, extension 5442, or by e-mail at MacmillanSpecialMarkets@macmillan.com.

First Edition: October 2015

10 9 8 7 6 5 4 3 2 1

Contents

PUDGE

Prologue

YOUR MOTHER ALWAYS WARNED YOU that nothing good ever happened after midnight. But your mother wasn't in a dugout at Fenway Park that night. It was 12:33 on the morning of October 22, 1975. The sixth game of the 1975 World Series had started the day before but, despite four hours of furious play, nothing had been decided yet. The Series had already mesmerized the nation; a back-and-forth affair with three games decided by one run, two involving ninth-inning come-backs. Both teams, laden with future Hall of Famers and unforgettable characters, had given much more than expected. The Series had res-cued the previously deteriorating baseball television ratings and revived interest in the game formerly known as the national pastime.

The Cincinnati Reds led three games to two heading into the night; a Boston Red Sox loss in this one would end the Series. By the time the clock passed midnight, Game Six was already being hailed as the greatest World Series game in history. A dramatic three-run pinch-hit home run in the eighth inning had tied the game and brought the home team back from the dead. The potential winning run had been thrown out at the plate in the bottom of the ninth. A miraculous catch against the fence in right field had saved the game in the top of the 11th. As word of the drama spread and late-night viewers tuned in to find their shows bumped but stayed on to witness the spectacle, it became the most watched World Series game ever.

Now, in the bottom of the 12th inning, Red Sox catcher Carlton Fisk made his customary slow, deliberate walk to the plate with a bat in his hand. The man known to all as "Pudge" was 27 years old. Although he had won the Rookie of the Year Award only four years earlier, it seemed as though he had been playing in Boston forever. Listed at six feet, two inches, his square-shouldered, erect posture made him appear much larger. He was recognized as one of the best catchers in baseball and, more importantly to Red Sox fans, he was a native New Englander who embodied the solid virtues of the region—a beloved homegrown hero who allowed millions of New Englanders to live their dreams through him.

Fisk had established himself as a leader who lived by a strict code—a man with a perfectionist's drive to excel and a single-minded devotion to duty who tolerated nothing less than maximum effort, from himself or his teammates. He had battled back from a horrific knee injury in 1974 and a broken arm in the spring of 1975, returning to his team on a white steed at midseason to help lead them to the postseason for only the second time in 29 years. The fact that two of his four major league seasons had been cut in half by injuries caused Fisk to be considered fragile. He had no way of knowing that he would overcome his injuries and go on to a 24-year career in which he would participate in the major leagues in four decades—a testament to his hard work and determination—and that he would eventually catch more games than any major leaguer before him and be selected to the All-Century Team and the Hall of Fame.

Fisk also had no way of knowing that both he and Major League Baseball were standing on the precipice of colossal change that in large part would be brought on by what transpired this night. He would be directly responsible for a spark that would combine with a historic court ruling that winter to ignite an uncontrollable chain reaction of increased fan interest, television revenue, and player salaries that would affect the game and its economics in unimaginable ways. He would not only live through the advent of agents, strikes, free agency, and court battles, but he would often be at the center of the triumphs and heartbreaks they would cause.

Everyone in New England made their best foxhole deals with their makers as Fisk approached the plate. Before he stepped into the batter's box, he went through his familiar routine, mannerisms that were mimicked and loved by Red Sox fans: he tugged on his sleeves, arranged the dirt of the right-handed batter's box with his feet, flexed his shoulders twice, then held the bat with his hands on each end and stretched over his head. He shook his head back and forth, held the bat in front of his face and examined the barrel. Then he stepped in the box and tapped the outside corner of the plate with the bat.

On the mound was rookie Pat Darcy, who had completed two innings in order. Darcy's first pitch was high and slightly inside and Fisk barely moved. The second pitch was low, between the belt and knees, starting on the outside part of the plate but moving in. The Reds' catcher, Johnny Bench, reached down and left to catch it, but the ball never got there. Fisk unleashed a powerful compact swing and met the ball squarely.

All good hitters learn, through repetition, the welcome sensation of when they get all of one—the unmistakable feeling that goes directly from their hands to their heart. Fisk knew as soon as he made contact that he had hit it hard enough to clear the 37-foot Fenway left field wall.

As Fisk, the umpire, Bench, on-deck hitter Fred Lynn, and millions more watched, the ball soared high into the foggy Boston night, directly down the left field line. For an instant, it appeared to have a slight tail to the left, toward foul ground. Fisk took two sideways crab hops toward first, but didn't run. He continued watching the flight of the ball that carried the fate of his team. He had certainly gotten enough to get it over the wall.

There was only one question now . . .

1 The New England Fisks

IN ORDER TO FULLY UNDERSTAND Carlton Fisk, his baseball career and his personality, it is necessary, above all, to know this: he was from New England. Carlton Fisk represented the region and all that it symbolized more than any major league baseball player in history. The principles, the strong will and beliefs, the work ethic, and, perhaps, the stubbornness—he bore New England as a badge of honor.

Carlton Fisk was as New England as any one person could be. He couldn't have been more New England if his great, great, great, great, great, great grandfather had come over on the *Mayflower*. He didn't—but Phineas Fiske did depart from Suffolk County, England, with his young family sometime between 1620 and 1640. He settled in an area of the Massachusetts Bay Colony that was soon called Middlesex County, a county that included settlements at Lexington and Concord, and raised his family near Groton, which today is just north of the I-495 loop around Boston.

The Fiskes (the "e" would be dropped from the family name in the mid-1800s) were like the other arrivals to that part of the New World— they came not to plunder but to build. They built farms, families, and eventually a new nation. Fiskes were not idlers or dreamers, they were doers. And they were not a wandering bunch. It was roughly 150 years before the first Fiske decided to see what was beyond the mountains: Samuel Fiske made the 80-or-so-mile trek northwest to Claremont, New Hampshire, in the late 1700s. Over the next 200 years, the clan would move exactly 11 miles, just south to Charlestown.

Like most of their neighbors, the early Fisks were farmers. As David McCullough wrote in *John Adams*: "The New England farmer was his own man who owned his own land, a freeholder, and thus the equal of anyone." Cecil Fisk was born into this line of proud, independent, hard workers in 1913. Cecil learned responsibility and self-reliance from his father, Sabin, who, in addition to farming, served as postmaster and delivered the rural mail around Charlestown in a horse-drawn buggy for forty years beginning in 1914. When snow piled up, teenage Cecil would have to help deliver the mail. He learned you didn't complain, you just did what needed to be done.

Cecil Fisk grew to love sports, both participating and watching. He was an excellent basketball player in high school, graduating from Charlestown High in 1931. A tough-as-nails competitor with a feared two-handed set shot, he starred for traveling semipro basketball teams that competed up and down the Connecticut River Valley as late as 1947. He and the few other tennis enthusiasts maintained the only court in town, and he won the New Hampshire state tennis championship in 1932 and 1933.

Cecil found his perfect complement in active, outgoing Leona Lundin. They were married in 1941 and soon thereafter bought a white, nineteenth-century clapboard house on Elm Street—just off Main Street—in Charlestown from his uncle. It was a homestead in which they would live together for the next 70 years. There were a lot of Fisks in the area; Sabin had been the youngest of six boys, all raised in Charlestown. Cecil and Leona's house sat just across a field from the house in which Cecil was born, the house that one of his sons, Cedric, would later inhabit (the Fisks still didn't move around a lot). Cecil and Leona had a son, Calvin, in 1944. They would add Carlton on December 26, 1947, then Cedric two years later, followed the next year by Conrad, and finally two girls, June and Janet. The kids were born in Bellows Falls, Vermont, because that was the closest hospital.

Like his father, Cecil was a large, powerful man. If he ever took your hand in his big paw, you had better brace yourself—he believed in the value of a firm handshake. With a square jaw and a steady gaze, Cecil was stoic, methodical, and not given to idle chatter. If something needed to be said, he'd look you right in the eye and say it, usually in as few words as possible. Serious and principled, he was known to be a man with an uncompromising value system of right and wrong. He expected 100 percent honesty and honor. He demanded hard work from himself and had little tolerance for others who didn't share his principles—*do something the right way or don't do it at all.*

And Cecil was tough. No one in Charlestown ever knew exactly how tough Cecil was because, quite frankly, no one ever wanted to find out bad enough. "He wasn't mean," says one friend, "but if you didn't know him you might think he was just by looking at him. He just wasn't very emotional or outgoing. But if something needed to be done around town, you could always count on him to be there to do it." Cecil was a solid citizen and his word was respected. He was a member of the town finance committee, town council moderator from 1954 to 1973, served on the school board, and was a longtime member of the Charlestown Historical Society.

A sober man, Cecil Fisk had exactly two drinks each year: a scotch and ginger on Thanksgiving and Christmas. Despite his serious demeanor, Cecil enjoyed music and was known to cut an impressive rug on the dance floor on special occasions. "He liked Lawrence Welk and Mitch Miller [of *Sing Along with Mitch*]," says his daughter Janet. "Other than ball games, those were the only two TV shows he watched."

Cecil didn't believe in excuses or concessions to trivial things like age or pain. He routinely played in the school's alumni basketball game into his seventies. One day, as an octogenarian, he was working up in a tree with a chain saw and came in bloody. "Got nicked on my calf," he said when asked. Concerned at the amount of blood covering his pants from the "nick," family members had to work to convince him to go to the clinic to get the thing taken care of—it took 14 stitches. Cecil's father, Sabin, would live to be 96; his only sibling, Beulah, 92. Cecil himself would pass in 2011, during his 98th year. It would be said that his passing was somewhat surprising; he had been looking good and was chopping wood only the day before. Hearty people, those Fisks.

Located along the Connecticut River in the southwest corner of the state, the town of Charlestown was small, having about a thousand residents by 1950. It was a rural area: a couple of stop signs, a flashing caution light, one drugstore, two small grocery stores, a few gas stations, several churches, a bar, and a post office. And that was about it. Bowling alleys, movie theaters, and restaurants were luxuries to be found in the towns 15 or 20 miles away. But Charlestown was a pretty little town, surrounded by beautiful rolling wooded hills, with tree-lined streets and well-maintained nineteenth-century Federal style homes along Main Street (actually Main Street was just an area where you slowed down temporarily on Route 12 while driving from Walpole to Claremont).

Charlestown didn't have a mayor. Town business was run by an elected board of three selectmen. Citizens were encouraged to voice their opinions at town meetings; everyone had an opportunity to have their say. It was the traditional form of New England democracy, with a natural distaste for tyranny or having one person telling everyone what to do. Independence was not just a word thrown around; it was a way of life, firmly representing the New Hampshire motto of "Live free or die."

There was no anonymity in Charlestown, for better or for worse. Everyone knew everyone else and also knew their parents and grandparents. They met and discussed their lives regularly at church, while walking in town and at school and public events. Houses and cars were left unlocked and nobody seemed to notice or care. It was a friendly, peaceful place with few problems. Typical was Chief of Police Ralph Willoughby's annual report to the Board of Selectmen for 1964, which revealed five arrests for assault, two for drunkenness, two citations for throwing refuse on the highway, and one for reckless driving—no one ever referred to Charlestown as "Little Chicago."

Charlestown residents were proud of their town and their upbringing. Those who later moved from the area frequently returned for the Old Home Days celebrations held every five years. It was the type of place where everyone always knew where they were from; the heritage was ingrained.

Also ingrained was their allegiance to the sports teams of Boston. Whereas during the previous century, residents of the region had aligned themselves politically and economically with Boston, so it was when it came to professional sports. Every town in the area big enough to have two churches with tall white spires had a radio station that blasted Red Sox games throughout the summer. Everyone was a Red Sox fan. There were no other teams as far as they were concerned. They'd listened to the games since birth. Their parents listened to the games. Their grandparents listened to them. The Red Sox meant a lot.

There were jobs to be had across the Connecticut River in the mill towns of Springfield and Bellows Falls, Vermont; the type of jobs in which useful things were produced with pride. The mills that dotted the banks of the river especially boomed during World War II, and made washers, bolts, nuts, rifles, parts for jeeps and tanks—everything a country needed for modern warfare. They also produced iron castings, organs, carriages, paper, and farm machinery. Cecil, like a lot of his neighbors, took employment over there. He worked as a machinist at the Jones and Lamson Machine Tool Company in Springfield for 39 years, until retiring in 1978. He was a hardworking craftsman, skilled with a lathe.

Cecil Fisk also worked his land. Good old Yankee resourcefulness was learned in the Fisk household. He had a 1950 tractor that he maintained himself and kept running well enough to pull a float in the Old Home parade in 2010 when he was 97 and the tractor was 60—and they both looked to be in good shape. Cecil and Leona grew most of what their family ate. They had vegetables, fruits, blueberries, blackberries, and strawberries. They kept a dairy cow, beef cattle, chickens, and pigs. Each year, Cecil took his vacation from the Machine Company to coincide with haying season. Cecil would later tell an inquiring sportswriter, "In these parts, survival meant hard work." They weren't idle words. His son Carlton would tell the same writer, "My parents provided for six kids very well on $6,000 a year."

It was a good thing that Cecil grew what the family ate. The boys were big eaters. "I never knew that all boys didn't eat like my brothers until I moved away," says Janet. "I had no idea. But it's unbelievable how much they would put away. They'd come home from school and eat five or six big cinnamon rolls and drink a quart of milk—each. During corn season, they would each eat four or five ears of corn, and that was with the rest of their meal. Looking back, they should have all weighed 400 pounds. You can't believe how much they would eat."

Dinner was a ritual in the Fisk family. Everyone was there, every night, no excuses. They all took their set spots around the large oval table, which dominated the small dining room. Cecil, at the head of the table, next to a stack of plates, presided. He dished out what he felt each kid should eat and passed the plates. No one left until it was all gone.

Cecil Fisk cast a giant shadow over the childhood of his kids. They learned to be accountable. The only "self" he taught them about came in self-effacing, self-control, and self-reliance. *Think before you do something. Don't let someone else do something for you that you can do yourself.* With Cecil, there was right and there was wrong; nothing else. Gray areas were for people who couldn't make up their minds. He made sure that he passed his work ethic and his ideals to his growing family. There were always jobs that needed to be done around the house and the kids were expected to do them as soon as they were old enough.

And old enough came pretty early—Janet learned to drive the family tractor when she was nine. If the chores didn't get done, there was no television that night or, sometimes, the long switch that hung above the back door got taken down.

The cow had to be milked every morning, no matter how cold (or through how much snow) the walk from the house to the barn. Each kid had a section of the garden to keep in the summer and an area of the driveway to shovel in the winter. "We had chores to do," Carlton said in 2000, speaking of his childhood. "We were expected to be involved and responsible, accountable within the family. A few of us sometimes decided we didn't want to be accountable and it turned out to be painful. There were consequences. I'm sure that had a lot to do with the work ethic we approached our careers by."

"He taught us a value system," says Calvin. "You shoveled your neighbor's walk because it needed to be done and you didn't ask for anything. If you didn't weed the garden right, you went back out and did it until it was done right. Be humble, don't brag or tell people how good you are."

Cecil didn't believe in giving allowances just for doing the chores. There was no reward for doing something that needed to be done. If the kids wanted money, they knew how to get it—work. Young Carlton had a paper route for years—not an easy task in the frigid New Hampshire winters. He walked to each house and placed the paper between the storm door and front door. Carelessly fling the paper toward the house from the road? Not acceptable. *Do the job the right way or don't do it at all.* He shoveled snow, mowed lawns, and, as a teen, worked for the sewer department and poured concrete for a contractor.

Along with the other town kids, Carlton and his brothers also worked in the fields on nearby farms during hay season. They'd spend the day helping get hay in, baling it and heaving it up to the barn lofts—hard, sweaty, itchy work. Once Carlton complained that a farmer paid him 50 cents an hour for baling when earlier he had gotten a dollar an hour from another. He got no sympathy from his father. "What would you do for money if you weren't getting the 50 cents?" was Cecil's reply. Unable to argue with that logic, Carlton resumed his haying career.

Cecil laid down the law and demanded a lot from his children. A lot. "He mellowed a bit later but when we were growing up he was a taskmaster," says Janet. "It was hard. Expectations were very high. It was just built into our personalities and character that we should succeed in anything we set out to do. Good enough wasn't acceptable."

"All their kids were grounded and well behaved," says one friend. "They made good grades in school and never got into any trouble. In high school, some of the rest of us might be out having a beer sometimes, but never any of them."

Whatever Cecil said was the way it was. His kids never won an argument, even if they were right, until he said so. Athletic even into his seventies, Cecil would occasionally remind the kids that he was still the top bull in the herd. Once when Calvin was in high school, he was shooting baskets when Cecil came in from work. Cecil took off his heavy coat and boots and challenged his son to a free-throw contest: "Shoot until you make one, then shoot until you miss." Calvin, who happened to be the state's leading free throw shooter as a senior, made 19 in a row and thought, "That should be enough for the old man." Cecil proceeded to sink 58 in a row. *Never be satisfied, you can always do better.*

Years later, in the clubhouse of the Boston Red Sox, a coach would say to Cecil, "Hey, you're Carlton's dad, huh?" Cecil replied matter-of-factly, "No, Carlton is my son."

The Fisk house seemed very small with all the big kids crammed into two bedrooms; and one bathroom for the whole house. Privacy was not something to be found in the Fisk house; or in the neighborhood. It was not a place for loners. The Fisk kids were active and competed regularly. "Everything we played was competitive," says Calvin. "But I think it was more of a personal competitiveness; you competed against yourself to see what you could do."

While they may have competed against themselves, they showed little mercy against their siblings. It was not uncommon for Leona to watch the kids head off to play basketball and then see them show up later bloody with black eyes. "Yeah, you bet we were all competitive in the family," says Janet. "It was 'Anything you can do, I can do.' Even for us girls."

No child of Cecil Fisk would have ever been happy with a mere participation trophy. All the Fisk kids were great athletes. Calvin, three years older than Carlton, may have been the best of the bunch. Not quite as tall as Carlton, but just as rugged and perhaps stronger, Calvin could play any sport. You name it, tennis, Ping-Pong, golf, anything he picked up, he was a natural. He was a star on the school's soccer, basketball, and baseball teams. He could throw an axe and split a block of wood from a dozen paces. Conrad pitched the local high school to a state championship in baseball, but a disc injury sustained in American Legion ball ended his career. Cedric had a higher batting average in high school than any of his brothers. June played on several state champion softball teams in high school (coached by her mother). Janet, in addition to playing on the championship softball teams, also won several state championships in basketball. She was such an athlete that while learning to play tennis in her early twenties, she beat one of her brother's professional baseball teammates, Dwight Evans.

Despite the talent and accomplishments, praise from their father was given about as easily as allowance for chores. Cecil was a perfectionist who raised his kids to be perfectionists. Once, Calvin scored 29 points in a basketball game, 14–16 from the field and 1 of 2 from the free-throw line. After the game, his dad had one comment: "How'd you miss that free throw?"

"I never heard Cecil compliment any of the kids about anything they did," says Jim Hogancamp, a friend of the kids who lived a few doors down. "That was their mother's job. I didn't think of Cecil as overbearing, but he always felt you could do better. That was the way it was for him. There was no room for error. No excuses. He always told us kids, 'whatever you do, you ought to do it right.' There was no reason for anything other than perfection."

"With him you didn't dwell on the things you did right," Carlton said of his father later. "Those were pretty much expected. What you thought about instead was the things you didn't do right. That was something my father taught all of us: you might not be good enough to be the best, but at least you were as good as you could be. You never accepted second best out of yourself."

"It was a motivating factor for all of us just to receive some sign of approval," Carlton said in 1990. "He had a hard view of sports. He wouldn't tolerate people who didn't bust their butts, no matter if it was just a pickup game." That trait would rub off on some of the kids.

Cecil Fisk loved his children and was proud of how they grew up, but he was not the kind of guy to show it. He was a man of his generation, only more so. His job wasn't to be their buddy, it was to make sure they turned out all right.

While Cecil was the undisputed ruler of the house, Leona Fisk cast a giant shadow in her own way. She was a woman of boundless energy, optimism, good spirits, and infinite talents. Known to everyone as Lee, she provided the emotion, the hugs, and the outward expressions of love for the family. Everyone in town loved and respected Lee Fisk.

A remarkable woman, Lee not only performed the multitude of daily tasks involved in raising six children, she embraced them. She took care of the garden and did all the cooking, cleaning, and sewing. Her flowers around the house were the envy of the town. She put up endless jars of canned corn, beans, jams, and jelly. She served as Cub Scout den leader (all the area kids wanted to be in her den), did crafts for church, taught kindergarten several years, and later coached the high school girls softball team. She had a beautiful alto voice and sang at church into her nineties. And she still took time to play with all the kids in the yard and never missed one of their athletic events.

Like Cecil preached, she wasn't satisfied with just doing these things, she excelled at them all. "If I needed a dress for something, I would tell her what kind of collar and sleeves I wanted and by the end of the week it would be made," says Janet. "And it would be perfect."

"She was a great cook," adds Calvin. She was renowned for her homemade cinnamon rolls, which she made almost every day and placed in a large stack on the kitchen table, ready for anyone who came by—and a lot of people came by just for the cinnamon rolls.

"They were great," says Walter Piletz, one of the kids' friends. "We'd stop by the house and there were always some there." Later in high school, she would bring a basket of them to pass out on the baseball bus.

"She had this shredded wheat molasses bread that was just unbelievable," says Janet. "We would all fight to see who got the middle piece—it just melted in your mouth. My mouth is watering now just thinking about it."

"Lee was the ideal mother in my opinion," says Jim Hogancamp, who, although he left town for college 51 years ago, still stops in to visit and take Lee to dinner. "If you went to the Sears and Roebuck catalog and ordered a perfect mother, it would be her."

Lee was also said to be one of the best athletes in town. She had been a great fast-pitch softball player growing up and had frequently played on men's teams. She once broke up a no-hitter with a late-inning hit in a men's game. She held records for years at the candle pin bowling alley in Claremont. Legend had it that she bowled so hard she once split a head pin in half. Lee frequently came out and joined in games in her yard with neighborhood kids. They got the impression that she was having more fun than they were. And they never ceased to be amazed by her athletic ability. "She could throw and hit as well as any man," says Brad Weeks, a year younger than Carlton. "You'd never want to get in a game of burnout with Mrs. Fisk."

"She could throw perfect spirals with a football," says Hogancamp, who later played college basketball. "When we were in high school, she could kick a football farther than me. And I wasn't exactly handicapped."

Sunday mornings Lee would fix a large breakfast, get dressed, put a roast in the oven, then walk everyone the four blocks to St. Paul's Episcopal Church, where she taught Sunday School. Afterward they would return home and she'd put a big Sunday dinner on the table. "Mom did all that stuff all the time," says Calvin. "She was a wonder woman."

"And she never complained," says Janet.

Lee gives a dismissive wave at Janet's comment. "What was there to complain about?" she asks. "It was stuff that had to be done." And there is the Fisk work ethic in a nutshell: Don't complain, just do it; because it is there and has to be done. It was a work ethic ingrained in the DNA of their children and reinforced by daily example.

2 The Forts

CHARLESTOWN'S HISTORY IS MOST SIGNIFICANT for an episode that occurred in 1747. The local log fort was besieged for three days by 400 marauding French and Indians. A total of 31 men defended the fort and eventually repelled the attack. The enemy, having had enough, never tried it again. By holding the strategic fort along the Connecticut River, the Charlestown men were credited with saving all of northern New England from the French. It was never recorded whether the men did it without thinking of the long odds they faced or whether they worried about their own comfort and safety. They stubbornly stood their ground and did it because it had to be done. It was a characteristic that would be found in the town's residents for years.

Although the second child of Cecil and Leona Fisk was given the name Carlton Ernest, he would never know a time when he was called anything other than Pudge, or Pudgy. The exact origin of the name remains a mystery, even to him. Some said it was given to him as an infant by an aunt who thought the little guy looked, well, pudgy. Young Carlton certainly fit the name. "I don't remember who first called him that," says Calvin. "It just seemed like he had always had that name."

Pudge weighed 12 pounds at birth; 35 pounds at 18 months. He appeared to be as wide as he was tall through grade school. "We were all shaped like that growing up," says Janet. "I guess that's just how we grew."

A six-inch growth spurt before his freshman year of high school assured that he would never again appear pudgy, but the nickname stuck. By that time, he was big enough that no one would have called him anything he didn't want them to, but he seemed to accept the name, or prefer it. He signed high school annuals, "Pudge '65" and his varsity jacket had "Pudge" stitched into the left chest. The local newspapers referred to him by his nickname also, as in "[the Charlestown Forts] will send senior Pudgy Fisk against the Royal, at West Canaan today." Every little town has guys named Whitey, Bruiser, Duck, or Big Ed, who are never referred to by their real name. That's the way it would be for Pudge. Even when he was more than sixty years old, he would remain Pudge; to everyone except his father, who always called him Carl.

There were a lot of kids in the area when the Fisk children were growing up and they played together constantly. "We'd ride our bikes down to town and meet and decide what we were going to do that day," says George Pebbles. They fished in the river or at other favorite spots, played in the woods, rode their bikes to local swimming holes, played sports.

"It was a tight-knit neighborhood," says Katy Shaw Gould, who was a year younger than Carlton and lived a few houses away. "Very safe. Kids walked to the other side of town. We walked through the woods. There wasn't a lot to do, so you made your own fun. We all played together. It was a nice place to grow up. The school was so small, it was like a big family. You formed friendships that stayed close your whole life."

"We would ride our bikes a couple of miles," says Jim Hogancamp. "We would play all morning, get in an argument, break it up, go home for lunch, then come back afterwards and start right back up again and play until dinnertime."

The entire village was involved. Wayward kids never had a chance. "News would get home before you did," says Hogancamp. "You had to be careful what you did because you knew you could never get away with anything."

The center of the universe for area kids was the large field beside the Fisk house. "There were about thirty kids in the neighborhood and we were all down there in the field at the Fisks' playing all the time," says Katy Shaw Gould. Cecil put up a chicken wire backstop at one end. It was home to many baseball games until Calvin and Pudge got big enough to start breaking windows with long hits.

"We played everything in the Fisks' field," says Hogancamp. "Kick the can, hide and seek, and of course every sport there was, baseball, football, kickball. They never locked their door. When we were kids, you would just walk in the house and announce yourself. You never knocked. There was always a crowd there."

Most of the time during the winter was spent playing basketball inside barns. There were several in the area, but the favorite was Carlton's grandfather Sabin's big barn, just across the field from their house. Up in the hayloft area, a basketball goal was hung and enough room for a half-court pickup game was cleared. Layers would slowly come off as the game heated up. Occasionally bales of hay or the post would be used for picks. Some shots had to arch over a beam. Of course, they had to be careful going for loose balls. At least one kid fell out of the loft during a game, but he just climbed back up and resumed playing. "Our parents always knew when we had been playing there," says Hogancamp. "We would come home smelling like hay or cow flop."

When they got bored with traditional basketball, the kids got creative. "Once we put on our ice skates and went over to Hogancamp's house and shot hoops on ice skates," says Pebbles.

"When it was real bad outside, we would cut the bottom out of soup cans and hang them up inside and shoot baskets with rolled up socks," says Roger Conant, who was two years older than Carlton.

It was a childhood spent working and playing outdoors, learning to interact with other kids, learning to compete and learning responsibility. It was a simple, yet fun existence, such as occurred in hundreds of other small towns at the time; the type of childhood that doesn't exist anymore—undone by progress, electronic sirens that keep kids inside and alone, and the fear of bad things that parents see on the nightly news. The Charlestown kids knew the serenity of sitting on the edge of a quiet lake watching their line lazily bob in the water, the independence of exploring trails through the woods, and the assurance of knowing exactly who they were and where their parents and grandparents had come from. The kids formed tight, lasting friendships and never felt deprived of the things that were available in bigger cities.

Charlestown High School was small. Carlton's graduating class had 42 and that was about as big a class as anyone could remember. Being at a small school, most kids participated in everything. Carlton was in the chorus one year, the band three years, the student council three years (president his senior year), did some hall monitor time, and was in the senior play. He was class president as a freshman and master of ceremonies at the class-night celebration before graduation.

Carlton is remembered as a friendly kid who got along with everyone. But he was very competitive. "Pudge and Calvin were both good guys," says Jim Hogancamp. "But here's the difference: they would both run over you when we were playing football, but Calvin would come back and pick you up, Pudge would keep on running."

Carlton wore his confidence in high school the way most kids wore their letter jacket. More mature for his age, never seen with a nervous grin on his face, he was the kind of guy that as soon as he showed up, no matter what the sport or activity, all eyes naturally turned toward him. He was the leader; it was never spoken, just understood. There was a presence about him, even in high school; a combination of masculine strength, graceful athleticism, and self-assurance that made everyone fall in under his command. He was the kind of guy you wanted to impress and always wanted on your side in any scrap.

He could come across as arrogant or full of himself at times but, to be honest, he *was* better than everyone else at most things. He had always been the biggest and best. "He would let you know he was pretty good sometimes," says one teammate. "He had no trouble telling people what to do. He definitely wasn't meek or shy." But in a town that size, it was difficult to get too bigheaded. Everybody had known everybody for years—they had ways of keeping guys grounded.

"If you took yourself too seriously you would hear about it," says Tom Herzig, a baseball and basketball teammate. "Also in his family, you couldn't get away with anything."

While Carlton had an easy smile and a quick laugh, knew everyone in school and was known by everyone else, he never really had what anyone would refer to as a best friend. He enjoyed the camaraderie of his teammates, and they all considered him to be a friend, but he never developed a deep, lasting personal friendship with anyone. He seemed to have a purpose and drive that separated him—destined to be the hero who rides into the sunset, alone.

Charlestown only had four sports for boys—cross-country and soccer in the fall, basketball in the winter, and baseball in the spring. There were rarely more than 70 or 80 boys in the entire school and some of them didn't like sports. Carlton, like most of the kids who were athletes, played a different sport each season. While the kids competed hard in all sports, basketball was the dream game in the region. The whole town supported the Charlestown Forts basketball team with a fervor and passion reserved for little else. The basketball team had a great tradition, going back to the twenties, and expectations were high every year. Being on the team was important. Winning was important.

Everyone in town had an opinion of how the team would do this year and what the coach should do differently. On Tuesday and Friday nights during the winter, the streets of the town were empty as hometown pride and community camaraderie were tightly packed in to the tiny gym. Think *Hoosiers* with a New England accent.

"If you weren't in the gym before the JV game started, you weren't getting in," says Hogancamp. The gym could hold maybe 500 or 600 and had bleachers only on one side. The curtain on the stage at one end of the gym would be pushed back, allowing another fifty or sixty people to sit on folding chairs there. Fans sat on the steps and stood lining the court, pushing in as close to the action as allowed. With the cheerleaders and band whipping up the crowd, the gym would get so hot they would open the windows in the dead of winter. When the team played rivals Walpole or St. Mary's of Claremont, overflow crowds would stand outside and get reports through the door. The basketball players owned the school; and, during a good season, the town.

The coach was 30-something-year-old Ralph Silva. Known to everyone simply as "Coach," Silva had only been in town a few years. Originally from Gloucester, Massachusetts, he had been good enough in baseball to catch the attention of the Washington Senators. He played in the deep minors a few years before his career ended when he was drafted into the Air Force. After getting a physical education degree from Springfield (Massachusetts) College in 1959, he showed up in Charlestown for his first coaching job. Soon after moving to town, Silva met one of the local youths, a junior high kid called Pudge who was his paperboy. He seemed friendly and dependable. That first summer Silva had no idea how much his paperboy would affect his success as a coach. "How lucky can you get?" Silva would later say about getting a Hall of Fame talent in his first job.

As a coach, Silva was knowledgeable and popular with kids. He could be gruff at times and demanding enough that he wanted to get each kid's best, but he didn't yell a lot—only occasionally when needed. "He knew he was coaching high school kids in a small town and never tried to pretend it was anything else," says Tom Herzig. Silva kept the kids in line—no sitting with girlfriends before games and no smoking—and was respected by his players. He was a stickler for fundamentals and playing the game right.

"Coach Silva was just an all-around great guy and a great influence on me growing up," says Brad Weeks. "He really took an interest in his players, not just on the field."

Silva was an incurable optimist who years later would tell every writer who asked, "I'm the luckiest guy in the world." He would coach into his seventies, and in his later years, slowed by a medical condition, continued to help out on the bench while his son coached high school baseball. "I love what I'm doing. I'm not going to get rich at it, and I knew that. I'm doing it because I love coaching and I love kids," he said in 2005 when he was elected to the New Hampshire Interscholastic Athletic Association's Hall of Fame after 363 baseball wins (seventh all-time in state history).

While he was primarily a baseball guy, as a coach at a tiny school, Silva was forced to coach all sports. At the time, New Hampshire had three classifications: S, M, and L (small, medium, and large). Charlestown was clearly one of the small schools, but in the early 1960s Silva, knowing the talent he had coming, petitioned to get the team moved up to Class M to face better competition.

The 1962–63 Charlestown Forts became a legendary team. While some future sportswriters liked to insinuate that Carlton Fisk was the sole reason the team was so good, that was an obvious embellishment. There was a lot of talent on the team. "Back then, everybody in town bled to play," says Carl McAllister, a senior center. "The guys on the team didn't need any encouragement, everybody worked hard. And we loved it." McAllister, the tallest player on the team at 6-2, was the leading scorer at around 19 points a game and also recorded double digits in rebound. He was a good enough athlete to throw a no-hitter in baseball and, in the fall, would scamper around the cross-country trail and then run over to the soccer field and make it in time for the games. The Class M state player of the year in 1963, he went on to play basketball at Plymouth State and became only the second player in the college's history to score 1,000 points. Ball-handling guard Jimmy Hogancamp was as slick and feisty as they came and ran the show on the court. Forward Roger Conant was a senior like McAllister and Hogancamp. George Pebbles was a junior starter. The only sophomore in the starting lineup was Carlton Fisk, a 6-1 forward.

Pudge was good at basketball. He could handle the ball and, with a huge vertical leap, he played above the rim. He was tough to keep from getting to the basket when he wanted to get there and also had a good jump shot from the elbow of the free throw line. While his scoring improved as the season progressed, it was his rebounding that defined his game and inspired awe from observers. He was an absolutely ferocious rebounder. With great hands and a natural instinct for the ball, he was quick enough to get position and strong enough that he couldn't be moved out. Playing much bigger than his height, his shoulders were so wide that when he boxed out no one else had a chance. And he went for the ball like a pit bull going after a mailman's ankle covered in A-1 sauce. "Pudge played hard," says Hogancamp. "I'd spend half the game trying to get him pissed off so he'd go even harder, and the other half trying to calm him down so he wouldn't foul out."

"Carlton was a great basketball player," says Ken Silva, the coach's son, who was the ball boy for the team. "He could dunk really easily. You weren't allowed to dunk in games back then, you had to lay it in. But Carlton had this thing he would do in practice. He would take the ball between his elbows, jump up, and lay it over the rim—with his elbows." With his elbows? "I saw him do it. That gives you an idea of how high he could jump. I think later they measured his vertical jump and it was something like 38 inches." It was an unexpectedly impressive vertical jump for a guy called Pudge.

Ralph Silva, a baseball coach at heart, quickly learned the game of basketball. "It was different than now," say McAllister. "We only played one defense [a 2-3 sagging zone] and really didn't have much of a set offense. We ran all the time. Our goal was to get the ball and fast-break, try to create mismatches and score quickly. It was continuous action, patterned after the old Bill Russell Celtics of the time. All we did in practice was run. We'd do the two-sided layup drill to warm up, then three-on-one and three-on-two the rest of the time."

The team was close. The guys had spent their youth hanging out together and competing at the Fisk house. Lee and Cecil had fed them and imparted their philosophy. "Mr. and Mrs. Fisk took an interest in all the kids on the team," says McAllister. "It was nice to have some adults who cared about us. The Fisks were always there and they supported all of us. They were always looking for ways to help. We appreciated that."

The kids knew each other's moves and moods. Carlton, while man-grown as a sophomore, was understandably a bit more immature than the seniors on the team. "Pudge could be kind of a baby back then, a little chip on his shoulder sometimes," says one of the guys.

One practice, Hogancamp, as high schoolers are wont to do, was having fun aggravating Carlton by calling him by his middle name. "Pudge hated to be called Ernest for some reason," says Conant. "So, of course, Jimmy kept doing it. But the thing was, every time Jimmy would say, 'Come on, Ernest,' Pudge's back was turned or we were running down the court, so he didn't know who was doing it. You could see he was getting madder and madder." Silva called for a break and when Conant approached the drinking fountain, Carlton shoved him.

"He thought I had been the one calling him Ernest," continues Conant. "He said, 'Who do you think you are?' I said, 'Push me again and you'll find out.' That was it. Pow. He slugged me. I got a real nice shiner out of it." Silva broke it up and threw both players out of practice.

"Silva never knew what started it, but he was going to kick Pudge off the team," says Conant. "We all took a vote and none of us would vote to have him removed—we knew we had a pretty good team and didn't want to mess it up."

Hogancamp, the toughest kid in school and the team leader, was having none of it. The Fisk house was near the high school and the kids routinely cut through their field on the way home. "That night Jimmy said, 'Come on, Mac, we're going to put a stop to this right now,'" says McAllister.

They knocked on the Fisks' door. "The only time I ever knocked on their door," says Hogancamp. When Lee opened it, Hogancamp explained that he had come to talk to Pudge.

"Jimmy really let him have it," says McAllister. "Right there in front of his parents. You could tell Cecil was mad at Pudge when he heard about it. He was a tough old dude and you knew he wasn't going to allow anything like that to happen again. I'm sure Pudge heard plenty about it later that night."

"I told him, 'I was the one calling you Ernie. If you want to fight someone, let's go, otherwise you need to talk to Roger and apologize,'" says Hogancamp. "I was lucky he had cooled off by then and didn't want to hit me or else I might have looked like Roger."

"Jimmy brought him over that night to apologize," says Conant. "When I saw him walk up I thought he was coming to finish the job. I came out and said, 'Come on, let's get this over with.' But he just said, 'I'm sorry. I never hit anybody in the face before.' I was glad that was all he came over for. We were okay after that.

"Later I read in a magazine where some guy said that Carlton was so competitive that he once hit a teammate for loafing in practice," adds Conant. "That's a bunch of baloney. It was me and it wasn't because I was loafing, it was because Jimmy Hogancamp was calling him by his middle name."

Carlton developed a reputation for working by his own clock—a reputation that would follow him throughout his professional career. "Pudge was slow getting to places in high school too," says Conant. "I remember one time we were having a game in Hartford. Coach told him, 'Be here on time or we're leaving without you.' Well, when it was time for the bus to leave, Pudge wasn't there so we left. His parents had to drive him. About halfway through the preliminary game, he showed up. We used to go out and warm up at halftime of the JV game. Coach saw him and said, 'I don't know what you're doing here. You're not playing.' He made him sit out. Pudge was on time for the buses after that."

Other than being late, there was no other trouble for the coach from Carlton Fisk. "There was a lot of respect for authority," Carlton later said, "because if you screwed around at school, you were going to get your butt kicked at home."

Whereas some parents of talented kids feel privileged or try to tell the coach how to do his job, there was none of that from the Fisks. They accepted their son's punishment and, although they never missed a game, didn't interfere with Silva. "They sat behind the bench at every basketball game and never said a word to me—'Do this, Coach'—like they do today," Silva said in 2005. "They never said a word. Whatever they did with the kids when they got home, I'm sure they got talked to, but never did he do it in front of me or anybody else."

On the court, the 1962–63 Charlestown team quickly proved to be the best in the area. Sometimes playing against schools with three or four times their enrollment, they had few close calls as they plowed through the schedule. "We ran up and down the court and blew people out," says Conant. "The coach of one team tried to slow us down by insisting on changing balls in the middle of a game."

"I was shooting free throws and he came out and made a big deal and made the referees switch from a narrow seam ball to a wider one," says Hogancamp. "He switched it right when I was getting ready to shoot. I guess he thought that would throw us off. All it did was make us mad. The game was kind of close at that point, but we ended up beating them by about 30."

"There was only one game that was really close," says McAllister. "We were playing St. Mary's in Claremont and we were down by one late in the game." The Forts, playing their third game in less than a week, came out flat in front of the crazed crowd of their traditional rival. St. Mary's took a 52–51 lead on two free throws with 1:11 left. McAllister missed a shot with 37 seconds left but Fisk, the leading scorer in the game with 17 points, was there to tap it in. McAllister then blocked a last-second shot and the perfect season was preserved.

The Forts were still undefeated when they traveled to Durham, New Hampshire, for the State Tournament, which was played on the campus of the University of New Hampshire. Using the sportswriter lingo of the time, the *Concord Monitor* put the "cagers" tournament into context: "On the year-round agenda of athletic strife, there is nothing quite like the hysteria that derives from tournament tussles. The sound and the fury always has been a unique segment of New Hampshire's tapestry of sports."

And Charlestown's tapestry was never better than in 1963. In front of the biggest crowd of their lives, which included seemingly the entire town of Charlestown, the Forts breezed to the Class M championship by 11 points. They returned home as conquering heroes—when their bus entered town it was met by a line of cars honking their horns, and an impromptu parade escorted them back to school. The Old Number 4 Fire and Hose Company Fire Department held a raffle to raise money and bought them nice jackets, which they wore proudly through the halls and around town—glorifying in the admiring glances from kids, old men, and girls. A banquet was held honoring the champions.

An even bigger thrill followed: they were invited to represent New Hampshire in the prestigious New England Invitational Tournament played in the Boston Garden. It was the chance of a lifetime for the small-town guys to get to play on the hallowed parquet floor of the Garden on March 23, 1963. "The only disappointing thing was that we didn't get to use the Celtics' locker room," says Conant. "I was looking forward to that, to get to sit in the same locker room as Bob Cousy and Bill Russell. But they made us change in the hotel."

The Garden gym floor seemed like the Grand Canyon. "When we walked in, we said, 'Oh my God, look at this place,'" says Hogancamp.

It was the first gym they had ever played in that had seats behind the baskets. A near-capacity crowd of 12,048—more than 10 times the population of Charlestown—was waiting for them.

"When I ran out on that court [as a cheerleader] I felt like an ant," says Katy Shaw Gould.

Charlestown's opponent, Winooski High School of Vermont, was a powerhouse with an imposing front line. They had soundly thumped a team from Maine in the tournament the previous year and were favored over the Forts. The different background and deeper corners led to some air balls early but Charlestown jumped out to a lead with their running game. Winooski fought back, continually feeding the ball inside. McAllister hurt his foot midway through the first quarter and had to sit out most of the rest of the half. The Forts fell behind by as much as four in the second quarter, but a late basket by Fisk tied it at halftime, 23–23.

During the break, Carlton watched McAllister and knew that the senior leading scorer was in pain but would try to gut it out in the second half. He also knew that, hobbled by the injury, McAllister would have his hands full with the Winooski big men. No one said anything specifically, but years later Carlton would tell a writer that he looked around the locker room and was struck by a sense of responsibility. He thought, "This must be me."

Then, as was written the next day in the *Claremont Eagle Times*, "With Pudgy Fisk, 6' 2" sophomore star, blazing the way, Coach Ralph Silva's Charlestown Forts outscored Winooski's Spartans, 32–18, in the second half to win the Twin State small school hoop championship 55–41." Playing with hunger and passion, neutralizing the taller opponents with his defense and rebounding, Fisk led a furious charge the second half. He was the leading scorer in the game with 17 and also led with 16 rebounds.

"Carlton just had a monster game that night," said Silva in 2004. "Anyone who ever saw that game knew he was something special." It wasn't just the number of points and rebounds that inspired, it was the way he played; physically overmatched, facing long odds and even longer arms. During the second half of the game Walter Brown, the owner of the Celtics, leaned over, pointed to Fisk, and asked an associate, "Who is that kid?"

The Forts finished the season 25–0. "People talked about that team forever," says Katy Shaw Gould. They were invited to appear in front of the State Senate as the only undefeated team in the state of any class.

The next two years, the Forts were almost as good, but came up just short in the tournament each time. In Carlton's junior year, they were 16–2 and lost in the state semifinals. By his senior year, he had added a consistent outside shot from what is three-point land now and was the top gun in that part of the state.

His final high school game, in 1965, was an epic battle that became a local legend. By the luck of the tournament pairings, the two best teams in the state met in the semifinals, Charlestown at 19–1 and Hopkinton, 15–1. Most observers felt that the team that won the semis would cruise in the finals. The defending state champion Hopkinton team was led by 6-10 Craig Corson, who would later play on a Final Four team for Dean Smith at North Carolina. Joining Corson on the front line was 6-6 George Sharp, who many felt was even better. Carlton Fisk, at 6-2, was the tallest Charlestown player. Hopkinton led 36–31 at halftime and pulled out to a 59–50 lead heading into the fourth quarter. Charlestown, led by Fisk, made a frantic comeback in the last period, but Carlton fouled out late. He left to a standing ovation. Hopkinton won 73–71.

"Carlton was like the Energizer Bunny that game," says Tom Herzig. "He was like a man possessed. Normally we had a fairly well-balanced team, but that particular game he was the whole show. He was constantly getting to the rim. They couldn't stop him." Carlton scored 40 points and grabbed 36 rebounds. His 19 field goals are still a state record for a tournament game.

"Carlton just didn't miss that night," says Glenn Herzig. "He was hitting his sweet jump shot from the corner of the free throw line and gathering seemingly every miss by teammates and putting it back in. There was a cop who worked the door at the state tournament, and he said he'd been covering the games for 30 years and had never seen anyone play a better game."

In an event that became ingrained in Fisk family lore, the first thing Cecil Fisk mentioned to his son after the game was that he had missed four free throws. "I was 2 for 6 from the free-throw line," Carlton said years later. "I look back on those times and maybe I didn't understand it at the time. In the scheme of things, it was a lesson in being competitive, never being satisfied, always striving to do better."

"Compliments from my father were few and far between," Carlton said in 1993. "It was a motivating factor. . . . I always thought I coulda done better. I never got a pat on the back."

"Maybe I should have [complimented the kids more]," Cecil said later. "But if I complimented them all the time, they might have thought they were doing everything right and didn't need to improve."

"I thought what I was doing was constructive," Cecil told Peter Gammons in 1990. "Maybe it wasn't."

The basketball team was 60–4 during Carlton's last three years in high school. He finished his high school career with 1,179 points, 641 in 21 games his senior year (30.5).

While basketball was a community affair in Charlestown, baseball was little more than an afterthought for everyone other than the players, their parents, and a few girlfriends. Because of the weather, the baseball seasons were very short—usually not more than twelve games. "Some years we only got in a few real practices where it wasn't freezing and snowy," says Tom Herzig.

"Playing so few games, it's ridiculous to think of the odds of someone coming out of that and not only making the major leagues, but the Hall of Fame," says Ken Silva. Indeed, of the 17 baseball Hall of Famers from New England, Carlton Fisk would be the only one of them who played after World War II, when players from warm-weather states took over the game.

Although he coached other sports, Ralph Silva was first and foremost a baseball man. More than anyone else, he helped prepare Carlton Fisk's professional chances by building up the game in Charlestown. "Baseball wasn't really much in town before he got there," says Herzig. "But Coach Silva worked on the field and he instilled a lot of pride in us. After he got there, everything started to improve for baseball."

After watching kids play baseball in local lots, a group of fathers had gotten together and formed a Little League when Carlton was young. Since there was no community diamond at the time, they carved one out of a cow pasture. The field was rough by modern standards. A true hop was a rarity. The field was sloped with a large hill in center field and left field—the center fielder was actually standing on the hill, well above the infield. An electrical fence surrounded part of the field. At least one kid couldn't resist temptation and tested an old legend.

"I found out real quick that urine conducts electricity," says Roger Conant. "I never tried that again." Players had to be careful where they stepped. "You had to watch out when you slid into second base," adds Conant, "there just might be a cow flop there." Players from other towns, wearing fancy complete baseball uniforms, would occasionally laugh at the Charlestown boys when they came in and saw them wearing T-shirts and blue jeans and got a look at the field. The laughter quickly died after they found themselves losing, not to mention after a few slides into cow flop.

It had quickly become apparent that Pudge Fisk was one of the best baseball players around, except maybe for his big brother. "He was always bigger and stronger than the other guys his age," says Tom Herzig. "And he had talent. We moved to town when I was in the fourth grade. I remember him from the first day of school. We were on the playground at recess playing softball and this kid hit one about four times further than anyone else. Everyone called the kid Pudge, but I never did think he was pudgy, he just had a huge chest and was stronger than anyone else."

Normally a catcher growing up, following in Calvin's footsteps, Carlton was forced into pitching in Babe Ruth baseball, at the age of 13 or 14. "We were playing in a big tournament in Claremont," says Glenn Herzig, whose father coached the Babe Ruth team. "Normally my brother Tom was the pitcher and Carlton caught, but in the tournament Tom had already pitched a couple of games and they had an inning limit. So Carlton was the obvious choice to pitch because he could throw hard. He only had a catcher's mitt, so he had to borrow my glove to pitch. He did great."

The high school field in Charlestown, like the Little League field, was a converted cow pasture. There were no dugouts; the few fans who showed up sat on a grassy hill behind the backstop. "It was like a sandlot," remembers Conant. "You had to run real hard to move because the sand was so deep."

"The field was pretty rough," says Brad Weeks. "And we were our own grounds crew, a half an hour before the game." Occasionally, snow lingered until May. Early in the season, players would have to chop chunks of ice off the trees near the field to keep branches from hanging over the foul lines. There was no fence, but in deep left field was the Charlestown version of the Green Monster—a giant pine tree,

30 to 40 feet tall. If a ball went over that, it rolled down a ravine into a brook. That was a home run. Calvin and Carlton Fisk each hit quite a few down there.

Carlton was physically dominant as a high school baseball player. One of the best pitchers in the area, he didn't waste time with off-speed stuff. He was a good, old-fashioned, reach-back-and-throw-as-hard-as-you-can pitcher. And, for Carlton Fisk, that was pretty hard. He had enough control to get through games and enough wildness to make high school batters pause and ask themselves exactly how badly they wanted a hit—it was gut check time before each at bat. Brad Weeks was the catcher when Carlton pitched. "He had one pitch, a fastball," says Weeks. "For a high school kid, he was fast. Not many guys caught up to it. He was big and intimidating to a lot of hitters. My hand would be sore after games. Nobody else wanted to catch him."

It was Fisk's hitting that inspired the most vivid memories. "Teams were afraid to pitch to Carlton," says Weeks. "He hit a lot of home runs." By the spring of his sophomore year, everyone in the valley knew who Carlton Fisk was. He could be gotten out with curveballs, but high school pitchers who were foolish enough to challenge him with a fast-ball often spent the next several seconds looking back and watching the ball grow smaller and smaller as it soared to previously unexplored places.

"We can go around now to the old fields in the area, and at every one of them you can point to something way out there and say, 'I remember when Pudge hit one over that or off that hot dog stand or something like that,'" says Glenn Herzig. "He hit the longest home run at about every field around here."

"I remember once when he played against St. Mary's he hit one out of Barnes Park [Claremont]," says Ken Silva. "It went completely out to left field. I remember going to get the ball and looking back at the infield and seeing how far it went. You knew you were watching something special. Once later, in American Legion, he hit one out at Barnes Park to right center and it hit a house way behind the field. Nobody had ever seen anyone come close to that."

"Carlton was my father's hero," says Roger Conant. "In the early seventies I went by his house and he had a big bag of baseballs. He said they were Carlton Fisk balls—he'd sent kids down into the ravine to get them whenever he hit a home run. I told him, 'You know I hit a few down there, too. How do you know some of these weren't mine.' He wouldn't hear of it. 'Those are all Carlton Fisk balls.' "

Charlestown played deep into the state tournament every year. When Carlton was a junior, he won two games in the tournament as a pitcher, one a three-hit shutout. Charlestown scored six runs in the sixth inning to win 7–6 in the semifinals. In the championship game, Fisk fired a two-hitter but lost when Woodsville squeezed home a run with a bunt in extra innings.

For the kids with talent and aspirations in baseball, American Legion ball filled the gap in the summers. Carlton played for the Claremont team his first year, as a 16-year-old, then switched to the Pierce-Lawton Post Number 37 in Bellows Falls. Vermont had a stronger American Legion system and Bellows Falls had won the Vermont state championship the year before. The switch almost didn't happen, though. "In the spring of '65, his dad called me and told me Pudge was unhappy with the program in Claremont," Bellows Falls coach Tim Ryan said in 2004. "He wanted to know if Pudgy could play for us. I told him I already had a catcher who had started three years of high school, but Cecil said it would be no problem. Carlton didn't care where he played." According to the American Legion by-laws, Fisk needed a release from the Claremont post in order to play for another team and Claremont was adamant about not letting him go. "Mr. Fisk went up there and talked to them and they wouldn't budge. So we held this meeting in Keene and Gubby Underwood [then New Hampshire state commissioner] told Claremont in no uncertain terms that they were to release him. 'We're not going to make this kid sit out,' he told them. The next thing I knew, I had his release in my hands."

"We were happy to have him," said Ryan. "He was a great leader and the team's most valuable player. . . . He'd do anything with no complaints. He was one of the hardest-working athletes I ever coached."

"I played American Legion ball in Bellows Falls with Carlton," says Tom Herzig. "By that time the difference in natural talent was obvious. The best pitchers we faced were not a problem for him. And every once in a while he would launch a home run 80 feet further than anyone else. One thing I noticed was the great economy of motion he had—running, swinging, throwing, there was just an efficiency of motion. He could do things easier and better than we could no matter how hard we struggled."

Lawrence "Poody" Walsh was a young sportswriter who would end up covering Fisk's entire career and still works his craft in the valley. "I had just started working for a paper in Bellows Falls the year Carlton played there in American Legion ball," he says. "I saw him hit some long home runs. We became friends. He had a nice family. They invited me to their house. I'm not sure he realized his own ability at that stage. He was a star in a small town, but when he came to Bellows Falls, he saw a lot of other good players, not as good as he was, but a lot better than what he had seen. It was a little humbling at first—he was kind of into himself in Charlestown."

Bellows Falls, about twice the size of Charlestown, was still a small town. "The people of the American Legion were great, they were very supportive," says Nick Anderson, a left-handed pitcher from nearby Walpole. "They provided the transportation; they would come by and pick us up in front of the Legion hall. Our uniforms were those old 100 percent wool things that weighed a ton after you sweated. They had pinstripes and the names of all the sponsors on them. It was a chance to travel farther than we ever had. It was hard to make the team, there were a lot of kids who tried out, from all the towns in the area. We had been rivals in school. I played against him in baseball and basketball in high school so I knew all about him. He was actually a better basketball player, I thought. I guarded him once in junior high and all I saw were knees. But we got to be friends on the American Legion team. Nobody worked harder than he did. He was a good teammate. He didn't act like he was better than anyone else.

"He had great power," Anderson continues. "He hit some mammoth home runs, but you could get him out with curveballs. I used to throw him curveball after curveball in batting practice and he'd get so mad he'd yell at me. He had all the tools. He was really fast for a guy that size, but you didn't think you were looking at a future major leaguer. We all had the same dream, but I don't think we thought it was possible for any of us. When he made it later it was like we all made it. We all felt a part of it."

Since the Bellows Falls team already had an established catcher, Fisk played shortstop and pitched, along with a little first base. The team traveled 180 miles to Cooperstown, New York, for a tournament on Doubleday Field for their first game. As part of the weekend, they toured the Hall of Fame. "It was a great trip for guys that age," says Anderson. "That was about as far as a lot of the guys had ever traveled. The big thing I remember about the Hall of Fame was listening to Babe Ruth's voice on a phone."

Coach Ryan would never forget the game in Cooperstown. In his first at bat at Doubleday Field, Fisk blasted a home run. "It went about 500 feet," Ryan said in 1972.

There were other tape-measure jobs. "Once we played in a tournament in Keene," says Anderson. "They had a nice field there with lights. They had a good team but we beat them. Pudge hit a home run that went over a pine tree that was about 40 feet tall and went over a shed in right field. There were a lot of scouts there for that tournament. They came up and talked to him after the game."

"How far did Pudgy Fisk's prodigious poke travel at the Falls Sunday?" the *Claremont Times* asked after one of his blasts at Hadley Field in Bellows Falls. "Well, BF's Poody Walsh was right out in left-center, near where the ball was driven, and he told us the blast hit about a foot from the top of the cyclone fence that surrounds the field. In other words—another foot and it would have cleared that fence. Since the snow fence is out about 380 there, the cyclone fence about 20 feet behind that—atop a steep bank—we figure the tape-measure-tap traveled about 420 feet—at least." The impressive home run grew to legendary status in the area; the distance grew as well—in a local 1967 article, it was referred to as 450 to 500 feet.

With more physical ability than experience, Carlton's results were not uniformly spectacular, but they were impossible to miss, such as the doubleheader he helped Bellows Falls sweep against Springfield. He pitched a one-hitter to win the first game 1–0, while striking out three times at the plate. The second game he hit two triples, including the game-winner to lead the team to a 2–0 win.

The first summer Carlton played for Bellows Falls the team went 16–3 and lost to Brattleboro in the finals of the state tournament. Some scouts were around and took note of him, but were not impressed enough to think of him as a future professional baseball player. Besides, Carlton just played baseball for fun. He was still convinced that his future was basketball. At the end of the summer, he headed for the college hardwood.

3 Joe College

UPON FINISHING HIGH SCHOOL, Carlton Fisk didn't really have a plan for his future other than a somewhat generic "go to college and play basketball and, maybe, baseball too." Despite his high school athletic heroics, he was little known beyond the Connecticut River Valley and New Hampshire borders. He had played for a tiny school tucked away in a corner of a tiny state; things like showcase camps and AAU tournaments didn't exist for kids in the area at the time. Carlton was offered a basketball scholarship to attend the University of New Hampshire and he jumped at the opportunity.

"We didn't really have many options for college," says Calvin Fisk, who after his own standout high school career also attended New Hampshire. In the fall of 1965 Calvin was beginning his senior year and was the captain of the baseball and soccer teams—playing well enough to later be elected to the school's Hall of Fame. "My dad was very conservative, a practical thinker. We came from a small town and didn't have a lot of opportunities or know of the opportunities. Because our school was so small, college scouts didn't really come around. Also, our family didn't have a lot of money and back then most athletic scholarships didn't pay very much, at least not at UNH. So it was just 'go to the in-state school.' The in-state tuition was definitely a factor. Looking back, I really wanted to play baseball and I should have gone somewhere further south."

The University of New Hampshire was not exactly the big time. Its teams competed in the Division I Yankee Conference, a strong conference led by two perennial favorites, University of Connecticut and University of Massachusetts (who a few years after Carlton arrived would trot out a pretty good player named Julius Erving), but the term "competed" was really just used to be polite. Good basketball was played in the Yankee Conference, but not by the home team in Durham, New Hampshire. Yankee Conference winners got an automatic bid to the NCAA Tournament. This had happened to the New Hampshire basketball team exactly zero times since the conference had been formed in 1946. By 1965, New Hampshire had not had a winning season in 13 years. They usually battled the University of Vermont for the cellar of the conference. Their record in the 1964–65 season had been 2–19. Lundholm Gym, which was built in 1938 and seated fewer than 4,000, was rarely even half-filled for games.

New Hampshire head basketball coach Bill Olson may or may not have been a good coach; no one will ever know—he never got a chance. He suffered from a terminal lack of support by the administration. Paid assistants or even a rudimentary recruiting budget were luxuries of which he could only dream. Even though the New Hampshire state tournament was played in his building, he rarely got any of the best players from his own state. Often, a majority of his players were those who had drifted down from Canada looking for a place to play. Olson's record from 1956 to 1966 was 60–146 (.291).

Baseball, if possible, was even lower on the evolutionary scale at the school than basketball. Games were played in front of a few girlfriends or parents who lived nearby, or maybe a few bored passersby who stopped for a look at a few innings. Hockey was the only game with any kind of support and the hockey players were the de facto big men on campus.

UNH had a beautiful campus, with about 1,700 students in Carlton's freshman class. The sixties hadn't really become "The Sixties" yet in the fall of 1965—maybe they were starting to in places like California, but certainly not in Durham. Campus life was still firmly rooted in the traditions of the previous decade. Freshmen were even required to wear beanies until the football team won their first game, although most did not due to harassment from upperclassmen, especially a group called the Sophomore Sphinxes (although any upperclassman would have had to be either severely myopic or inebriated to consider harassing Carlton Fisk no matter what he had on top of his head). Freshmen were required to live on campus in the tiny cinder block dorm rooms and to buy a meal ticket for the Dining Hall, which had an enforced dress code—no T-shirts, jeans, or shorts allowed and jackets and ties mandatory on Sundays.

All male students were acutely aware of the military draft, which awaited those not in good academic standing, but patriotism was still in style and there was no on-campus opposition to the growing war in Vietnam. The first antiwar demonstration at the university occurred in the spring of 1966 and was organized not by students, but by a small group of local pacifists. It was sparsely attended except for some students who jeered the demonstrators.

Although Durham did not have bars at the time, beer wasn't hard to find, but drug use was rarely seen or talked about on campus. Curfews and rules prohibiting males from being in the female dorms were in place to protect the virtue of coeds, although rumor had it that females could be found who did not seem to want their virtue protected.

While the basketball team had been a perennial loser, for 1965 things were supposed to be different. For the first time, the administration had showed a willingness to help recruit good athletes and it had paid off. In addition to Carlton Fisk, several other top-notch basketball players arrived on campus in the fall of 1965. A 6-3 jumping jack from Worcester Academy Prep in Massachusetts named Jeff Bannister was the best of the lot. A remarkable athlete, Bannister not only played basketball but was a great track man—good enough to win several national AAU competitions in the pentathlon and decathlon. He would later compete in the 1972 Olympics (after he beat another decathlete named Bruce Jenner at the trials) and only a fall on a wet track in the hurdles kept him from the medal stand. Bannister was a good enough athlete to do a 10.4 100 meters, a 4:10 1,500, and high jump 6-6 in the 1972 Olympic trials.

"It was just kind of lucky for them to have two world-class athletes on the team at the same time," says Joe Rahal, the starting point guard, who had played with Bannister at Worcester, where they had won the New England Prep School title. "We made the nucleus of a very good team."

Carlton quickly fit in, with college life and with his new teammates. "Pudge was very down-to-earth," says Rahal. "No pretense, just a down-home country New Hampshire style. He laughed a lot. We had a lot of fun together."

Since freshmen were not eligible for NCAA competition at the time, they were forced to play on the freshman team. The 1965–66 UNH freshman squad raced up and down the court, averaging 99.4 points a game, led by Bannister's 26.7. "We beat UConn's freshmen by 30 points," says Bannister.

"Between Jeff and Pudge, with their speed and athletic ability, people had a hard time keeping up with us," says Rahal. The fact that they were much smaller than most other teams, several of whom had taller guards than 6-3 center Bannister, didn't make any difference once the games started. "Everybody could run. We ran people out of the gym. We scrimmaged the varsity three times. We beat them to the point where they stopped having us scrimmage them—it wasn't doing either of us much good. I don't want to say they got discouraged that the freshmen beat them so bad, but that's probably the right word."

"Yep, we beat them pretty badly," Bannister concurs.

It was the best freshman team in the school's history with a record of 15–1. While not the big scorer he had been in high school, Fisk was still one of the stars. "Carlton was a jumper and got *all* the rebounds," says Bannister. "He was a man among boys. We used to leave him towels in his locker to dust off the boards while he was up there."

The freshman coach, Bill Haubrich, later described Fisk as "a terrific kid. He was always in a good mood, a happy kid—except when it came to competing. Success and failure meant everything to him."

"All the guys on that team had been used to winning," says Rahal. "No one wanted to lose, but Carlton was especially intense. His intensity made him stand out. He had a desire to win and, coupled with his athletic ability, that made him special."

Although Carlton would later downplay his basketball aspirations by telling reporters that at 6-2, he found himself outmatched by a bunch of 6-5 and taller forwards, in reality that never caused a problem. Even if his future did not lie at forward, he could have easily made the transition to off-guard. Most games, he and Bannister were the best players on the court. Carlton Fisk was good in college basketball. Good enough to start for UNH as a sophomore? Most likely. Good enough to eventually be All-Conference in the Yankee Conference? Probably. Good enough to make the NBA? Who knows. But there was certainly nobody who could handle him during his freshman season.

"I volunteered to be the trainer for the freshman basketball team," says Calvin. "I watched all the games that year. It was an impressive team. Carlton dominated the boards. Nobody could rebound with him. They were undefeated until the last game at Rhode Island, where they lost by one point. A last-second shot by Rahal almost went in but wedged between the rim and the backboard. And that's the only game they lost."

Carlton took the loss hard. "After the URI loss, all the kids were showering, getting ready to watch the varsity game," Haubrich said in 2000. "Not Fisk. He stayed in the locker room, in uniform, his head in his hands. Finally I said, 'Okay, Pudge, time to get on with your life.'"

And getting on with his life meant baseball. Up to this point Carlton had much preferred basketball over baseball. He had grown up dreaming of one day playing for the Boston Celtics, of triggering fast breaks like Bill Russell, hitting bank shots like Sam Jones, and hustling all over the court like John Havlicek. Baseball had only been something to do while it was in season. But while he was finding that his height could possibly limit his objectives in basketball, it was evident that in baseball he was on an altogether different plane than other players. No one was even close. As a catcher, pitcher, and part-time shortstop and outfielder, he was the star of the freshman baseball team. He ravaged hapless freshman pitchers. "Carlton used to tell us what he was going to hit in the next baseball game," says Bannister. "We used to go to the game and tell the pitcher what he was going to do . . . line drives today to right field, then he would do it. Lots of fun. He was a man among boys." Carlton Fisk began to realize where his future might lay.

But playing college baseball in New Hampshire was not the best way to get there. University of New Hampshire baseball seasons were almost as short as his high school seasons had been. "My junior year, our last two games were snowed out," says William Estey, who was a year ahead of Carlton. "And they were in May. We usually only played about 20 games or so, and six of those were on our so-called southern tour in New Jersey and Philadelphia."

"At UNH I played in less games in my entire career than some kid I met in Florida at spring camp had played in one year of high school in California," says Calvin Fisk. "We went to New Jersey for spring training if that tells you anything. One year we were supposed to play Princeton down there, but it snowed. The next day, it cleared enough to play, but there was still a sheet of ice between first and second. It wasn't the best place for baseball. We were 4 and 16 my senior year."

But good players still could draw notice. The Major League Baseball draft was instituted in 1965. Calvin Fisk became the first player ever taken in the draft from New Hampshire when he was picked by the Baltimore Orioles in the 48th round, the 712th pick overall that year. Calvin, who had hit .424 as a freshman, decided to stay in school one more year to graduate. "I got drafted by the Orioles after my junior year," he says. "I didn't sign. I thought, 'I'll just wait until next year.' I really didn't have any guidance or plan."

While athletics went very well for Carlton in his first year of college, academics were another matter. After years of a somewhat sheltered existence spent under the intense discipline of his parents, Carlton eagerly experienced college social life, at times at the expense of his studies. "I was only 17 when I went to college, and I was still pretty immature," he explained years later. "I spent more time on the basketball court than in class." He struggled academically. He wasn't stupid; in fact, in 1964 he had made the highest score in Charlestown on the annual National Mathematics Exam given to kids in the advanced math and algebra II classes. The problem, he explained, was that "I hadn't learned how to apply myself in anything but sports. . . . I couldn't stay still long enough to keep my nose in a textbook for very long."

The University of New Hampshire's academic standards for athletes were much higher back then compared to most Division I schools now. At the conclusion of his freshman year, Carlton was notified that his grades were lacking; he would be welcomed back to the school for the fall of 1966, but only on academic probation. Already losing his enthusiasm for school, the prospect of attending classes and practice, but not being eligible for games for a whole year, did not sound particularly enticing. Also, the outlook for the basketball team was not good. The nucleus of the great freshman basketball team had been gutted by trouble with grades, injuries, and transfers. It is difficult to go from a constantly winning environment to the exact opposite—a situation in which there is virtually no chance of being successful. It didn't take Carlton long while watching the UNH varsity basketball team slog through a 3–21 season (0–10 conference) his freshman year to see what might lay ahead. College life had lost its luster. He chose not to go back.

"He came back to Charlestown after he left college," says Claremont sports reporter Poody Walsh. "He came in to see me. He was down. He wasn't sure what he wanted to do. I helped get him a job with the local rec department."

Carlton Fisk would work at various jobs in the area, but he was not entirely finished with the University of New Hampshire—he would visit frequently in the next few years. One day in the cafeteria line his freshman year, he met a pretty coed from Manchester, New Hampshire,

Linda Foust. She was tall, slim, blond, and outgoing. They began dating, and would continue to date until they were married in 1970. More than forty years later, Linda would still be Mrs. Carlton Fisk.

Although he didn't know it at the time, leaving college was the best thing Carlton Fisk could have done for his baseball career. If he had remained at UNH, playing 15 to 20 baseball games a year while also playing basketball, it would have been hard for him to start in professional baseball as a 22-year-old college graduate with so little experience. He might have eventually made the majors, or he might not, but even if he did it would have been at an age too old to compile Hall of Fame–worthy numbers.

In the summer of 1966, there was still amateur baseball for Carlton Fisk. Calvin was playing in his third summer with Orleans in the Cape Cod Baseball League and arranged for Carlton to play there also. Carlton had previously committed to Bellows Falls for his last year of American Legion baseball, but once the Legion team was finished he joined Orleans for the end of their season. The Cape League was one of a handful of summer leagues for select college players—a chance to evaluate their talents against a higher level of competition than that provided by the usual college schedule. The manager for Orleans in 1966 was 29-year-old Dave Gavitt, an energetic young man who, during the school year, coached baseball and basketball for his alma mater, Dartmouth. Within six years, Gavitt would lead the Providence Friars to the NCAA Final Four in basketball. He would later help organize the Big East Conference and become CEO of the Boston Celtics in the 1990s.

Calvin moved to first base and Carlton caught the last two weeks for Orleans. Once again, Carlton made an immediate impression. In his first at bat in the Cape League, he slammed a home run. The more experienced pitchers didn't seem to faze him. "He went 6-for-9 with a home run, two triples, and two doubles," says Calvin. "One game he single-handedly beat Chatham, who was something like 33 and 3. He had a two-run triple and another hit and we won 3–2."

All this time, professional scouts had kept their eyes on the big, slugging catcher. Back then, New Hampshire and Vermont were not considered fertile mining grounds for professional baseball talent. But word got around. The bird dogs had originally perked up their ears at some of Carlton's monster home runs. "The bird dog for the area for the Red Sox was an old, short, toothless, cigar-chomping guy from

Chester [Vermont] named Bert Stewart," says Calvin. "Once he came to one of our high school games [when Calvin was a senior and Carlton was a freshman]. Unfortunately I went 0-for-3, but Carlton hit a grand slam and a couple of other hits." Stewart kept tabs on Carlton and dutifully filed reports to the team.

While bird dogs for other teams also noticed Carlton, the nearby Red Sox showed the most interest. The Red Sox scout covering New England was Jack Burns. A native of Cambridge, Massachusetts, the 58-year-old Burns had been a slick-fielding first baseman for six major league seasons in the 1930s, mostly with the St. Louis Browns. After coaching third base for the Red Sox a few years in the late fifties as part of the Pinky Higgins regime, he became a scout. It was Burns who would be most responsible for recommending and signing Carlton Fisk. And Fisk would be the best player he ever signed. "Jack Burns was nice," says Legion teammate Nick Anderson. "He was short, always wore a hat with a wide brim that had a card tucked in the band. He followed us around a lot."

Although Carlton played all over the field, Burns viewed him primarily as a catching prospect. He could see the tools that could be refined, the take-charge personality. "He had a good swing and a strong arm and he could run like hell, but he had an awful lot of passed balls," Burns said later. "To tell the truth, he didn't look that good as a catcher. The kid was raw. . . . But he had good hands in the infield and tremendous power. They kept showing me places where he'd hit balls out beyond the field. . . . Anybody who could poke a ball that far had a chance."

Other scouts talked to Carlton as well. Like Burns, they all agreed that the best fit for his talents in professional baseball would be as a catcher. At their request, Tim Ryan had Carlton catch in several tournaments his last year of Legion ball to give them a better look.

In the 1966 American Legion State Tournament, Carlton put on a show. He went 18-for-24 at the plate and pitched 12 innings with 14 strikeouts and only two unearned runs. Bellows Falls ran out of pitchers and lost in the championship game but Carlton was named the tournament MVP. Afterward, he was approached by scouts from the Reds, Orioles, Mets, Pirates, and A's. And scouts from the Yankees and Braves spoke with Cecil.

Burns had been hovering around Carlton for the past two years and was a step ahead of the other scouts. He had watched him at UNH, his last year in Legion, and in the Cape League, and was impressed that he seemed to hold up against the increased levels of competition. Burns considered him a prospect.

At the time, there were two baseball drafts, one in June and one in January. The January draft, frequently called the supplemental draft, would be dropped in 1986. It contained far fewer players than the June draft and was for players who had graduated high school or college during the winter. It was also for other special cases, such as players who went to college for a time, but stopped for whatever reason. Carlton Fisk was selected in the first round of the January 1967 draft by the Boston Red Sox. He was the fourth player taken in the draft, just behind future major league star Ken Singleton, who was picked by the Mets. Alex Distaso, a right-handed high school pitcher from Los Angeles, was the first pick in the draft (he would hurt his arm within two years and only pitch in two major league games).

Some observers—and also Carlton himself—were surprised the Red Sox took Fisk so high. Bob Wilber, who coached the Chester, Vermont, American Legion baseball team and also helped bird dog Bert Stewart, later told a reporter that Jack Burns initially didn't regard Fisk as first-round material. "At the time they didn't think Pudgy was a number one draft pick," he said. "I told them I knew the Reds and the Pirates had him number one and if they wanted him, they better take him with their number one pick."

It was later routinely stated that Carlton and his family had let it be known that they would only sign with the Red Sox. That made a nice story for the hometown folks in Boston and may have had a little truth, but since the baseball draft had been instituted, players had to go where they were selected. It is very doubtful that if Carlton had been drafted by, say, Pittsburgh, he would have turned them down to stay and work at the Claremont rec department.

Carlton signed with the Red Sox within a week of the draft. Bonuses for the first-round picks of the supplemental draft were not as lucrative as those in the June draft. Ken Singleton received a signing bonus of $10,000 and Fisk's was reported to be the same. Carlton's college days were officially over. So were his basketball days. He was now going to cast his lot with professional baseball.

4 Waterloo, Pittsfield, Pawtucket, and Louisville

IT WAS A TIGHT SITUATION for the 1968 Class A Waterloo Hawks. The bases were loaded with their opponents, no outs. Since several big wheels from the Boston Red Sox front office were in town to look at the prospects, the Hawks players felt pressure to make a good showing. The team's catcher, Carlton Fisk, slowly walked to the mound and informed the pitcher, "If it's hit to you, throw it to me and we'll get a double play." A few pitches later, the batter bounced one back to the pitcher, who fielded it cleanly and threw home. Fisk relayed to first as planned; double play. He happily ran off the field, but was surprised to find the team's manager on the top step of the dugout, screaming that there were only two outs. Fisk hustled back to home plate. Luckily, the runner had held up at third (he had asked the third baseman where the catcher was going, and the alert third baseman told him he had called time-out). Embarrassed by the gaffe, Fisk tried to hurry out of the clubhouse after the game, but he was caught by Sam Mele, an old-timer from the Boston staff. "Son, I don't know how you play baseball up there in New Hampshire," Mele told the young catcher, "but around here we play three outs to an inning."

Upon signing with the Red Sox, Carlton Fisk was initially ticketed for the Class A team in Greenville, South Carolina; however, his professional baseball career was immediately sidetracked. At the same time he was drafted by the Red Sox, he was in danger of another draft—the military one. With the undeclared war in Vietnam becoming more taxing, President Lyndon Johnson had doubled the draft pace in August of 1965 to 35,000 per month. As an unmarried guy no longer possessing a college deferment, Fisk was fair game. He had recently received a notice to report for his pre-draft physical.

The war hung over the heads of all young baseball players at the time. "Most of us had a military obligation back then," says Jimmy Powers, a catcher who was taken out of high school by the Red Sox in the 15th round of the June 1967 baseball draft. "The Red Sox gave us advice and helped line us up with the Reserves or the National Guard so we could still try to play baseball, but it set guys' careers back." The Red Sox also warned their players to toe the line in the service—legend had it that in the mid-sixties a player, believed to be Tony Conigliaro, gave an officer a suggestion for what he could do in his hat and angry military officials reported to the Sox that future players could enter the draft like everyone else if they didn't behave better.

Carlton Fisk joined the Army Reserves and was assigned to the nearby Chester, Vermont, 393 Supply and Service Battalion. Instead of wearing a baseball uniform and swinging a bat, he spent the spring and summer of 1967 wearing GI-issued khakis and swinging an M14 rifle. First up was eight weeks of basic training at Fort Dix, New Jersey. From the First Call bugle in the morning until Taps at night, he enjoyed constant PT, practiced close order drilling, and learned how to mop a floor, scrub a latrine, police an area, make a bunk, and stand guard. He learned to answer every order with "Yes, Drill Sergeant" and never "Yes, Sir," lest he be reminded that the drill sergeant was not an officer but worked for a living. Closing his eyes at night was followed seemingly by reopening them five seconds later in the morning.

In the Army, Carlton was not a celebrity; his athletic ability gained him no favors. He was merely serial number AR-11-4-8-5-5-2-9, a nameless soldier in an olive-drab uniform, just like any other ground-pounder. He had to take orders whether he agreed with them or not. But there were no problems from Private First Class Carlton Fisk, he fit right in. He later said of his military time: "I don't know if it changed my attitude, my discipline, but it might have helped a little bit on the coachability end of it. Because of my talents, I was like a loose cannon on deck. I had all the firepower but no direction." After Basic, he was attached to the Chester Reserve unit for the next four years. Minor league managers would have to work around his required Army duties of one weekend a month and an annual two-week summer camp.

Fisk was released from active duty in 1967 in time to report to Sarasota to join Boston's Florida Instructional League team. Running for six weeks in October and November, the Instructional League was where teams sent the most promising prospects from their farm systems—a chance for the brass to get a good look and for the kids to get more experience against better opposition. "It was pretty fast competition," says Powers. "Me and Carlton were the two youngest players. Most of the guys had been in the system a few years. Of course they always needed a bunch of catchers to catch all the pitchers. Me and Carlton were both pretty quiet down there. We just did our work. He was a nice guy. He was a hard worker and obviously a step ahead of everybody else physically."

In Sarasota, Carlton met another catcher in the Red Sox system, and a good one. Jerry Moses was 21, two years older than Carlton, but he already had four years, 329 games, and 1,134 at bats of pro ball experience. A high school All-American quarterback in Yazoo City, Mississippi, the 6-3, 215-pound Moses had spurned football offers from the entire Southeastern Conference—including one from Bear Bryant at Alabama, who was searching for a replacement for the recently departed Joe Namath—to sign with the Red Sox in 1964 for a $50,000 bonus. He got into four games with Boston the next year and managed to become the youngest Red Sox player to ever hit a home run, at 18 years and 289 days. Moses was a solid-hitting catcher with a strong arm and was considered to be the Red Sox catcher of the future—an obvious roadblock to Carlton reaching Boston.

As in spring training, a lot of catchers were needed and they were always busy. They worked out in the morning and played games in the evening. Moses, Powers, and Fisk split the catching duties during the 51-game season. There were a lot of instructors and coaches prowling the grounds, watching over the prospects and giving advice. The coach who made the biggest impression on Carlton Fisk during his introduction to professional baseball was 58-year-old Mace Brown. A gray-headed, tobacco-spitting, laid-back, down-home man with a big nose and an equally large grin, Brown was an Iowa farm boy who pitched in the major leagues in the 1930s and 1940s and then worked for the Red Sox as a scout and instructor for years (his prize find as a scout would be Jim Rice in 1971). Mace had been one of the first full-time relief specialists in the major leagues, and the first to pitch in the All-Star Game. He threw one pitch for which he would always be remembered and, unfortunately, it was not a good one. He had given up one of the most celebrated late-season home runs, the "Homer in the Gloamin," to Hall of Fame catcher Gabby Hartnett on September 28, 1938, which helped the Cubs win the pennant. "Mace Brown was considered the pitching guru in Sarasota," says Powers. "He was just a good old country guy; everybody liked him. He especially liked to teach pitchers the overhand curveball that dropped straight down."

One extremely hot day, the kind of day in which the oppressive Florida heat lays on your arms like a blanket, Fisk labored through the task of catching the numerous hotshot pitchers, all of whom had great arms, but most of whom also had difficulty finding the plate. Carlton had caught six or seven of the sessions, each lasting about 20 minutes. When the young pitchers weren't firing missiles over his head that he had to jump to try to catch, they were bouncing Mace Brown's 12-to-6 curveballs in the dirt, ricocheting them into his knees and body. After finishing with the last pitcher, Carlton trudged toward the clubhouse, his hair matted, his uniform soaked, his legs and back aching. When he was stopped by a coach and informed that he still had to do some running, he exploded: "I just spent two and a half hours catching a bunch of prima donnas who couldn't throw the ball sixty feet six inches in the air. I got my bleeping workout in, then some. I'm not running." Exhausted, he stalked off.

Mace Brown calmly walked over, put his arm on Carlton's shoulder, and looked into his filthy, sweat-streaked face. "Son, I want to tell you something my daddy told me a long time ago," he drawled. "If you hadn't wanted to work, you oughtn't have hired out." The words struck Carlton like a foul tip off the face mask. It sounded like one of the most profound statements of truth and essence he had ever heard. In reality, it was just a southern-fried version of what his own daddy had told him all his life, but he later said those words made him realize that baseball and life were hard work and full of challenges. "From that moment on—continuing through today—whenever I face a challenge I think of Mace's words," he wrote years later.

Carlton Fisk reported to Waterloo, Iowa, of the Class A Midwest League for the 1968 season. Flying in to Waterloo, the first thing a New England native would notice was the incredibly flat land; a perfectly level, brown checkerboard of cornfields as far as the eye could see. This was Carlton's first taste of the Midwest. Along with the flat land, there would be other new experiences for New Englanders, such as when someone would yell, "Get in the dugout, there's a tornado warning."

The manager of the Waterloo Hawks was a tough Texan named Rac

Slider. Blessed with perhaps the perfect name for a low-level manager, the 35-year-old Slider was a cocky little dude, standing barely five feet, eight inches and weighing maybe 160 pounds. In his 11-year minor league playing career as a shortstop he had never made it above Triple A. After getting his start as a rookie-league manager in 1965, he became a ubiquitous presence in the Red Sox farm chain, managing various minor league clubs for the next 21 seasons.

Slider was intense. He didn't hesitate to jump all over players who committed a mistake on the field, frequently bringing the offenders back early the next day for remedial work. Most of the time, just to make sure everybody got the message, he would have the entire team come back early as well. And heaven help the rookie player who dared utter his given name of Rachel. "Rac was hard on us, but he was a good manager," says pitcher Charles Prediger. "He would yell at you when you messed up, but usually you deserved it. Some days we'd be there from 10 to 11:30 working out, then go home and be back at 4:30 for batting practice and infield and pitching practice, then play a game that night."

The team was composed mostly of guys right out of high school. It was the first time away from home for most of them; the first taste of freedom, the first time to play baseball every day without distractions. No school. No parents. Just baseball. "We were young and naive and didn't know what to expect, it was all new," says Prediger. "But it was great. We were playing baseball and getting paid for it. Pudge was a great guy, he fit in real quick." As it seemed to everywhere he went, the nickname somehow caught up with him quickly although he hadn't looked pudgy for years.

"At that stage nobody knew anybody," Prediger continues, "so you just sort of watched and felt your way around until you knew who you were comfortable with and then split rent with them and shared groceries. You grouped together with guys you enjoyed and had things in common with. Pudge was fun to hang out with. Me and Pudge and an outfielder named Charlie Day ran around a lot together. For a while we were like the Three Musketeers."

There were no assistant coaches at this level of the bushes—Slider was drill sergeant, mother, priest, and warden to the players. When they played, he ran the game, coached third base, and worried about lineup moves and pitching changes all at the same time. "It was tough," says Slider. "I had to do everything. There were so many players who needed help; more than I could get to. There's only so much time and you can't show any favorites. They were all kids, but they thought they were grown up. Some of them found out later they still had some growing to do. My main goal was to keep them out of trouble—sometimes that was hard to do."

Waterloo was a medium-sized city of around 70,000. It was a nice place as far as the minors went, much larger than most Class A towns, but it was slow, as were most of the stops throughout the Midwest. A theater or local bar was the usual off-field recreation, but mostly the players entertained themselves. Being young and experiencing freedom for the first time, they did what most guys their age would do—stupid stuff. There was a standing bet on the team: anyone who could drink a gallon of milk in half an hour, and keep it down, would win a hundred dollars. Many tried. No one could do it. But it was great fun to watch the challenger's stomach swell like a ripe watermelon and then see him race from the room before the projectile white flood spewed out. Occasionally, if there was doubt, someone would aid nature's course by cannonballing off the top bunk onto the poor guy's stomach. Great fun when you're 19 years old and on your own.

The players spent almost all their waking hours together, working, sweating, and dreaming. They developed friendships that would last several years as they moved up in the organization together. Some of the players found out they barely had the talent to play at this level. Others had the talent, but lacked the discipline to get much further. Spending so much time together, teammates learned each other's limits. "Pudge was on a mission," says Prediger. "He wanted to be the best. He was always taking extra batting practice, running extra sprints. You could see the talent in Pudge. I made it up to AAA. You could always pick out the guys who had a good chance to make it all the way—he was one of those."

"The talent was there," says Slider of Carlton Fisk in Waterloo. "It didn't take long watching him on the field to see that. You can never predict who's going to go on to a good career at that stage. You can see the raw talent, and if he is a player and what kind of a work ethic he has. I saw a lot of big league talent that got wasted over the years because some guys didn't want it bad enough or got into trouble or just didn't work and make adjustments. But Carlton had a good work ethic. It didn't surprise me that he went on and got better at each step up."

Players were all too aware that if they couldn't hack it here, there was no place else to go. "There was a restaurant in Waterloo that we used to go to a lot," says Prediger. "The owner was nice to ballplayers and he'd let us run up a tab. He knew we got paid every two weeks. During the season we hit a bad stretch and were losing a lot, making a lot of mistakes. After one game we were all at the restaurant and Rac came in—he knew where he'd find us." Slider silently reviewed his young troops for a long moment, then ambled over to the jukebox, fished a coin out of his pocket, and put it in. "He punched up the old country song 'Please Release Me.'" It didn't take a college kid to get the not-so-subtle symbolism in the manager's choice of music. "I'll tell you what, that scared me more than anything he did that year."

There was some talent on the Waterloo pitching staff: Lynn Mc-Glothen, a tall, hard-throwing right-hander who looked like Bob Gibson, and Roger Moret, a lefty from Puerto Rico who spoke little English. Both would be in the majors with the Red Sox within four years. The team had been together a few weeks when they got another left-handed pitcher, this one straight off the campus of the University of Southern California.

Bill Lee got more mileage out of being both left-handed and a Californian than any man in baseball history. Possessing a curious, inquisitive mind, he lacked even the remotest amount of resistance to speaking that mind—a fact that did very little to ingratiate him with the old-school Slider. A man who has spent 14 years hacking through the backwoods of minor league baseball does not appreciate a smart-mouth college kid with a few days of professional experience telling him how to do his job.

Lee, who temporarily shared an apartment with Carlton and a couple of other guys, immediately noticed the ability of his catcher, along with his tendency to be slow and methodical. "He was also slow at putting down signs," he later wrote. "I used to think, 'Jesus, what's taking him so long? I've only got two pitches.' . . . He was a fine receiver right away, he had a great arm and despite being sluggish off the field, he was very fast on the bases."

The first month Lee pitched infrequently and only in relief. He otherwise spent his time showing an unsurpassed ability to get on Slider's nerves. But Bill Lee had real talent and the higher-ups knew it—they sent orders for Slider to give him a start. In his first professional start, Lee gave up a single to the first batter and then promptly picked him off. He proceeded to retire the rest of the lineup in order for a one-hit, near-perfect shutout. The next day he was on a plane to join the Red Sox' higher Class A team. It was not the last Carlton Fisk would see of Bill Lee.

Fisk, with his competitiveness, had difficulty coming to grips with one of the realities of minor league baseball: the main purpose of the team was to train players to move up in the organization; winning, on the whole, was of secondary importance. Carlton had never done much losing in any sport; he hated it. But Slider was forced to take looks at players who weren't quite able to compete professionally—they had been signed, so somebody thought they could play and there was nowhere else to see if they could but here. Others who had definite talent, like Bill Lee, were soon kicked up a level. The Waterloo Hawks were in the process of finishing in eighth place in 1968 with a record of 53–60. Ralph Silva later told a reporter that Carlton had voiced frustration in letters home and was so exasperated with the losing that he considered giving up. That was most likely an exaggeration, however. A son of Cecil Fisk would never quit anything.

Fisk was soon recognized as the best catcher in the league. July 8, the Midwest League All-Stars played the Quad Cities Angels, the first-half champs, in the league's version of an all-star game in Davenport, Iowa. Carlton was behind the plate for the All-Stars and hit the game's only home run in front of one of the biggest crowds most of the kids had seen all year, 2,117. He finished with a good season at Waterloo, hitting .338 in 62 games, and leading the team with 12 home runs.

Fresh off his impressive first year, Fisk was invited to major league camp with the Red Sox in 1969. He was a young prospect there for a look—a kid with a future but essentially no chance of making the team. But the Red Sox were definitely not set at his position. The only catcher in camp with major league experience was Russ Gibson, a veteran of only 125 major league games, despite the fact that he had been in the Red Sox system for 12 years.

Fisk got noticed. "I remember exactly the first time I saw him in Winter Haven [the Red Sox spring training site]," says veteran pitcher Ray Culp. "He was very imposing, just a huge guy. He looked like a linebacker. He really stood out. He got in the batting cage and started ripping balls out of the park; the ball kept going. I said, 'Who's this?' And one of the guys just said, 'Some kid.' I've only seen two young guys who hit like that, where the ball just jumped off their bat—Pudge and Richie Allen when I was with the Phillies."

Carlton's arm and athleticism quickly impressed the bosses; so did his confidence. Sox manager Dick Williams told of having a contest to see which catcher could last the longest without dropping a foul pop. Williams kept hitting fungo flies, straight up, two and three at a time, and eventually Fisk was the only one left. Then Williams told him, "I'll keep hitting fungoes until you drop one."

"Fine with me, Mr. Williams," Fisk answered. "But you might be here all day." Williams also said he liked Fisk's ability to get on pitchers when they needed it.

While being properly deferential to veterans, Fisk had enough confidence to expect others to respect his time. One day as he walked through the clubhouse he passed pitcher Jim Lonborg, who was talking to reporters. Lonborg, a certified Boston hero less than two years removed from a Cy Young Award–winning season, called to him, "Hey Carlton, I'd like to warm up for a couple of minutes. Will you catch me?"

"Love to," Fisk replied.

"I'll be there in five minutes," Lonborg responded.

Five minutes turned into fifteen as Lonborg continued talking to the writers. Finally the door opened again and Fisk yelled in, "Hey Lonborg, you're on my time. How about getting out here to do that throwing you said you wanted to do."

Carlton got a few reps with the first squad and showed enough to have some in the press asking if he was ready for the bigs now. The *Sporting News* noted, "One of the most impressive young players in the Boston camp is 21-year-old Carlton Fisk, a catcher from New Hampshire. People are wondering if he can leap from Waterloo to Boston in one jump."

While "people" were wondering, the men who made the decisions were certain he could not. Personnel director Dick O'Connell told reporters Carlton wouldn't make it in 1969, but allowed, "The boy is very advanced for his age."

Fisk was sent to the minor league base in Ocala for reassignment in early April and joined the Pittsfield AA team of the Eastern League. Pittsfield was a pretty town in the mountains of northwestern Massachusetts, about an hour and a half south of Charlestown, New Hampshire. They played in Wahconah Park, one of the oldest wooden stadiums in the country. If they got 1,000 fans out to a game, it was considered a big crowd.

Bill Lee started the season in Pittsfield also, but after a month was called to Boston and stuck. There were several other guys from the Waterloo team in Pittsfield. "I roomed with Pudge in Pittsfield," says Charles Prediger. "He would come home with me on off days. I lived in a small town just north of Philadelphia. We would stay with my parents and go fishing during the day. His parents would come see us in Pittsfield and we'd go out to eat. They were nice people."

It was a treat May 20 when Carlton made his home-state professional debut against Manchester, New Hampshire, in front of his family and friends who drove over from Charlestown. The only New Hampshire player in the league, he was the star as he hit his first home run of the season in the fourth inning and added a double and a walk and scored the final run to help Pittsfield to a 4–2 win.

At Pittsfield, Carlton met Rick Miller. A speedy outfielder from Grand Rapids, Michigan, Miller had been the Big Ten batting champ and an All-American at Michigan State before the Red Sox drafted him in 1969. The two became good friends. Carlton introduced Miller to his sister Janet and they began dating. They would be married three years later.

Although he had the great arm, Fisk was still pretty raw in the field. "At Pittsfield, Carlton really wasn't a very good catcher," says infielder Buddy Hunter. "He struggled. But he worked hard. He was the first person on the field every day. One of the problems was that he had one of those old round catcher's mitts without a break in it. He dropped a lot of balls. He was slow getting the ball out of his glove."

Despite Hunter's impression, Prediger remembers that Carlton seemed more polished behind the plate than he had been in Waterloo and was also becoming a student of the game. "In Double A, we started sitting in the locker room after games if I pitched and he caught and we'd talk and go over the game, just talk baseball for a long time. He was always very knowledgeable. He knew the hitters and knew their weaknesses. He would come out and talk to you on the mound and tell you 'be careful, this guy likes the slider away,' that sort of thing.

"Pudge was a great guy to have on my team," continues Prediger. "He was bigger than most guys and I always knew he had my back. If anyone started out to the mound after getting hit or something, he would jump out and get right in between. He protected his pitchers. Don't think guys didn't know that and appreciate it."

Unmindful of the clock, on or off the field, Carlton's pace frequently irritated his teammates. "As a middle infielder, I want things to move fast, but we always had to wait on Pudge," says Hunter. "We had to wait on him in the game and again after the game. He was always the last one out of the clubhouse. We would all be on the bus, getting ready for an eight-hour drive and he would still be in there. He was a nice guy, but we hated him when he did that.

"What I really remember about Pudge from those early years in the minors is that he was so loose," adds Hunter. "We would be doing exercises before games and he could turn his body and put his legs in places I wouldn't dream of. And I was a skinny infielder. I couldn't believe a big guy like that had that much flexibility. I think that helped him last all those years squatting."

Carlton struggled at the plate much of the year at Pittsfield and hit only .243. It was a pattern that would be repeated throughout his years in the minor leagues. He would start the seasons hitting well, then fade and end up at .243, at .229, at .263. He would later hit much better in the major leagues than he did in the minors. Most guys fare better in the minors than they do against the obviously better pitching in the majors. How could Fisk do the opposite? He always blamed the poor lighting and poor hitting backgrounds in the minor league parks. Pittsfield was a particularly difficult place to hit, especially when the sun set directly behind the center field fence, shining into the batter's eyes. He also frequently said that he felt more comfortable in the batter's box in the majors because minor league pitchers could throw just as hard, but they didn't know where the ball was going. Another factor was the paucity of games he had played in high school due to the weather. He hadn't seen that many good pitchers (or good curveballs) before entering professional ball. "I found out why so few hitters ever come out of northern New England," he later said. "It's pretty tough going into professional baseball when most of the guys you're playing against had more games in one year than I played in my entire life."

The other impediment to his minor league batting average was the military obligation: one weekend a month and two weeks in the middle of the summer. Each year, just when he would get in shape and start hitting, he would have to leave. "The reserves interrupted your flow," he said later. "You'd be doing well, and then it would be time to go, and when you returned, it would take time to regain your rhythm, especially at the plate. But I wasn't complaining, because the sacrifices being made by the guys who were on active duty in Vietnam were far, far greater than the ones I was making."

One of the guys in Vietnam making a sacrifice was his own brother. Calvin had graduated from the University of New Hampshire in 1966 and signed with the Orioles. But as an ROTC graduate he was called to active military duty soon thereafter. He had been able to attend spring training camp with the Orioles and was assigned to the Class A Miami Marlins in 1967 and was hitting .296 with five home runs when the Army called him back for good. By the time Carlton was in Pittsfield in 1969, Calvin was a first lieutenant with the 25th Infantry Division in Vietnam. He was the subject of an article in the September 1, 1969, issue of the Army's *Tropic Lightning News* titled "Catcher in the 'Nam: Fisk Eyes Baseball Career." Appearing between articles covering a jungle ambush and a sweep through an enemy bunker complex was a picture of a smiling Calvin Fisk, in green fatigues, swinging a weighted bat he had brought with him. He discussed his dream of returning to baseball: "I've kept in good shape since I entered the Army. My arm is strong and I'm still throwing well, only my hitting maybe is a little rusty." Calvin kept his baseball dream alive, but upon returning and attending camp with the Orioles he was told he was too old. He returned to school, got his PhD in anatomy, and became a professor at Indiana University.

Carlton's military duty in the Reserves at least allowed him to continue playing professional baseball. Bob Wilber, who as the coach of the Chester, Vermont, American Legion squad had known Carlton as a player, befriended him during his time in Chester. "We'd spend a lot of time together during those two weeks each year," he said in 2000. "He used to make me take him with me to Rutland to play softball. He'd play under an assumed name, but everyone knew who he was."

While Carlton tried to remain as anonymous as everyone else in his unit, occasionally his full-time job would be discovered and someone would make a big deal about it such as happened on a unit training trip to an Army depot near Scranton, Pennsylvania, in the summer of 1969. One of the base workers was a big baseball fan and arranged a photo op and impromptu baseball lesson for his son. That week's issue of the *Pocono Record* (Stroudsburg, Pennsylvania) had a picture of Carlton Fisk, in his Army fatigues, squatting in a catcher's stance next to the boy. The accompanying article, "Little Leaguer Gets Big League Advice," explained: "Bobby Clemens' smile was about as bright as the sun on Tobyhanna Army Depot's parade field where he met big leaguer Carlton Fisk. Carlton looked like almost any other member of the Chester Vt 393 Supply and Service Battalion at the depot for two weeks. However, it didn't take long for word to get around that he regularly wears another uniform—that of the Pittsfield Red Sox. . . . Dressed in his Army khakis, swinging a bat at his side, Carlton took Bobby onto the parade field to give him some pointers and present him with an autographed ball. It was quite a present for Bobby, whose ninth birthday fell the day before. This is the Little Leaguer's first year with his hometown group. . . . It is an especially proud father who watches Bobby in the field for the boy was born with a club foot. Through corrective surgery in September of 1967 Bobby's foot was repaired and he was soon able to take up normal activities. As for Fisk, chances are that he'll soon be the starting catcher for the Boston Red Sox and if he does Bobby's thrill at having met him will probably double."

Back on the baseball field, Carlton continued to show progress and gave hints that he might indeed soon be the starting catcher for the Red Sox. Once again he was regarded as one of the best catchers in the league and sportswriters voted him to the All-Star team. In the play-offs at the conclusion of the 1969 season, against York, Carlton had an RBI triple and a home run as Pittsfield won 7–4.

When Pittsfield's season was finished, Carlton was called up to the Red Sox for the classic cup of coffee. He knew a few of the guys on the club he had worked with in the spring and in the Florida Instructional League in 1967. Also, Bill Lee was already there. But Fisk kept mostly to himself, as he was awed by the surroundings and the much older players. "I didn't feel like I was part of the team," he said later. "I felt more like the batboy."

He had been to a few games in Fenway as a fan, but sitting in the stands was nothing compared to the view of the park from the dugout. It was amazing how green the grass and the stands were, how close the Green Monster felt, and how majestic the whole place seemed. "It was a little intimidating to walk in the Boston clubhouse, because of all the history that had taken place there," says pitcher Mike Garman, who was called up from Class A Winston-Salem at the same time. Babe Ruth, Ted Williams, Jimmie Foxx, Lefty Grove, there was an aura to the place. "We were tickled to be there."

Carlton made his major league debut in a start against the Orioles in Boston on September 18. The Fisk family and a horde of others made the trip from Charlestown. Ralph Silva and Poody Walsh visited Carlton in the dugout before the game. In a tough assignment for a guy in his first game, Carlton faced Mike Cuellar, a left-hander with some of the most baffling off-speed pitches in the majors. Cuellar was putting the finishing touches on a 23-win, Cy Young Award season.

Carlton stepped into the box in the bottom of the second with one out for his first major league at bat. He hit a grounder to the third base-man, who vacuumed it up and threw him out at first (apparently no one told him that few men made a living hitting ground balls to Brooks Robinson). He went 0-for-4 with one strikeout against Cuellar.

It was a tumultuous time in Boston. The Red Sox were struggling to stay above .500 and headed for a third place finish. Draconian manager Dick Williams, who had led the Sox to the 1967 pennant, had worn the nerves of his players thin. There had been a celebrated incident in which he fined star Carl Yastrzemski for loafing in August. Rumors were swirling that Williams was on the way out. Four days after Carlton's debut, Williams was fired and third base coach Eddie Popowski was named interim manager. Some players openly applauded the firing, others were upset that the man who helped turn around the franchise had been let go. The rookies kept quiet and drank it all in. Carlton got to travel with the team and see the difference between life in the majors and life in the minors, but he only got in one more game, striking out in his only at bat in a 10–3 loss to Detroit on September 28.

Carlton and Linda were married over the winter. They had weathered the difficult geographical separation while she was still in college in Durham and he was in Waterloo in 1968. Playing in nearby Pittsfield in 1969 had given them the chance to visit much more frequently. The marriage took place in Manchester, New Hampshire (Linda's hometown). Calvin Fisk served as best man.

The Red Sox, still looking for an answer behind the plate, brought six catchers to camp in 1970. Jerry Moses was there and was considered to be the front-runner for the job. Russ Gibson, who had hit .251 in 85 games in 1969, Tom Satriano, Don Pavletich, and Bob Montgomery were also there. Fisk hurt his back early in camp and it cost him any chance to compete. He was optioned to AAA Louisville in late March. The Colonels' manager, Billy Gardner, initially told him he would be the number one catcher, then on the last day of spring training called him into his office. Bob Montgomery, who had been the International League's All-Star catcher in 1969, was being sent down by Boston. Carlton was headed back to AA, this time to Pawtucket. He once again got off to a fast start, hitting five home runs with 13 RBIs in the first 12 games for Pawtucket while batting .316. But, as before, nagging injuries, weight loss, and slumps caused a big drop the second half of the season.

Carlton felt like he had a solid spring with the Red Sox in Winter Haven in 1971 and thought he deserved to stick with the team. Jerry Moses had been traded over the winter for pitching help, removing a large obstacle to Fisk's major league ambition. Fisk battled Montgomery for the Red Sox catching job through most of camp, but Boston picked up veteran catcher Duane Josephson from the White Sox in a trade March 31. The 29-year-old Josephson, after being a habitual .230 to .240 guy, had hit a career-best .316 in 1970. He was regarded as a tough, dependable defensive catcher. Fisk was sent to Deland, Florida, to finish spring training with the AAA Louisville Colonels. He didn't like it. It was reported in Boston that before Fisk left Winter Haven, Red Sox manager Eddie Kasko told him he'd "have to go out and earn his letter in the minor leagues."

Carlton gave a different account to a sports reporter at a Springfield, Vermont, American Legion banquet that fall: "He [Kasko] told me they kept me around [spring training] because they needed someone to warm up the pitchers. He said they had sent out waiver feelers on me and seven clubs were interested in me. He said he hoped I would have a good season [in the minors] because it would increase my trade value." Not exactly an award-winning motivational speech.

Fisk had been progressing up through the Red Sox farm system, getting better each year, but he was still missing something to distinguish him from other catchers; something in the way he handled a game behind the plate, something that would give him the assurance and confidence to take charge of a team of older men and tell them what to do. He found that something in Louisville in the summer of 1971.

The manager for the Louisville Colonels was Darrell Johnson. A 43-year-old former catcher, Johnson had experienced the classic life of the baseball traveling yeoman. Signed by the St. Louis Browns, he spent six years in the minors before making his major league debut in 1952. He proceeded to play for the Browns, White Sox, Yankees, Cardinals, Phillies, Reds, and Orioles—seven teams in parts of six seasons. Never able to earn a regular playing job, he was finally released in 1962. He played in only 134 games in those six years, compiling a .234 lifetime average.

While not possessing the cannonlike arm or hitting prowess to allow him to have a lengthy stay on the field anywhere, Johnson became an excellent handler of pitchers and was known as a great mentor for younger teammates. And Johnson didn't just waste all those hours he spent on major league benches sneaking hot dogs and checking out girls in the stands—he watched and learned from some of the best minds in baseball. "I got a lot of slivers in my butt, but I got them sitting next to men like Ralph Houk and Casey Stengel and Fred Hutchinson and Earl Weaver," he told a reporter in 1974. "I didn't play much, but I learned a lot of baseball. They didn't make a move I didn't analyze." After retiring as a player, Johnson worked his way up through a succession of minor league managing and major league coaching positions.

Johnson was serious, taciturn, and not at all charismatic. He was demanding with his players, almost a perfectionist. "He expected you to come to the ballpark ready to play every day," says Mike Garman, who pitched for Louisville in 1971. "Otherwise, you might not hear from him for days."

Johnson recognized the potential in Fisk. He saw the tools he never had himself; tools he would have sold his soul to be able to possess. As an insufficiently talented bench academic, Johnson understood that the lot in life of a minor league manager was to train guys with more talent to be able to have better careers than he was able to have himself. He dedicated the 1971 season to honing the physically impressive, but raw, undisciplined game of Carlton Fisk.

In Johnson, Fisk found a professional mentor. He would later point to the 1971 season as the turning point in his career. "I always worked hard, but I never knew what I was doing," he said. "He taught me pitches, pitchers, sequences and the difference between being a catcher and someone who goes behind the plate to catch and throw."

"Pudge and I spend a lot of time together, just talking baseball," Johnson said in midseason 1971. "In spring training, I gave him pitching charts from previous games and asked him to grade them. He was calling the whole game over again. He was to ask himself if that was the right pitch to call in each situation. He used a red pencil to make his marks. I asked him to explain why he did it this way."

After every game, Fisk and Johnson went over the scorebook pitch by pitch. They were constantly talking baseball, constantly quizzing one another. Talking, studying, and learning. How do you get guys out? Learning how to call a good game. "He broke the job [catching] down into different parts and put them all back together again for me," Fisk said in 1973. "Darrell Johnson taught me in Louisville that the catcher has to run the ball game. He has to make his pitcher bear down and stay away from mistakes. This isn't always easy to do with some pitchers."

Johnson taught Fisk how to become a professional catcher. Study the hitter. What does he like? What did he do last time? Watch his feet, watch his hands. Study and watch. Know your pitcher. What's his best pitch? What does he want to do when he needs an out? Know how well he throws each of his pitches, on each day. Watch the pitcher for signs of weakness or mechanical faults. Learn which pitchers to prod, which ones to coddle, how to call the correct pitch in the correct spot, how to block low pitches to give pitchers the confidence to throw their best low stuff in key situations without worry of a passed ball, how to work umpires. He had to learn it all. They spent hours together. Carlton had always charged ahead full speed, brimming with testosterone and muscle. Now he had a method to control the aggression. And more importantly, a method to control the game, to impose his will on the game. The constant study greased the synapses of his gray matter—information that once traveled from his eyes to his brain by snail-mail carried on a winding New Hampshire road by a horse-drawn wagon now raced through on a high-speed Internet connection.

"I think that also helped him be a better hitter in the majors," says Garman. "He knew what was going on in the pitcher's and catcher's mind after that. It helped him know what to expect when he was up there hitting."

Louisville had a strong team, loaded with young players who would make their mark in the majors soon: Ben Oglivie, Lynn McGlothen, John Curtis, Roger Moret, Dwight Evans, Juan Beniquez. Carlton once again got off to a good start hitting. In the first 16 games he drove in 16 runs and was hitting .380. After missing a few games when a foul tip off his own bat on a checked swing broke his nose, he continued to play well. In mid-May he was over .300 and among the league leaders in RBIs. One game against Winnipeg he had 8 RBIs (a new club record) on a grand slam, a 3-run homer, and an RBI single.

In May, Louisville players got a look at a peculiar pitcher for the Richmond Braves who would play a major role in the lives of the ones who made it to the Red Sox over the next decade. Luis Tiant was a Cuban right-handed pitcher, already balding, with a round face, puffy jowls, and a stocky build modeled after Yosemite Sam. He had the most unusual windup and delivery any of the players had ever seen, corkscrewing around, turning his back on the hitter, rolling his eyes up and every way except at the batter, and releasing the ball from a multitude of slots.

Tiant had been a flame-thrower when he torched the American League with the Indians in 1968, winning 21 games with a 1.60 ERA. Arm trouble got him traded to Minnesota in 1970, then the Twins gave up on him in 1971, cutting him and leaving him at the hotel in Orlando as the team headed north at the end of spring training. After every other major league team passed on him, the Braves had signed him to a 30-day trial with their Triple A Richmond team, only as a favor to former teammate and friend Stan Williams. Richmond used him sparingly and soon released him.

But the seasoned eyes of Darrell Johnson saw something. Although Tiant was struggling with his control, which he blamed on the sporadic use due to bad weather and rainouts, the arm looked strong. Johnson passed on the word and the Red Sox, like every team, always looking for one more good pitcher, picked him up and assigned him to Louisville for a trial.

Carlton Fisk was immediately impressed with Tiant, both on the mound and in the clubhouse. He was remarkable in that, even though he hadn't been pitching well, even though he was hanging on the edge of the end of his baseball career, he always displayed confidence in himself and was a cold-blooded competitor. He was also a delightful human being off the field with a wit and easygoing attitude that made him impossible to dislike.

Johnson quickly realized the team had made a steal. And Tiant quickly started bedeviling International League hitters. May 22, he struck out 13 batters for the Colonels. June 1, he pitched a five-hit shutout. Not long after that he was on his way to Boston. Carlton Fisk and Luis Tiant would be seeing much more of each other later.

Fisk had a solid year at Louisville and was named to the International League All-Star team. The work with Johnson paid off. "Pudge was great to pitch to," says Mike Garman. "I later pitched to some pretty good catchers in my career, Jerry Grote, Steve Yeager, Gary Carter, Ted Simmons, Tim McCarver—some pretty good catchers, but Pudge by far was the best catcher I ever pitched to. He had such great quickness, nobody was ever quicker than him behind the plate. He called a great game. Also his arm was just that much better than any other major league catcher I ever saw. He had a phenomenal arm. When we played in Louisville, you actually wanted guys to try to steal second. All I had to do was throw the ball and then dive out of the way and it was an out. It was an easy way to get out of trouble. He was so quick, though, you really had to move fast or he would nail you with the ball. He could be tough on you on the mound when things weren't going the way he wanted. He would come out to the mound and tell me, 'Have an idea.' Sometimes, I'd have to tell him, 'Get back there, I'll do the pitching.' We would go back and forth in games, but we were great friends off the field.

"You really developed some great friendships in those years coming up through the minors," adds Garman. "You played with a lot of the same guys at each place, met them in the fall and in spring training. We were all about the same age. We went through a lot together, long bus rides, worrying 'Are we ever going to make the majors?' You really formed a close bond with those guys. Spending that much time together in those years, you got a pretty good idea of people. Pudge was rock-solid. I really respected him a tremendous amount. He was a gamer, one of the best teammates. He got upset when we lost. It meant a lot to him. He was really committed and cared about winning."

"We ended up being on several teams together in the minors—Pittsfield, Pawtucket, and down in the Florida Instructional League [in 1969]," says Prediger. "I roomed with him in Pittsfield and in Florida. We got married on the same day. Then our wives became good friends. We went everywhere together."

"We got very close in the minors," says Hunter, who in addition to playing with Fisk at Pittsfield also played at Pawtucket and Louisville. "Our wives were friends. We later had kids about the same time. We did a lot together. He was a fun-loving guy; always had a smile on his face, always happy. We joked around a lot. There was a lot of camaraderie back then. That's the main thing I remember about those guys. We did everything together. After games, we'd take the bus together, went out together, drank beer and talked baseball together. And you learned an awful lot about baseball from going out with the older guys and talking over beers. Now, even in the minors, everybody has their separate cars and other activities and they all take off—they miss a lot. The camaraderie and team atmosphere was great."

"I guess we were the family-oriented guys," adds Garman. "We were all married, at about the same stage of our families. Our wives were best friends, they hung out together away from the field, did things together when we were on the road. We would drive together to the ballpark. Later, when we were in Boston and would go on a road trip, my wife would drive up and stay with Linda Fisk at their house in New Hampshire. Some guys went out and drank a lot in baseball, but Pudge was not one of them. There was never an issue with alcohol. We might sit around and drink a beer and talk baseball, but that was it. Most of the guys we hung around with, like Charlie Prediger, Buddy Hunter, me, and Pudge, we've all been married over 40 years now. That's rare for baseball, rare for anyone nowadays, but you don't have marriages that last that long by accident. We weren't the guys going out and drinking a lot. Linda was really kind and friendly to everyone, very easy to get along with. She wasn't overly outgoing, never got loud or was like some of those baseball wives who always wanted the spotlight. She was just classy and nice."

It was a good life, but uncertain. Carlton and Linda's first child, daughter Carlyn (a combination of Carlton and Linda) was born late in 1970. In the off-season, they lived in Keene, New Hampshire, a larger town about 20 miles south of Charlestown. Making only minor league money ($4,000 a year), Carlton was still concerned about his future and how to pay the bills for his growing family. In the winter after his AA season he told a reporter from nearby Springfield, Vermont, that he was only going to give it a few more years—he had no intention of "pulling a Russ Gibson" and toiling in the minor leagues for 10 years. As a precaution, he began taking classes at Keene State.

Baseball players of the era were not afforded the luxury of working out all year like their modern counterparts. They had to have jobs during the winter. Carlton took a job in a clothing store in Keene. "He just walked in one day and asked for a job," the store's owner, Ron Russell, said in 2000. Of course Russell, a big sports fan who years earlier had played semipro basketball against a block of granite named Cecil Fisk, knew who Carlton was. "He was well known up and down the Connecticut River Valley. . . . He was a smart kid. He said if he didn't make it to the big leagues within a year and a half he was going to get his (P.E.) degree and become a teacher." Russell enjoyed his new employee. He worked hard and was good for business. A lot of girls would come in and just hang around, looking at him. "He was a regular clerk, helped clean, inventory, and waited on people. He was a great employee. Very cordial. A model of perfection."

"He was on the edge, trying to figure out what was going to happen with his career," says Mark Russell, the son of the store's owner. Mark was in college at the time and became friends with Carlton. "He had been in AA; promising, but still not a sure thing. They really didn't have much back then. He wasn't making any money from baseball. He had to have a winter job to pay the bills. He was living in a trailer park, working and taking college classes. He was trying to make sure he had an education in case things didn't work out with baseball. He was a good guy. Grounded, friendly, knew where he was from. He's stayed that way over the years."

Carlton became friends with the Russells and was particularly kind to Kevin, their mentally handicapped son. Later, when he made the majors, Carlton treated the entire store, about 15 people, to a trip to Fenway, giving them a grand tour before the game. Russell and his family would make many trips to Boston to see Kevin's favorite hero.

"Kevin was huge into sports," says Mark Russell. "When you can introduce a kid like that to a major league ballplayer, it's just great. Carlton was very generous with his time with Kevin. He always had time for him."

With the progress Carlton Fisk made at Louisville in the 1971 season, it appeared that the struggles and uncertainty of his minor league days would soon be over. He was called up to the Red Sox in September.

5 Boston

CARLTON FISK HAD BEEN TO THE MAJORS for the brief two-game sightseeing trip in 1969, but this time it was the real deal. He had earned his way up and he was here to play. He arrived with five others from the minors, guys with a lot of talent who would help in the near future: Cecil Cooper, Roger Moret, John Curtis, Ben Oglivie, and Rick Miller. It was said that with the Sox out of the race, manager Eddie Kasko wanted a look at the future. The press called the youngsters Kasko's Kiddie Korps.

The Boston Red Sox had not won a World Series since 1918, when their best player was a left-handed pitcher named Babe Ruth. Since then, they had won American League pennants twice, in 1946 and 1967, with seasons of mediocrity interspersed with dismal futility in the intervening years. But 1967 had proven to be a watershed after which they had been perennial contenders.

The Red Sox had a unique owner in Thomas A. Yawkey. Along with the Cubs' Phil Wrigley, the 68-year-old Yawkey was one of the last of the true barons of baseball team owners. Orphaned as a child and the sole heir to a vast timber and mining fortune, he had owned the Red Sox since buying the team and Fenway Park for $1.2 million in 1933, at the age of 30. Since Yawkey never needed the Red Sox to make money (what would he do with more of the stuff?), the baseball team became his plaything. He was often spotted on the field or in the clubhouse, enjoying the vibes. Few owners ever loved their players the way Thomas Yawkey did. He frequently worked the room in the clubhouse after games, chatting up players and asking about their families. He was especially enamored with his biggest stars, Ted Williams and Carl Yastrzemski. The Red Sox players, for the most part, loved both Yawkey and his money.

"Tom Yawkey was great," says pitcher Gary Peters, who joined the Red Sox in 1970 after seven years with the White Sox. "He used to come in and play pepper with me. I would usually be there early, doing player rep stuff, and he'd come in and say, 'Come on, let's go play pepper.' Me and the batboys would go out there with him, on the field at Fenway Park, and play. After I got here and was the player rep, he told me, 'Anything the players want to be comfortable, just let me know.' He was really great to players."

Yawkey never wanted for anything in his life except for a major league championship but, like the overindulging parent who spoils his child, he couldn't buy one and didn't know how to go about earning one. Although he lavishly poured money into the system on salaries for his players and bonuses for unproven prospects, he presided over years of losing teams, mainly due to mismanagement caused by an overreliance on ill-prepared, inept cronies in key positions.

Yawkey had made a major change in this philosophy, which in turn resulted in a major change in the team's fortunes, in 1965 when he hired Dick O'Connell to be his general manager. The mild-mannered, bald, cigar-smoking, universally respected O'Connell had been a Naval Intelligence officer in World War II, serving on the staff of Admiral Chester Nimitz. O'Connell got his start in baseball after the war at the suggestion of several members of the Red Sox organization he had met while serving at Pearl Harbor.

The former intelligence officer had worked in various positions for the team, gradually learning the business and moving up, until he was named general manager in 1965. He was the first nondrinking partner that Yawkey had hired at the important position—an honest to goodness baseball man—and he proceeded to be singularly instrumental in turning the Red Sox from the highest paid bunch of losers into one of the best teams in the league. He proved to be a shrewd trader and an astute judge of talent who didn't give a Fenway Park rat's ass about what color the player was (a marked change to a problem that had plagued the organization for years). He took over a team that had finished no higher than sixth place for the previous seven years and that drew barely 600,000 fans, and within two years engineered the Impossible Dream pennant winner of 1967. Thereafter, the Sox regularly led the league in attendance and the modern Red Sox Nation was born.

In 1971, baseball owners still operated under the age-old reserve clause and held all the cards in relations with players. But under the influence of Yawkey, the Red Sox players were treated much better in contract talks with O'Connell than the rest of major leaguers. New players obtained in trades, used to fighting for every cent, were amazed at the ease of negotiations in Boston. "When I got to Boston, Dick O'Connell, the general manager, said to me, 'How much would it take to make you happy?' " said Gary Peters. "I gave him a total, which I thought was a little high and he said, 'Fine, I'll get the papers for you to sign.' I remember thinking if it was that easy, I would have asked for more."

When Carlton Fisk joined the Red Sox in September of 1971, they were playing out the schedule, playing for numbers, and for next year's contract. They had been in first place for a total of 32 days and contended as late as July, but the powerful Baltimore Orioles had caught fire, as everyone expected, and pummeled the field into submission, eventually winning both 100-plus games and the Eastern Division title for the third consecutive year. The Sox were on their way to an 85–77 record, good for third in the division, 18 games back. They had experienced a poor second half, going 36–40.

Even though they were considered to be underperforming, the Sox had drawn well at the gate with over 1.6 million fans. Red Sox fans were among the most knowledgeable, loyal fans in the game. They shouldered a combination of uninhibited love and pathologic pessimism due to the plethora of tantalizing near-misses of the past; near-misses that became embedded in their DNA and were passed from generation to generation, such that a kid born in 1965 might, during a bout of self-pity and depression, throw his hands to the heavens and cry out, "Why did McCarthy skip Parnell and Kinder and throw Galehouse at the Indians in the playoff in '48?" Most of all, Sox fans cared. But they expected a lot. "The Red Sox fan base was very demanding," says former Boston utility infielder John Kennedy. "They're great, great fans. They know the game and they support the team no matter what. But you better produce. You're being paid, they expect you to perform. If you don't produce, you're going to hear about it." And one of the things people had been hearing about in 1971 was that the team should've had a much better record in view of the obvious talent they possessed.

That talent started with Carl Yastrzemski. Yaz had achieved mythical status in New England with his otherworldly performance in the waning days of the 1967 pennant race, leading the Sox to the pennant and capturing the Triple Crown. A magnificent athlete who could do virtually anything better than anyone else, he possessed speed and defense (five Gold Gloves), power (three 40-homer, 100-RBI seasons between 1967 and '70), could hit for average (three batting titles, missed a fourth by .0003), a strong arm, and played the peculiarities of the left field corner of Fenway Park better than any man who ever lived. By 1971, he had been one of the best players in baseball for a decade, but he was finishing his worst season as a major leaguer, hitting only .254 with 15 home runs and 70 RBIs.

Yaz was an enigma, to those who played with him, those who covered him in the press, and those who worshipped him from the stands. He was the de facto leader of the team by reason of sheer talent and force of personality, but he didn't seem to readily accept the mantle of authority placed upon him, preferring to lead by his actions alone. At times he could appear moody, prideful, or selfish. He was said to be an intractable loner; some said shy, some said self-centered. In Jim Bouton's seminal book *Ball Four*, a former Red Sox teammate was quoted as saying "Carl Yastrzemski is for himself, first and second and the hell with everybody else." After being the highest paid player in the game at $140,000 in 1970, Yaz had signed a monstrous deal: three-years, $500,000. When word of that contract came out he immediately became public enemy number one among fans and the media. The fact that he proceeded to have a poor season after signing the contract made him fair game. Fans, disappointed at his inability to do the impossible on demand, began booing him at Fenway. Teammates strongly defended Yaz in the press as did manager Eddie Kasko. They all agreed that no one on the team worked harder at his craft. He frequently played hurt and seldom missed a game for any reason.

Besides Yaz, there was plenty of other talent. Outfielder Reggie Smith had 30 home runs and 96 RBIs in 1971. Smith was blessed with the type of athleticism that had never been seen in Boston. He had speed, power, and one of the strongest arms (if not necessarily the most accurate) in the majors. Third baseman Rico Petrocelli, the emotional leader of the team, hit 28 home runs and had 89 RBIs. Petrocelli was a scrapper, loved by fans; a fierce competitor who had earned a reputation as one of the toughest guys on any field. He was a great-fielding third baseman and would have been a Gold Glove winner if Brooks Robinson hadn't been playing in the same league. Shortstop Luis Aparicio, obtained from the White Sox before the 1971 season, was on everyone's short list of the greatest fielding shortstops in history. But, at 36 years old, the future Hall of Famer had lost a few steps from his range and had slumped at the plate as well, hitting only .232 in 1971.

The Red Sox pitching, while including some quality arms, was relatively thin. It was mostly a veteran staff, led by Gary Peters, Sonny Siebert, Ray Culp, and Jim Lonborg, with one of the league's best relievers, Sparky Lyle, in the bullpen. Bill Lee, Fisk's brief minor league teammate, was in Boston concluding a fine season in which he had gone 9–2 with a 2.74 ERA, mostly as a reliever. There were only a few holdovers from the 1967 pennant winners: Yaz, Smith, Petrocelli, Lonborg, and first baseman George Scott. The team had failed to capitalize on the promise of '67, which was cause for great discontent among fans and media.

If printed reports of the time were believed, it was not a happy clubhouse that Carlton Fisk and the other new guys joined. It was a clubhouse on edge. Young *Boston Globe* sportswriter Peter Gammons facetiously referred to the team as "Unity University" due to all their spats. The favorite pastime in Boston seemed to be ripping teammates and management. A 1972 baseball guide magazine summed up the national media sentiment about the Red Sox when it stated, "The only question [about the team] is 'who's going to be unhappy in Boston this season?'"

The biggest blowup of 1971 had occurred in July. Part-time outfielder Billy Conigliaro, upset on the occasion of his brother, former Red Sox star Tony, retiring from the California Angels, griped to the press that a jealous Yaz had gotten his brother traded from the Sox. He added that the Sox clubhouse was divided with Yaz and Smith on one side and everyone else on the other, that the two stars influenced who played and who sat on the bench, and who got preferential treatment from management.

Smith responded, telling reporters that Conigliaro's remarks were a "cop-out on his part because of his lack of ability. I don't want to play with him anymore because he's not acting in the best interest of the club." The story seemed to keep the national press happy and interested for a week, the local press for much longer.

Looking back, most observers and players feel that Boston didn't have any more disagreements than any other baseball team, they just had a much more aggressive press to deal with. It wasn't just the

Boston papers. Every town in New England had a newspaper and citizens who were red-hot Red Sox fans. And they were all looking for the big scoop. "The Red Sox had a great team atmosphere on and off the field," says Buddy Hunter, who was called up earlier in 1971. "A lot of the stuff written was because the writers were constantly looking for stuff. I had writers come up to me and try to get me to say things."

"That's how it happened in Boston in those days," says Leigh Montville, who got his start with *The Boston Globe* about the same time Carlton arrived in Boston. "I remember one of the first games I covered, Billy Conigliaro was playing. A crucial fly ball dropped in front of him and they lost. I was down in the locker room after the game and I heard somebody ask Carl [Yaz], 'Do you think Billy was playing too deep?' And he said, 'Yeah, I guess so.' That was it. That was all he said.

"The next day everybody else's headline was 'Yaz Blasts Billy C.' I was the only one that missed it—I wrote about the game. I guess I hadn't been there long enough to know."

"They usually had someone to write about the game and somebody walking around looking for stuff," says pitcher Bobby Bolin. "If you've got 25 guys together for that long, 162 games, every once in a while you're going to have somebody say something, especially when something bad happens on the field and people are frustrated. Usually it's forgotten as soon as it's over. But they always made a big deal out of it."

"I played on four other clubs," says John Kennedy. "After a game with some teams, there might be three or four writers in the clubhouse. Here there would be 30. You'd come upstairs and see them standing there. Once everybody got in the clubhouse, here they came. If we lost, all 30 would go straight for the manager's office and start peppering him with questions: 'Why did you do this? Why didn't you do that? Why didn't you hit this guy or move that guy?' And there was always somebody snooping around trying to get a big story."

If any team in baseball lived in a glass clubhouse, it was the Boston Red Sox. And the members of the New England media regularly walked in ready to hand out stones. "There were some good writers in that bunch, but some of them wished they were writing an Ann Landers column instead of baseball," says Kennedy. "Someone might come in and say Yaz and Smith and Conigliaro were having problems, 'What do you think about them?' Then they would go to each one and say, 'Did you hear what Tony said?' Then they would go to the other guy to get his reaction—all the time trying to get somebody to say something." This annoying media tendency in Boston would prove to be influential in one of the biggest episodes of Carlton Fisk's rookie year in 1972.

Easygoing Red Sox manager Eddie Kasko was 39 years old. Almost studious-appearing with his wire-framed glasses, Kasko seemed an unlikely inhabitant of what was probably the hottest managerial seat in the majors. Originally signed by the Browns, he had spent eight years in the minors before making the Cardinals in 1957. Despite limited athletic ability, he survived in the majors the next eight seasons on guts, brains, and determination, hitting .264 as a shortstop and third baseman. A favorite of Cincinnati manager Fred Hutchinson, he had been obtained by the Reds soon after Hutchinson moved to Cincinnati in 1959 and had been instrumental in the Reds' pennant in 1961 and had hit .319 in the World Series.

Kasko retired after his only season with the Red Sox in 1966 but had impressed observers with his attitude and had been particularly helpful in assisting talented young shortstop Rico Petrocelli. Viewed as a manager with potential, Kasko was given the Red Sox AAA teams in Toronto and Louisville from 1967 to 1969. He had replaced the embattled Dick Williams in Boston in 1970.

Unlike the abrasive, demanding Williams, Kasko was much more amenable to his players. He didn't seem to particularly enjoy confrontations. Rather than order someone to get a haircut, for instance, he might call the player into his office and discuss the image the team should project, then leave it up to him to get his hair cut. Not overly emotional, Kasko maintained an even keel. He had rules, but they didn't seem to get in anyone's way.

"Kasko was a super guy," says relief pitcher Bobby Bolin, who, like Kasko, was a southerner from the Carolinas. "Everybody liked him. He didn't get on guys too much. He let players play. And he didn't get too uptight. One night we were playing the Orioles and I came on in the bottom of the ninth to relieve Sonny Siebert. The bases were loaded with Orioles. Eddie looked at me and flipped me the ball and said, 'Good luck.'"

"I liked Eddie," says Kennedy. "It was just, 'Go out and play the game and play hard.' He didn't bother you. He got along with everybody."

Kasko had immediately taken heat because the Red Sox had failed to live up to expectations. They had a winning record, but didn't seriously contend. Whether Kasko would be retained for 1972 had been a regular source of debate in barrooms, cabs, and newspapers all over New England as the Sox stumbled through the second half of the 1971 season. The team had settled that debate by giving him a one-year renewal on September 5.

In reality, the reason the Red Sox had not won the last three pennants was due neither to the managers nor team harmony. It was because the Baltimore Orioles routinely had three or four 20-game winners, three or four Gold Glovers, and the slugging of Brooks Robinson, Frank Robinson, and Boog Powell. They were just an exceptional team and won 109, 108, and 101 games from 1969 to 1971. Had the Red Sox manager joined hands with the players and sang "Kumbaya" before and after every game they still wouldn't have beaten the Orioles of that era.

Carlton Fisk had little trouble fitting in when he arrived in Boston in early September of 1971. Buddy Hunter had been called up earlier in the summer when second baseman Doug Griffin was hurt. "The only guys I knew when I got there were Luis Tiant and Lonborg, because they had both been in Louisville for a while," says Hunter. "But they were great. Lonborg had been in Louisville rehabbing; a prince of a guy, he actually invited me to stay at his house when I first came up, until I found a place."

"The veterans were great to us new guys when we came up," says Mike Garman, who arrived in September also. "They knew most of us; me and Pudge had been going to spring training with them since 1969. Everybody in the clubhouse from Yaz on down was great. Once you were in the Boston clubhouse, you were treated like royalty."

By September, the "Unity University" episodes were a fading memory and the rookies found a loose team. "There was a lot of laughter in the Red Sox clubhouse," says Hunter. "Tiant was just the funniest guy I ever saw. He kept everybody loose. Sparky Lyle was another guy who was always doing things to make us laugh. Once we had been playing kind of bad and Kasko called a team meeting. You knew we were going to get chewed out—they don't call team meetings to tell you how great you've been doing. We get in there and Kasko counts and we were one short. 'Who's missing?' From the bathroom we hear, 'It's Sparky, I'm in the shitter. I'll be right there.' He comes out, naked, carrying the biggest chocolate cake you've ever seen. He put it in the center of the clubhouse and sat in it. We were all choking, trying to keep from laughing. Kasko's face turned redder and redder. Finally, he said, 'Meeting's over.' We started a winning streak right after that."

Fortunately for Fisk, the Red Sox catching situation was still unsettled. Duane Josephson had started most of the first half, but he suffered from the same malady that plagued all catchers: injuries. He damaged some ribs in a catcher-versus-pedestrian accident at home plate in 1971 and spent three weeks on the disabled list and several more weeks not feeling right afterward. As the season wore on, he played less and less. Bob Montgomery caught most of the games in July and August. Kasko decided to see what young Carlton Fisk could do. He gave him a starting assignment September 6 in New York. Fisk went 0-for-3. Despite another 0-fer the next day, Kasko left him in the lineup.

Teammates were impressed with the change in Fisk. "To be honest, in 1971 I thought he must have had one of the worst spring trainings ever," says Petrocelli. "We knew he was the catcher of the future, but he really didn't look that good. He was chasing balls in the dirt when he hit, balls were getting by him catching, he wasn't blocking the ball that well. We thought, 'Man, he needs a lot of work.' When he came back from Triple A that September, I couldn't believe it was the same guy. He was polished. He had a better idea of the strike zone. What an improvement."

While Fisk looked much better behind the plate, he was understandably a bit hesitant about bossing around the grizzled vets of the pitching staff. In one of his first games, 34-year-old Gary Peters was pitching. Peters had been one of the better left-handers in the league ever since winning the Rookie of the Year Award in 1963. He was finishing two good years with the Red Sox in which he won 30 games. Peters was a fun-loving guy off the field, but was not someone to mess with. He once held a steak knife to Reggie Smith's throat in a restaurant to let him know that he was tired of pranks for one night. He was an equally serious, deadly competitor on the mound.

Late in the game, Peters gave up a couple of ground ball hits and appeared to be laboring. "I thought, 'Well, I'm supposed to take charge here,' so I went [out to the mound]," Fisk said later. "When he saw me coming, he walked away."

Peters stood behind the mound, with his back to Fisk, and rubbed the ball for an eternity. Fisk, not knowing what else to do, patiently waited. "I was a little mad at the time," says Peters. "You give up a couple of cheap hits, you're not happy. I finally turned around and he's still standing there on the mound. I won't repeat what I said, but it wasn't too pleasant."

"What the bleep do you want?" Carlton remembered Peters demanding. The young catcher, momentarily taken aback by the assault, shrugged.

"The next time you come out here, you better have a pretty good idea how we're going to get out of this situation," snarled Peters. "Get your ass back behind the plate."

"I thought, 'Gee, is that the way pitchers are supposed to talk to me?'" Carlton said. "And I went back behind the plate." It would be the last time a pitcher ever chased Carlton Fisk off the mound.

After a few games, Carlton started feeling more comfortable with a bat in his hand. His first major league hit was a home run in Detroit September 12 off Les Cain. He put together a modest eight-game hitting streak before being blanked the last game. He finished with a .313 batting average in 48 at bats with two home runs and six RBIs. He also registered six assists and threw out the first four runners who tried to steal on him. The press mentioned that he looked like the best catcher to hit Boston in the last 40 years.

It was during this period that Carlton had an encounter which foreshadowed an unforgettable future relationship. Facing the Yankees, Fisk squatted behind the plate when Thurman Munson came to bat. Munson, the Yankees' catcher and the 1970 Rookie of the Year, hit a ground ball and started toward first. Fisk, as was his custom then, hustled down the baseline in his long-legged, athletic stride, ready to back up first on a bad throw, and nearly beat Munson to the bag. According to Yankee teammates, Munson, who prided himself on being fast for a catcher, felt Fisk had been trying to show him up. He didn't say anything to the smart-ass rookie, but seethed when he returned to the bench. Munson didn't know it at the time, but he would be seeing a lot of this kid during the next decade.

6 Rookie of the Year

WHEN THE RED SOX PITCHERS AND CATCHERS reported in the spring of 1972 Carlton Fisk was ready. He had put in the time. He was 24 years old. This was the year. The Red Sox had experienced troubles at the catching position for quite a while. Although Jerry Moses had made the All-Star team as a backup in 1970, he had actually only played well for half of a season. Only once in the previous 12 years had a Red Sox catcher caught more than 120 games in a season. From 1967 through 1971, Mike Ryan, Russ Gibson, Elston Howard, Tom Satriano, Jerry Moses, Bob Montgomery, and Duane Josephson had all spent time as the number one catcher. There wasn't exactly a lot of heritage for Carlton Fisk to live up to; nothing like, say, Mantle had to deal with replacing DiMaggio.

Fisk had impressed both teammates and media members in September of 1971, and no less an authority than Carl Yastrzemski had told reporters that he had the potential of a Johnny Bench (the highest praise possible for a catcher at the time). While many felt that Fisk had earned the job, manager Eddie Kasko was still uncertain, wary of turning over the reins to a rookie. "When Carlton Fisk came up at the end of the season in 1971, we all saw the enthusiasm and potential that he had," says Kasko. "Everyone would like to have an everyday catcher who can hit. Josephson was good, but he got hurt a lot. Montgomery was a solid backup guy—we knew what we had with him. Fisk had the confidence and looked like he could be a leader someday. He could really throw, but the question, as it is with everyone who comes up, was can he hit major league pitching. Everybody has a weakness and pitchers find it in a hurry and word gets passed around the league. Then they're going to keep getting you out that way until you make an adjustment."

Fisk split time equally with Josephson and Montgomery in Winter

Haven, but had only a single in his first 13 spring training at bats. While fizzling at the plate, he was more than adequate behind it. He particularly impressed observers with his arm, such as on March 15 when he gunned out a runner trying to steal in the first inning and later started a double play by pouncing on a bunt and throwing to second. "I've always liked him as a catcher," Kasko told reporters after the game. "I've been waiting for him to do a little more hitting. He has a job for many years to come if he can hit major league pitching."

It was hard for the other players not to take notice of the rookie catcher. His physical stature alone assured that. Even among professional athletes, Carlton was an impressive specimen, much more impressive than the mere numbers on the roster of 6-2, 210 pounds. It was how those 210 pounds were layered on that 6-2 frame that was notable. He had huge hands and a broad back. His appearance exuded natural strength. "The first thing you noticed about Carlton Fisk was that he was such an imposing figure," says John Kennedy. "I don't remember seeing many catchers who were his size. The other thing, though, was he was very fast. He was one of the best at going from first to third on a ground ball to the outfield."

Teammates also noticed the way he went about preparing to play. "He had a stretching program he went through every day in the outfield," says Bobby Bolin. "I never saw another catcher do that in the 13 years I played in the majors. I guess that's what helped keep him loose to play all those years. I tried it once but it was too hard."

"He was a hard worker," says Gary Peters. "He ran with the pitchers. That surprised us because that was a lot of running, a lot of wind sprints. We did more running than the other players. He was the only one who ran with us."

Other players took note of Carlton's play, his hustle and his attitude. "I knew he was going to be good," says reliever Ken Tatum. "He was gung ho, always doing something extra. He stood out. In the spring, I mentioned to one of our players, 'Pudge is going to play for a long time.' Everybody noticed. You saw him prepare himself for a game the same way every day. Whatever he was called on to do, he did more. Yaz was the same way. You know, some guys work hard, but others are damn lazy. You knew Pudge had the work ethic to go far."

"The thing I remember about him was that he always wanted to learn," says veteran pitcher Ray Culp. "He was always asking questions in the clubhouse and everywhere else. He wanted to know how I wanted to pitch to him. We had an apartment in Winter Haven and he and his wife would come over, we'd barbecue and he would want to talk baseball—how did I like him to set up behind the plate on certain pitches? How did I like to set up certain hitters? He wanted to know how we would work together best. I'm sure he did that with the other pitchers too. That helped him fit right in as a rookie."

Always talking baseball. Talking and learning. Learning how to call a good game. The subject would never go stale.

"He had that look in his eye," Culp continues, "that determination that he wanted to be a big leaguer. He certainly had the physical talent and ability, but you knew with his attitude, that he couldn't miss."

But Josephson was a veteran; a professional; a known quantity. And he was having a better spring offensively, hitting over .300. Late in the preseason, Fisk began hitting—eight hits in 17 at bats; he was suddenly comfortable in the batter's box, the ball looked as big as a beach ball, a few more games and he would put away any doubt that he could do the job. Then . . . baseball stopped. Players went out on the first strike in major league history.

The rookies in Carlton Fisk's class were the first to enter the game completely under the new politico-economic atmosphere of collective bargaining and players' rights. As Carlton and the other rookies were given a crash course in the new management relations, they had no way of knowing the changes that were coming—changes that would alter the game and their careers over the next two decades. Carlton Fisk would never know a time in which owners and players were not locked in an all-consuming, hate-filled struggle for money and power. The changes would make him a wealthy man, but they would also bring heartbreaking consequences.

Collective bargaining for baseball players was still a relatively new undertaking in 1972. Traditionally, "bargaining" for baseball had been what they called it when the general manager mailed the player a contract and the player signed it—or chose not to sign it and bought a lunch pail to try another line of work. Owners had all the power and they knew it. The original Players Association had been created by the owners and was largely for show—it had no staff and no power. Little was accomplished other than a nominal player pension plan. All that changed when the players hired Marvin Miller in 1966. A true labor lawyer, Miller immediately made his presence felt; and he made those in baseball management shudder.

"I remember the first spring when Marvin Miller came by to talk to all the players in each camp," says John Kennedy, who was with the Dodgers at the time. "Al Campanis [Dodger general manager] called a team meeting the day before Miller was coming and told us, 'You don't want that guy. He's trouble. He's a labor lawyer and that means strike.' When he said that, we all knew: 'If they're that scared of him then maybe we've got the right guy.'"

"I had been a player rep for all those years," says Gary Peters. "It was really hard early on." Being a team player rep was a high-risk job for those who weren't irreplaceable on the field. Some years more than half of the player reps in the majors would be mysteriously traded or released. "The owners wouldn't listen to anything we tried to negotiate. There were three or four owners who wouldn't even talk to us. That's why we got Marvin Miller."

Miller was able to force the owners to negotiate. He got the first Basic Agreement—the general contract that covered all collective working conditions—signed in 1968. He started small; it increased the minimum yearly major league salary from $7,000 to $10,000 among other things, but his sights were set on the holy grail: the reserve clause.

The first serious battle between players and owners arrived in the winter of 1968–69 as they negotiated a new pension plan. Stonewalled by the owners, the players were led by Miller to adopt the position that they were not going to sign contracts until the pension agreement was concluded—this was the first time a mass holdout had been considered. Realizing the threat to the game if the owners did not at least show a little good-faith bargaining, the new commissioner, Bowie Kuhn, quickly helped change the owners' stance and settled the fight to avoid any disruption of the schedule. But the first blow had been struck.

In 1972, the major issue was a refinement of the pension plan (a more equal share of television revenue to be placed into the players' retirement fund) and health benefits, but the real cause was player solidarity—the ability of players to stand together and negotiate as a whole against the owners. When the owners refused to budge on their position, players were left with an unpleasant choice: knuckle under or stand together and fight. Players-only meetings were held around the majors and a vote was taken on whether to authorize a strike for March 31, 1972, four days before the scheduled major league opener.

Most clubs voted unanimously for the strike, but there were mixed opinions in the Red Sox clubhouse. Carl Yastrzemski, Reggie Smith, and Rico Petrocelli were all against striking, mainly because they had always been treated very well by Red Sox management. Yaz particularly felt a loyalty to Thomas Yawkey. Smith did not endear himself to the low-paid youngsters when he stood up and said he was voting no because every week out was going to cost him $4,000, while it would cost most of the other players less than $800.

"The Red Sox had the best owner in baseball," says Peters. "They were the best treated; it was the best place to play. It was difficult for the Red Sox players to strike. They wanted to get on the field for Mr. Yawkey. We had to convince them that they weren't striking against Yawkey, but all the players in the league had to stick together. It was a difficult time in the spring. If all the owners had been like Yawkey there never would have been a strike in the first place. Actually, we never would have hired Marvin Miller—think how that would have changed the history of the game."

The player reps flew to Dallas to meet with the other player reps and the votes were tallied. The strike was on. The reps flew back and held a meeting with the Sox players at the Holiday Inn in Winter Haven, where they told them to pack up. "We didn't know how long it was going to last," says Culp. "There was a lot of confusion."

"O'Connell came in after our last game [after the strike vote] and said, 'You guys are on strike, everybody has to leave,'" says Kennedy. "The next day we put everything in garbage bags—we couldn't use any of the club's ball bags or trunks. We went to the airport carrying all our stuff in garbage bags."

Most of the players made their way to Boston after a few days. Some went back to their hometowns to wait it out. There were no organized workouts during the strike; players weren't allowed to use team's facilities or equipment. A lot of the Red Sox worked out at Tufts University in Boston, where they had an indoor infield and batting cage; others wherever they could. But it was hard to stay sharp.

The first baseball strike was tough. "We knew why we were doing it," says Kennedy, "but it was awfully hard. We weren't making a lot of money to begin with and we wouldn't be getting paid. But it was time. When I first started in the majors [1962] the minimum salary was $4,500. By 1972 it was still only about $12,000. Most guys weren't making much." The loss of money certainly hurt a guy like Carlton Fisk, who, after the addition of a son, had two children, and was scheduled to make the league minimum—and now he wasn't even getting that. He had a little money in the bank from the clothing store job, but how long would that last? Players, and fans, waited.

On April 14, Commissioner Bowie Kuhn triumphantly informed the world that the owners and Players Association had agreed to end the strike and the season would open. It was a day of rejoicing. "Finally, Some Good News—Baseball Starts Tomorrow," trumpeted one headline. It was reported that Kuhn had held a closed-door session with all the owners in a Chicago hotel to hash out the details of the settlement. During the four-and-a-half-hour meeting, the National League owners had argued for a complete 162-game schedule to be made up, but the American League owners had wanted an abbreviated schedule. Buried in the last paragraph of the happy announcement was the mention, hardly noticed, that none of the canceled games would be rescheduled—the AL owners had gotten their wish. This small tidbit would prove to be very important before the season was finished.

The strike had cost Fisk much more than a few weeks' worth of pay—he lost irreplaceable time needed to win and hold the Red Sox catching job. He started the season with the Sox, but on the bench as Josephson remained the starter. "The strike hurt everybody as far as getting ready," says Kasko. "But it probably hurt a young guy like Fisk more. It hurt him because he didn't get to play as much as he needed and didn't get a chance to take the job. Nobody knew what was going to happen with the strike and we didn't know how guys would stay in shape, so the veteran Josephson got an edge in my mind to start the season." In the third game of the season, however, Josephson suffered a severe pulled muscle. While Fisk, like most team observers, felt he would get the call, Bob Montgomery started the next game and got two hits.

Fisk was down. He had felt that at worst, his role for the season would be platooning with Josephson, with Fisk appearing against running teams, and that he was considered to be the backup. Now it looked as if he was the third catcher—relegated to watching games and warming up relievers. Bill Lee shared his misery. Lee, slated again for relief duty, wanted to start. "My buddy, Bill Lee, and I used to talk about it in the bullpen during games," Fisk told a reporter in 1973. "He convinced me that one of these days I'd get a chance. And when I got that chance, I had to be ready. He showed me that I was actually an awful lot like a relief pitcher and that I had to accept my role. I didn't find out that I was really the number three catcher on the team until Josey got hurt in the first home game against Cleveland. Instead of me going in there Monty [did]. During that time I was moaning and groaning in the bullpen to Lee. I told him I felt I had to be in there catching. He just told me to stay ready."

Carlton stayed ready and opposing base runners stepped in and gave him a break—they ran Montgomery and the Red Sox crazy. After watching the Indians steal four bases, Kasko decided to give his strong-armed rookie a chance. Carlton Fisk's first action of 1972 came April 21 in Boston against the Yankees. Carlton flied out to center field his first time up. Next, he rapped into a 6-4-3 double play and some Boston fans began to wonder who the catcher at Pawtucket was and how soon he could get to Fenway. The Red Sox held a 4–3 edge when Fisk stepped into the batter's box to lead off the seventh. He blasted a line drive over the center fielder's head and two quick left turns later pulled into third base with a triple. Left fielder Tommy Harper plated him with a single and the Sox went on to win 5–4.

Fisk put in another good effort the next day, going 2-for-5 with an RBI as the Sox beat the Yankees 11–7. After that, Kasko wrote the name Fisk into the lineup on a regular basis. "He didn't set the league on fire at first," says Kasko, "but he looked good, looked comfortable. You say, 'Let's catch him a little more, see how he handles this pitcher, see how he hits certain pitching.' Before you knew it, he was playing every day and we didn't want to take him out of there." Josephson didn't realize it at the time, but he'd had a Wally Pipp moment. His leg would heal, but he would never get the Red Sox catching job back, nor would anyone else for a long time.

Carlton gave up only five stolen bases the first month while throwing out five attempted thefts. In an early game against the Angels he twice threw out the lead man on attempted sacrifice bunts and later cut down a runner trying to steal second. His hitting was solid, if not spectacular, but the sound defense kept him in the lineup. He quickly showed that he had matured enough to handle a pitching staff. "I liked pitching to him," says Culp. "Of course he was slow and deliberate. He was slow getting into the batter's box too. I didn't like him to come out to the mound very often, so he didn't do that with me. But he had that middle linebacker mentality. He was very competitive. That's comforting for a pitcher. Sometimes a pitch gets away from you. It's good to have a guy that big back there in case the batter starts to come out. We didn't have to worry with Carlton back there."

"Right off the bat you could see that he was a take-charge guy," says Kennedy. "No nonsense, he ran the show. A lot of times, a rookie doesn't want to step on toes, just wants to fit in. Somebody had taught him that the catcher runs the show. He was an aggressive player and wasn't afraid to say the things that needed to be said."

His hustle and arm were quickly noticed around the league. He routinely charged down the baseline on infield ground balls, ready to stop a wild throw from going into the dugout. He fearlessly flung his body over rails and into dugouts chasing pop-ups. He was especially quick getting out from behind the plate to pounce on bunts. And he protected home plate like he was defending Old Fort Number Four against 500 French and Indians. Everyone could easily see the passion; how much winning meant, and how much he hated to lose. Every play, every pitch was important. He attacked the baseball field with the same fervor and energy that had allowed him to grab 36 rebounds in a single basketball game.

After a month it seemed like Fisk had been in Boston for years. His maturity was settling and he showed no hint of a lack of confidence. In fact, he had a self-assurance that strayed to the side of cockiness. The field was in front of him and he owned it. He didn't hesitate to slowly saunter out to the mound to talk things over or to do some butt-chewing if he saw the need. The game progressed when he said it did. The slow walk to the mound came to be known as the Pudge Trudge.

"Fisk took charge of our pitching staff and really turned it around," Lee later wrote. "He had learned the importance of working a pitcher and nursing him along when he didn't have his best stuff. Fisk also demanded your total concentration during a game. If you shook him off and then threw a bad pitch that got hit out, he had a very obvious way of expressing his displeasure. After receiving a new ball from the umpire, he would bring it out to you, bouncing it on the grass like a basketball all the way to the mound. There would be an expression on his face that said, 'If you throw another half-ass pitch like that, I'm going to stuff this ball down your throat.'"

It wasn't as easy as he made it look. "A rookie isn't going to come in and take over, tell the pitchers what to do right away," says Kasko. "That doesn't happen. We had a veteran staff with Culp and [Marty]

Pattin and Peters and Tiant. They would get with him and tell him how they were going to pitch and how they're going to handle certain situations. He would soak it all up. He learned fast. Then it was his job to keep them on an even keel in the game. He did seem to have a very high level of maturity for a rookie, though. He was the type of person who knew exactly who he was. He was very stable and levelheaded. That's exactly what you want in an everyday catcher."

As Fisk proved himself, the pitchers gradually gave him more attention and respect. They learned to rely on his instinct, preparation, and knowledge of the game. "As a reliever, I didn't have to worry about what was done from the catching standpoint," says Tatum. "There was no trouble. He knew what he was doing. He knew how to call a game."

"Back then, the pitcher had the right of refusal on a catcher's sign, I don't know how they do it today," says Peters. "I didn't shake him off much, but I was a veteran, so he wouldn't argue with me. With the younger pitchers, though, he'd put down a sign and they'd shake him off, and a lot of times he'd put the same sign down and shake it. He'd make them throw his pitch."

Despite the play of their rookie catcher, the Sox were as cold as the New England spring weather. They ended April with a 4–7 record, lost five in a row in May and dropped to 9–17. Yaz was out with an injury and it seemed as though most of the starting rotation was either hurt or battling control problems. They ended June 27–34, eight games out.

Fisk's batting average climbed with the temperature. In June, a streak in which he hit safely in 15 of 16 games and had 25 hits in 58 at bats (.431) pushed his average well over .300 and he was suddenly fighting for the American League lead in doubles and triples. He was hitting better than anyone predicted; better than anyone else on the team—he was hitting major league pitching better than he had ever hit the minor league stuff. He was one of the most talked about players in the league. People looked up the single season Red Sox record for home runs by a catcher and found that it was Bob Tillman with 17 in 1964 and it was suddenly in jeopardy.

By midseason Carlton Fisk was one of the most popular Red Sox players in recent memory. He was receiving more fan mail than anyone else on the team, even Yaz. Sox fans had taken to him immediately. Part of the appeal was his style of play, full of blue-collar grit and hustle; part of it was certainly the pleasant surprise of a productive everyday catcher, something the team had needed for years. He was a catcher with power—even better. And his confidence and leadership on the field were reassuring. But most importantly, he touched a nerve deep in the core of the Red Sox fan base: he was homegrown; unquestionably one of their own—a true New Englander. Sox fans were perhaps the most provincial in the major leagues and there had been precious few New England stars for the team over the years.

Pudge didn't come from a baseball factory in some sun-soaked state or big city, he grew up playing with the local guys in his tiny community and made it the old-fashioned way. He had waited through frigid winters, and shoveled snow off frozen baseball fields to scratch out a few meager high school games. He knew what it was like to walk through a subzero New England winter morning to the barn, to have baseball games snowed out in May, to have his heart broken by the Red Sox for decades. His play validated the entire region. Every town in New England, from Brattleboro, Vermont, to Van Buren, Maine, had kids who dreamed of growing up and doing what Carlton Fisk was doing. He was unquestionably one of them. And they loved him for it. If he could do it, what did that say about the rest of them?

He wore his New England pride for all to see. In interviews, he referenced his upbringing more often than most guys say they have to get the breaks, it's a game of inches, or they're going to take them one at a time—it was his go-to line. He was a man who undeniably exemplified all the attributes they wanted to believe about themselves as New Englanders: he was tough, independent, and principled. Stoic and in control, he spoke what he believed, said what needed to be said and little else. He was Calvin Coolidge in John Wayne's body. And his posture: tall, ramrod straight; just hand him a musket and he could pose for a statue of a minuteman, keeping faithful watch to protect the citizens from tyranny, marauders, and even Yankees.

While their rookie catcher was a sensation the Red Sox continued to blunder through June, battling slumps and injuries. In addition to Yaz, Smith had an assortment of ailments all year. Second baseman Doug Griffin was hit by a pitch on the hand, sustaining a hairline fracture that put him on the disabled list. Aparicio missed time with a broken finger and Harper pulled a hamstring in early July. The team would not break .500 until July 7.

Luckily for the Sox, however, while they were floundering no one else was doing any better. The Orioles had been having their own problems, particularly a severe power outage, and battled the Tigers for first, with the Yankees lurking not far behind. The Sox fell no further out than eight games (on June 29).

Carlton was selected by manager Earl Weaver to be a reserve on the All-Star team. He was hitting .310 with 15 home runs and 36 RBIs at the All-Star break. Despite the fact that his name was not on the ballot, he had drawn a heavy write-in vote. He admitted this was beyond his hopes for the year: "In spring training, the chances of my catching in the All-Star Game this year was about 100 to 1." The game was held in Atlanta's Fulton County Stadium on July 25. The National League won 4–3 in 10 innings. Carlton entered the game in relief of starter Bill Freehan and went 1-for-2, with an eighth inning single. Perhaps feeling a little awe at his surroundings, he did make one rookie mistake: after handling knuckleballer Wilbur Wood flawlessly in the eighth inning, he congratulated Wood on his win. "It's not over yet," Wood reminded him.

After the All-Star break, Fisk resumed his assault on enemy pitchers. For the month of July, he pounded out a .354 average with nine home runs and 19 RBIs in 28 games. With Fisk getting key hits seemingly every day, the Red Sox put together two separate seven-game winning streaks, went 20–12 for the month, and vaulted back into the race.

At the beginning of August, Carlton was hitting .312, second in the league to Lou Piniella's .315, but he refused to show satisfaction with his play—there was too much Cecil Fisk in him. "To tell the truth, I'd rather be a better catcher than hitter," he told reporters. "As a catcher you're involved in all 27 putouts, but you might only come to the plate three or four times in a game. . . . I've had a lousy season behind the plate and I admit it. . . . I thought I threw the ball much better last season and blocked out better." His defense *had* slipped over the course of the summer. Opponents had been successful on about 75 percent of steal attempts and he had recently allowed 12 steals in a row before throwing out Roy White of the Yankees. "I'm disappointed in myself," the All-Star catcher concluded.

On August 8, Carlton Fisk woke up early and climbed into his car for a two-hour drive west to Springfield, Massachusetts. The Red Sox, a frustratingly talented team going nowhere, were 51–50 at the time, mired in fourth place, five and a half games behind Detroit. The rookie was enjoying the spoils of his newfound stardom: the demand for him across New England had grown throughout the summer. He was going to make an appearance—no speech, just pose for pictures and scribble his name for adoring fans—at a Springfield Parks and Rec event, picking up a little extra pocket cash in the process. There was plenty of time to get back for the game that night. What could be simpler? A nice, easy day amid fans, away from the pressures of Boston, followed by playing baseball.

After finishing with the formalities in Springfield, Carlton was making his way to the exit when he found himself surrounded by a group of seven or eight people who exchanged pleasant banter. "All of a sudden, one man [later determined to be the mayor of Springfield] leaned over to me and asked me why I thought the Red Sox weren't doing better," Carlton explained in 1973. Carlton gave what he thought was a reasonable, honest answer, thanked them for inviting him, and drove back to Boston, giving it little further thought. Except that the rookie had severely underestimated the New England media.

One of the members of the group, unknown to Carlton, was Gene McCormick, a reporter for the *Springfield Union*. The newspaper ran his words: "Carl Yastrzemski and Reggie Smith are not lending inspiration to the team. . . . Maybe huge salaries have something to do with a player's attitude. . . . The veterans are supposed to be leading the team but the younger players have been doing it. . . . They [Yastrzemski and Smith] don't realize the effect they have on the club as a whole. When they aren't aggressive in the outfield or when they don't show drive, the whole team droops."

The story was picked up by the Boston papers and blasted from headlines. "The Fisk Furor: Rookie Charges Yaz, Smith Fail to Hustle," screamed *The Boston Globe*. Various paraphrases went out over the wire services to the entire country.

The Boston press lived for this—stuff that could make good copy during an otherwise boring season for at least a week. It fit the prevailing theory of a clubhouse in turmoil. As Ray Fitzgerald of the *Globe* wrote, "The Red Sox should put it on the regular schedule. Father-Son game in May, Cap Day in June, Bat Day in July, and in August, Name-Calling Night." Members of the press were more than happy to have this lucky beach ball land in their midst and they gleefully batted it about.

Carlton was noted to be somewhat sheepish when he showed up at the park the next day to find a throng of media-types waiting; some of them crammed around Kasko's office door, some of them skulking about, looking for the reaction among players, jabbing their pens deeper to see what they could stir up. Carlton told them he didn't want the thing blown up any more than it was (as if that would be possible) and tried to downplay its significance. "What I said was twisted around, the emphasis was put in the wrong places. Everybody respects Yaz and Smith for their talent. Nobody can make the plays all the time.

"It certainly looked different when I saw the things I said in print," he said later. "But I really never meant to say anything against them personally." He tried to appear apologetic for the clamor he had caused: "I was severely misunderstood. I guess it's a lesson to learn, but you have to learn the hard way, I guess. Maybe I'm too naive, I don't know. I just won't say anything to anybody anymore. I'm completely disenchanted. The story made it sound malicious when it wasn't meant that way.

"That's what I get for talking to someone like it's my mother," he added. "I guess I'm still sort of naive, the country boy in the big city."

Fisk, Yaz, and Smith were called into Kasko's office for a ten-minute, closed-door session before the game. "I told them in the meeting, 'Ya gotta be honest with each other,'" says Kasko. "'If you have something to say, you say it to the player, don't go to the papers.' They talked about it. They [Yaz and Smith] had been a little upset at first, but then when we got in the room and they all three had a chance to talk about it and voice whatever they had to say, they got it straight and went on from there."

"I'm not a rah-rah guy," Yaz told Fisk in the meeting. "You want to do that, go ahead. That's the manager's job, not mine."

"Pudge and I always got along great," Yaz later wrote. "Fisk had the same intensity I did. He wanted me to be a rah-rah guy, but . . . I led by example. . . . It wasn't in my nature to go around and tap everybody on the back and say, 'Let's go.' I had enough problems trying to hit the baseball."

When Kasko emerged from the meeting, he told reporters, "As far as all parties are concerned, it's a dead issue." He said Fisk explained that he was severely misunderstood and Smith and Yaz accepted his explanation at face value. Kasko refused to castigate, or fine, his hot-hitting catcher, explaining that while he didn't agree with players calling out teammates in the media, sometimes it could have a good effect on the team. He added that he was not worried about Fisk—he might get on pitchers but he was not a pop-off.

"Things like that happened in Boston all the time," says Kasko. "If it wasn't that it was going to be something else. They [writers] all looked for some type of story because they had so many writers and they couldn't just all write about the game because then they'd be writing the same thing. So they had to always try to find a little extra. I had a meeting with the team every year and told them, 'Look, if you read something in the paper that I said or supposedly said, before you make any comment to the press, come to me and ask me if that's what I said or not and I'll tell you. And, by God, when I read something that you said that I didn't like I'm not going to say something to the newspaper guys. I'm going to come to you and ask you if you said that, and we'll talk about it and hash it out.' There's no use in letting stuff like that get worse. So I tried to downplay it and hoped the writers would find something else."

Yaz refused to add to the drama. He smiled and told reporters he didn't want to comment, adding with a chuckle, "You guys would just print it wrong anyway."

The more emotional Smith did not take it well, however. At first he didn't want to go to the meeting, telling Kasko, "I don't even want to talk about it. I don't have anything to say." After the meeting, he seemed calm and told reporters he was satisfied with Fisk's explanation. "He said he was misquoted, so that's enough for me . . . it's not a big deal."

He added, "There's no problem. There never was any problem to begin with." Smith quickly changed his attitude, however, and it became evident that there was a big problem. After the game, he was noted by reporters to appear irritated as he read a Boston paper which contained comments from the press stating that what Fisk said was correct. He flung the paper across the room and stormed to the refuge of the trainer's room.

The next few days, Smith was reported to be visibly sulking in the clubhouse and dugout and wordlessly stared straight ahead on the team's flight. After a few more days of reading the incendiary comments in the paper, he announced that he was finished talking to reporters for the foreseeable future: "I have nothing to say to the press. . . . That's the way it's going to be."

The cloud of the incident didn't settle for two more weeks; an annoying cloud for the players, but a glorious thing for the press. They kept stirring it up. McCormick defended his article. "The comments were all accurate. I don't retract anything. He said it all. I think he just thought that since he was away from Boston stuff like that wouldn't get in the paper. Maybe he thinks we just write goody gumdrop kind of stuff here."

The comments had little effect on the other Red Sox players. They knew the Boston press and the players involved. "Yaz was always a good team leader," says Peters. "He was the captain. He worked harder, played harder, and had more talent than anyone else. He would say things to the young guys if they needed it. There wasn't any doubt that he was the leader."

"I think Pudge wanted to win so bad, I think that's why he said that," says Petrocelli. "He was still young and thought it might be Yaz's or Reggie's place to get the team motivated. Both guys were quiet, though. Yaz's leadership was always by example. We didn't have any rah-rah guys. By this time everybody on the team knew Pudge and knew he didn't mean anything bad by it."

Players ripping each other in the press was nothing new for the Boston Red Sox. As Fitzgerald had stated, it was part of the usual summer's schedule. The surprising thing this time was the reception—most fans were clearly in Fisk's corner. The comments were not viewed as those of a troublemaker, as in some previous episodes, but rather those of a winner who wanted everyone to try as hard as he did. It certainly helped that the guy making the remarks was seen scrambling all over Fenway Park, diving into the stands, fearlessly blocking the plate with his body, and showing the emotion that had been sorely needed by the team. He was walking the walk and they appreciated that. Fisk had been the primary reason the team had not fallen out of contention during the summer while others battled injuries and slumps.

But what kind of guy was this Fisk? Here was a rookie, who barely three months ago was just happy to be here, and now he's calling out two All-Star teammates; not only that, but *the* All-Star teammate—the great and mighty Yaz. Managers had been fired and fellow players had been traded for less. Fans viewed Fisk with newfound respect. The Boston media also seemed to take Fisk's side, albeit while some noted that the rookie should learn to show better diplomacy for the sake of team harmony. They generally applauded the statements and indicated that they bore an element of truth, something everyone in New England had wanted to say, but lacked the guts. Harold Kaese's headline in the *Globe* said it all: "Many Have Thought . . . Only Fisk Has Spoken."

Yaz, the highest paid player in the game, *was* having a miserable season. He hit so many routine grounders to second the first few months of the season that the wise guys in the press box (in a pun relating to the current movie hit *Summer of '42*) were starting to call Yaz's 1972 season the "Summer of 4 to 3." By the first of August, Yaz was hitting .248 with only two home runs and 29 RBIs. The über-talented Smith also had been struggling, hitting .260 with 11 home runs and 40 RBIs. And, even worse, he appeared to loaf in the outfield at times. In a game earlier in the week, Smith had two straight balls hit over his head in right field against Baltimore. It was well known among players that Smith would sometimes go in the tank when he was mad at the press, a teammate, or a manager. They would see him take a few halfhearted swings in batting practice and know it was going to be one of those days. These were the two big guns of the offense. The team needed them to play better.

While it was frustrating for fans and the press to watch these two highly talented players perform poorly, they had good reasons for their subpar efforts in 1972. Yaz, who frequently played hurt without complaining, had severely strained ligaments in his right knee in early May while sliding into home plate in Anaheim and had spent most of the month on crutches, missing 26 games. He had also hurt his wrist in 1971, which was responsible for his power outage. Smith also was slowed by injuries, particularly his elbow in recent weeks.

After a few days, Yaz let the incident go, at least publicly, and returned to his normal routine. In his time in Boston, he had learned to do two things better than anyone else in the league: manage the unpredictable bounces in the left field corner at Fenway and manage the unpredictable bounces of the Boston-area media. He was usually concise, sometimes pithy, rarely rude, and usually left some room for the imagination but little doubt as to his true meaning. He managed to say all the right things for each situation while coming off like a good guy and almost never threw a teammate under the bus, no matter how he truly felt. Yaz got over the "Fisk Furor."

Smith, however, never did. Smith had experienced a difficult time in Boston trying to adjust to life as the city's first African American baseball star during a period when off-field reminders of race relations such as the fight over forced school busing and the continuation of an unofficial color line in the real estate market were constantly in the news. Smith had embraced the Black Power movement of the late sixties and seemed to chafe at every perceived slight—often seeing racial insults where none existed. He had more natural ability than anyone this side of Yaz, but the pressure of great expectations caused by that talent weighed heavily on him. He also had a temper that was quick to ignite; even with friends, he could go from happy and relaxed to murderously angry in a matter of seconds. Smith's relations with the New England press had been a mixture of tentative friendship and adversity over the previous five years—aggravated by continuous predictions of superstardom he seemed unable to achieve. He always reacted harshly to negative comments and had numerous well-publicized blowups and feuds with the media. This, of course, caused more bad press. They wrote that he was surly and grumpy and had a habit of arriving late and being difficult to coach. Some in the media openly questioned whether he even liked baseball. Fans picked up the refrain and frequently booed him at home. Smith, who had previously gotten along well with Fisk, had feuded with other teammates before and he would add the name Carlton Fisk, perhaps in large gold letters, to his list.

Carlton wished the incident would go away, but he didn't apologize when asked by out-of-town writers. "If I go out and bust my hump for nine innings, there is no reason why anybody else can't," he told *Sports Illustrated* later in the season. "I'm not trying to be a martyr. It's just that I'm going to be there doing the best I can all the time and I think others should, too."

It is worth noting that while others claimed he may have been misquoted, Fisk used terms such as "twisted around" or "misunderstood" and said that he didn't really mean to hurt their feelings, but he never backed away from the words themselves. For a decade it had been felt throughout New England that a major problem with the Red Sox was that players, coddled by owner Yawkey's largesse, were too comfortable. "Country club" was the term bandied about most often. True or not, that was the reputation. In the winter of 1971, after being with the big club a total of one month, Carlton had spoken to Lee Maidrand of the *Springfield* (Vermont) *Times-Reporter* at an American Legion banquet and "touched on the so-called country club atmosphere of the Red Sox and knocked some of the Sox for a 'stagnant, complacent attitude.'"

The comments were premeditated. A stagnant complacent attitude was not acceptable.

"I think after that Pudge started showing more leadership himself," says Petrocelli. "He realized the other guys weren't the type and he said, 'If nobody else is going to do it, I'm going to do it.' If we were behind, he'd come in the dugout and scream, 'Let's go, you guys.'"

Bill Lee later summed up: "By the time Carlton spoke his piece to the writers—something I thought took a lot of guts, whether I agreed with him or not—we had already found our leader. And it was him."

Suddenly the Sox began to play like everyone knew they could. For the first time all year, the key players were healthy and the whole team seemed to be energized. The rest of the season would be a tight race between Boston, Detroit, New York, and Baltimore, with none of the teams putting more than a few games' distance between the pursuers. August 1, the Red Sox had been seven games behind the Tigers, but in five weeks, they took over first. While some national reporters pointed to the Springfield incident as the spark, players downplayed its importance in the turnaround. But there is no denying that the Sox played at close to a .650 clip from that point through the end of the season.

While Carlton continued to hit well, his biggest contribution to the team effort the second half of the season came in helping the pitching staff. The original rotation had been shredded by injuries. Ray Culp tore his rotator cuff, had surgery in July, and was lost for the year. Sonny Siebert and Lew Krausse were ineffective and dropped from the rotation. Two rookies, Lynn McGlothen and John Curtis, were called up from Louisville and installed as starters. Fisk had played with both in the minors, McGlothen in Waterloo and Louisville, and Curtis in Pawtucket in 1970, and he was invaluable in assisting their adjustment to the major leagues. Curtis, a crafty left-hander, won 11 games and the hard-throwing McGlothen eight.

Fisk was also a calming influence on 29-year-old Marty Pattin, a talented pitcher who had started the season at 2–8. Pattin was an intense competitor, so high-strung he often threw up after the first inning. "Carlton would make him stay within himself, getting him to take out his anxiety on the hitters," said Lee. Sometimes that took going out to the mound and saying, "When are you going to put the ball over the plate, Martha?" Pattin got hot the second half of the season and ended with 17 wins.

As the season played out, a major factor in the resurgence of the Red Sox was the rebirth of Luis Tiant. The onetime castoff had experienced an up-and-down season in 1971 following his call up to the Sox in mid-June. He had gone 1–7 with a 4.85 ERA and few expected much more from him. Tiant was used almost exclusively out of the bullpen the first half of 1972, usually in mop-up situations. His record stood at 4–4 on July 30. He had been gradually throwing better, however, and Kasko began pitching him in key situations.

Tiant won a complete game victory August 5 as a last-minute replacement for Siebert, who was scratched due to dizziness. Tiant repeated the feat seven days later. Back in the starting rotation regularly, he strung together four consecutive shutouts. He proceeded to go 11–1 with 11 complete games and six shutouts from August 5 to September 29.

As he became more comfortable and played better, Tiant emerged as the major presence in the Red Sox clubhouse. With a big cigar (which somehow managed to stay fully lit even in the shower) and keeping a constant running commentary in his high-pitched Cuban accent, he was impossible to ignore. Tiant was always happy, smiling, and joking. He rarely lost his temper, even after a bad game. Possessing the ability to criticize someone in a way that made them smile, and also able to crack people up with just a look, he seemed to instinctively know when the clubhouse or bus needed a laugh.

Tiant was one of the biggest practical jokers in baseball. The Red Sox clubhouse became a loose, happy place in 1972, and Tiant was invariably in the middle of things: slithering along the ground like a snake to give someone a hotfoot, cutting ties, ripping up suits—everything was fair game. Outfielder Tommy Harper, who had played with him in Cleveland, joined the Red Sox in the off-season before 1972 in a trade from Milwaukee and was his closest friend. As such, Harper frequently bore the brunt of Tiant's practical jokes. Once Yaz brought in a prized fish he had caught to show off in the clubhouse. Tiant borrowed the fish, put tongue depressors in its mouth to make it smile, got into Harper's dressing area, and dressed it in Harper's cap and uniform. When Harper came off the field, the whole clubhouse broke up watching his reaction to a smiling fish wearing his uniform.

Teammates learned not to savor the hot water in the showers without first checking on the whereabouts of Tiant—they never knew when a bucket of ice water might appear in mid-shower. No one could take themselves too seriously around Tiant. Reggie Smith, who liked to impress with his groovy threads, was also a frequent target. "We were in Oakland and Reggie Smith came in with a solid orange polyester jumpsuit," says Buddy Hunter. "During batting practice, Luis went in and put it on. It was extremely tight on his body, he had a funny-shaped body anyway, and he had to squeeze to get it zipped up. He put two benches together and walked sideways down the benches; then he put a ball bag around each arm, like a parachute, and jumped off and yelled 'Geronimo!' I laughed so hard it brought tears to my eyes."

Yaz enjoyed the pranks more than anyone else. "Once during a game, Yaz went back in the clubhouse and took a pair of scissors to Luis Aparicio's suit," says Petrocelli. "Aparicio was a great dresser, sharkskin suits and all that. And Yaz cut off a sleeve of the jacket and taped it on the other side and put it back in his locker. Aparicio comes in, puts on the jacket and the sleeve falls off. We were all dying. Aparicio yells, 'I'll get you, you son of a bitch.' Then he did it to Yaz a few days later. But Yaz didn't care because he wore such bad clothes on the road anyway. He had an old trench coat he wore that must have been 15 years old. We called it the Columbo coat. You couldn't make his clothes look any worse."

As the summer wore on, pennant fever grabbed the city of Boston. Fenway crowds had been growing steadily throughout August. Each day a much keener interest was paid to the American League East standings and the results of the other teams. The closest the Sox had come to a pennant since the 1967 season had been 1968 when they finished, 17 games out. The four teams arrived in September with only the slightest difference in their records. The Sox opened September by winning nine of 11. September 7 they moved into first by mauling the Yankees in Fenway 10–4. A week later the Sox beat New York 7–2, starting a streak of six losses in seven games for the Yankees, knocking them out of contention. Yaz, as he always seemed to, played best when all the chips were on the table. After hitting just two home runs in the season up to that point, he hit 10 in September while batting .350 with 23 RBIs. Fisk hit .308 in the September pennant race, including one stretch in which he hit near .400 at 23-for-60.

About this time, astute observers noticed that there was a disparity in the schedules. Because of the delay to open the season and the fact that the missed games in April were not replayed, some teams had more games than others. The Tigers would end up playing one more game than the Red Sox. Therefore, a tie was an impossibility.

And the remaining schedule was not kind: the Sox played the last six games on the road, three in Baltimore followed by three in Detroit. On the last day of September, the Red Sox and Orioles battled into extra innings, with aces Jim Palmer and Luis Tiant both going the distance. The Sox won it on a two-run home run by Yaz in the top of the 11th. The next day Marty Pattin beat the Orioles 3–1 to knock them out. It was now a two-team race.

Boston's first two wins in Baltimore had put them up by one and a half games over Detroit. It was the largest lead of the season for the Sox and there were only four games to go. The next day, they faced Baltimore's tough left-hander, Mike Cuellar. The game was tight and tense all the way. Trailing 2–1 in the last inning, the Red Sox put two runners on base, but the game ended with a double play. Meanwhile, Detroit won over Milwaukee.

The Sox boarded the plane for the trip into Detroit for the final three games of the season with a one-half-game lead; the two pennant contenders playing the final series—a chance to make their own destiny. Since the Tigers had played an extra game, the Red Sox had to win two of the three games to take the pennant.

On October 2, a Monday night crowd of 51,518 packed Tiger Stadium. John Curtis took the mound for the Sox, facing Mickey Lolich, the Tigers' ace. The portly portsider Lolich was one of the best left-handed pitchers of the era. He ate innings the way he ate hamburgers— abundantly and with gusto. In 1971 he had thrown an astounding 376 innings while winning 25 games. Manager Billy Martin had taken it easy on him in 1972—he entered having thrown only 318, while looking for his 22nd win. Lolich had beaten the Red Sox all three games he had faced them in 1972, all three with complete games. The first game of the season, Lolich had been aided by a base-running gaffe that saw both Yaz and Aparicio on third base at the same time.

After the Tigers scored a run in the first inning, the Sox rallied in the third. Harper lined a one-out single to left. Aparicio followed, grounding one between third and short and the speedy Harper made it to third. First and third, one out, with Carl Yastrzemski at the plate; a few more hits and the Sox could run Lolich out and get to the soft underbelly of the Tiger bullpen early. Yaz came through, blasting a tremendous drive deep to center field. Harper trotted home, tying the game. Tearing down the first baseline, Yaz saw the ball hit the top of the center field fence and bounce toward the infield. He kicked into gear, thinking triple or possible inside-the-parker. As he approached third base, however, he was startled to see Aparicio lying there. Luis Aparicio, one of the greatest base runners in baseball history, had misstepped while rounding third base, landed on top of the bag instead of the inside corner and then slipped on the wet grass beyond the base, spiking himself when he fell. He scrambled back to third where he met up with the streaking Yaz, who pushed him off the bag, yelling that he could still make it. Aparicio got halfway and fell again. By this time, the shortstop's relay had arrived to the Tiger catcher. Aparicio returned to third and Yaz, with nowhere to go, was ruled out 8-6-2-5. Smith followed by striking out looking and the rally was over. Instead of a 3–1 lead with one out and Lolich on the ropes, the Sox had merely tied the score at 1–1.

"We couldn't believe it," says Kennedy. "It was a fluke play. But it was almost the exact same thing that happened to open the season."

Lolich, as great pitchers often do after escaping an early threat, cruised the rest of the way, scattering two singles, four walks, and two hit batters while striking out 15. The Tigers scored in the fifth, sixth, and eighth and took the heartbreaker 4–1, climbing into a half-game lead with two games left.

The next night, over 50,000 fans showed up again. This was the game the Sox had to win. Luis Tiant, pitching on three days' rest, took the mound facing Woodie Fryman, a mediocre left-hander with a 13–13 record. But Fryman had been hot lately since coming over from the Phillies, going 9–3 with a 2.40 ERA in his last 13 starts. The Sox jumped out with a run in the first, but could get no more. Tiant battled brilliantly, holding a shutout until the sixth when the Tigers scored on a walk, a sacrifice, and single to right. The Tigers scored two more in the seventh and won 3–1, clinching the pennant.

Reporters entering the Red Sox locker room were struck by the unabashed emotions they encountered. The room was like a funeral parlor, the only sound the hushed questions from writers and the sobbing of players. The writers were respectfully restrained as they worked the room. Tom Yawkey, so excited by the pennant race that he had gone on his first road trip with the team since the 1940s, patrolled the tear-stained clubhouse, patting his soldiers on the back and offering words of consolation. Carlton Fisk, who had been 1-for-12 in October, sat hunched in front of his locker, crying and clenching his fists as Yawkey patted his shoulder. "Don't worry, we'll get them next year," the owner said.

Boston won the meaningless last game and the Tigers took the division by one half game with a record of 86–70 to the Red Sox' 85–70. One half of a game! The canceled games due to the strike cost the Sox the chance to play for the title. "The sad thing is to work so hard and then when you get down to the end and lose by half a game," says Kasko, who still is mad 42 years later. "You say, 'That's no fault of ours. Why the hell didn't they straighten this out when the strike was on.' They had to see that this might happen. You play an uneven schedule, you might run into that situation. But they didn't think about that." Among the canceled games had been four head-to-head contests between the Tigers and Red Sox, one in Detroit and three in Boston.

"It's hard when you lose the race like that," says Petrocelli. "You can look back at the whole season and think, 'One game.' Who knew? Anything in any game you lost could have been the difference."

"You could look at what happened as another of those 'Red Sox lose again' stories," wrote Carl Yastrzemski later. "Or you could see it, as I do, as the beginning of building another championship team, and failing because we weren't quite there yet. . . . You get so close with guys who are giving their all, who weren't as good as the talent on Detroit or Baltimore, and then miss out."

It had been a great year for Carlton Fisk. He caught 131 games and led the team with a .293 batting average and also with 22 home runs. He tied for the league lead with nine triples, an impressive number for a man who spent half of each game squatting on his heels. Down the stretch of the pennant race, he had caught 64 of 69 games. Although he had struggled with his throwing in midseason, he recovered to nab 21 of 39 would-be stealers after August 3.

Fisk received all 24 votes for Rookie of the Year in the American League, the first AL rookie ever chosen unanimously. He was only the second catcher in league history to be named Rookie of the Year. (Thurman Munson was the first in 1970.)

After leading the league's catchers in assists and having only seven passed balls, Fisk won the American League Gold Glove for catchers. He finished fourth in the Most Valuable Player voting, behind Dick Allen, Joe Rudi, and Sparky Lyle.

Larry Claflin noted in *Sporting News* that "he probably will receive as big a raise as any player in the game." There was speculation that he could jump to as high as $30,000 a year—big bucks for a second-year player.

With the expected increase in money, Carlton and Linda felt secure in moving out of the trailer park in Keene. They purchased a home on four acres of land in Raymond, New Hampshire, a rural area about an hour north of Boston, ten minutes east of Linda's hometown of Manchester. They liked the quiet setting and small town. Carlton and Linda were still somewhat dazed by both the sudden success and the adulation from fans. After the agonizingly slow, poorly paid four-year journey through the minor leagues, the newfound fame caught them both by surprise. They initially were overwhelmed and enjoyed the bounty; reveling in the recognition, the commercial opportunities, the demand for Carlton as a speaker and the fact that they frequently got comped for meals whenever recognized throughout the region. Everyone in New England wanted him as an after-dinner speaker. He was feted in front of a packed crowd at the Charlestown Elementary School gym, speaking to townsfolk under a banner that proclaimed, "Welcome Pudgy." Carlton and Linda were no longer a private couple, but celebrities. There was no going back.

7 New England Grit

CARLTON FISK WAS ONE of the last Red Sox players to sign in 1973. After several talks with Dick O'Connell, amid rumors among writers in camp that he was seeking as much as $50,000, he finally inked his contract on February 28, two days before the deadline. "I'm very pleased," Fisk told reporters afterward. "The Red Sox always have treated me fairly, and that goes for now. I'm ready to go."

National writers watched closely for Carlton to fall prey to a malady that seemed to afflict every young Boston star; some called it the Affluent Athlete Syndrome. *Sports Illustrated* described it like this: "Leroy (Whiz) Kidd [a composite drawn from the Boston experience] appears out of nowhere, hungry and on the make. He tears Fenway Park apart, a real hero with the left-field wall. In the off-season Leroy plays Jesse James on the banquet circuit. . . . He asks for, and gets, a raise about the size Charlie Finley considers reasonable for the whole Oakland squad. In his second season Leroy really moves into what is called Outside Activities. . . . Before games Leroy spends a lot of time in the whirlpool, talking stocks. . . . He gives the impression that he's incorporated, and that the part of the corporation that plays nine innings is the least of it. Toward the end of the season Leroy begins to complain that the manager doesn't understand him. But by then he has his own private manager anyway." The combination of outside interests, overinflated self-worth, and the pressure of expectations from the media then combine to cause a chronic, irreparable bad attitude, leading to poor performance, boos in Fenway, and a not-so-graceful exit from the city soon thereafter.

Boston fans and writers, perhaps jaded by pessimism from past experience, had not even waited until 1973 to start worrying. In August of 1972, Harold Kaese of the *Globe*, already conceding that Fisk would be the Rookie of the Year, ran an article titled "Here's Hoping Fisk Beats Jinx," detailing the Red Sox' long list of previous rookie stars who flopped in their second seasons.

They needn't have been concerned. Carlton Fisk was not going to be susceptible to the Affluent Athlete Syndrome or any of those other problems for one simple reason: he lived by a code that would not allow it. Never spoken or written down as such, it was a definite code, rigid and personally enforced; a code that had been forged in the crucible of expectation and accountability of his childhood. His code gave him a drive for perfection and prevented him from being satisfied, no matter how well he did.

Fisk got off to a big start in 1973. He hit two home runs opening day, including his first career grand slam, as the Sox beat the Yankees 15–5. He had five home runs in the first seven games. But the Red Sox were not the same team that had narrowly missed the pennant in 1972. Starting pitching especially hurt the team. Other than Tiant, who continued the dominance he had shown in 1972, the starters were either injured, feuding with Kasko, or both.

Fisk rarely left the lineup now; he caught 51 of the first 54 games. Eddie Kasko compared Fisk's competitiveness to former Cincinnati teammate Frank Robinson—a man known as one of the most intense competitors in the game. "He [Fisk] and Frank are a lot alike," he told reporters. "If you play against him, you hate him but if you play with him and want to win, you love him. He is an extremely competitive player who unlike many of his counterparts, plays as if he were on the Crusades."

Fisk *was* on a crusade; he was on a mission. The fact that his zeal sometimes made enemies did not seem to bother him. "I know a lot of people don't like me," he said, "but I can't worry about those things. I'm paid to play the hardest I can and to win."

The fiery 37-year-old Frank Robinson showed his displeasure with Fisk in a midseason game. When Robinson was targeted by Bobby Bolin brushbacks in retaliation for pitches thrown at Tommy Harper's head, he threatened to charge the mound. Fisk intervened and the two exchanged angry words and nearly came to blows as the benches cleared. "Tell him [Fisk] that people don't like him in this league,"

Robinson told a reporter after the game. "He's got a lot to learn. He's the most disliked player in the league because of the way he won't give in to anyone."

Fisk didn't give in, and he made no apologies. "The idea is to win, not be a contender for a congeniality prize," he added later.

Fisk firmly believed that he and the pitcher owned the inside part of the plate. He knew that at Fenway it was especially important to keep right-handed hitters from crowding the plate and jerking outside pitches toward the Green Monster. He didn't hesitate to call for well-placed inside pitches, sometimes butting heads with reluctant pitchers. And he made no effort to hide his intentions. "Our pitchers have to gain the respect of the hitters," he said. "And the only way they can do that is to come in close to them with pitches and keep them loose. It might even mean they'd have to nail a few guys in the ribs to get them from taking away too much of the plate. I'd never be in favor of hitting anybody on the head, but you can't allow a batter to stand up there and dig in with no fear." Because of this practice, Carlton became a frequent target of opposing pitchers, protecting their peeps who had been hit by Boston pitchers. He would be near the league leaders in being hit by pitches throughout his career.

Carlton was the kind of guy other guys naturally dislike when viewed from afar; the kind of guy they might like once they get to know, but just don't like watching: cocky, no trace of self-doubt, no trouble telling everyone else what to do and how to do it. He seemed to enjoy being the alpha male. He took himself a little too seriously. He thrust his jaw out in defiance when challenged, or when arguing an umpire's call. Then there was the funny way he ran, picking his knees up too high, like a dainty gaited horse—a run especially infuriating as he made his way around the bases after a home run. "If you could only teach him to run differently, people wouldn't dislike him," said Milwaukee manager Del Rice.

Perhaps the number one reason opponents disliked him, from first sight, was The Walk. He had a most distinctive stride and posture. Deliberate and slow, with his back and head impossibly erect, it was an incredibly arrogant walk; a purposeful walk that at once signified confidence and command and damned little regard for what others thought about him. It was particularly irritating when he took his all-too-frequent, measured promenades to the mound—with his mask audaciously cocked on top of his head—delaying games and frustrating opponents eager to get in the box against an embattled pitcher.

But to Boston fans, all these things only made them love him more. Kids mimicked him in backyard games and on Little League fields. He was theirs and they knew, without a doubt, he would always be there, fighting for them. He was invariably in the middle of most run-ins, such as the one at Fenway May 30. It started when the Angels' Alan Gallagher was caught in a run-down between third and home. An easy out, he unnecessarily crashed into Carlton when tagged. The next time Gallagher came to bat, Luis Tiant's first pitch was a fastball high and tight, knocking him down. Gallagher exchanged words with both Fisk and Tiant after getting up. He then grounded out. Gallagher, known to teammates as Dirty Al, intentionally bumped Fisk on his way back to the dugout. Fisk responded with a word and a shove and both dugouts emptied. It would not be the last fight for Carlton and the Red Sox that year.

By the All-Star break Carlton's average had slipped slightly to .275, but he had 18 home runs, well above his pace from the previous year. Now viewed by most outside of New York as the best catcher in the league, he was voted to start the All-Star Game by fans—nearly doubling the second place finisher, Thurman Munson.

As a two-time All-Star, Carlton was now comfortable in the role of asserting his will on the team, particularly the pitchers, during a game. "I realize that I have a very important job, and I'm going to do it right," he said. Typical was the August game against the Indians in which a struggling Marty Pattin gave up a couple of long foul balls into the left field seats to Charlie Spikes. Fisk stalked to the mound to tell him to be more careful. "You do the catching and I'll do the pitching," an already irritated Pattin, who was one of Carlton's better friends off the field, told him. With Fisk and Pattin face-to-face, exchanging heated words, pitching coach Lee Stange raced to the mound to separate them.

In a July article in *Sports Illustrated*, Fisk said he liked to get his pitcher mad at him because then he might try to throw harder and get the batter out. "If I can get a pitcher mad enough, he'll want to throw the ball right through me. He can't do that. But he might get a couple of batters out trying."

Fisk was becoming a leader, showing the type of leadership a good team needs. Mostly, like Yaz, he led by example and there was no mistaking his example of hard work and all-out hustle. He had little tolerance for the guys who didn't seem as dedicated to winning as he was and he didn't bother with polite etiquette when a point needed to be made. "I know he rubbed a few people the wrong way sometimes," says Kennedy. "Anybody who says things is going to get that reaction. Sometimes there might be things I wanted to say but I didn't because I didn't want to hurt the other guy's feelings. Pudge didn't care if he offended somebody; if there was something that needed to be said, especially if something was hurting the team, he said it."

"Too many guys want the baseball life—the booze, the broads, the celebrity status," Fisk told a reporter. "Too few guys really want to play baseball." It was not the type of attitude that made him the most popular player in the clubhouse—certainly not the guy who knew how to have the best time in every city on the road. But while not everyone in the clubhouse particularly liked him, or agreed with his philosophy, everyone respected him and his judgment.

Although he could appear aloof at times to guys he didn't know, Fisk was friendly and got along with most teammates, and loved the revelry of the clubhouse. He was certainly not the center of attention, happy to allow Tiant and others to dominate the pranks, banter, and insults—but he enjoyed just sitting in the clubhouse while the team swirled around him, and especially enjoyed talking baseball for hours after a game with teammates, learning about the game and feeling a male closeness available in few other adult pursuits. He cooperated and was engaging with the media, at times even witty, but mostly he developed a reputation as a man who liked his privacy; who tolerated intrusions by strangers, but certainly didn't enjoy them. Whereas in his first year he had frequently spent time talking to fans and signing autographs, he began to grow irritated when they were rude or demanding. He was comfortable with a small circle of friends, but much preferred the company of his wife and growing family after games at home and in the off-season. He kept most others at a certain distance, careful not to allow them into an uncomfortable closeness or to reveal any personal thoughts.

He was rarely spotted out and about in Boston. He didn't like the traffic or the fact that his private life was exposed to everyone in the city. At the time, alcohol was pervasive in the game. Players had time and a lot of players drank. A lot of players drank a lot. Young players were eager to fit in. Not Carlton Fisk. After a road game, he would have a beer or two with the boys, to be social, but told *Sports Illustrated* four was his limit. " 'Some guys have to work for a living' is his getaway line when a good time seems about to be had by all." He was often one of the first players back to the hotel, famous for the hours he spent sleeping. In 1973, by request, he roomed alone—costing him $6 a day out of his pocket. He admitted to a reporter that he frequently had bouts of insomnia, lying in bed brooding about things he may have done wrong in the day's game; the perfectionist in him still nagging, What did I do wrong? What could I have done better?

The rivalry between the Red Sox and Yankees had been present for generations, but it had simmered beneath the surface for much of the previous decade as the two teams had rarely been good at the same time over that period. It had heated up in 1967 when, with the Red Sox driving for the pennant, a couple of beanballs ignited a vicious brawl at Yankee Stadium. The genuine dislike between the two teams and their fans had grown in the early seventies as both teams crawled back into contention and realized that now each stood in the other's way.

On August 1, the Red Sox played the Yankees at Fenway in front of 30,000 fans, the third game of a four-game series. The Yankees had been in first place in the division since July 11, but their lead had shrunk to only half a game. The Red Sox were in fourth place in the tight division, only two and a half games out, at 55–49. The first two games of the series had been split, both decided in the last inning. The day before, the Yankees had stunned the Sox by scoring three times in the ninth. As New York's Roy White scored the final run, he mysteriously tripped over Fisk's leg, which was allegedly blocking the plate as the catcher waited in vain for the ball. The Yankees, naturally suspicious, had felt that Carlton tripped him on purpose.

The next day, the first time Fisk came to bat, Yankee pitcher Mel Stottlemyre sent a fastball straight for his head, a reminder that the incident the previous day had not gone unnoticed. Carlton seemed to accept it as the normal course of things and nothing else was said. John Curtis pitched a gutsy game for the Sox and the score was tied 2–2 in the top of the ninth. Felipe Alou was on first and Thurman Munson was on third as Yankee shortstop Gene Michael, nicknamed Stick for his slight physical build, approached the plate. The stage was set for an event that would go down in Red Sox–Yankee lore.

As Curtis prepared to deliver the pitch, Munson broke from third and Michael squared around to bunt, a suicide squeeze. Michael whiffed, however, and Munson, lumbering home, was hung out to dry. Only a few weeks earlier Fisk had beaten Munson out for the All-Star team (a fact that Munson had loudly dismissed as a preposterous outrage). That week, Fisk had appeared on the cover of *Sports Illustrated*—strutting that annoying walk, looking back at the camera like a friggin' Sasquatch. Perhaps these things ran through Munson's mind as he raced toward his increasingly intrusive rival. Or perhaps he was just playing the way he always played: hard.

Having failed to get the bunt down, Michael refused to get out of Fisk's way for the play at the plate; he stood there like a slug—it was his only defense. Fisk roughly elbowed Michael aside and braced himself as Munson, increasing to ramming speed, lowered his shoulder. There is a certain point when a person recognizes unmistakable sinister intent and physical threat in another and the expectations of conflict cause an immediate adrenaline rush—fight or flight. Carlton Fisk knew what was coming, and flight sure as hell wasn't going to be his choice; he held his ground. The collision carried Munson on top of Fisk as they both sprawled in the dirt, doing headstands before landing. Fisk held on to the ball. Munson was out, but lay on top of Fisk, allowing Alou to continue running the bases. Fisk kicked Munson off and all hell broke loose. This was no ordinary pushing, shoving, dancing major league brouhaha—this was an all-out rumble that would have made the Jets and Sharks proud.

Curtis, Griffin, and Yaz were soon in the middle of things, along with several Yankees, and the area around home plate quickly resembled a Black Friday crowd at Walmart going for the last Xbox. While Fisk and Munson were holding and punching each other, Michael jumped over Munson and started hitting Fisk, flailing away with great zeal, but little effect. Fisk, who still had the ball securely in his hand, retaliated on Michael with a haymaker. He grabbed Michael with one arm and held him in a headlock, while still swinging at Munson with the other. They were then buried under the contents of both benches and bullpens. The brawl lasted about 10 minutes and Fisk remained in the middle while others tried to push and pull teammates and opponents out of the scrum. For the next 10 minutes, Fisk and Kasko chased the umpires around the infield, demanding an interference call on Michael (a rule Carlton would learn in intimate detail in two years), but the umps weren't buying it. They threw out Fisk and Munson, but not Michael.

After the game, writers and fans gave little thought to the fact that the Red Sox had won the game in the bottom of the ninth. They only wanted to talk about the fight. When asked who threw the first punch, Munson said proudly, "I did. We said a few things and I hit him. He kicked me off him with his foot pretty good. I don't know what he was doing. Is he scratched up?" He smiled evilly. "What a (bleeping) shame." And to make sure they understood this was no random accident, Munson added, "Fisk was lucky he didn't get into a fight last night the way he blocked the plate on Roy White."

Yankee manager Ralph Houk, a veteran of many baseball brawls, told reporters he feared for his scrawny shortstop's life when his neck was caught in the viselike grip of Fisk's elbow. "Fisk had him in a stranglehold and I thought it might really be serious. Michael couldn't breathe. I had to crawl underneath the pile to try to pry Fisk's arm off his throat to keep him from killing Stick. All the while he had Michael pinned down, he was punching Munson underneath the pile. I had no idea Fisk was that strong, but he was scary."

Over in the Red Sox clubhouse, Bill Lee, as usual, got off the best lines. He inspected Fisk's face, which had a small mouse under the left eye and a scratch on the right cheek, and said, "You know how I know you were in a fight with Michael? Your face is scratched. Michael must have hit you with his purse." Liking the sound of that, he loudly told everyone the Yankees fought "like a bunch of hookers, swinging their purses."

Once the dust cleared, the Sox had knocked the Yankees out of first place and a new era had been launched. Over the next four decades, as the Red Sox–Yankees feud grew and outdistanced the famously bad-blooded Dodgers-Giants as baseball's number one hate-fest, this game came to be viewed as the spark that reignited the smoldering embers of hostility. It was Ali-Frazier number one, the Hatfields and the McCoys, Coke versus Pepsi, all rolled into one. It was the end of that ridiculous détente that had existed when neither team was relevant. As the two teams both rose to the top of the standings in the seventies, it was inevitable they would eventually get back to the serious business of hating one another; they had only been waiting for an incident to rally around.

Before the 1973 Yankees fight, Red Sox fans loved Carlton Fisk. After it, they absolutely idolized him. He had achieved the New England–kid trifecta: make a basket on the parquet floor of the Boston Garden, hit a home run for the Red Sox over Fenway's Green Monster, punch a couple of New York Yankees. The fact that he did it while holding another Yankee in a headlock with the other arm only added style points. It couldn't have been more beautiful. New Englanders now saw in Fisk what they had been waiting for: someone who would stand up to the Yankees, someone who would never back down. After decades of being pushed around, always coming out second to the Yankees, the Red Sox were now on equal ground. For the next seven years and beyond there would be good old-fashioned back-and-forth hatred between the two teams. And fans loved it. And for Carlton Fisk and Thurman Munson, who had known about each other for several years and grown increasingly antagonistic, it was the beginning of a beautiful relationship.

Fisk hit .255 in July and then his average plunged. He was noted to look tired by the press. He continued to look and play worn down as he crawled toward the end of the season. He hit .198 in August and .186 in September. He sat out some games in September with sore ribs and finished with a .246 average, 26 home runs (none after September 2), and 71 RBIs. Although he bettered his 1972 home run total, the drop in average was an obvious disappointment. He had always had trouble keeping up his weight during the season. In 1973, he dropped from 218 pounds in spring training to 191 by the end of the season. Part of his deteriorating batting average was due to fatigue and weight loss, but also part was due to adjustments by pitchers. He had opened his stance and moved his hands in while hitting home runs early in the year. Soon pitchers fed him a steady diet of outside breaking pitches. He was trying to pull everything and was easy prey for junk away. He would have to adjust to their adjustment.

The Red Sox caught and passed the Yankees and finished in second place in the division for the second straight year, this time to the Orioles. Although they were in second, they had not been close the last month as the Orioles comfortably cruised to the crown. Eddie Kasko was fired the final day of the 1973 season. Despite the fact that the Red Sox' 1973 total of 89 wins was their most since 1967, and that he had a four-year record of 346–295 (.540), it had not been enough to save his job. The official word was that he may have been too nice and didn't communicate well enough, but the reality was that he had not brought a pennant.

Intent on resting a little and then working to come back in better shape in 1974, Carlton cut out all diversions over the winter. He hibernated in his home in Raymond; no speaking engagements, no telephone calls. "Until maybe a couple of weeks ago, I'd sleep a few hours every night, get up and feel like I'd just caught an August doubleheader," he told Peter Gammons in December. His code and the perfectionism instilled by Cecil took their toll. "I really feel wiped out. I'd think about things I didn't do, things that got screwed up." He vowed to stay in all winter and rest and get mentally prepared for next year. The previous winter he had gone to as many as five banquets a week. In addition to the Army duty, which was now finished, he hadn't had time for rest.

He planned to make only one appearance: he had signed an agreement in March with a bank to make nine appearances and this was the last one, a Little League banquet in Salem, Massachusetts, away from the media and spotlight of Boston—or so he thought. As Carlton was leaving the banquet, a reporter approached and asked for Carlton's opinion on the recent trade of Reggie Smith to the Cardinals for Bernie Carbo and Rick Wise.

It had not been an amiable split between the Red Sox and Smith. The tempestuous outfielder had been in and out of the lineup with nagging injuries in 1973 and his relationship with fans, the media, and some teammates had deteriorated and turned toxic. Smith and Bill Lee had a memorable mid-game, dugout fight May 24 in Boston that resulted in Smith landing several punches to Lee's head and then throwing him to the ground. Late in the year Smith had worn a helmet in the outfield in Fenway due to fans throwing things and was booed for not running out balls. Boston writers had mercilessly ripped him all season. With these things in mind, Carlton answered, "He is gone and we'll be a better club because of it. He was one of the chief causes of friction on the team."

As expected, Fisk's comments made headlines in Boston and on the wire services—great stuff for those slow off-season sports pages. Reporters, following standard operating procedure, scurried to Smith for a response and he didn't disappoint: "It only shows the gutlessness that has characterized him [Fisk] throughout his career. He showed his cowardice at a meeting with Kasko last year . . . now that I'm traded, he goes behind my back once again. If they were so worried about what Reggie Smith was doing and that's what stopped them from doing their jobs between the lines, then they're a bunch of babies. It's nothing but petty jealousy on the part of Fisk and he's only trying to disguise and cover up the fact he fell flat on his face and his batting average will prove that out."

"Some things were taken out of context," Fisk told Peter Gammons when reached at his New Hampshire home for a counter-counter-comment about the affair. "But I refused to come out and scream that and look like a fool. . . . I felt that way about Smith. I'm not saying I'm right, it was my opinion. . . . But from now on, I'm staying up here with my mouth shut."

Fisk was not the only one on the team who had problems with Smith. Many of the other players and virtually the entire coaching staff felt the same way. "When he [Smith] was traded, it was the happiest day of my life," said Lee. "It's like a can of tuna. If botulism begins to grow in it, you have to open the can and eliminate the botulism before it's edible."

When Fisk, true to his word, refused to discuss the matter further, reporters, not being ones to give up easily (what were they going to write about in November in New England, the Patriots?), went to his mother. "It's true there's no love lost between Pudge and Reggie," Leona Fisk told them, speaking as straightforwardly as her son. "The situation stems from the story of a year ago. Reggie has never forgotten it." She then added, "Maybe Reggie is jealous."

Carlton Fisk signed his 1974 contract on February 11, the deadline for filing—once again one of the last players to sign. When word leaked that the two-time All-Star had initially asked for $60,000, it provoked outrage among indignant writers. "What does a pipe fitter think when he hears that Carlton Fisk is demanding $60,000 after two major league seasons?" wrote Ray Fitzgerald in *The Boston Globe*. Fisk was proving to be as tough and unbending a negotiator as he was a player, a fact that would not bode well for Boston-area pipe fitters in the future.

The man chosen to replace Eddie Kasko was Darrell Johnson, Carlton's old manager from Louisville. Johnson was the ultimate loyal organization man. He had worked in most aspects of the Red Sox system, as a manager, scout, and coach. He was familiar with the city of Boston, and its effect on managers and coaches, as he had been Dick Williams's pitching coach for the 1968 and 1969 seasons. After managing Louisville in 1971 and 1972, Johnson had won the league championship with AAA Pawtucket in 1973. He had managed most of the Sox players at some point in the minors so they knew what they were getting.

When Johnson took over he promised a more aggressive style of play and no palace revolts. Disgruntled players Reggie Smith and Lynn Mc-Glothen had been traded away. In the spring he dumped aging veterans Aparicio and Orlando Cepeda (who had a good hitting year in 1973 as a DH but was so slow on the bases that Fisk, who batted behind him, estimated he cost him at least 15 RBIs) and replaced them with youngsters from Pawtucket with speed: Cecil Cooper, Dwight Evans, and 23-year-old shortstop Rick Burleson.

Burleson was a scrapper with an average level of physical ability except for an absolute gun for an arm. Called Rooster because of his flaming crimson neck when he got mad, which seemed to be very often on the baseball field, Burleson quickly gained the reputation as a 100 percent certified red-ass. He wasted no time in taking charge of the infield. He was a guy who did the little things to help a club win. He bunted, he fouled off enough pitches to drive pitchers nuts, and he moved runners along by hitting to the right side. His spark was a welcome addition to the team.

Unfortunately Carlton Fisk would not be a part of the new aggressive trend of the Red Sox. He sustained what was politely described as a severe "groin" injury March 17, in St. Petersburg, when he took a foul tip off the bat of Cardinal Joe Torre into his nether regions.

Peter Gammons later wrote that as Carlton rolled on the ground, writhing in agony, Reggie Smith, now a Cardinal, showed little sympathy for his former teammate. He cheered the injury and shouted wildly at him from the opposing dugout, "I hope you die, you mother****er," yelling with such zeal that teammates finally forced him to shut up.

Perhaps because they all understand how painful these incidents are, a certain type of gallows humor usually results from teammates. Bill Lee, who threw the pitch, had recently been volunteering with the Zero Population Growth Earth-loving activists. He said the pitch had been his contribution to the cause.

But it was no laughing matter for Fisk. After the game, he had so much swelling that he was told he would be out for a week. He was no better after two weeks, however, and was placed on the disabled list to open the season. He finally rejoined the team April 8 for a workout, expecting to play. He caught batting practice wearing special protection and initially felt fine. But when he finished and stood up, he became nauseated and doubled over in pain. The doctors ordered four days of complete rest.

On Carlton's first day off the disabled list, April 26, he was in the lineup as designated hitter in Kansas City. He walked the first time up and came around to score, sliding across home plate headfirst. He didn't return to action behind the plate until two days later, the season's 20th game. It was a struggle getting through games. Every few innings he would noticeably flinch, have to call time-out, and walk around. He was wrapped in more pelvic protective devices than the wife of a crusading medieval king. The severe stomach cramps and nausea continued for the next month. Doctors told him it was something he would just have to live with, possibly for the entire season. In the meantime, he got hit in the same place four or five more times. "It's ridiculous," he complained to reporters. "I've never been hit there more than twice in a year in all my life. Now this. It seems like I'm getting hit every day."

On May 5, Carlton finally started feeling comfortable and started pounding the ball. Over the next six weeks, he hit .340 and the Sox, who had been a game under .500 when he returned, went 30–13. They took over first place after a Tiant shutout over the White Sox June 1. With the exception of one day, the Red Sox were in first the entire month of June.

As they neared the end of June, Boston was the best team in the league. Earlier in the week, they had won back-to-back shutouts. Yaz was back on track, the young players were fitting in, and the pitching, led by Tiant and Lee, was solid. Lee had moved into the starting rotation in early 1973 and had immediately been effective, using a wide assortment of off-speed pitches including (appropriately) a screwball. No longer viewed as just a weirdo Californian, he was now recognized as one of the best lefties in the league and was an especially rare pitcher: the left-hander who could win consistently at Fenway. He was in the process of winning 17 games for the second of three consecutive seasons.

Lee was also recognized in the clubhouse as a very intelligent pitcher and one of the most competitive men on the team, a man totally dedicated to winning once he stepped across the line. Carlton appreciated Lee's unique outlook on life and his ability to let bad games go and focus on the next day. Once, after an unsatisfactory day at the plate, Fisk was sitting in the clubhouse with his head down, beating himself up. Lee put his arm around him and said, "Cheer up, Pudge. Even a gynecologist has a bad day every once in a while."

Starting in Waterloo, the two had known each other longer than any other teammates and they maintained a friendship throughout their time together. While they went for separate pursuits off the field, each respected the other's intensity and competitiveness, even as they sometimes drove each other crazy during games. They had public shouting matches in the middle of the infield, over Carlton's preference for frequently strolling to the mound and over pitch selection. Lee sometimes liked to experiment with different pitches, throwing by a cosmic inspiration which he might not understand until the ball was about to be released—a tactic that would cause Fisk to explode. "Bill Lee and Fisk used to have some very good conversations out there on the mound," says Petrocelli. "Fisk would start coming out and Lee would turn around and start walking toward second base. It was a riot watching them go at it."

"We did have our disagreements," Lee later wrote about Fisk. "I would shake him off, and that would drive him nuts. . . . One game, I shook him off six consecutive times. He came out to the mound and yelled, 'How the hell can you shake me off six times! I've only got five fingers!'

" 'My point exactly.'

"Whenever Carlton came out to the mound to chastise me for shaking him off, I would ask him who knew better than I what kind of stuff I had. He would answer, 'Your catcher.' Then we would yell at each other for five minutes. By the time we finished and he had returned to his crouch, it was forgotten.

"There were other times when he would get on my case during a game in which I needed it. . . . He believed I should be more stoic out on the playing field. I agreed, but I had those moments when I bugged out. Carlton calmed me down. By screaming at me. 'Cut the shit, bear down, and we'll get two.'

"Fisk was my best friend in the game. We may have argued with each other, but he could never lose my respect or friendship."

On June 28, 1974, more than 33,000 fans sat through an early-evening downpour in Cleveland's Municipal Stadium to watch the Red Sox take on the Indians. Fisk was hitting .299 with 11 home runs and had recently been named as the leading American League catcher in All-Star votes—his third consecutive All-Star Game. He was in his prime, playing better than he ever had before. The game was tied going into the bottom of the ninth. With two outs, the Indians' Leron Lee was on first base when George Hendrick drove a line drive to the base of the wall in left center. Lee tore around third and raced for home. Center fielder Rick Miller scooped up the ball and made a perfect throw to the cutoff man, shortstop Mario Guerrero. Fisk stood by the plate and waited for the relay, anticipating a close play. The throw from Guerrero was high and to the third base side of home plate. Fisk tried to hold his ground and reached up for the throw, fully extended and defenseless. The 190-pound Lee, charging full speed, slid hard, crashed into Fisk's exposed, planted leg like a blitzing linebacker, and scored the winning run.

Before the dust settled, Carlton was rolling on the ground, holding his left knee and screaming in pain. Teammates were sickened as they helplessly watched him thrash about with his left knee flopping lifelessly. "I never saw anything like that," says Petrocelli, who ran in from third base. "His leg was bent the other way at the knee. You know how it bends back? This was bent all the way forward. It hurts just to think about it. I'll never forget it. I said to myself, 'Oh my God, he'll never play again.'"

Fisk was carried off the field and taken to Lutheran Medical Center, where he was kept overnight. Doctors gave a gloomy report—he would need surgery. He flew back to Boston and was taken to Hahnemann Hospital where he underwent an operation the next day. The knee had been shredded: the medial collateral ligament, medial meniscus, and anterior cruciate ligament were all torn. The doctor told Carlton he had operated on over 200 knees in his career and this was the second worst one he had ever treated; it looked worse than the knee injury that had recently ended the football career of Gale Sayers. There was a good chance he would never be able to play baseball again, and an even better chance he would be left with a permanent limp. Then, trying to offer some hope, the doctor said with luck he might be able to play again in 18 months.

Hospital switchboard operators were overwhelmed with phone calls checking on the city's most famous patient. In order for Fisk to get any rest, the doctor instituted a no-visitors rule except for immediate family. Carlton was on crutches for over a month, unable to do anything except wonder what the future held—making a living squatting and getting up a hundred times a night was difficult for a man with a bad knee. He attended the All-Star Game in Pittsburgh on crutches, a long slit up his blue jeans to allow for the thick cast, and received encouragement from Brooks Robinson and Reggie Jackson.

When the cast was taken off after a month, he had lost two inches around the leg. He made a few road trips with the team late in the season and hung around the park doing some running and weightlifting. The initial workouts were painful as the adhesions, formed by the healing process, were torn and stretched. Although the Red Sox had not immediately crumbled as many predicted after Fisk was hurt, an 8–20 swoon in August doomed their pennant chances. They hit .203 as a team for the month of September as the Orioles caught fire, won 28 of their last 34 games, and roared past everyone. The Red Sox finished in third place, seven out. The team that had been the class of the league the first three months would have to wait until next year.

Carlton went home to Raymond for the winter to try to build his knee back into playing shape. He had enough lack of knowledge of medicine and enough naive hope that he actually thought hard work could get him back on the field. He made no scheduled appearances or commitments for the entire winter. Other than driving the kids to school a few times and doing some odd jobs around the house, he was totally focused on fixing his knee. His progress was checked by Red Sox trainer Buddy LeRoux at a Boston area rehab hospital once a month, but otherwise there was no contact, or help, from the team. During this time, seeds of discontent with the organization and, perhaps a realization of the business aspect of the game, were planted. "The Red Sox just said, 'Too bad you got hurt,'" Carlton said in 1981. "'Go rest over the winter and we'll see you in the spring.' I had no postoperative advice from the Red Sox and if I hadn't had a little something down deep inside, I would've never made it.

"They could have at least given me some idea of what to do," he told Peter Gammons. "Everything I did, I did on my own, so it's a miracle that I came back."

He was a 27-year-old formerly successful Major League Baseball player looking at an uncertain future with no road map. The doctor's words reverberated throughout the winter: *a chance you will never be able to play baseball again, a chance you will be left with a permanent limp.* He set out to make sure that didn't happen. But what to do? With nothing to go on, he came up with his own regimen. He made up exercises. He went to the local YMCA to lift weights. He wrapped weights on his ankles and ran bleachers, aware that one misstep could ruin his knee for life. He ran in the mornings with the pastor of the family church (true, it never hurts to get divine assistance). He tried to cover all the bases. It wasn't easy, but with Linda's encouragement and his *little something down deep inside,* he made it through the long and painful winter of sweat and discontent.

8 The Best Game Ever

"Everybody in America saw that game, and all of the sudden baseball was great again."

JOHNNY BENCH, DISCUSSING GAME SIX OF THE 1975 WORLD SERIES

ENTHUSED BY THE STRONG showing throughout most of the 1974 season, the Red Sox and their faithful had high hopes for 1975. They also had some concerns. The team had essentially stood pat all winter while the Yankees, who added perennial All-Stars Bobby Bonds and Catfish Hunter, appeared to be loading up. The only trade the Red Sox had made was to deal the popular Tommy Harper to the Angels for utility infielder Bob Heise. Fans originally were not happy about the move, but they soon forgot about it when they got a good look at new outfielders Jim Rice and Fred Lynn.

Jim Rice had been the Red Sox' number one draft pick in 1971 out of high school in Anderson, South Carolina, where the 6-2, 200-pounder had also been a standout running back. He had bludgeoned his way through the minors, battering International League pitchers for a .337 average with 25 home runs and 93 RBIs while winning the league's Triple Crown in 1974. Rice had unparalleled physique and his strength was legendary—he would snap at least three bats on checked swings in his career.

Fred Lynn, a second round pick in the 1973 draft after his junior year at the University of Southern California, possessed the type of overall athleticism that came along rarely in a generation. He had returned punts and served as a backup receiver to Lynn Swann in college before giving up football to concentrate on baseball. He then led the team to three NCAA championships. He did everything smoothly, as if he didn't even need to break a sweat. He had speed, a great arm, power that seemed to come from just dropping the bat head, and body control that allowed him to make tumbling, diving circus catches in the outfield on a routine basis. Boston writers were soon touting him as the package of Ted Williams at the plate and Carl Yastrzemski in the outfield.

But no matter how good rookies look in spring camp, no one knows how they will perform once the season starts. Along with the questions about the rookies, there were apprehensions about several of the veterans. Petrocelli, still only 31 even though he seemed to have been in Boston for ages, had been seriously beaned in September of 1974 and also had been slowed by a pulled hamstring. Pitcher Rick Wise, expected to be a mainstay of the rotation after he was obtained from the Cardinals for Reggie Smith, had hurt his arm pitching on a cold April start in 1974 and had never thrown well all season.

The major concern for Red Sox fans and management in the spring of 1975, however, was whether Carlton Fisk could recover from his horrific knee injury. All winter, the refrain in Boston, when discussing the upcoming season, had begun "With a healthy Fisk . . ." The Sox had looked like the best team in the majors for a large part of 1974 before fading after the loss of not only their defensive leader but their cleanup hitter.

"We didn't hear or see much of him in the off-season," says Petrocelli. "He stayed to himself. I understand he worked his butt off rehabbing. When we came to spring training, he was like new. He looked as good as ever. It was amazing he could come back from that. I had even greater respect for him."

Fisk had indeed worked his butt off rehabbing, but he was worried about the knee as spring training started. It felt good to be on the field, though; to be back with the team—one of the guys again, not a hanger-on. He was swinging the bat well in practice and his arm, although sore, seemed sound. His mechanics weren't smooth, but that was to be expected after the long layoff; that would come around. He was looking forward to putting the injury out of the way and getting back to the business of herding his team to a long-awaited pennant. But when he took the field for the first time in a game situation in March against Montreal, it was apparent that the knee was far from ready. He felt stiff and uncomfortable and was slow getting out of his crouch on plays. He gave up five stolen bases in the five innings he played. Chasing one pitch in the dirt, he noticeably winced and came up limping.

Clearly disappointed after the game, he was sore and walked through the clubhouse like an old man. "Before I got down here, I thought I was okay," he told anxious Boston writers. "But now everything seems to be going downhill. The knee is sore, my arm is sore, and I seem to be unhinged doing everything."

The original plan was for Fisk to have the next day off, to work back in slowly, but when he arrived the next morning, he told Johnson he felt good and wanted to play; he was a late addition to the lineup for the day's game against the Tigers. The good news was that after the game he was able to forget all about his knee trouble. But there was a bad news bit. In his first at bat, a pitch from Detroit rookie Fred Holdsworth sailed inside. Carlton checked his swing and flinched to avoid the ball but it nailed him solidly a few inches above his right wrist. He left the game immediately, his forearm swollen and painful. The trainer examined it and took him for X-rays; there was a broken bone.

The arm was put in a cast and Fisk was told it would remain there for at least six weeks. He hung around the team, feeling like an outsider once more. All he could do was run to try to stay in shape. And wait. The cast came off April 22, but he had to wear a splint another three weeks. He was not allowed to take batting practice until early June.

Meanwhile, the Red Sox started very well, especially the youngsters. Lynn was hitting .429 with 13 RBIs after the first 12 games and had made several great plays in center field. He would be ranked at or near the top of almost every offensive category by midseason. Rice was nearly keeping up with him at the plate. The two were soon being called the Gold Dust Twins. Major League Baseball had rarely seen two such dominating rookies on the same team.

The Red Sox took over first place May 21 and maintained a tenuous lead, never able to pull ahead more than a few games. At first glance, the 48-year-old Johnson appeared to be quite adept in managing not only the ball club but the politics of Boston. And quite adept meant that he won just enough games to stay ahead of calls for his head—the inevitable fate of any Red Sox manager. An impersonal, no-nonsense boss, Johnson was a classic textbook manager with a slow trigger finger on changes or moves—he left his talented players alone and let them perform while he remained content to prowl in the shadows of the dugout.

But Johnson seemed to be a different man than Carlton Fisk had known in Louisville. The pressures of Boston did weigh heavily on him. He was quiet and often had trouble articulating, with players and the press, and that made him seem paranoid at times. Some veteran players butted heads with him early over their roles. As the team began piling up victories, the troubles were forgotten, but Johnson became more detached from his players and grew more tense and defensive with writers' questions as the season, and the expectations of success, proceeded. Johnson also battled a drinking problem. He had been nailed with a DUI over the winter back home in California. He was noted to show up for games impaired at least twice during the season. The bullpen coach, Don Bryant, was rumored to be there mainly to help keep the manager intact after hours and to get him to the ballpark on time.

Amid questions of whether Fisk could make a comeback, or whether he was destined to be another broken-down catcher relegated to part-time duty, he finally took the field on June 23. The Red Sox were at home, playing the Indians. They were 37–26 with a one-and-a-half-game lead over the second place Yankees. A standing ovation rocked Fenway when Fisk was introduced. He received more warm applause when he stepped into the batter's box the first time. He went 0-for-2 and played five innings as the Red Sox lost 11–3, but the knee felt great. He couldn't help but be happy after the game. "It's just like getting married," he told reporters. "You plan for it, you know it's coming. And when the day arrives, you're still nervous. It was really nice the way people treated me. You can say a lot about the fans around the country, but none are more appreciative than those in Boston."

The next day he went 2-for-2 with a single to right field and a bunt single. Carlton played five innings each the first two days, then six the third, each time relieved by second-year backup Tim Blackwell, who, along with Montgomery, had played solidly in his absence. Carlton's activation coincided with a little discord in the clubhouse. Veteran catcher Tim McCarver, 33 years old in 1975, had been picked up off waivers in August of 1974. He had proven to be a good pinch hitter and a good guy to have on a team: intelligent, with postseason experience, and a great influence on youngsters as well as a general all-around cheerleader. With Fisk available, the Red Sox elected to drop the popular McCarver, prompting some grumbling from players. When the team lost the three-game series to the Indians, Bill Lee went on a tirade after the game because he heard some boos. "This town doesn't deserve us," he railed. "After we win the World Series, I'm going to get the hell out of here and ride into the western sunset. The writers are lousy, so are many of the fans." It was nice to be back in good old

Unity U. again—business as usual (although some felt that Lee's outburst was actually a calculated move to spare his friend unwanted media attention in his first series back).

The Yankees followed the Indians into Boston for a four-game series. Although it was only late June, these were the Yankees, they had been hot (19–5 in June), and they held a one-and-a-half-game lead. The series drew 136,187 fans, a Fenway record for a four-game series. The fans and media realized that the two teams were coming to be characterized by their catchers; both gritty, proud battlers who seemed to have little affection for one another. Munson, hitting .341 entering the series, offered some backhanded comments about Fisk and his injuries, noting that he had failed to repeat his outstanding rookie season. "I have no ill feeling toward Carlton," he said. "I feel sorry for anybody who gets hurt the way he has. The only thing I've ever said detrimental about him is that he seems to get more publicity while I'm having better years. I've played six years, a couple of them pretty good ones. He's really only had one good year."

Fisk countered diplomatically, if also more blandly. "Munson and I have been running one-two for the past few years. Anytime we play against each other, it's a big thing personally. I don't know whether it's contagious with the rest of the players."

Fisk homered in the first game, a 6–1 Sox win, and proceeded to go 4–11 in the series with three RBIs, including a run-scoring double in the 3–2 win in the final game as the Sox took three of four. The return of their field commander gave the Red Sox a needed lift just as a few of the other starters had slumped. "It was so important to get him back in there," says Petrocelli. "We had a big lead early in the season but Baltimore and some other teams were starting to catch up. Bob Montgomery played well as a replacement and had some key hits, but Pudge was just the best catcher in the history of the team. He always got hits when we needed them and seemed to rise to the occasion, especially when we were on the Saturday *Game of the Week*. Every time we were on the *Game of the Week* he got a home run. I used to kid him about wanting to be seen by the rest of the nation." Fisk would have his chance to be seen by the rest of the nation before the year was out.

Six days after Fisk's return, the Sox took over first place for good. They won 10 in a row from July 7 to July 19, and pulled out to a six-and-a-half-game lead. But it was not without drama. The pitching staff was hit by sore arms and bad luck in July. The sore arm came from

Luis Tiant, who would languish for the next two months. The bad luck came from fourth starter Reggie Cleveland and Roger Moret, who had near-fatal car accidents. Both would not only survive but become key members of the staff down the stretch, with Cleveland winning 13 games and Moret 14.

July 25, the Red Sox pulled into New York for a four-game series at Shea Stadium, the Yankees' temporary quarters while Yankee Stadium was being converted to the House That George Built. The Sox were in first place with a seven-game lead over the Yankees, eight over Baltimore, but a Yankee sweep could plunge the race into chaos and resurrect ghosts of past Red Sox tragedies. Fisk had three hits and two RBIs in the opener, but Boston lost 8–6.

The second game was tight. Fisk doubled in a run in the second inning. The score was tied 1–1 going into the ninth. The Red Sox rallied, loading the bases for Jim Rice, who hit a sacrifice fly to score one. Fisk then followed with a hit to drive in two more. The Sox held on to win 4–2 and even the series.

Bill Lee and Catfish Hunter locked up in the third game, taking a scoreless tie into the ninth. The Sox scored on a Rick Miller single to take the lead, but the Yankees made it interesting in their half. With one out, Graig Nettles drove a line drive to deep left field. Fred Lynn raced to his right and, just short of the warning track, dove and snagged the ball in the webbing of his glove before tumbling and rolling to a stop, saving the game. The Sox then won the nightcap of the doubleheader, giving them 17 wins in the last 20 games. Fisk went 6–13 with six RBIs in the series.

The next night, back in Fenway, Fisk was 4-for-4 with a run-scoring single in the first, a two-run homer in the fourth, a solo homer in the seventh, and a bases-loaded, tie-breaking, walk-off single in the bottom of the ninth (five RBIs in all) to give the Red Sox a 7–6 win over Milwaukee. In his first 31 games back, he hit .330 with five home runs and 21 RBIs.

The Red Sox reached September with a six-game lead. The specter of the squandered leads of 1972 and 1974 weighed heavily on the minds of the press and fans as they nervously counted down the last days of the season—afraid to give themselves over to too much euphoria until the deal was officially settled. Players were constantly reminded of past Red Sox collapses.

Young relief pitcher Jim Willoughby later talked about the keys to the team staying loose and focused during the pennant stretch: "We were fortunate to have Luis Tiant, who had the ability to get people to relax, to step back from the intensity of the moment, look around, and see what the real values are. . . . Luis and Rick Wise were two great guys to have around the clubhouse because of their sense of humor. . . . Carlton Fisk was a real steady kind of guy. He was a family man, in control all the time. He very seldom became angry or frustrated. . . . He would be excited about something, but never demonstrative. He was one of the solid members of the team that held it together. Him and Rico Petrocelli."

With barely three weeks to go, the Orioles came to Fenway for a crucial two-game set. Winners of five of the last six Eastern Division titles, the Orioles had spent the past two months trailing within striking distance, like a silent pirate silhouette in the fog following a ship loaded with bullion. They arrived in Boston having won 14 out of 17 to pull within four and a half games.

September 16, in front of a Tuesday evening overflow crowd that Red Sox officials later admitted was close to 45,000 (before strict fire marshal rules clamped down on standing-room-only sales), Baltimore sent their ace, Jim Palmer, to the mound. Boston countered with Tiant. Luis had struggled all season to stay above .500, fighting back and having arm trouble while also undergoing the painful mental process of reuniting with his parents, whom he hadn't seen since 1961, from Fidel Castro's Cuba. He had missed a few turns in July and August and hadn't looked sharp when he returned. But in mid-September, when the team needed him most, the old warrior had finally put it together. He had pitched a three-hit, 10-strikeout win over the Tigers September 11.

Facing Palmer, Petrocelli led off the third inning with a home run to put the Sox up 1–0. In the fourth, Fisk homered to make it 2–0. That was more than Tiant would need. He cruised, tossing a five-hit shutout in front of delirious fans who gave birth to the chant "Loo-ee, Loo-ee," which would follow him the rest of the year. The game put the Sox up by five and a half games and all but sealed the race.

When the Red Sox officially clinched the division, it was somewhat anticlimactic. With the magic number at one, the Sox lost to Cleveland September 27, but the Orioles lost both ends of a doubleheader. Everyone had already gone home when word came of the final Oriole loss. It was still sweet nevertheless.

In retrospect, the arm injury may have saved Carlton Fisk's knee. It had clearly not been ready in March. The rest with the arm gave the knee time to fully heal. Had he played all spring, it may have been on a damaged heel that nagged him and never fully recovered. He finished the season hitting .331, with 52 RBIs in 263 at bats. As the team pushed toward the pennant in September, he hit .400, drove in 20 runs and finished with a 16-game hitting streak. "That really meant a lot to me," he said later. "Doing it when I did it like that. When it counts."

After coming back, Carlton had firmly reestablished himself as a team leader, along with Yaz, Petrocelli, and Tiant. By this time, he had a definite presence wherever he went. "Pudge was just one of those guys that when he came into a room, everybody noticed," says Fred Lynn, who became one of Carlton's closest friends on the team after rooming with him during a late-September call-up in 1974. "He was our field general, he was in charge out there. He was a gregarious guy if you knew him. If not, it might take you a little while to get to know him.

"In the clubhouse, he wouldn't be the first guy to say something, but he had a big booming voice," Lynn continues. "When he chimed in, you heard him. But he didn't stand up on a soapbox and lead the charge, that wasn't his style." It was the same with pranks. Carlton enjoyed watching the skullduggery going on around him, watching Tiant and Yaz keep up the funniest two-man show in baseball, but he rarely started anything himself. "We had a lot of fun, a lot of laughs, though. Once we were out at a restaurant in New York City. Rick Miller, Pudge, and another guy. We went to P. J. Clarke's. I had on a cashmere sweater. There were some hooks behind me for a coat rack. Pudge grabbed me and picked me up and hung me on the hook by my sweater. I felt like the scarecrow in *The Wizard of Oz*. My feet couldn't quite reach the floor to get off, so I'm just hanging there. He was laughing. That was the sort of thing he thought was funny."

Tiant, who had a nickname for everyone—Polacko for Yaz, Pinocchio for Petrocelli—called Fisk Frankenstein. "That's because Pudge walked like that," says Lynn. "When Pudge would come out to the mound, that's probably what LT thought he looked like; clomp, clomp, clomp. It took him like two minutes to walk from home plate to the mound." Tiant would yell, "Hey Frankenstein," in the clubhouse and walk stiff-kneed with his arms held straight out.

Although Fisk was getting over the knee injury, Lynn doesn't remember it slowing him down. "Of course, he was so slow, you wouldn't have noticed if he was hobbling anyway. We were always waiting on him. Anytime we needed to go somewhere, it was 'Pudge, come on.' If you wanted to be anywhere on time you had to tell him you were leaving 15 minutes ahead of when you really wanted to leave. We'd say, 'Didn't they have clocks up there in New Hampshire?'"

The 1975 pennant was a team effort. In winning 95 games, the Red Sox led the league in slugging, on-base percentage, and batting average (.275). Rick Wise, who had been hurt with a bad shoulder most of 1974, came back to win 19 games in 1975. Tiant won 18, Lee 17. The hitting was led by Lynn's .331 average with 21 homers and 105 RBIs and Rice with 22 home runs, 102 RBIs and .309. Cecil Cooper hit .311 and Bernie Carbo contributed 15 home runs in part-time duty. Otherwise, no one had anything close to a career year. The team really needed Carlton Fisk's additional punch in the second half. Yaz hit only .212 after the All-Star break due to an injured shoulder. Second baseman Doug Griffin was unable to fully recover from a horrific beaning by Nolan Ryan in 1974 and was eventually replaced by Denny Doyle, who was picked up in a June 12 trade. Petrocelli had similarly struggled in 1975 while coming back from injuries but in September he finally regained his stroke.

Boston's opponents in the playoffs, the Oakland A's, were heavy favorites. In terms of the all-important factor of postseason experience, they had a decided edge. The A's had played in the last four American League playoffs and won three consecutive World Series. The Red Sox had Yaz and Rico left over from the '67 team and Bernie Carbo, who had played as a rookie for the Reds in the 1970 Series. But the A's dynasty had run its course. Even though the major players were still in their prime, the team had grown weary due to a fractured atmosphere; the owner and players had so much animosity with impending money troubles weighing heavily on everyone's minds that it was difficult to focus on baseball.

Luis Tiant took the mound for the Red Sox in Game One at Fenway Park and showed he was clearly over his midseason troubles. He was at his vexing, twisting, turning, speed-changing, arm-slot-altering, batter-confusing best as he pitched a three-hitter to win 7–1. The Red Sox scored two in the first on three errors on two consecutive plays. With two outs, Yaz singled off Ken Holtzman. Fisk followed with a sharp hopper to third that got through third baseman Sal Bando and rolled down the line. As Yaz rounded third, outfielder Claudell

Washington's throw sailed over one cutoff man's head and off Bando's glove. Yaz scored and Fisk took second. Carlton then scored on an error by the second baseman. That was all Tiant needed.

Jim Rice had suffered a broken right hand when hit by a pitch September 21 and was lost for the postseason. With the injury to Rice, manager Johnson moved Carl Yastrzemski from first base to left field for the playoffs. There had been some concerns in the press over whether the 36-year-old could adjust to the outfield so late in the season. But questioning Yaz's ability to play left field at Fenway Park, at any age, was like questioning Mozart's ability to play "Chopsticks." He demonstrated that in the second game of the playoffs. Twice he held Oakland's Sal Bando to singles by perfectly playing rebounds off the wall. He threw out Bert Campaneris, who was trying to go from first to third, on one of them to end a threat in a third inning that could have been a disaster for Boston. As it was, the A's still had a 3–0 lead heading into the bottom of the fourth. Then Yaz hit a two-run homer off Vida Blue into the net in left field. Fisk followed with a bullet to left center for a double. He moved to third on Lynn's single and then scored when Petrocelli hit a sharp grounder that was turned into a double play. The game was tied.

With the A's bullpen ace Rollie Fingers on the mound in the sixth, and the game still tied, Yaz hit a double off the wall. Fisk came to the plate. Fingers worked the corners carefully, but Fisk refused to bite. The count went 3–0. After taking a strike, Fisk drilled a single to left center to break the tie. "They really came out smoking with that lead," Fisk said after the game, discussing the refusal of the Red Sox to be intimidated by the powerful A's. In the key at bat against the future Hall of Famer Fingers, "He threw me some nasty sliders, I just laid off them [until getting a good one to hit]." The Sox headed to Oakland with a 2–0 lead in the best-of-five series.

In Game Three, once more Yaz stole the show with dazzling defensive plays and timely hits. A three-run rally in the fifth inning, keyed by a Burleson double and singles by Doyle, Yaz, and Fisk, put the Sox up 4–2. In the eighth inning, with A's runners on first and third and starter Wise still on the mound, Reggie Jackson hit a line drive in the gap that headed for the wall. Yaz sprinted to his left and dove, fully extending himself and barely stopped the ball. He bounced up and fired it in, holding Jackson to a single. Had it gotten by to the wall, Jackson would likely have had a triple and two runs would have scored.

Instead, the score was 5–3 with runners on first and second and the dangerous Joe Rudi at bat. Johnson brought in Dick Drago and he got a one-pitch double play ground ball to Burleson. Drago finished the A's off in the ninth and the Red Sox were the American League champions.

It was a three-game sweep over the defending world champs, the first Boston postseason series victory in 57 years. While Yaz was the obvious choice for playoff MVP, Carlton Fisk had also played brilliantly, going 5-for-12 (.417) and preventing the A's, who had stolen 183 bases during the season, from swiping any in the three games.

Champagne flowed in mouths and over heads in the victorious clubhouse. Soon in addition to champagne, eggs, shaving cream, and other things were being used in varied, unique ways. Carlton smiled as he held up a glass of champagne and told reporters, "Very good. But I don't know if this stuff feels better when you drink it or have it poured on your head."

Thomas Yawkey worked the room with a smile on his face and a paper cup filled with champagne in his hand. "I hate this stuff," he said. "Never touch it. Tears my gut apart. I don't know when I last had it." He grinned. "Yeah, I guess it was eight years ago [1967]." Yawkey invited the players to a victory celebration he had previously and optimistically scheduled for that evening.

Fans began to congregate at Boston's Logan Airport within minutes of the final out of the third game, about 11 P.M. The crowd grew steadily through the night, as some came from a hundred miles or more. A number of the fans brought blankets and sleeping bags and slept on the concourse floor; others read, hung up homemade signs and banners, and enjoyed the atmosphere of a pennant. After a drought of 31 years, they now had two pennants in eight years—it was getting to be a habit.

The players expended all their emotion in the joyous clubhouse. The ride home on the plane was subdued with everyone enjoying a quiet kind of happiness. The crowd, estimated at 1,500, cheered the team as they got off the plane shortly after 7 A.M. and made their way through the airport. Fifty state troopers cleared a path down the stairs to the first level. Fans greeted each player by name and shouted encouragement and congratulations; some reached over and slapped their backs or grabbed hands as they passed. Carlton wore dark sunglasses and a big smile as he and his wife waded through the crowd. Outside the terminal the players boarded three chartered buses. Rooters reached through windows for a final handshake as it pulled out. The buses took the team to Fenway Park to pick up their cars. Another crowd was waiting outside Fenway, already in sleeping bags to buy tickets for Saturday's opening game of the World Series, even though sales wouldn't start for one more day.

All over New England, fans were giddy at the reality of an American League pennant. After the near-miss of 1972, and the collapse of 1974, this was sweet to finally have in hand. "The American League Champion Boston Red Sox. Say it trippingly on the tongue," wrote Ray Fitzgerald in the *Globe*. "Savor it, like a swallow of rare burgundy. Announce it, the way they do at the Garden: 'Here come the American League Champion Boston Red Sox.'"

It was not just any team that waited for Boston in the 1975 World Series, but the Big Red Machine, one of the most dominant teams in the history of the game. The Reds had won 108 games in the regular season, the most in the National League since 1909. And they hadn't really started playing well until manager Sparky Anderson moved Pete Rose from left field to third and put George Foster in left regularly. Since the switch was made full-time on May 20, they were 88–24 (.786). A team specifically designed for the artificial turf of their home park, Riverfront Stadium, they were a staggering 64–17 at home. They combined power and defense with speed; they had stolen 168 bases in 205 attempts during the season and another 10 in their three-game playoff sweep of the Pirates. Going into the Series, comparisons between the two catchers were inevitable. The Reds' Johnny Bench was viewed as the best in the majors, some already said the best ever, both offensively and defensively. But Fisk, if not quite at that level, was not far behind.

Before the World Series, NBC executives were worried. Television viewership had fallen sharply the past few years. The 1973 and 1974 Series, particularly bland affairs between the A's and Mets and Dodgers, had brought disastrous ratings. Baseball was losing ground to football as a spectator sport. Those who predicted the demise of baseball pointed to the fact that the pace was too slow and the game too boring, especially as a televised spectacle. Those people would find that they were premature.

Game One was played in Boston on October 11. It had been a cold, raw, damp New England afternoon. Despite the weather, Boston fans were ready. Ten thousand standing-room-only and bleacher tickets had been sold in two and a half hours two days before the Series opened. The first in line, 25-year-old unemployed musician Andy Harp, had waited 46 hours to buy his quota of four tickets. With "Sold Out" posted on the Fenway Park ticket windows, scalpers did a brisk business.

Luis Tiant kept the powerful Reds hitters off balance and scoreless, but the Red Sox had trouble offensively as well. Only one left-handed starter had won for a visiting team in Fenway in 1975, but Reds lefty Don Gullet matched Tiant, allowing nothing but round numbers on the ancient left field scoreboard through six innings. In the Reds' seventh, George Foster singled. When he tried to steal second, Fisk cut him down, saving a run because Ken Griffey followed with a double.

The Sox then broke it open in their half of the seventh. Tiant, who hadn't batted since 1972 due to the designated hitter, started the rally with a single to left. Gullett misplayed Evans's bunt and Doyle got a hit to load the bases. Then Yaz singled to right and the Red Sox took a 1–0 lead. Or did they? When Tiant strolled home, he missed home plate. Fisk, waiting on deck, noticed it and jabbed him on the butt with his bat and nodded, not wanting to attract too much attention because the Reds' first baseman Tony Perez had the ball only a few feet away. Tiant snuck back and touched home. "You gotta understand," Carlton told reporters after the game. "Luis hasn't been on the base paths in three years."

Fisk then walked, bringing in another run. Two singles and a sacrifice fly later, the inning ended with the Sox up by six runs. Tiant retired the last six Reds in order for the 6–0 win, finishing with a brilliant five-hit shutout. Although he had an RBI on the bases-loaded walk, Carlton didn't get a hit in Game One—breaking a 19-game hitting streak counting the playoffs.

Bill Lee took the hill for the Red Sox in Game Two. Lee had slumped late in 1975. He didn't win a game after August 24 and had been sent to the bullpen at the end of the season. But scouting reports said his off-speed stuff would be better suited to stop the Reds than Reggie Cleveland's sinker-sliders. Lee's quirky ways and pithy comments had long been known in Boston, but now under the scrutiny of the nation in the World Series, he had become a media sensation—thrilling and filling every reporter's pad with witty, sometimes knowledgeable, sometimes nonsensical, but always welcomed, comments and observations—on baseball and the cosmos at large. The press ate it up. The other Sox players were happy he took away some of the constant badgering from themselves. And Lee reveled in the attention. Now they would find out if he could pitch.

A steady rain had fallen throughout the night and morning. Because of the wet field, neither team took batting practice. A second straight, strained-past-capacity crowd huddled and shivered in the chilly wind blowing in off the Charles River. Rain fell through most of the game, including a 27-minute delay in the seventh.

The Sox scored first but should have had more. Cooper led off with a double on the first pitch from Reds starter Jack Billingham. Denny Doyle followed with a bouncer off Billingham's glove and Boston had runners on first and third, no outs. Yaz then hit a sharp one-hopper to the mound, Billingham fired to Concepcion for a force-out, conceding a run to Cooper. But Cooper hesitated, then broke for home late. Instead of throwing to first for the double play, Concepcion alertly fired home and Cooper was an easy out. Fisk salvaged a run for the Sox by singling to right field to score Yaz, who had taken second while Cooper had been in a brief run-down. The missed opportunity for Cooper would prove fateful.

Lee set down the first 10 batters in order. The Reds scored a run to tie it in the fourth on a Joe Morgan walk, a Bench single, and a Perez groundout. That was the only threat the Reds mounted through eight innings.

The Sox took the lead in the sixth. After Yaz singled, Fisk hit a sharp grounder to short that took a sudden hop on the soggy field and Concepcion couldn't handle it (the first error of the Series). Yaz then scored on Petrocelli's single. That's the way it stood as the game went into the ninth inning: Red Sox 2, Reds 1.

But the Reds, who won 48 games in which they had trailed in 1975, 25 times in their final turn at bat, were not the types to give up. In the days before the lights-out, one-inning closer, Lee took the mound for the ninth. Bench, who had told the television audience during the rain delay that he would be looking for something outside from Lee to take the other way (unfortunately no one thought to relay this bit of info to Lee), promptly got a low outside pitch and laced it into right field for a double. Dick Drago replaced Lee and retired Perez on a grounder to short as Bench took third. Foster flied to Yaz in shallow left and the Sox were one out away from a two-game lead in the series. But Concepcion hit a seeing-eye bleeder to the right of the mound and beat the play to first while Bench scored. Concepcion then stole second and scored when Griffey doubled to left center, putting the Reds up 3–2. The Reds' bullpen ace Rawly Eastwick came on and retired the Sox in the bottom of the ninth. The Series was, as Bill Lee told reporters after the game when they asked for his impression of the first two games, "tied."

Interestingly, the famed Green Monster was a mere spectator in the first two games. Not one ball was hit off or over the wall. That would change when the Series returned.

But first, the teams flew to Cincinnati, switching from the classic, real-grass park filled with character and history to the antiseptic, plastic-turfed, perfectly round, concrete Riverfront Stadium. Game Three was marked by a record-tying six home runs. Despite the power barrage, it would forever be remembered for a ball that traveled less than two feet and resulted in one of the most disputed umpire calls in history—and Carlton Fisk was right square in the middle of it.

Rick Wise started for the Sox. Wise had good memories of Riverfront. In 1971, while pitching for the Phillies, he had the kind of day usually only seen in Little League by 12-year-olds with mustaches: he pitched a no-hitter and hit two home runs. He would have no such luck in this one.

The Red Sox took a one-run lead when Fisk led off the second inning with a home run off a Gary Nolan curveball. Not to be outdone in his own ballpark, Johnny Bench countered in the fourth with a two-run homer. The Reds added three in the fifth on back-to-back home runs by the unlikely tandem of shortstop Dave Concepcion and skinny centerfielder Cesar Geronimo and a sacrifice fly by second baseman Joe Morgan.

The Red Sox, down 5–1, battled back dramatically with a Bernie Carbo pinch hit home run in the seventh and a two-run job by Dwight Evans with one out in the ninth to tie it up. Then things got interesting. After the Sox went down scorelessly in the 10th, Jim Willoughby, who had pitched gamely while keeping the Reds in check for three innings while the Sox mounted their comeback, took the mound for his fourth inning of relief.

Geronimo led off with a single. Ed Armbrister walked to the plate to pinch-hit for the pitcher. A 160-pound, seldom-used outfielder who hit .185 in 65 at bats in 1975, with exactly one sacrifice, the 27-year-old Armbrister was the kind of guy Sparky Anderson liked to have on his bench—just happy to be there and willing to do whatever the team's big stars needed him to do. Now in the 10th inning of a tied World Series game, they needed him to sacrifice Geronimo to second base so Rose or Morgan could drive him in with a single. And everyone in the ballpark knew it.

The right-handed Armbrister squared around, his right foot inches from the plate, and slid his right hand up the barrel of the bat as Willoughby reached back to throw. The pitch hit the bottom of Armbrister's bat. The ball ricocheted straight into the dirt in front of the plate and bounced 10 feet high. It was a fair ball. The speedy Geronimo, as Reds radio man Marty Brennaman liked to say, was on his horse, headed for second as soon as he saw the ball hit the dirt.

Fisk jerked his mask off and flipped it away with his right hand and was in front of the plate going for the ball before Armbrister could react. They were both looking up at the ball and Armbrister, semi-crouched, had barely taken a step with his left foot when they collided. Fisk had his left forearm on Armbrister's neck while he reached up and barehanded the ball. Then, with the ball in his right hand, Fisk shoved Armbrister away with his left forearm, took a short step to his right, and fired to second. Armbrister, still in front of the plate, only started to run to first after Fisk threw. The throw had a tail on it, sailed high, glanced off the leaping Burleson's glove, and continued into center field. Geronimo popped up out of his slide and scampered to third ahead of Lynn's throw. The entire episode around the plate lasted slightly less than two seconds from the time the ball hit the bat until Fisk released his throw. The controversy would last much longer.

Darrell Johnson immediately charged out of the dugout and he and Fisk angrily confronted home plate umpire Larry Barnett, demanding an interference call. The 30-year-old Barnett, a veteran of six major league seasons, refused to budge. Johnson and Fisk walked up the line and pleaded their case with the first base umpire, who, not surprisingly, backed up Barnett.

In the television booth, the announcers clearly sided with the Red Sox. After viewing the slow-motion replay, Tony Kubek said, "Armbrister is right in his way. I've got to say, right there, he interfered with him."

"Boy is Fisk hot," Curt Gowdy said as they watched the argument.

Kubek: "I don't blame him." Another slow-motion replay once again showed the collision.

Kubek: "Armbrister is definitely in his way."

The call stood. After order was restored Barnett appeared to be trying to talk to Fisk as they prepared for the next batter, but Fisk turned away wordlessly. Fisk was given an error on the throw and the Reds were given an excellent chance to put the game away. While new pitcher Roger Moret was warming up, someone in the television booth handed Curt Gowdy a rule book and he read the relevant rule out loud. Now, even more convinced that the rules were on their side, Gowdy and Kubek reiterated their opinions that interference should have been called.

With men on second and third and no outs, Boston's options were limited against the Reds' lineup of Hall of Fame–worthy men who couldn't wait to get to the plate in a situation such as this. Rose was intentionally walked. After pinch hitter Merv Rettenmund struck out, Joe Morgan singled past the drawn-in outfield and the game was over. As the ball left Morgan's bat, Fisk took off his mask and flung it into the screen behind home plate.

Few writers went to the victors' clubhouse after the game—they all wanted the Red Sox' reaction. They got good stuff, all right, but the censors had to bleep out the best parts before it could be printed in family newspapers. Boston writer Ray Fitzgerald called it "the angriest losing locker room I have ever seen." A torrent of untargeted towels and a profusion of profanity filled the air.

Initially Fisk didn't say anything as he was surrounded by a large throng of writers, instead doing a silent, slow burn as the questions bounced off his hardened exterior. Finally, he said, "You saw the play, didn't you? What did it look like?" He paced around, fired a scorecard magazine across the room, then yelled, "If that wasn't interference what was it?" The words flooded out now. "As I went for it he took two steps in front of the plate. He stood under the ball. I have to go for the ball. . . . I probably tagged him coming down." (Review of the play shows he did not.) Fisk continued to fling papers about the clubhouse. "It's a damn shame to lose a ball game like that. One call from an umpire can change the complexion of the whole Series. If I don't think I've got a legitimate complaint, I'm not the kind who will beef and moan and make a show."

"We should have had a double play on that ball," he continued, "but the umpires are too gutless under pressure. We asked Dick Stello at first to rule on it, too, and he backed up his fellow thief. . . . This is a game that would have given us the edge and now we're just bleeped."

In the past, umpires were picked for the World Series based on their perceived talent and reputation; on merit. A 1974 bargain with the umpires' union had changed that so that now all umpires had a shot at the $9,000 paycheck for the World Series. They were rotated through with the only prerequisite being six years of major league experience. The 1975 World Series was the first for all six umpires on the team. "Baseball owes it to the fans to have only the best umpires in the Series," said Yaz. "Maybe we ought to rotate the teams, too. I think this is a disgrace."

"Next year they'll have San Diego and the Chicago White Sox in the World Series," he added. "The umpires aren't chosen by ability, only by that rotation system. Maybe the players shouldn't be chosen for talent, either."

"Bleep the umpires," Drago was quoted as saying. "Let's just do away with the rotten creeps and use the honor system. It couldn't be worse than anything you saw tonight. That bleeping slob of a plate umpire, Larry Barnett, has been bleeping the Red Sox all season long."

"They stole this game from us," said Cleveland. "It was the most raw, unfair thing I have ever seen. Barnett is the most gutless slob who ever umpired a baseball game."

Bill Lee said if you watched the NFL all season you wouldn't see a better body block by an offensive lineman and called it the worst bleeping miscarriage of justice since he was in Little League. He said that he would have bitten the umpire's ear off if he had been close. "I would have Van Goghed him," he said, adding a new verb to the lexicon. "The Series is now even: one for us, one for the Reds, and one for the umps."

But how do you guys really feel? Stop beating around the bleeping bush.

When Fisk calmed down a bit, he tried to explain the play to reporters. "It was obviously interference because I had to push him out of the way. When I did shove him aside, he stopped. . . . I don't know. It sure is a shame to lose a game this way."

When questioned by reporters, Barnett defended his decision. "I ruled that it was simply a collision. It is interference only when the batter *intentionally* gets in the way of the fielder." When looked up, the rules that covered this, numbers 6.06 and 7.08, say nothing of intent, however.

Darrell Johnson said that in his argument with Barnett, the umpire never mentioned intent, but said only that it was a judgment call. A judgment call cannot be protested, but an interpretation of the rules can be. The protest would have needed to be made before the next pitch, however.

All parties agreed that a collision had taken place. And it had taken place in fair territory. In the opinion of Dick Stello, who was umpiring at first, "The batter has as much right to go to first base as the fielder has to go for the ball." Had Armbrister taken an inordinate amount of time getting out of the box, or had Fisk been unusually quick reacting and getting to the ball? Or both?

Over in the Reds' clubhouse, Armbrister said, "The ball bounced high and I stood there for a moment watching it. As I broke for first base, Fisk reached over my head for the ball before I could continue on. I stood there because he hit me in the back and I couldn't move."

On careful review of the film, it appears that Armbrister started to run but was stopped by the collision when he was rear-ended by Fisk. The collision did not interfere with the throw, as Fisk was set before throwing. A good throw by Fisk would have eliminated the controversy. With Geronimo's speed, it would have been a close play at second for the force. The relay to first would have easily gotten Armbrister, due to his late start. There was not time to tag Armbrister and then throw to second for a tag play on Geronimo. The most damaging factor to Fisk and the Red Sox was the unusual quickness of Carlton Fisk in getting out of his crouch to make a play. Most catchers would have gotten there more slowly, would not have collided with Armbrister, and would have been forced to make the easy play at first. Lost in the confusion, but clearly shown on the video, was the end of the play, which backed Petrocelli's later claim that Geronimo's legs overslid third base and he ended sitting on his butt, a few inches off the base. Petrocelli applied the tag before Geronimo could reach back with his hand. But the umpire apparently didn't see it.

The next day the *Boston Globe* headline screamed: "A Call They'll Never Forget." A large sidebar displayed the applicable rule: "Offensive interference is an act by the team at bat which interferes with, obstructs, impedes, hinders or confuses any fielder attempting to make a play." There was no mention of intent in this version of the rule. Not surprisingly, each city's press and fans seemed convinced the call should have gone their team's way. Everyone recalled the play from their point of view: either incidental contact or a perfect shoulder block by the runner and obvious interference, causing Fisk to have to leap as he threw to second. As such, the call received very little attention in Cincinnati's two papers, but was the topic of debate in Boston for several days.

After reviewing pictures and tape of the play, the next day Barnett sat with reporters and told them he had slept well and "if I had to do it again, I would do it all over again. I know that I am right." He went through the play, step by step. "There was a collision. I was quoted as saying there was no intentional interference on the play, but I did not say that. I said there was a collision."

He noted that pictures showed Fisk using his left gloved hand and shoving Armbrister aside. "I would certainly say that my decision was justified by the way Fisk is pushing Armbrister away from him." He said he and the other umpires sat around for over an hour after the game discussing the play and there was no doubt among the group that the call had been correct. He added that he hoped the Red Sox wouldn't hold it against him for the rest of his umpiring life. "If they do, then shame on them." They would, and longer.

Another unnamed National League umpire was quoted as saying "As far as I could see, it looked to me as though it were more interference on Fisk's part than anything else. He just made a lousy throw to second base. And he's trying to take it out on Barnett, but it shouldn't happen that way."

After a day of reviewing all the arguments, Ray Fitzgerald's *Boston Globe* headline concluded: "Call Was Bad . . . So Was Throw."

Not satisfied, others in the Boston press tried to consult the highest authority available, Secretary of State Henry Kissinger. The gravel-voiced Kissinger, like the seasoned politician he was, refused to take sides, however. "I'm a Red Sox fan, so I'm a little biased," he told them.

Fisk soon wished the play, and the arguments, would just go away. When he had finally returned to his hotel room that night, in frustration, he had pulled the curtains down while drawing them. The next day he was in the coffee shop of the team hotel when a photographer from UPI came in and took a picture. When he and Rick Burleson tried to leave the hotel for a walk with their wives, an AP photographer interrupted them and started shooting away.

The call would be debated through the winter. In February 1976, NBC ran highlights of the World Series and had Kubek, Joe Garagiola, and some of the participants in the studio to rehash the Series for more than two hours. While reviewing new camera angles and footage, Kubek continued to argue for the interference call. He and Barnett took turns reading the rule book, each offering support for his interpretation. A view from the first base side was shown in which Barnett was removing his mask just as the collision appeared to be finishing— raising the possibility that he was unable to see the crucial step.

Barnett would later have his life threatened in a letter that demanded he return $10,000 the writer claimed to have lost on a wager due to the call. But Barnett also enjoyed benefits from the fallout. He noted in the spring that he had made between $10,000 and $15,000 over the winter in speaking fees based on the call. "Tell me, when's the last time you can remember anybody, I mean anybody, paying money to see or listen to an umpire?" He also was signed to do some commercials. He received hundreds of letters over the winter to his Prospect, Ohio, home, which ran about 2 to 1 against him. One memorable letter was addressed to "Larry Barnett, Home Plate Umpire, Third Game, 1975 World Series, Prospect, Ohio." It read, succinctly and eloquently, "You stink!"

Like any good umpire, Barnett would never have any public doubts. Even today, almost 40 years later, he is satisfied with his decision. "When a catcher and batter have contact, the runner has just as much right to run to first base as the catcher has to get to the ball," he says. He points out that Major League Baseball has always maintained that the call was correct and, in fact, video of the play was used for years to teach umpires the interference rules.

Fisk and Barnett would never appear together on a show or at an event. They would work behind home plate together for the next 18 years but would never talk; until Carlton's last major league game. "I worked home plate for his final game," says Barnett. "Afterward, he shook my hand and said, 'We had good careers,' and that was it."

Larry Barnett would go on to complete 31 years of service as an American League umpire, including three as supervisor of umpires. He still holds the record for being the youngest major league umpire at 24 years old (after working five years in the minors). He would work four World Series and seven American League Championship Series. He would make thousands of calls on close plays in his career, and yet, when he dies, Game Three of the 1975 World Series will be listed on the first line of his obituary.

It wasn't easy, but the Sox were able to put the controversial call behind them and focus on the next game, aware of the fact that with only the slightest change in fate, they could have easily held a three-games-to-none lead. Days earlier Luis Tiant had baffled the Reds hitters, keeping them off balance with his assortment of vertigo-inducing change-ups and curves. After the Reds scored two runs in the first inning of Game Four, Fisk, sensing the live arm coming back on his pitcher and seeing that the Reds were sitting on off-speed pitches, put the hammer down. He called for almost all hard stuff. The Reds were blown away early.

Trailing 2–0, the Sox mounted a comeback in the fourth. Fisk started it with a single to left. Lynn singled, Evans tripled, the score now tied. The Sox scored three more times in the inning to go up 5–2.

The Reds came back with two in their half of the fourth and it was 5–4 Boston after four innings. And that's the way it ended. It was a gutsy performance by Tiant, who continually teetered on the edge but managed to keep the Reds off the scoreboard. When Rose walked in the fifth, the first two fastballs had nothing on them and Tiant's breaking pitches were drifting dangerously high. Fisk motioned to Johnson that he might be nearing the end. Tiant came back and fought through it, though; his fierce competitive nature never burned brighter.

In the ninth inning, Geronimo singled and Armbrister successfully bunted, dropping it along the first baseline (afterward Fisk said wryly, "I wish the same thing would've happened, because maybe this time somebody would've gotten it right"). Rose followed with a walk: two on, one out. Johnson walked to the mound for a conference. Tiant had no intention of being relieved. Fisk felt that Tiant was throwing harder than he had earlier and, knowing what a fighter he was, told the manager, "Let him go after 'em." Griffey followed by drilling a liner to deep center that Lynn ran down on the warning track, making a great over-the-shoulder catch with two hands. Morgan then popped out and the Series was tied again. Tiant had thrown 163 pitches in the complete game victory, giving up nine hits, four walks, and four runs.

In Game Five, the Reds jumped on Reggie Cleveland for five runs in six innings. Perez hit two home runs. Reds pitcher Don Gullett was even tougher than he had been in Game One, giving up only two hits in the first eight innings. In the ninth, Yaz and Fisk singled and Lynn doubled, but the Red Sox rally died under the arm of reliever Rawly Eastwick. The Reds won 6–2 and the series moved back to Boston and destiny.

And then they waited. And waited. The gloomy New England skies darkened, opened up, and it poured. The game was originally scheduled for Saturday afternoon. Three days in a row Commissioner Bowie Kuhn slogged across the soaked field and conferred with the Fenway groundskeeper and declared the field unplayable. Some thought the field could have been ready on the Monday, but felt Kuhn didn't want to risk matching his prize jewel against the NFL's *Monday Night Football*—such had been the interest in baseball the past half-decade.

Hordes of press, stranded in Boston, eating and drinking up their expense accounts, running out of rainy-day stories, followed both teams everywhere they went, looking for something to fill up space in lieu of game accounts. It was noted that they were nearing the record for longest delay in a World Series, six days, which had occurred in 1911. They rehashed the Armbrister incident from every conceivable angle with no one changing their opinion. Bill Lee energetically entertained the masses with quotes about baseball, the socio-political-theological universe, and life in general.

The players anxiously awaited the news of when they could resume. The delay messed with their well-established routine. Sitting around the clubhouse, playing cards, taking a little indoor batting practice at local college facilities, they just wanted to get it over with.

In reality, the three-day rainstorm was served up by the gods as a meteorological sorbet, to cleanse the palate for the best course to come.

Finally, Kuhn gave the go-ahead for Tuesday night. It was cloudy but only a few spits of rain fell and soon subsided. Helicopters had been brought in during the morning to help dry the Fenway turf. In view of all the rain, it was a surprisingly warm night, 64 degrees at game time. The canceled afternoon starts on the weekend made Game Six the first World Series game ever played at night in Fenway Park. Originally the pitching matchup was to be Jack Billingham vs. Bill Lee but with the three-day delay, both managers had adjusted their rotation. Johnson had planned to bring Tiant back for Game Seven, if needed, but felt that the delay gave him enough time to rest after his marathon Game Four outing, a decision that did not sit well with Lee. Anderson planned to go with his entire staff except for projected Game Seven starter Gullett.

The Fenway faithful had barely settled in their seats when Fred Lynn gave the Sox a quick 3–0 lead with a home run. Tiant, obviously showing wear from his effort six days ago, was not his usual self, but he still managed to keep the Reds scoreless through four.

In the fifth with one out and runners on first and second, Griffey launched a drive to deep center field. Lynn gave fearless chase, barely missed it, and hurtled his body against the wall, whacking it with an audible thump and crumpling on the warning track as Griffey raced to third and two runs scored. Dazed, Lynn lay there as the crowd fell silent. But he refused to come out, getting up and waving off the trainer. Bench then followed with a shot off the wall in left and the game was tied. The runs broke a 40-inning scoreless streak for Tiant at Fenway.

The Reds got two more in the seventh. Tiant, clearly laboring and having little left on the ball, was allowed to start the eighth inning. It cost the Red Sox as Geronimo turned on the first pitch and hit it just over the fence in right, barely inside Pesky's Pole, making it 6–3 and knocking out Tiant.

An eerie silence fell over Fenway Park. The Red Sox were down three games to two and trailed by three runs. Six more outs and the Series would be over. Since Lynn's home run in the first, the Sox had produced only three harmless hits. In the press box, writers began typing their leads, anxious to make deadlines. Dick Schaap, editor of *Sport* magazine, passed out ballots for Series MVP. NBC cameramen lugged their equipment to the Reds' clubhouse to set up for the victory celebration.

But just when things looked bleakest for the hometown nine, Lynn singled off the Reds pitcher's leg and Petrocelli walked. Anderson quickly gave his pitcher the hook and brought on his rookie closer Rawly Eastwick, who had already notched two saves in the Series. After Eastwick retired Evans and Burleson, Johnson sent Bernie Carbo up to hit for Moret, who had replaced Tiant in the eighth. Carbo had helped carry the Red Sox early in the year, but had lost playing time as the season wore on—displaced by the magnificent seasons of Rice, Lynn, Cooper, and Evans. Other than his pinch home run in Game Three, he had been to the plate only one other time in the Series, making an out as a pinch hitter in Game Two. With a two and two count, Eastwick threw an absolutely perfect pitch. Carbo was going to let it go, then realized it was tailing in and would catch the black. He flicked his bat awkwardly and barely managed to foul it off. As Ray Fitzgerald wrote in the next day's *Globe*, "The patient was still breathing. But the 35,205 relatives were gathered at the bedside and saw no hope."

The next pitch was a fastball, high and over the outside part of the plate. Carbo got all of it. Everyone in the dugout and stands stood and watched as the ball sailed over the center field wall. The game was tied. Fenway exploded.

The game then turned into a mighty struggle that no one could finish off. Doyle led off the bottom of the ninth for the Sox by walking. Yaz followed with a single, sending Doyle to third. The winning run was 90 feet away with Carlton Fisk coming to the plate. How many times had he played this scene out in his mind growing up in Charlestown? But Sparky Anderson was not going to allow Fisk the chance to beat him in the ninth. He ordered him intentionally walked, loading the bases. Fred Lynn followed with a shallow fly down the left field line. Reds left fielder George Foster had an average arm with questionable accuracy, but Don Zimmer, coaching third, felt the ball was too short for the pedestrian-footed Doyle to risk with no outs. He yelled, "No, no, no." Doyle, standing on third with the close Fenway crowd almost in his lap, heard "Go, go, go," tagged up, and took off with the catch. Foster fired straight and true. The ball took a large hop off the damp turf, but Bench blocked the plate and Doyle was out—double play. It was the fourth Red Sox runner thrown out at the plate in the six games of the Series. Petrocelli ended the inning by bouncing to third.

On into the foggy night, nearing midnight, they played. After Carbo's home run, as phones rang to spread word of the game, the number of televisions tuned in to NBC spiked to the highest level ever recorded for a World Series Game, over 76 million. Joe Garagiola announced that Johnny Carson and *The Tonight Show* would not be seen. Few people cared.

In the 11th, it was the Reds who appeared to have a chance to win the game. Rose led off and was spun around by an inside 1-and-2 fastball. Umpire Satch Davidson immediately said the ball hit him and waved Rose to first. Acting mortally wounded, Rose summoned up the strength to sprint down to first, where he grinned as Fisk violently objected to Davidson. Replays showed that the ball clearly missed him, but Rose wasn't about to give back a free base in this situation. The percentage play for the next batter, Griffey, was a bunt and that's what Anderson called. But Griffey laid it down too softly and it died a few feet away, along the third baseline. Fisk was out from behind the plate in an instant, flung the mask, made a quick barehanded pickup, and threw to second to nail Rose.

The brilliant play by Fisk kept the winning run out of scoring position with the dangerous Joe Morgan coming to the plate. Morgan then hit a sharp liner deep into the right field corner that seemed destined to be the World Series–winning hit. The only question was would it clear the fence, or bounce off for a double? Evans took one look and ran back toward the sharply angled fence. With no room left, he leaped and threw his glove up in an awkward-looking, apparently futile gesture. But Evans was a superb defensive player and he knew how to play right field in Fenway Park. The ball stuck in his glove just in front of the fence. He almost fell over the short fence into the stands, but quickly righted himself and threw toward the infield. Yaz, at first, fielded the ball well to the dugout side of the base and threw to Burleson, who had dashed across the infield to cover first. Griffey, who had been near third when Evans made the catch, was an easy second out and the game had been saved yet another time.

The game was nearly four hours old now, only minutes away from being the longest game in World Series history. Those in the press box had already anointed it as one of the best. Fenway Park had taken on a surreal atmosphere. In the version of the story Carlton would tell for years, he had been tired late in the game, but was snapped back to reality and energized when Rose had turned to him in the 11th and, like a kid jazzed up on lattes, remarked, "This is the greatest game ever." As Fisk moved into the on-deck circle to prepare to lead off the bottom of the 12th, he felt that something good was going to happen.

Fred Lynn, following him in the batting order, was standing close, watching the pitcher warm up. "Pudge came up and said, 'I'll get on and you knock me in.'"

"Sounds good to me," Lynn replied.

The Reds' Pat Darcy, a 25-year-old rookie who had filled in for injured starters with an 11–5 regular season record, was about to begin his third inning of work. The eighth Reds pitcher of the game, Darcy had retired the side in order in the 10th and 11th. Sparky Anderson only had Don Gullett (the presumed starter for Game Seven) and Clay Kirby in the bullpen, but Kirby was buried so deep in Anderson's doghouse he would not throw a single postseason pitch. Darcy, a good sinkerball pitcher, had only given up two home runs since April. "But Pudge was a good low-ball hitter," says Petrocelli. "We were looking for him to do something." The Green Monster, such a prominent feature of Fenway Park, had not been cleared by a ball so far in the Series. It was 12:33 A.M. when Carlton Fisk, carrying a Rick Burleson model bat, stepped into the batter's box after doing his usual deliberate pre– at bat stretching, shaking, and twitching routine.

Baseball is a team sport, but the thing that separates it from other team sports is the one-on-one confrontation between pitcher and batter. There is nowhere to hide. Everyone watches, only one can triumph. The right-handed Darcy's first pitch was a fastball that sailed high and Carlton watched it. The second pitch was a low, inside sinking fastball. Carlton reached down and uncorked a quick, short, powerful swing. He immediately knew he had gotten it all. The ball rose high into the night, but appeared to be curving, drifting dangerously close to the left field foul line.

In the broadcast booth, Dick Stockton roared, "There it goes, a long drive. If it stays fair . . ."

In the on-deck circle, with a perfect angle on the ball, Lynn knew at once that it had the distance. "He hit it so hard, it didn't have a chance to hook foul."

As everyone in the park, and at home on television, watched the flight of the ball, Carlton took a few hops down the first baseline and began waving at the ball. He shouted and motioned frantically with his arms, waving to his right. Once, twice, three times. The ball appeared to straighten out about 30 feet from the fence. It struck the inside of the top of the foul pole and bounced down in left field where George Foster caught it and put it in his pocket. (It would remain at his house until 1999 when he sold it at auction for $113,273.)

". . . home run!" yelled Stockton.

Carlton threw both hands over his head and jumped straight up, then clapped his hands as he began high-kneeing it toward first, reaching out to shake hands with the jubilant first base coach Johnny Pesky; shaking hands with the man for whom the right field foul pole was named, not yet comprehending that he had just provided the reason that, years later, the left field pole would bear his own name. Pandemonium broke loose in Fenway Park. Rapturous fans were already pouring over the rails and storming the field as Carlton rounded first.

He toured the bases, slapping hands with fans, careful to step on each base. As more fans rushed the diamond, he resembled a running back in open field as he zigged and shouldered his way past defenders between third and home. He triumphantly jumped on home plate with both feet and was mobbed by the entire Red Sox team. Fenway organist John Kiley launched into the "Hallelujah Chorus."

Watching in the NBC truck, producer Roy Hammerman ran the live camera shot of the ball soaring into the pole, then cut to Fisk euphorically rounding the bases. But he also noticed something on another monitor, a sight that would change the way future athletic events were televised and ensure that this home run would forever hold a place in the pantheon of sports moments: the shot of Carlton Fisk, seconds after connecting, dancing along the baseline, watching, hoping, shouting, waving—willing the ball fair. He immediately recognized what they had and quickly set up the replays.

The camera shot had actually been something of an accident. Forty-eight-year-old cameraman Louis Gerard had been stationed inside the left field wall at ground level, peering through a small hole in the scoreboard the entire game. But Gerard wasn't alone in his perch. He had a furry companion who contributed to his historic shot. In an interview in the *Sporting News* in 2012, Gerard said as Fisk stepped into the batter's box, the director told him over the headphones, " 'Follow the ball if [Fisk] hits it.' I said, 'I can't. I've got a rat on my leg that's as big as a cat. It's staring me in the face. I'm blocked by a piece of metal on my right.' So he said, 'What are we going to do?' I said, 'How about if we stay with Fisk, see what happens.' "

What happened was pure gold. The television audience, already exhilarated at the magnificence of the game and the thrilling ending, was mesmerized by the replays of the sight from Gerard's camera. Over and over, they witnessed Carlton's real, unrehearsed reaction, the ultimate exhibition of the thrill of victory. "And Joe, Carlton Fisk had a lot of little boy in him right there," Stockton said to Garagiola during one of the replays. Never before had a television camera captured an athlete's spontaneous emotions, the human drama—the essence of why we play and love the game—so completely and so powerfully.

"They didn't even know they had that shot at first," John Filippelli, an associate director that night and later an executive producer for ABC, said in 2000. "It was a wonderful aberration that changed television. No one had ever thought of isolating on an individual."

As Gerard was leaving the park later that night, someone called to him from the NBC production truck. "Louie, come in here. I want to show you something," said the executive producer, Scotty Connal, who later helped start ESPN. "Do you know what you've got here?" Gerard answered, "Yeah, I got Fisk waving his arms, trying to keep the ball fair."

Connal said, "Yeah, but we've never done that before. It's going to change what we're going to have to do every time we take a shot. You changed television."

It became the camera shot "heard 'round the television industry." Before Game Six, there was no such thing as a reaction shot. Cameramen followed the action, focusing on the trajectory of a hit ball or a thrown pass or a shot. Forever after, there would be the isolation shot, looking for the reaction of the athlete to what happened. The home run, coming when it did, in the classic venue, to end such a memorable game, with the stakes so high, was great by itself. But when the public got a look at Fisk's raw emotions, waving the ball, then exploding in joy, it became an all-time classic; one of the most memorable and iconic shots in television sports history. "I've always wanted to find the rat and thank him," director Harry Coyle said to the *Los Angeles Times* in 1987.

Gerard would win an Emmy for his camera shot of Fisk that night. It would be one of a dozen Emmys he captured during his 35-year career, but this one would always hold a special place in his home. "My father was very proud of that shot," says his daughter Julie Hartley. "He was very humble and didn't talk about it, but you could tell he was proud of it. I have a scrapbook with all the articles about it." Gerard filmed Super Bowls, Stanley Cup Finals, major golf tournaments, as well as numerous television shows, but Fisk's home run shot was the high point of his career. It made him a legend in the business. In 2013, a retired NBC cameraman said whenever former employees met, Gerard's shining moment invariably was brought up. "It was such a novelty. He made himself famous." In the ultimate expression of pop culture fame, the event and Gerard's name later became the answer to a question on *Jeopardy!*

So tied together would Carlton Fisk, the Game Six home run, and Gerard's camera shot be that upon Gerard's death, at the age of 86 in 2013, Fisk released a statement: "Though I never had the pleasure of meeting Mr. Gerard, I am forever grateful to him for capturing my reaction to the home run. Rest in peace." When have you ever heard of another athlete issuing a statement at the death of a photographer or cameraman?

Back at Fenway Park, after Carlton's triumphant tour of the bases he emerged from the dugout for an on-field interview with NBC's Tony Kubek to the ecstatic roar of the crowd. Organist Kiley hammered out "For He's a Jolly Good Fellow," then launched into "Give Me Some Men Who Are Stout-Hearted Men" and continued playing every upbeat, celebratory tune he knew. The fans stood in their seats and on top of the dugout and on the field, clapping, waving pennants, and singing along. Even though it was now nearly one in the morning, no one wanted to go home. No one wanted the moment to end. After so much tension, the release of emotions was overwhelming. Once he concluded the interview, Carlton jogged all the way around the warning track, shaking hands and waving to the fans. "I don't think I've ever gone through a more emotional game," he said in the clubhouse. "I don't think anybody in the world could ask for a better game than this one."

Carlton stayed in his sweaty uniform and lingered in the clubhouse longer than usual, soaking up the moment, trying to put it all into perspective. He couldn't. This was the reward for all the hard work and lonely hours put in over the winter getting his knee back into shape. It was the imaginary home run every kid who ever picked up a bat alone in his yard had dreamed of hitting: last inning, World Series, home team has to win to stay alive, whole world watching on television . . . here's the pitch. Everyone had dreamed it, but only Carlton Fisk and Bill Mazeroski had done it; two men out of two hundred million. No matter what else he would do for the rest of his life, he would always be remembered for this home run, remembered for his three-second dance up the first baseline. He would always be remembered.

In Charlestown, New Hampshire, David Conant, Fisk's high school teammate Roger's father, ran down to St. Luke's Episcopal Church after watching the home run on television, climbed up to the belfry, and began ringing the bell. Hearing the racket, a local policeman went to the church with his lights flashing, intent on arresting the joker who was making all the noise in the middle of the night. When Conant told him the reason he was ringing the bell, the cop said, "Hell, if I'd known that, I'd have come and helped you."

"The church later had a patch made up that said, 'The day the bells rang,' to honor the event. They put that patch in the Hall of Fame. My father got there before Carlton did," says Roger Conant proudly.

The next day's *Boston Globe* ran a huge picture of Carlton waving the ball. Ray Fitzgerald's headline summed up: "The Best Game Ever."

"The sixth game of the 1975 Series will be the standard by which all future thrillers must be measured," wrote Ron Fimrite in *Sports Illustrated*.

Game Seven; oh yeah, Game Seven, the rules said it *was* necessary. And they had sold all those tickets. They couldn't really, as some suggested, just call them both winners and have everyone go home happy. But how do you come back, in less than a day, and play after experiencing the mountainous fluctuations of emotions, the incredible plays, the . . . perfection of Game Six?

Lee started against Gullett. Fisk was greeted with thunderous applause when he came up to bat for the first time. The Sox took another 3–0 lead, thanks to wildness from Gullett, who walked in two runs. Perez got two back with a sixth inning home run off Lee's famous Leephus blooper pitch. Rose singled in a run in the seventh to tie it at 3–3.

In the Reds' seventh with the bases loaded and two outs, Johnny Bench popped up behind the plate. Fisk raced back, leaned deep into the stands, and made the catch to keep the game tied. But the Sox couldn't get any more runs. Joe Morgan blooped home the go-ahead run for the Reds in the ninth on a pitch he hit off the end of his bat. The Red Sox had one more chance, but with the bases empty and two outs, Fisk watched helplessly from the on-deck circle as Yaz flew out to center to end it.

The mood in the Boston clubhouse after Game Seven was sedate, but not catastrophic. Players quietly gave interviews and went about the business of closing down another year. They all realized they had come as close as possible to a championship; little breaks and bloop hits and questionable calls all contributed to the outcome. But they could be proud of their finish; of taking the great Big Red Machine to the limit. "Yes, I'm drained," said Fisk in answer to a writer's question. "I think we all were right after last night's game." Then he admitted that the emotional roller coaster of the past 24 hours had taken its toll. "That's probably why we couldn't take advantage of the opportunities we had early in the game."

After the game Sparky Anderson said, "I don't know that there's ever been a better World Series." Neither did anyone else.

As time went by and the warm glow of the aftermath of the 1975 World Series faded, the magnitude of what had been accomplished began to become apparent; of how special this Series had truly been. And it couldn't have come at a more important time for the game of baseball itself. Shirley Povich, who had covered every World Series since 1924 for *The Washington Post*, later wrote, "If there was a single time frame in which it happened, a decent guess would be that America rediscovered baseball as the game of its heart during those glorious Twelve Days in October of 1975." The Series "recaptured for baseball every fan it ever lost and bred millions more."

The Series had contained everything: big-name players doing what they were known for, oddballs doing what *they* were known for, bit players seizing the opportunity of the big stage, close games, brilliant defense—great players making great plays, late-inning heroics, a new crisis with each base runner, it had it all. Fans were reminded of how much fun baseball could be. Five of the seven games had been decided by a single run. There had been come-from-behind heroics and controversy. The numbers were as close as the Series: the Red Sox scored 30 runs, the Reds 29; the Red Sox got 60 hits, the Reds 59; the Red Sox won three games, the Reds won four. A record 75.9 million viewers had tuned in on television—the most in history. The Series took NBC from a dismal third to a runaway first for the month in TV ratings. In the ensuing months, people would continue to talk about this as one of the greatest, if not the greatest, World Series in history. Time would not diminish that sentiment.

Carlton Fisk enjoyed all the spoils of the conquering hero. Over and over that winter, it seemed as if everyone forgot, or didn't care, which team had actually won Game Seven and the World Series. It was often said that the Red Sox won the Series three games to four. In late October, "Carlton Fisk Day" was celebrated in New Hampshire. The statehouse plaza was filled. The crowd included the four state champion (each class) baseball teams, Carlton's parents, sister Janet and Rick Miller, Ralph Silva, Governor Meldrim Thomson, and general wellwishers and fans, about 800 people in all. Carlton stood on the statehouse steps with Linda, three-year-old son Casey, and five-year-old Carlyn as the crowd yelled, "Carlton Fisk for governor." He laughed and said, "And if I am elected . . ." The crowd roared with laughter and yelled with every word.

Broadcaster Curt Gowdy was the master of ceremonies for the affair and said, "I became a big fan of Carlton Fisk right away in his rookie season when he had the guts to stand up to some of his teammates and say he was right to get out there and hustle."

Carlton told the adoring crowd, "I couldn't have been born or raised in any greater state." He thanked his parents and advised youngsters in the crowd, "No matter how great the odds are against you, if you hang in there and keep swinging you're going to have a chance to at least make contact." After the lovefest concluded, Carlton and his family drove their station wagon to the governor's home for lunch.

An even bigger political elbow-rubbing affair followed. Carlton and Linda were guests of President Gerald Ford at a state dinner at the White House January 26, honoring Israeli prime minister Yitzhak Rabin. It was reported that Fisk invited Ford to stay at his house while campaigning in the upcoming New Hampshire primary.

Amid all the postseason revelry, one of the reasons the Red Sox players, fans, and press didn't feel too bad about losing the Series was that they could look at the roster and dream of the days ahead. These guys had taken one of the greatest teams in baseball history—winners of 108 games, a team with possibly the greatest one-through-eight everyday lineup—to the brink. Other than old man Yaz, indeterminately aged Tiant, and Petrocelli, the Sox players all had long futures with a B on their caps: Fisk was 28, Cooper 26, Burleson 24, Rice 22, Lynn 23, and Evans 24. These guys were just going to get better. And there was a power-hitting kid in the minors named Butch Hobson who looked ready to step in at third when Petrocelli hung it up. This was undoubtedly the team of the future; an unbelievable blend of youth and talent; a dynasty in the making. How many pennants would they win over the next decade? How many World Series? It helped ease the sting of defeat that winter to know, without a reasonable doubt, that this Red Sox team would return to the World Series, soon and often.

But they never did.

9 The Holdout Three

THE 1976 BOSTON RED SOX were the obvious choice to repeat as American League champs—they had talent, youth, and now postseason experience on their side. The off-season pickup of future Hall of Fame pitcher Fergie Jenkins only reinforced that opinion. Jenkins, 33 years old, had won 20 or more games in seven of the previous nine years and was coming off a 17-win season with Texas. But the Red Sox were never able to capitalize on the potential of their great team. The reason, as stated later by Yaz, is that they "got caught in the crap that surrounded free agency. It affected the attitude and the future of the Red Sox."

As the 1976 season approached, it became apparent that the game of baseball was changing drastically. It would remain the same on the field—the bases were still 90 feet apart, the pitching rubber 60 feet, six inches from home plate, three strikes were still an out—but off the field it would become unrecognizable. Almost as soon as Carlton Fisk's Game Six fly ball bounced off the foul pole, an era had ended. Radical, relentless changes to the economics of the game were now in motion; changes that would alter rosters, players' salaries, attitudes, and expectations over the coming decades.

Above all, players would finally get theirs: representation, respect from owners, and money. Lots of money. But these things would not come without a cost. Gone forever would be the days of a team made up of guys who had come up through the system, taking the field and winning together; of players settling in the city they played in and becoming part of the community for decades; of players signing a contract and then going out and playing baseball without constant talk and worry about money throughout the season. Clubhouses would change; inhabited by strangers, new each year, perhaps tied to the same agent, but little else. For fans, the cut would be deep: no more sense of loyalty, no stability for their favorite teams, no more ability to even remotely identify with the players who made up the game—future players would be multimillionaires as inaccessible and unreal as kings—and no more assurance that the baseball season would even be completed each year. The cost to players would also be significant. The next two decades would be filled with near-continuous battle with owners, acrimony with fans and writers over escalating salaries, and uncertainty over the length of their playing careers and cities of employment.

The new era had been coming ever since the Players Association had banded together and hired labor attorney Marvin Miller in 1966. Each Collective Bargaining Agreement (CBA) Miller negotiated, along with adding to players' pensions and health benefits, had added key steps to increase players' rights. A major prize was won in the 1970 agreement—the right to pursue binding arbitration in front of an independent panel to resolve owner-player disagreements over salary and contractual issues. Miller used this arbitration to win the release of A's pitcher Catfish Hunter from his Oakland contract in 1974, then watched as a feeding frenzy took place among owners that resulted in Hunter signing a five-year, $3.5 million contract with the Yankees with a $1 million signing bonus; unbelievable numbers for the time— dwarfing Hank Aaron's highest-paid-player salary of $225,000.

The sledgehammer to the wall came on December 23, 1975, when an arbitrator ruled that pitchers Andy Messersmith (a 19-game winner in 1975) of the Dodgers and Dave McNally of the Expos were free to listen to all offers after playing a year without a new contract. This officially struck down the reserve clause and introduced a new term to the everyday vernacular of the baseball world—the free agent. It also sent a chill through the hearts of baseball owners. But while feeling the chill of losing their beloved reserve clause, the owners once more did exactly what Miller hoped they would—they cut their own throats by trying to outbid each other for Messersmith's services. (McNally retired as planned.) When Messersmith signed a deal with the Braves for $1 million over three years, players and agents everywhere sat up and took notice.

Carlton Fisk had always been a tough negotiator. Usually one of the last to sign each year, he realized his own value early, reasoning that a large number of those 1.7 million butts a year in the seats at Fenway

Park were there in no small part due to his actions. While some play-ers didn't like the confrontations of hard-nosed contractual debates and took what the club offered while making only token resistance, Fisk never avoided skirmishes, particularly when it came to defending his worth. The troubles he had while rehabbing his knee after the 1974 season made him realize how fleeting glory could be in the major leagues. Also, the apathy he felt the team showed that winter made him appreciate what disposable property damaged baseball players were and brought the stark realities of the business of the game into focus. Fisk had been one of the early players to sign with an agent. In fact, when he showed up with counsel for negotiations in 1974, it was the first time Red Sox management had ever faced an agent. Fisk was informed by Dick O'Connell that he would have to speak for himself because, "I do not talk to agents." That year Fisk had discussed with his agent what he should ask for, then went into the talks alone. Things had changed since then.

To make matters worse for the Red Sox, Fisk hadn't signed with just any agent. He had signed with Jerry Kapstein, a man whose name would soon inspire fear and loathing among baseball executives. In the early days of baseball agents, in the early 1970s, anyone could have the job; there were no requirements, no certifications. All you needed was a client willing to let you negotiate on his behalf and a briefcase; and the briefcase was optional. Kapstein became one of the original players in the game. A native of Providence, Rhode Island, the Harvard-educated lawyer was highly intelligent, gregarious, cool under pres-sure, well informed, and a workaholic. Kapstein loved baseball and had an encyclopedic grasp of facts and figures. "No one knows more baseball than Jerry Kapstein," Fisk said. Initially Kapstein represented only Carlton, Pittsburgh's Richie Zisk, and Baltimore's Bobby Grich. He got his big break in 1974 when he prepared the salary arbitration case for pitcher Ken Holtzman of the Oakland A's. Holtzman had proven himself to be one of the better left-handers in the league while helping the A's to three consecutive world championships and Kapstein was determined to get him the big raise he deserved—previously unattainable from the thrifty hands of A's owner Charlie Finley, but now possible through the arbitration process. While working on the case, Kapstein met and signed up A's relievers Darold Knowles and Rollie Fingers. Brandishing stats, charts, and big-time lawyer savvy, Kapstein won all three arbitration cases.

After Kapstein's early success, word spread through locker rooms and he was soon a rich and powerful broker of baseball talent. Kapstein was highly protective of his players and encouraged them to let him do all their talking, a tactic that irritated baseball officials, who preferred face-to-face discussions with outgunned players. Kapstein was a brilliant negotiator who fully understood the position of power from which he now dealt. Most general managers and owners, stubbornly clinging to a now antiquated system, were no match for Kapstein. He rarely left a nickel on the table and became universally hated by executives throughout baseball.

Kapstein and a few other major agents helped shape the new world of baseball economics. They realized that they were in control of the singular thing that owners were in most need of, and were willing to undermine the opposition to get—talent. Few men comprehended the dramatic shift and its ramifications earlier than Jerry Kapstein. He knew that the average major league salary of $44,000 a year was due to explode. "Most owners will be fair, but they have to recognize that times have changed," Kapstein told *Sports Illustrated* in June of 1976. "A player can now become a free agent and seek his fair price on the open market." And seeking a "fair" price on the open market was the strategy Kapstein wanted for all his players; it was the gateway to untold riches.

By 1976, the 32-year-old Kapstein had 60 clients, including some of the biggest names in the business: George Brett, Steve Garvey, Joe Rudi, Bert Campaneris, Don Gullett, Don Baylor, and Bobby Grich. He also had Red Sox players Fred Lynn, Rick Burleson, and Carlton Fisk. "I'd never had an agent," says Lynn. "Usually you just asked the older guys, 'What should I do here?' But after 1975 I knew things were going to change pretty quickly. I remember talking to Pudge in the dugout about it toward the end of the year and asking him who he was with." Fisk recommended his man. "Kapstein knew his stuff. He was so far ahead of the owners, they didn't have a chance. He was a sharp guy, full of fire, and a great negotiator. And he could foresee what was coming. I had made 20 grand my first year. He said, 'I can see guys making $1 million a year soon.' And we said, 'What?' That was crazy."

After losing the reserve clause, the owners soon realized that their enthusiasm in pursuing free agents was the very thing driving up salaries and, unable to control themselves, they decided they needed to do something to reverse the process. As spring training of 1976 approached, the owners resolved to beat the Players Association back into submission with talks on the new Basic Agreement. At stake in 1976 was the number of years required before being eligible for free agency. The Players Association, feeling the momentum from recent victories, was not in a mood to give in. The two sides were at an impasse.

On February 23, major league owners announced they were locking the players out of spring camp in 1976 until a new Basic Agreement was reached. Commissioner Bowie Kuhn, acting to avoid another catastrophic strike so soon after the one of 1972, stepped in and ordered them to open camp after 17 days. Players reported, labor talks resumed, and no games were lost, but the two sides were still far apart. Meanwhile, Kapstein told all of his clients in need of new contracts—including Fisk, Lynn, and Burleson—to sit tight and not sign until they found out what the terms of the new CBA would become.

In early March, Fisk signed the renewal paper, indicating he would play the season without signing his contract—technically playing out his option. He became the first Red Sox player ever to take advantage of the new rule. "I fully expect to sign," he told reporters at the time. "I had a good talk . . . we're still talking. We have been bargaining in good faith all along. I expect to sign."

In the next few days, Lynn and Burleson also signed their renewal papers. The news hit New England like a late spring nor'easter. The Red Sox had three holdouts! If they didn't sign for the entire year they would become free agents and Boston would get nothing in return for losing the heart of their team. Unthinkable. The good feelings left over from the great 1975 season evaporated in an instant.

Red Sox players had always been treated much more fairly, some would say coddled, by management under the direct instructions of Thomas Yawkey. It was not unheard of for Yawkey to give a player a needed loan in midseason for some unexpected expense, such as a down payment on a house, and when the player tried to pay it back later, wave him off with a simple, "Thanks for the memories." Carl Yastrzemski took heat from players around the league for not totally backing the rebellion in the first strike, but he had never faced the kind of fight guys on other teams had faced just to get a token raise. Yaz had retained an agent since 1970, but only for outside deals—he had handled his salary negotiations himself. Those contract talks, while routinely resulting in some of the biggest deals in baseball, had always taken place with O'Connell at a Boston restaurant, concluding amiably before dessert, at which point O'Connell would smile, shake hands, and instruct the waiter to bag up a dozen lobster tails to go for Mr. Yastrzemski.

Yawkey wasn't just that way with his favorites or the stars. Buddy Hunter remembers that soon after he was called up in 1971, he met Yawkey in the clubhouse and introduced himself. A month later when Hunter was sent back down after the regular second baseman came off the disabled list, he was told that Yawkey had ordered that he keep his major league salary when he went back to Louisville—an unheard-of practice.

"When I first came here, George Scott had been playing third and broke his hand," says utility infielder John Kennedy. "So I played every day at third. I knew no matter what I did, when he came back I was going to the bench. So when Scott got back after about a month, Kasko came up to me in the clubhouse and said, 'Dick [O'Connell] wants to see you in the office.' I thought, 'Oh no, I'm traded again.' I went in there and he handed me a check for $2,000. He said, 'You did a good job.' "

Many viewed the refusal of the three to sign as an ungrateful act of disloyalty to Thomas Yawkey and his goodwill. But, at the urging of Kapstein, they knew the time was right to make a stand. "It was a calculated risk," says Lynn, "because we were anticipating the courts upholding the Messersmith and McNally ruling [the owners had appealed to a higher court], and we knew free agency was coming. We were pretty sure that whatever happened was going to be good for players. We thought we could get a multiyear contract if we waited. But our necks were on the line. If anything happens to us, an injury or something, we're toast. We're at the mercy of the club. If that stuff hadn't been in the courts at the time, we would have just signed our typical one-year deal and it would have been over." And Red Sox history would have been drastically altered.

Because there had always been such collegial relations over contracts, and because it was Boston, with all the media and fan pressure, there was much more at stake for the Red Sox holdouts than for those in other cities. The reaction for the three was immediate and almost uniformly negative. "We caught a lot of flak over it," says Lynn. "Back then, the club had control of the press pretty much, with the exception of a couple of guys like Gammons and [Will] McDonough. Most of them just fell in line with what the club said. They started printing bad stuff about us every day. It was brutal."

There was an immediate effect in the clubhouse also. In the past, once contracts were signed and players were together and playing baseball, the only thought given to money was over who would suddenly grow alligator arms when the check came after dinner. Now, money threatened to disrupt the entire season. Players who were happy with the team and their own contracts, who realized what the loss of the three would do to their pennant hopes, were not exactly supportive. "It changed the club around," Yaz later wrote. "Things got only a little better when they finally showed up for spring training—late. As long as they were unsigned there was a cloud over the team. Everyone knew it was affecting our club, but we didn't talk about it much."

Even with the negative attention on the salaries, few expected anything other than continued good times for the Red Sox once the season started. The young Sox players had known only success—usually first or second place finishes. They took for granted that they were going to win; they were the team of the future and the future was 1976. They were unanimous picks to return to the Series. With their new ace, Jenkins, on the mound, the Sox lost their opener 1–0 when Burleson made a bad throw on a routine grounder that ended up being the deciding run—it was a sign of things to come.

The Sox stumbled to a 6–7 record in April, then opened May with a 10-game losing streak (the team's longest since 1960) and sank to the bottom of the division. A team-wide hitting slump, bad pitching, and sloppy defense all contributed. Fisk hit .347 in April, then lost 80 points off his average in May, at one point going 2-for-26. Meanwhile, negotiations continued, mostly in the press. Both sides issued deadlines and ultimatums. The Red Sox continued to state they were unhappy dealing with Kapstein but, advised by Kapstein, the three players refused to be present during talks. Kapstein became convinced that owners were bugging his phones and began insisting on an ever-increasing array of cloak-and-dagger tactics. He refused to take calls; he would only return them, often from a pay phone. He would leave instructions to call him at certain pay phones at specified times, varying the location and time, lest any spies catch on to his routine.

Fans were definitely in the corner of the owners at this stage of the money game. The country was battling a recession. Guys making

$18,000 a year had no sympathy for someone who appeared to be ruining their team by trying to get $200,000 or $300,000 for playing baseball. Writers, most of whom were making much closer to the average fan than the average ballplayer, seconded the thought, and fanned the flames. "The label 'mercenary' is applicable," George Vass wrote in *Baseball Digest*. "For there's no other way to categorize [free agents and holdouts]. No loyalty to team. No loyalty to city. No loyalty to anything but self-interest. Above all, no loyalty to baseball, which makes their gains possible. No sentiment for the game, no concern for its future. Just get it while it's there."

As the Red Sox continued to lurch through their schedule, Boston media blamed the slump on the contentious contract talks and holdouts of Lynn, Fisk, and Burleson. The issue was an open wound that, continually picked at by the media, proceeded to fester. Lynn was hitting for a good average, but the defensive flair from the previous season seemed to be missing, and soon, so was his power. He sat out an annoying number of games with injuries, prompting those in the press to call him Fragile Freddy and question his heart. Fisk battled several nagging injuries and continued to slump badly. Burleson was a mess in the field, making uncharacteristic errors. "[They] became a good excuse for our losing, but an unfair one," said Dwight Evans later in the season.

Matters were made worse when Boston executive Haywood Sullivan leaked some of Kapstein's demands to local writer Clif Keane. Keane had a popular radio talk show with fellow writer Larry Claflin called the *Clif and Claf* show (referred to in the Red Sox clubhouse as the *Syph and Clap* show) in which they regularly ripped Red Sox players. They railed on the shameless numbers over the radio, further inciting the scorn of fans.

The three holdouts received hate mail along with loud boos and taunts from the home crowd. Fans at Fenway were so close to the field that conversations with players had always been possible. Now they became venomous and the abuse grew throughout the summer, intensifying as the team underperformed. The players clearly showed the strain from the negativity of the multitude. Burleson, neck raging crimson, would swear back at fans while returning to the dugout. The normally emotional Fisk kept frustrations bottled inside. But the friendly fire hurt. And, being the local guy, the boos hurt him more than the other two; these had been his people. Just a few months ago they were ready to make him governor and now the sonsabitches were booing? "It was very difficult to play at home," says Lynn. "I personally couldn't wait to get back out on the road. With the writers and talk shows like that—it was tough. It went from the fans going crazy every time you walked on the field in 1975, to now they wanted your head. At Fenway, you know the fans are there—one way or another. There's always a big crowd and they are so close. Gosh, that was a difficult season."

Teammates noticed that Fisk appeared troubled; his mind was weighted before and after games. Even though the negotiations were technically out of his hands, he couldn't dissociate the complex feelings of team and city vs. personal security. It was impossible to relax and just focus on the game. Later in the year Carlton told *Sports Illustrated* how the stress and boos affected his play: "As a catcher, I have to be totally involved to be effective, but I just couldn't concentrate. I was denying myself the emotional involvement that I need to play well."

Speaking of the response from the fans in 1976, he later said, "I would never want to go through that again. It was hell."

In addition to the press and fans, the holdout affected the relationship with their teammates who could recognize what the turmoil was doing to their pennant chances. All the harmony from the success of 1975 seemed to disappear by the end of May. Differences of opinion that would have quickly been forgotten a year ago now sparked resentment. Burleson said, "My teammates would never say so, but I could tell that the little arguments that arose and the nitpicking I sometimes heard were really caused by our holdouts."

It was no longer a unified locker room but a collection of businessmen with differing agendas. "When the three were going through their trouble, Kapstein would telephone them in the locker room on the road," wrote Yaz. "They'd talk to him while they were in the clubhouse, which is a no-no."

"It seemed to take something away from their game," Bill Lee later wrote. "They had lost that spark that had come out of the youthful dive-for-every-ball enthusiasm that all three of them had. They still played hard . . . but they had lost their edge. Free agency seemed a burden for them. It was tearing at their brains. Over the course of the full season, I could see it playing havoc with the concentration, impairing their ability to give one hundred percent. . . . The game itself is demanding enough. They didn't need the albatross of unsigned contracts and front office mind-games wrapped around their necks. The press compounded the pressure. Fisk's locker was near mine, and, after every loss, I knew I would be hearing at least one writer asking him if his contract squabbles were hindering his performance."

"Nobody else said anything directly," says Lynn. "I'm sure some of the veterans might have been wondering, 'What are these guys doing?' But nobody ever came out and said anything. Also I'm sure they were waiting to see what happened. Because they would do the same thing next year."

"There weren't really a lot of bad feelings for those guys because we all knew what they were doing," says Jenkins now. "We understood. Nobody knew how long you had to play. This is the livelihood for these guys. Back then, everybody got a one-year contract. You knew that if you got hurt or something, your career could be over. To be able to get even a two-year contract would have been huge. It just wasn't done. We all knew we were expendable as soon as management didn't want us. And we had all been in the situation of being forced by management to take less than we thought we deserved because we never had a choice. Now, it looked like there might be a choice."

Regardless of the cause, the collapse of the team, with essentially the same roster that had won the pennant the year before, was mystifying. "We were shocked," says Petrocelli. "We were saying, 'What the heck happened? What's going on?'" No one had any answers.

The Red Sox and their fans tried everything to shake the team out of the slump. A Boston radio station flew in a real Salem witch May 11 to try to break the losing streak. Fisk reacted with indignation to the 42-year-old teacher of "Witchcraft as a Science" at Salem State College. "This is a rap against the players," he griped to reporters. "It makes us look unprofessional. This is a business, not a sideshow. We don't appreciate making a joke of the game. Nothing's funny right now." Due to the witch or not, the Sox did win that day, 6–4 in 12 innings. They proceeded to win six of their next seven, climbing into third place. Then they traveled to New York to play the Yankees.

If the 1973 Munson-Fisk-Michael fight launched the 1970s blood rivalry between the Yankees and Red Sox, the 1976 fight defined it. The mother of all Red Sox–Yankees fights occurred on May 20 in Yankee Stadium and, as expected, Carlton Fisk was there at the beginning.

The rivalry had progressed over the past few years as both teams improved and was now red hot. "It was a different atmosphere than anything else," says Jenkins, who was getting his introduction to Yankee–Red Sox combat in 1976 and, after playing years with the Cubs and Rangers, had never faced the type of contempt and loathing that awaited him. "It definitely wasn't like playing Cleveland or Detroit. At Yankee Stadium, as soon as you went in they'd boo the snot out of you. People would throw paper cups at you in the bullpen. They hated you because you played for the Red Sox."

Nothing in sports could compare to the reception when the Boston Red Sox bus pulled up in front of Yankee Stadium. "I used to take the train out at two o'clock so I could avoid the bus pulling up," said Fisk years later. "Going from the ballpark to the bus [after the game] you'd better wear your equipment." The air would be filled with everything from metal objects to moons, expletives, and references to players' mothers. Of course the feeling was mutual and Red Sox fans returned the favor to welcome the Yankees to Fenway.

"We had a great rivalry, both teams were very competitive," says Petrocelli. "Fisk and Munson had that great ongoing competition; who's going to be the best catcher? Who's going to be the All-Star? Things were said in the newspapers for both teams. The two teams really didn't like each other on the field. Fights broke out. And they always seemed to be mad at Fisk. He never backed down."

"I'd be warming up guys between innings and you'd hear stuff hitting the ground around you," said Fisk. "Once I heard something and I look around and it's a piece of aluminum foil and inside the foil is a tuna fish sandwich, thrown from the third deck, if that ever hit you . . ."

"With the way the teams felt about each other, playing in the same division, with each game meaning so much, you know something is going to happen," says Lynn. "Every time we played them you were just waiting for something to happen. A routine ground ball for a double play, whoever slides into second, they're not just sliding into second, they're looking out for somebody. Every chance you had to hit them, you did. Same way with them. It's not like it is today, with guys smiling and talking before the game and stuff. There was no way you talked to any of those guys. We didn't like each other. There was so much emotion, it didn't take much to light the powder keg."

The Sox entered the game May 20 with a 13–16 record. The Yankees were 19–10 and threatening to run away with the East. Players on both teams knew the series was crucial to Boston's hopes of getting back in the race. Bill Lee, normally a Yankee-killer, was on the mound for the Red Sox and pitched brilliantly, giving up only one unearned run over the first five innings. In the sixth, Lou Piniella and Graig Nettles singled. The next batter, Otto Velez, stroked a hit to right field and the powder keg was lit.

Piniella, either forgetting or not caring that Dwight Evans had the best outfield arm in baseball, tried to score. The fiery Piniella was one of the slowest and worst base runners in the game, a man so unaware of his own shortcomings on the base paths that he once was thrown out at three of the four bases in a single game—thus only narrowly missing the rare accomplishment of being thrown out for the cycle.

Piniella took a huge swing around third base, chugging far wide of the baseline, looking like he would stop in the dugout for a drink. Evans threw a one-hop laser beam to Fisk. Out by a good 10 feet, rather than admit defeat Sweet Lou maintained his speed and, two steps from the plate, lowered his shoulder and prepared to swing both forearms toward the catcher's face. Fisk, squarely straddling the base-line while holding the ball, playing without a contract, less than two years removed from a near-career-ending injury on a collision at the plate, held his ground. He recognized the intent to maim in Piniella's actions, dipped his own head and shoulder, and tagged low, sending Piniella sprawling. Fisk held on to the ball as the impact knocked him down. He quickly rolled up and shoved Piniella to the ground. Piniella had a grasp on Fisk's chest protector and pulled him down with him as he fell. While both players were on their knees, Fisk grabbed Piniella in a headlock with his left arm and slugged him in the face with his right. Players from the benches and bullpens flooded onto the field.

Lee, backing up the play, saw Velez sprinting for Fisk and tried to tackle him, catching a sucker punch in the back of the head from Yankee Mickey Rivers in the process. Nettles then grabbed Lee in a bear hug, flipped him up, and drove him into the Yankee Stadium turf on his left shoulder. Meanwhile, Rivers danced around the outside of the mass of combatants, cheap-shotting anyone wearing a Red Sox hat. "I grabbed Velez with both arms to pull him away and then I got hit in the jaw from behind," says Lynn. "I never knew who did it. I had never been hit like that in a baseball fight. This wasn't like most baseball fights. This one was dangerous."

After a few minutes of general melee, the fight appeared to be running out of steam with a lot of dancing and holding and threatening. Then Lee stood up and realized that his left arm—his moneymaking arm—was hanging lifelessly at his side. He wandered through the mob looking for his hat and glove, then spotted Nettles and popped back into the middle of the pile, intent on unleashing his lethal linguistic armament. Nettles, apparently aware that he could not match vocabularies with Lee, sent a right-handed haymaker to Lee's face. Unable to raise his damaged left arm, Lee took the full blow and dropped for the second time and fists started flying all around home plate again. Rico Petrocelli, one of baseball's most accomplished true pugilists, and Jim Rice, who nobody wanted a piece of, finally worked their way to the middle and separated the antagonists. Fisk, with his hair disheveled and his back covered in dirt, stood up and held his catcher's mitt high to show everyone that the ball was still firmly in place.

After the 1973 fight, Lee's comment about the Yankees fighting like a bunch of hookers swinging their purses had enraged New Yorkers. Years later, Nettles said of his blow to the unarmed Lee's face, "I wanted to make sure he knew he wasn't getting hit with a purse." The Yankee Stadium crowd stood and cheered as Lee was helped off the field with his left arm dangling.

The Red Sox won the game 8–2, but the damage was done—Lee had a separated shoulder with torn ligaments and was finished for months. In the aftermath, it was hoped that the fight would at least light a spark under the Red Sox, but it did not. They lost the next two nights in Yankee Stadium—by one run in extra innings each time—and their dismal season continued.

All three players were still unsigned and daily reports had them on the verge of being dealt away before the June 15 trading deadline. On June 10, the Sox had just finished a 5–7 home stand by blowing a 5–2 lead in the eighth inning to Oakland. As the team bus pulled out of Fenway, headed for Logan Airport and a 13-game road trip, Burleson began singing, "Goodbye Fenway, Goodbye Fenway . . ." Lynn soon joined him, laughing and singing louder. Darrell Johnson sat stone-faced in the front of the bus.

Carlton Fisk did not laugh either. He was playing the worst baseball of his major league career. There was no rest—he faced stress over the contract business, stress over his poor play, stress over the team's slump, stress over the boos at Fenway. A lot of stress. He was miserable.

That night, it got worse as Fisk and Johnson had a shouting match in the dugout. Playing in Minnesota, the frustrated Red Sox had quickly fallen behind. With Rod Carew on second and catcher Butch Wynegar on first, Johnson told Fisk to throw to second (to try to get the slower Wynegar) if Carew tried to steal third. Fisk argued that Carew usually runs on his own and so Wynegar probably wouldn't be going. Johnson refused to back down. It was a seemingly small disagreement and normally would have been forgotten quickly, except for the tension of losing and the other problems. There were several additional heated exchanges about Fisk's pitch selection during the inning as the Twins continued to hammer the ball. At the end of the inning, Johnson shouted, "I don't want any more of your lip." When Fisk returned to the dugout after striking out in the sixth inning, Johnson, at the other end of the dugout, continued the argument. "Then *you* call the pitches," Fisk retorted as he threw his helmet in Johnson's direction. The helmet skipped off a step and hit the manager in the leg. Fisk then stomped down the steps into the clubhouse.

That night, over a drink, Carlton told *The Boston Globe*'s Peter Gammons, "He's been second-guessing me all season. . . . Every time someone gets a hit off us, it seems that Darrell's blaming me for calling the pitch. It's been going on all year and I'm sick and tired of it. I'm sorry in one way, because it hurts the team, but it was bound to open up. I thought after my knee, the groin, the broken arm . . . I thought that I'd be able to just go and play and everything would be the way baseball's supposed to be. But this has turned out to be the worst year yet."

Gammons later wrote that Fisk, still trying to sort things out, was sitting by himself late that night, waiting for his meal, when two young ladies sat down at his table. Within a few minutes, Fisk had pulled out his wallet and lined the table with pictures of his children. Looking at family pictures not being exactly the type of late-night entertainment the two girls had in mind, they politely got up and left. "Right now my family is the only stability I know," Carlton told Gammons. "Everything else seems out of kilter. . . . All this stuff has definitely affected my concentration, and I'm certain it's affected Rooster, Freddie, and probably some of our teammates. I'm trying to play. My arm's killing me. Darrell's on my case. And there's [assistant general manager John] Claiborne coming around talking to me."

The next day Fisk missed the team bus to the park and arrived too late for batting practice. He was fined by Johnson and benched. He was back in the lineup the next day and he and Johnson were reported to soon settle their differences. "It was simply an argument about baseball," Fisk told reporters in an official-sounding statement.

Johnson said he appreciated that "a lot is going through his mind that sometimes may have left his thinking a little fuzzy. . . . I hope this all is just the contractual thing, because everyone's on edge, no one's himself on or off the field."

And no one being himself on the field was certainly not a good thing for a team with the talent of the Red Sox. Their season of great expectations was rapidly slipping away. "It was like a nightmare," Yaz wrote later. "I couldn't believe it was happening. After 1967 we came apart because of injuries. But now, in 1976 and the years afterward, we came apart for a different reason . . . baseball went from a team orientation toward an individual situation. Nobody kidded around. It became . . . I guess the word is 'businesslike' . . . the free agency thing turned us upside down. . . . We pulled fewer and fewer pranks. . . . Nobody would do anything to anyone anymore because a guy would get ticked off. . . . All of a sudden, it became a quiet clubhouse."

As Johnson continued to fiddle with the lineup, searching for an answer, he only caused more frustration and unhappiness among his players. Butch Hobson was brought up from AAA to play third base and Petrocelli temporarily played second, a move that quickly fizzled. The Red Sox' much publicized agreement to purchase the A's Joe Rudi and Rollie Fingers for $2 million was nixed by Commissioner Bowie Kuhn, who invoked the "best interests of baseball" clause in nullifying it. The Sox didn't get the two Oakland stars, but the players whose lives would have been changed by the addition remained resentful and felt unwanted.

In August Fergie Jenkins summed up to a reporter, "Coming to Boston from Texas, I had high hopes this year. I expected one of my best seasons, but I soon learned that the team I was playing for was not the one I had played against the year before. Neither the hitting nor defense was as good as I thought it'd be, and I was very surprised at the poor fundamentals. There also seemed to be a lot of players with bad attitudes."

Trade rumors continued to swirl—that the Red Sox would dump the three players for anything they could get, rather than let them walk as free agents at the end of the year and get nothing. "I can't win," Carlton said about the contract situation, "whether I get what I want or not.

I've been criticized everywhere for not sitting down with the club, but every day in spring training or early in the season it seems I was talking with Claiborne and that took my thinking away from baseball. I'd never thought of being anything but a Red Sox. All of a sudden I was threatening to leave and become a free agent, the club was threatening to trade me, and I was up in the air." Every time the news on the field slowed down, another Boston writer would bring up the contract issue. Not long after Thomas Yawkey died of leukemia July 9, it was even suggested that he had died of a broken heart—due to the holdouts.

On July 17 the desperate Johnson called Yaz and Petrocelli into his office and asked if the two veterans had any thoughts as to what they could do to stop the hemorrhaging—hoping they had a magic cure. They didn't. Still, when the Red Sox decided to fire Johnson two days later and hire third base coach Don Zimmer, it came as a surprise— the quick-triggered move of panic from a team with unmet expectations. Johnson had led them to an American League championship and had been selected *Sporting News* Manager of the Year less than a year earlier. But the Sox were 41–45, 13 games behind the division-leading Yankees. Johnson had insisted all along that the three unsigned players were not his area of concern and that they wouldn't affect his team's play, but few actually believed that.

General Manager Dick O'Connell, citing the usual suspects of lack of discipline and poor communication, told the press, "We cannot blame everything on Darrell Johnson." He then added a statement that should be inscribed on every ex-manager's tombstone, "But it's easier to change managers than the team."

"There are a lot of reasons besides Darrell Johnson why we haven't done well this year, and everybody knows what some of them are," Yaz told the press.

Johnson had been a mentor for Carlton Fisk. He, above all others, had been responsible for molding Fisk into a professional catcher. But the relationship had soured amid the frustration of losing. Fisk, at the time mired in an 0-for-26 slump, told reporters, "I guess it had to happen. That's the way baseball is. A team should win, and when it doesn't the manager gets the blame."

In response, a New England journalist wrote, "How tragic that Johnson had to suffer for the failings of his spoiled brats. I hope Fisk took a hard look at the reflection in the mirror the next morning when he showered."

In 1976, the 45-year-old Don Zimmer more closely resembled the thin, former fiery infielder of the 1950s than the ubiquitous, round-faced cherub he became in the 1990s. He had been popular with the team as a third base coach. All baseball, rarely seen without a huge wad of tobacco stretching his cheek to the limit, he was an extremely competitive, conservative, no-nonsense manager who was quick to get on players who didn't hustle. For those who did hustle, he left them alone. Fisk would later say that Zimmer was "the easiest guy I ever played for, the easiest manager ever. Put your name in the lineup and he said, 'Go get 'em, boys.'" One of Zimmer's first moves was to call Burleson, Fisk, and Lynn into his office. He told them he wasn't getting involved in their salary negotiations, but their play on the field could be much better.

The new Basic Agreement had finally been agreed upon during the All-Star break and was due to take effect in August. Kapstein signed contracts for the three just under the wire. All three got five-year contracts; Lynn would receive $1.65 million over the five years, Fisk $900,000, and Burleson $600,000. Everyone was happy they wouldn't need to worry about contracts for five years—the three would remain Red Sox. It was announced that they would be covered by the old Basic Agreement, which included an option year with the Red Sox after the contract expired (a seemingly small detail that few noticed at the time). Under the new BA, effective August 9, they would have been eligible to become free agents immediately upon the expiration of the contract.

The nearly yearlong contract squabble was finally over. When asked about the poor seasons by the three and their contracts, Don Zimmer said, somewhat diplomatically, "Baseball, because it demands so much more concentration than people think it does, is a tough game to play when you have other things on your mind. . . . I have to think that the contract difficulties Lynn, Fisk, and Burleson had earlier had a lot to do with their failure to play up to what they did a year ago."

Future baseball players would reap the benefits of the efforts of guys like Lynn, Burleson, and Fisk in 1976. For better or for worse, player salaries would grow exponentially. In 1972, when Carlton Fisk broke in, the minimum major league salary was $12,000—about what a young schoolteacher would make—and the average was $34,000. By 2010, the minimum salary would be $480,000 and the average would be $3.3 million. "It worked out for everybody in baseball," says Lynn of the first free agent season. "It's kind of a forgotten thing with how high salaries are now. We were the whipping boys. Was it worth it? Yeah, I guess in the long run. But we were out there by ourselves that year. It was the toughest year of my career."

The players may have gotten what they wanted, but not necessarily what they needed. As concluded in *Sports Illustrated*, "[They] won a lot of money for their obstinacy, but they suffered a lot of mental anguish as well." How much was the mental anguish really worth? The effect on their team, their personal happiness, and ultimately their careers, was immeasurable. Paradoxically, players in the future would be making much more money, but they seemed to be less happy with their situation. Salary beefs, which had rarely taken up much print during the season, would become ubiquitous. The more they got, the more they wanted; and the more they wanted, the more fans expected. A lot of the fun left the game of baseball.

Soon after signing, Fisk went on an 18-game hitting streak in which he was 28-for-74 (.378), raising his batting average 30 points. (He would end at .255.) The Sox were hopelessly out of it, though, as the Yankees charged to the pennant. The Sox finished in third place, 83–79.

Over the winter, players got their first look at what wholesale free agency would do for salaries. The Red Sox management initially gave indications of trying to stay in competition with the free-spending Yankees. They signed relief pitcher Bill Campbell from the first free agent draft. Campbell, who had been one of the best relievers in the league for three years, had become a free agent when he asked for $27,000 per year, but Minnesota owner Calvin Griffith refused to budge from $22,000. Campbell then signed with the Red Sox for a bit more—$1,050,000 for five years. Welcome to the new era.

In 1977, Carlton Fisk had no contract worries. And he was completely healthy for the first time in three years. He got off to a blistering start at the plate. His batting average hovered between .340 and .360 through the end of June. It tailed off somewhat, but he was never below .292 for the entire season. He was once again selected to start the All-Star Game. Munson, the 1976 American League MVP, was not happy. He told reporters the AL would have "a heckuva backup catcher."

The 1977 Red Sox could score runs. Butch Hobson, an ex-Alabama football player, had taken over at third base and quickly became a fan favorite by hurtling his body around Fenway Park. Hitting in the eighth or ninth spot most of the year, he hit 30 home runs and 112 RBIs. George Scott had been obtained from Milwaukee in a trade for Cecil Cooper over the winter. Scott, a big Mississippi Delta farmhand, had come up with the Red Sox in the sixties and had been a key member of the 1967 pennant-winning team. Nicknamed Boomer, he was popular with fans for his graceful fielding around first base and his colorful language, little of which was found in dictionaries. With his uniform, he wore a shell necklace, which he claimed was made up of the "teeth of second basemen." He had led the American League in "taters" with 36 in 1975.

The Red Sox had staggering power throughout their entire lineup: Rice hit 39 homers; Scott 33, Hobson 30, Yaz 27, Fisk 26. Only Lynn, who had severely strained ligaments in his ankle during spring training and missed the first five weeks of the season, had an off year.

The season was fun—and maddening. They were a team of extremes. The lineup, nicknamed the Crunch Bunch, could explode at any time. They went through a stretch in which they hit 33 home runs in 10 games. They hit five or more in one game eight times. They hit 16 in a three-game series with New York. It was home run derby with Wiffle balls in the backyard every night.

But Red Sox pitching was terrible at times. No lead was safe until the final out of the game. "Going into each game I never knew what I was going to do," Fisk said the next year. "The starters didn't have good stuff, and I had to be a magician to get a good game out of them." Red Sox games became a contest to see if the offense could score enough runs to stay ahead of their opponents' inevitable outbursts. Reliever Bill Campbell led the team with 13 wins. Tiant was 12–8 with a 4.53 ERA, the worst of his career. Wise and Cleveland each won 11 games with ERAs of 4.77 and 4.26. Lee's arm was still not completely healed from his injury and he was only able to win nine games. The Red Sox pitching staff became a patchwork of rookies and injured veterans. Zimmer jerked starters in and out of the bullpen, further frustrating them.

"He started moving us around," says Jenkins, who was slowed by an Achilles injury. "You'd miss a start, go to the bullpen. Then go back again. It was frustrating. We were veterans and knew how to win. He was searching for something, playing hunches. But that really hurt us."

During this period, a renegade group of disgruntled players who called themselves the Buffalo Heads emerged. The Buffalo Heads were united not only in friendship and love of partying (this was the seventies after all), but in a growing dislike of Zimmer. The ringleader was, to be expected, Bill Lee—Lee was never one to conform to authority and the conservative Zimmer particularly drew his ire. The other members, Wise, Jenkins, Willoughby, and Cleveland, were similarly frustrated pitchers, driven to distraction by Zimmer's continued tinkering with the rotation. They were joined by Bernie Carbo. The name of the group was coined by Jenkins in a nod to Zimmer, because he said the buffalo was the ugliest creature on earth. They made no attempt to keep their opinions secret. The open insubordination by the group—Lee frequently held forth in the clubhouse to reporters on Zimmer's inadequacies and referred to the field leader as a gerbil—caused further problems with team morale. Zimmer hated them passionately and the feeling was mutual. Whereas Darrell Johnson had largely ignored Lee's off-field comments, chalking them up to a minor cost of his competitiveness, Zimmer read every paper and listened to every sports talk radio show and took the insults to heart. And since he couldn't defeat Lee in a battle of wits, his only recourse was to move him and his cohorts in and out of the rotation and, later, to lobby his bosses to rid the team of the divisive group. One by one, the Buffalo Heads were dumped, mostly in one-sided deals. The team would miss the lost talent.

The Yankees, who had spent liberally on free agents and were much stronger than they had been in 1976 when they had won the pennant, were neck-and-neck with the Red Sox all year. Neither team was able to open more than a three-game lead through early August. Once again, a September series with the Yankees proved fateful. On September 13, the Red Sox went to Yankee Stadium for a three-game series—games they had to win. The Yankees took the first game 4–2. A perfect example of the feelings between the two teams occurred in the first inning the next day. Yankee leadoff batter Mickey Rivers had pounced on three first pitches the day before, two going for hits, one a home run. When Rivers, whose cheap shots in the '76 fight were never forgotten, stepped in to start the second game of the series, Red Sox starter Reggie Cleveland drilled him in the ribs with his first pitch. As New York fans screamed and booed rabidly, Fisk slowly walked to the mound for a word with his pitcher, wanting to make sure he wasn't unsettled by the start or the fans' reaction. "Let's see the little bastard hit that first pitch," Cleveland said when Fisk reached the mound.

The Yankees won again, 2–0, and a week later they won six in a row and pulled away. The Red Sox ended in a tie for second place with the Orioles at 97–64, two and a half behind the Yankees. It was the fourth-highest win total in Red Sox team history but that did little to mollify disappointed fans.

Down the pennant stretch, Fisk played great, ending with a 16-game hitting streak. He had 35 RBIs in his last 26 games and was named the Red Sox MVP. In his finest year at the plate, he hit .315 with 26 home runs, 106 runs, and 102 RBIs and became only the third catcher, after Yogi Berra in 1950 and Roy Campanella in 1953, to hit .300 with more than 100 runs and RBIs.

Behind-the-scenes changes were taking place in the Red Sox front office—changes that would affect all of their futures. When Tom Yawkey died in July 1976, the Red Sox had become part of his estate. In essence, the executors of the Yawkey will—his wife, Jean, and his two lawyers—became the owners of the team. Not overly interested in baseball, and advised by her lawyers of the devastating tax implications, Mrs. Yawkey decided to sell the team, letting word leak out of her intentions in April 1977.

There were several interested parties, but the most intriguing was a couple of former Red Sox employees. Haywood Sullivan had been an All-SEC quarterback at the University of Florida, where he had also played baseball. He signed with the Red Sox for a bonus of $45,000 in 1952 and became one of the long line of Red Sox bonus babies that wasted the team's money. As a catcher, he played mostly in the minors until 1960, then played briefly for the Red Sox, and A's, hitting .226 in 851 major league at bats.

After his playing career was over, Sullivan managed briefly in the minors and then was recruited to the Red Sox front office as part of the Dick O'Connell reorganization in 1965. He was instrumental in several trades that helped shape the 1967 pennant winners; however, after 1970 he lost favor with O'Connell, but remained very close to the Yawkeys, particularly Jean. In his bid to purchase the team Sullivan partnered with former Red Sox trainer Buddy LeRoux, who provided needed cash. LeRoux was a hustler who had made a bundle of cash in Florida real estate and also had some personal contacts who provided more money.

Mrs. Yawkey officially put the team up for sale and accepted bids on September 1, 1977, in an unusual public auction. A-T-O Inc. (an Ohio-based conglomerate that owned, among other things, Rawlings Sporting Goods) bid $18.75 million. Two Boston businessmen offered $16 million, and the ownership group organized by Sullivan and LeRoux came in at about $15 million. With Jean Yawkey's connections, a deal was worked out in which Sullivan reportedly put up $100,000 and received a $1 million loan from Jean. With that, he and LeRoux were able to get 52 percent of the club for the $15 million total price tag. The other bidders screamed foul and a lawsuit was filed by A-T-O Inc., feeling they had been maneuvered out of the deal in which they had been the high bidder. Nasty legal wrangling ensued. So much press coverage was given to the fight, investigating every political, financial, and sports angle of the deal, that Red Sox publicist Bill Crowley said, "If nuclear war were to break out, it would only make page two in Boston."

The suits were finally settled, other American League owners were pacified, and the deal was made with the team of Sullivan, LeRoux, and Yawkey taking control of the Red Sox. After the sale went through, Mrs. Yawkey fired Dick O'Connell and installed Sullivan as the team's general manager in October of 1977. This drew fire because under O'Connell's tenure the Red Sox had gone from perennial bottom-feeders to one of the most important franchises in the majors, averaging 88 wins and 1.72 million in attendance during his last 11 years. O'Connell came to be seen as the victim being persecuted by Sullivan and his patron, Mrs. Yawkey. Few realized at the time that the court cases and political front-office skullduggery were only omens of things to come, for the franchise, its fans, and its star players.

10 The Massacre

THE 1978 SEASON APPEARED to be the year the Red Sox would break through. The murderous lineup that slugged its way through 1977 was back and the team had made some definite upgrades. A trade with California brought second baseman Jerry Remy, who had stolen 41 bases in 1977, giving the Sox the one offensive measure they lacked— speed. And, finally, it appeared that the Red Sox had a pitching staff that could match their hitting. Management made a noble effort. They signed Mike Torrez as a free agent. The 31-year-old Torrez had won 17 games for the A's and Yankees in 1977 and two more in the World Series and had won 68 games in the past four years. He was solid and reliable. They bolstered the bullpen with free agent signings of Dick Drago and Tom Burgmeier. Then, in late March, the Red Sox pulled a major trade, getting Dennis Eckersley from the Indians.

Only 23 years old, Eckersley already had three seasons of major league experience and had averaged 13 wins a season over that period for bad Cleveland teams. The California-raised Eckersley was supremely confident, to the point of openly taunting opponents from the mound when he had his good stuff, but he was popular with both teammates and the media. He threw heat and spoke a unique language all his own—a peculiar marriage of hipster-jive and baseball-slang spoken nowhere else on the planet. Eckersley and George Scott could have a fifteen-minute conversation in the clubhouse without using one recognizable English word. A "cheese for your culo" meant you were going to be nailed in the butt with a fastball. A breaking ball was a "yakker." He might excuse himself from a group of writers and announce that he was going to get oiled and then drop some heavy iron on his beef tonight for some high-class grease, meaning he was going to have a drink, then take a date out for a nice meal.

When Eckersley reported to the Red Sox, he sat in the press room at Chain O'Lakes Park in Winter Haven and told Boston writers that he liked to work fast: "One thing I can't stand is for the catcher to come out to the mound to talk to me." This statement was met with hearty laughter throughout the room. In response to Eckersley's puzzled look, they said, "You're in for a good time here, then. Fisk is out there after every pitch."

Torrez, who also didn't appreciate his catcher slowing him down, had some adjustments to make with his new catcher along with Eckersley. "We had a little bit of a falling-out early when I first got there because I liked to pitch fast," says Torrez. "Get the ball, get the sign, and throw, before the batter has time to think. Carlton was methodical and liked to work slow, always positioning the fielders and stuff. You had to wait on him. I told him, 'Stay down. You don't need to do all that stuff. We have pregame meetings to go over the hitters, you don't need to move everybody around.' He got a little upset. But once we talked it over we were fine."

"He would come out and get on a pitcher," adds Torrez. "He'd say, 'What the hell are you doing out here?' That was fine. Sometimes you need a reminder. If he saw something that could improve what you were doing on the mound, that was good."

The new players quickly fit in with their Boston teammates. Fisk, all business, got with the new pitchers and discussed how to attack enemy batters and gave them his view of surviving in Fenway Park. "Other than that, Carlton was kind of hard to get to know," says Torrez. "He was one of the guys and had fun, but he also didn't say a lot. He was more into observing. On the road, he kind of stayed within himself. But once you'd been with the team awhile he loosened up."

Under the intense pressure of expectations and payroll, the Sox started slow, losing close games with frustrating mistakes. After losing three of the first four, they righted themselves and won 10 in a row. Then, a short time later, they won eight more in a row. Wins were coming every day. Their sluggers bludgeoned other teams as expected, but they were now getting great starting pitching also. They reached 20 wins earlier than any Red Sox team since 1946. Fans, anticipating great things, piled into Fenway ahead of 1977's record pace in which they hit two million for the first time.

As in 1977, Carlton's presence behind the plate helped the young pitchers who contributed to the staff. Rookie Jim Wright moved into the starting rotation in early May and stayed there most of the year. "Carlton was an outstanding teammate and leader," says Wright, who went 8–4 with three shutouts. "It was great to have him back there as a young pitcher. As a rookie, I was in awe. I was thinking, 'Jeez, this is the guy who hit the home run in the World Series a few years ago. Maybe we'll get back there again.' But he was great. He treated me the same as anyone else. He told me a lot of things to help. He told me when I first came up, 'A lot of pitchers fail in Fenway because they don't throw inside.' You'd think with the fence so close you have to keep the ball away, but he said the fence could be reached easily with outside pitches too. He liked you to throw inside, not to hit people, but you had to work inside to get them out.

"He would come out to the mound when he thought you needed it. He was different with everybody. Some guys he really got on, others he was more of a cheerleader. He learned what worked best with each pitcher. And he was great about knowing what was working each game. I was a curveball pitcher, but I remember one road game I had given up a few runs and my curveball was hanging. He came out and told me, 'You don't have your curveball today, it's getting you in trouble. So we're going to do it with your fastball. We'll show them a few sliders, but it's going to be the fastball mostly.' The rest of the game that's what we did. I just threw wherever he put his glove and I made it into the ninth inning.

"Once in spring training, the year I made the club, I had pitched two and two-thirds innings without giving up any hits, then gave up a broken-bat single. Johnny Bench came up and just mashed one—a line drive home run. It was gone as soon as he hit it. Pudge strolled out to the mound and said, 'Don't worry, that wouldn't have gone over the Green Monster. It might have gone through it . . .'"

The Green Monster weighed heavily on the psyche of all Red Sox pitchers. It felt so close, like someone was looking over their shoulder; so close that they thought they were going to scrape their fingers on it if they reached back too far in the windup. "Carlton made it easy for me," says Don Aase, who came up to the Red Sox as a rookie in the middle of the 1977 pennant race, was forced into the rotation by injuries, and won six games with two shutouts. "I didn't have to do any thinking. I relied on his knowledge of the game and the hitters. That really gave me confidence having him back there. I just had to throw where he told me to. He was good at taking the pressure off. Sometimes he would come out and crack a joke. You have to be relaxed to pitch good." Sometimes he provided a firm nudge in the backside. Once when Aase was struggling and told Fisk he was tired, Fisk snapped, "Bear down. You've got all winter to rest."

The Red Sox continued to blow through the league; every day they went to the park knowing they were going to win. It was one of those rare, charmed times when everything lined up right: most of the players were in their prime, everybody was healthy, and nobody was in a slump. The good times rolled every day. They had a lineup that looked like an All-Star roster: Remy, Burleson, Rice, Lynn, Yaz, Fisk, Scott, Evans, Hobson—there wasn't a weak bat in the bunch. By June 26, the Sox were 50–21 (33–6 at home) and had won 24 of their last 30. Starting pitchers Eckersley, Lee, Tiant, and Torrez were a combined 33–8. They looked unbeatable. The only question seemed to be whether they would clinch the pennant by Labor Day.

Meanwhile, the Yankees were having a frustrating season. Injuries and manager Billy Martin's increasingly unstable behavior had decimated the team. It was a testament to their considerable high-priced talent that they had managed to stay as close as they did. New York came into Fenway in early July a battered, demoralized team. After losing the first day 9–5, the Yankees were so desperate for healthy pitchers that they summoned a rookie who drove to Boston from their AAA team. The game was rained out, however. It was announced that the game would be made up as part of a three-game series in early September. Few gave it much thought, but the one game missed against the ravaged Yankees at that stage would prove to be huge.

Even while the Red Sox appeared invincible, manager Don Zimmer was constantly under pressure; not only from the fans and media, but from his own team, many of whom questioned every move and found him to be dull and slow in his decisions. And Zimmer, always intense, unable to relax, amd ecstatic at the way the team was playing, may have put the throttle down too hard in midseason and burned some players out. Lee threw 146 pitches on May 6, Tiant 159 later in May. Torrez threw 160 in an 11-inning loss July 1. The starters never got a rest. "Zim's philosophy was to play the same guys all the time," says Lynn. "But sometimes that can backfire. If you are blowing people out, you might want to get other guys some playing time because you might need them later. When guys got hurt the second half, the guys on the bench hadn't played. It's really hard to get thrown into the fire when you haven't had much playing time. You can't be comfortable."

The team began to show cracks. Bill Lee, who got off to a 10–3 start, would never win another game for the Red Sox after July 15. He had staged a one-day walkout June 15 to protest the trade of his fellow Buffalo Head Carbo to Cleveland. He apologized and returned the next day. "Fisk stood by me," Lee wrote later. "He didn't necessarily agree with my action, but he would defend my right to take it. He said he thought it was a bit selfish on my part to walk out the way I did, but he respected me for standing up for my convictions." Zimmer, however, did not respect Lee. As the left-hander's performance continued to slip in the second half and he increasingly offended Zimmer with his comments to the press, he sank further in the manager's doghouse. Lee rarely saw the field the last few months.

A series of injuries soon followed. Yaz had recurrent back pain. Rice hurt his foot. Reliever Bill Campbell, who had pitched brilliantly in 1977, was bothered by elbow and shoulder soreness, possibly due to overwork the previous year. And in the biggest blow, Burleson suffered torn ligaments in his left ankle while sliding into second the day before the All-Star break. He was out almost three weeks and the team severely missed his influence in the middle of the infield.

Despite the injuries, there seemed to be little cause for concern. The team continued to win. July 20, the Sox were 62–28, on a pace to win 112. Eckersley was 11–2, Torrez 12–5, Tiant 7–2. They were nine up on second-place Milwaukee, 14 ahead of New York. Then, the worst thing that could have happened to the Red Sox occurred: Billy Martin finally imploded and got axed. Drunk and upset, he made the infamous "One's a born liar and the other's convicted" statement about his best player (Reggie Jackson) and boss (George Steinbrenner). The next day, July 24, he was forced to resign. Had Martin continued as manager, it is unlikely the Yankees would have had either the ability or inclination to climb out of their hole—and Red Sox Nation would have been spared one of their most painful episodes.

The new Yankee manager was Bob Lemon, essentially an anti-Martin. Under the laid-back guidance of Lemon, who treated his players as adults and seemed content to write down names on the lineup card and stay out of their way, the Yankees took off. This was a very strong Yankee team, stars at every position, most bought with the deepest pockets in baseball. The turmoil and the injuries had masked how truly great they were, but now they were playing loose, and they were healthy. They began eating into the Sox' lead.

And the Red Sox began slowing down; more injuries and slumps. Torrez was hit on the throwing hand by a come-backer off the turf in Kansas City in July, sustaining a bone bruise on his middle finger, which affected the way he gripped the ball for two months. Tiant, at least 37 years old, began showing his age, struggling to get through games. Second baseman Jerry Remy went down with a leg injury. George Scott, always fighting a battle with weight, began losing as his waste size and batting average went in opposite directions. Zimmer played him less; he grew unhappy and griped. After hitting 33 home runs in 1977, he would hit only 12 in 1978. Dwight Evans was beaned by a pitch and had dizzy spells the rest of the season. Butch Hobson had developed a serious elbow condition which worsened to the point that fans behind first base were at constant risk. Zimmer continued to play Hobson at third, however, and it became a familiar sight for fans to see Hobson rubbing his elbow after every throw—he was actually working loose bone chips back into place so he could move the joint. Hobson would make a staggering 43 errors, mostly on bad throws, in 133 games, with the majority occurring in the last two months. By contrast, New York third baseman Nettles made only 11 in 159 games.

The Sox slumped to 13–15 in July. They bounced back in August and won 20 out of 29, but now they found they could not shake the Yankees. No matter how well they played, the Yankees kept gaining. Zimmer ran his horses at full gallop, crossed rivers, climbed mountains, ran across rocks, and when he looked back the once distant cloud of dust was not only still there, but was now a noisily closing thunder of hooves. *Who are those guys?*

The embattled Zimmer could scarcely poke his head out of the dugout without incurring the wrath of fans. He tried everything to snap the team out of their slide. Every starting pitcher except Tiant was sent to the bullpen at some point. The purge of the Buffalo Heads had contributed to the Red Sox having a dangerously thin bench—almost no depth at all. When the pitchers faltered and the injuries occurred they had no reserves to fall back on.

Late in July, a month in which he batted .365, Carlton Fisk broke a rib when he crashed into the stands trying for a pop foul. Although he later said it made him feel as if "someone is sticking a sword in my side" every time he threw, he played on as though nothing happened.

As he continued to play, the pain worsened and he unconsciously changed the way he threw to protect the ribs—a change that would have severe consequences. But he suffered in silence.

Every day Zimmer wrote his name in the lineup and every day Carlton Fisk gamely went out and played, regardless of the pain in his ribs, and now in his elbow. He never asked for a day off, and Zimmer, watching the scoreboard and seeing the Yankees win almost every day, didn't want to take the field without Fisk in there. Fisk had always had trouble keeping weight on during the season; catching every day combined with the strain of the close race, he lost 34 pounds over the 1978 season. Despite the weight loss and the rib and arm pain, he would play more games than any other Red Sox player—squatting behind the plate in 154 games, one shy of the American League record for catchers. The Red Sox had an open date August 24. Starting August 25, Fisk caught 36 games in 37 days. The only day he didn't catch during that period was September 25—the Sox had the day off. Bill Lee later told reporters he could see the pain in Fisk during the pennant race and urged him to take some time off. "I can do one more," Fisk told him.

"I looked into his eyes," said Lee. "He looked like a raccoon. You could see he was playing in pain and it was just sapping his body. . . . Fisk is a guy you've got to put a governor on. He's just going out there because of his puritanical upbringing—you know, staunch, quiet, arch-conservative, play-with-an-arrow-in-your-heart type of thing.

"Pure Connecticut River granite. Pudge wouldn't ask out of a game if he had both legs cut off."

In the tight race, "I wasn't about to let a little pain and agony stop me from playing," Fisk said in 1979. Zimmer? "He came up to me a couple of times. It was never, 'I want to give you a day off.' It was always, 'You're all right, aren't you?' Or 'You can play, can't you?'"

Fisk later told Peter Gammons that Zimmer made the lineup out at 1:30 and he didn't want to go into his office and beg off with an injury and make him scratch his name out. "There shouldn't be anything wrong with saying, 'Look, I'm hurt,' but somehow the whole thing made you feel like a puss." And Carlton Fisk's code made no allowance for being a puss.

On September 7, the Yankees came to Boston, not so much as a second place team, but more like the Nazis rolling into Paris. The Yankees had won 12 of their last 14, were now healthy, and were flying high. Since falling 14 games behind the Red Sox July 17, the Yankees had been 35–14. The Red Sox had gone 25–24 over that period, and were coming off a 3–5 road trip. Boston had a four-game lead with 24 to play, but the object in their rearview mirror was much, much closer than it appeared.

The four-game series started poorly for the Sox. A Hobson error in the first inning gave the Yankees two unearned runs. The Yankees had seven runs and Munson had three hits himself, before the ninth man in the Red Sox lineup came to bat for the first time in the third inning. When the carnage was over, the Yankees had 21 hits and a 15–3 victory. They smelled blood in the water.

Rookie pitcher Jim Wright, who had pitched well all year, entering with an 8–2 record and an ERA of 3.12, was on the mound for the Red Sox the second game. Rivers singled on the first pitch, stole second, and cruised into third when Fisk's throw bounced away from Burleson. Wright lasted into the second inning, getting one more out than Torrez had the night before, and left losing 4–0. His replacement, Tom Burgmeier, immediately gave up a single, a walk, and a home run. Meanwhile, Yankee pitcher Jim Beattie, recently recalled from Tacoma, retired 18 Red Sox in a row at one point. The Sox continued to self-destruct in the field. Evans, who had not dropped a fly ball in his entire major league career, dropped his second one of the week as he was still dizzy from the beaning. Fisk had two throws get away for errors. The game ended 13–2 with seven Red Sox errors. Seven.

The next day, the Red Sox had to face Ron Guidry and his 20–2 record. But Boston had Eckersley, who at 16–6 was no slouch. When Eckersley set down the Yankees in a scoreless first and the Sox got two on with one out in their half, it looked like a new story. Then Guidry got Yaz on a weak grounder and Fisk on a called third strike and the Sox were done for the day. More errors, a wind-blown pop fly that fell in for a double, three walks, a wild pitch, and a passed ball and Eckersley was gone after seven runs. The Yankees won 7–0. "This is the first time I've seen a first-place team chasing a second-place team," said NBC's Tony Kubek.

With a chance to keep New York from leaving with a sweep in the last game, Zimmer passed over both Tiant, who begged to pitch on three days' rest, and Bill Lee, who had been banished. Some questioned whether Zimmer was letting his personal feelings affect his choice, but Lee had lost seven consecutive starts since July 20. Zimmer picked

22-year-old rookie Bobby Sprowl to try to slow the Yankee onslaught. Sprowl, who had recently been called up from Bristol, was making only his second major league start. He lasted two thirds of an inning, walked four, and was charged with three runs. The Yankees built a 6–0 lead before coasting to an 18-hit, 7–4 victory.

"How can a team get 30-something games over .500 in July and then in September see its pitching, hitting, and fielding all fall apart at the same time?" a demoralized Fisk asked no one in particular in the club-house. He had gone 4-for-11 with four RBIs in the series but it had been much too little to help. The Yankees had outscored the Red Sox 42–9, with 67 hits to 21 in the four games. Red Sox starting pitchers had combined to retire only 20 Yankee batters. At the conclusion of the four-game series, which was tagged the "Boston Massacre" by media, the Yankees had caught the Red Sox; they were tied at 86–56.

Five days later, Boston went to New York and lost the first two games of a three-game series, making six straight losses to the Yankees. They were now three and a half back—they had blown 17 and a half games in two months. The team was stunned. Players sat and asked them-selves, "How can a team with so much talent play this way?" No one had an answer. The Sox managed to salvage the last game 7–3 behind Eckersley.

With 15 games to go, the Yankees held a three-and-a-half-game lead. The Red Sox had lost 14 of 17 and appeared finished, done in by yet another late-season collapse. The C word was beginning to be thrown about by fans and media. "Why do the Red Sox skitter and fall?" wrote Leigh Montville in *The Boston Globe*. "The word is 'choke' and the word is appropriate. That is what they do. They choke. They have surren-dered to the fear inside their minds." Is that what they did? Choke. Really? Or was it just bad luck, injuries, and slumps? Everyone had an opinion.

The true story of the 1978 Red Sox was not how they blew the big lead, but how, after the disaster, when everyone had ridiculed them and written them off, they somehow were able to come back. "It was different from the 1967 team, which played on emotion," Yaz wrote. "In 1978 we became very tough, very businesslike, and we said that nothing was going to stop us." Knowing they needed to win every game, they almost did. They finished at a 13–3 pace and won the last eight in a row. They played inspiredly and brilliantly. They made one error the last eight games; the pitchers allowed only three earned runs in the last 60 innings of the regular season.

But the Yankees were winning also. Since late July, the Yankees had won nearly three of every four games. Each day the Red Sox would go out and, against all reason that said they should be hanging their heads and giving up, win their game, all the while watching the scoreboard to see how the Yankees were doing with their slim one-game lead. And each day the answer on the scoreboard was the same: those damn Yankees won also.

"The last two weeks, it was win or go home every game," says Torrez. "We knew the situation we were in. We had to win every day and hope someone beat the Yankees. We knew we could play and we hit a hot streak at the right time."

"The last two weeks, we had to win [every game] and we did," says Lynn. "That's really a testament to that ball club and their heart. We were out of it, but these guys just dug in and said, 'We're not losing.'" Down the stretch, September 21 to 30, with his body at the point of exhaustion, with the pain in his side growing worse, Fisk hit in eight of nine games, going 13-for-35 (.371). On September 24, he caught all 14 innings at Toronto in a 7–6 win. There was no time to worry about personal discomfort.

The entire city was consumed by the drama taking place at Fenway Park. When Pope John Paul I died September 28, a local television personality famously led with, "Pope dead, Sox still alive, details at eleven."

Finally, there was a single game left and the Red Sox still trailed the Yankees by one. Luis Tiant took the mound against the Blue Jays for the final game of the year, with all of New England knowing that the Red Sox had to win and the Yankees had to lose. The Yankees were playing in Cleveland, sending future Hall of Fame pitcher Catfish Hunter against the sixth place Indians. "But Rick Waits was pitching for the Indians," says Lynn, pointing out that hope sprang eternal in the Red Sox clubhouse. "He didn't throw hard. That was the type of pitcher the Yankees didn't like. We knew we had a chance if we won our game."

Tiant pitched and the team and fans watched the scoreboard. One of Toronto's outfielders snuck through an open door in the scoreboard and posted a fictitious "8" next to Cleveland, which temporarily sent the crowd into a frenzy. After the fraud was discovered a real number

"2" flashed up beside Cleveland in the first and a roar went up once again. The Red Sox continued to win and periodic eruptions arose from the stands as word came over the radio or scores posted on the scoreboard showed the Yankees falling further behind.

"It was the transistor radio era," says Bill Campbell. "Everybody in the stadium had the Yankee game on. It was weird. There would be nothing going on in our game and all of a sudden a big roar would go up from the crowd—they had heard the Indians score another run." Bob Stanley kept a transistor radio on in the Sox bullpen, relaying news to the team from the Yankee game, leaping to his feet to lead hundreds of fans in ovations for Cleveland runs. Finally, with Boston leading 5–0 and New York trailing 9–2, the scoreboard announced: "Next Red Sox Home Game Tomorrow" and the fans went wild. After 162 games, the two teams were tied with the best record in baseball: 99–63. One of them would have to win a 100th.

On Monday, October 2, they met at Fenway Park on a bright sunny afternoon in a one-game playoff to settle things once and for all. A few weeks earlier, with the possibility of a tie, officials from the teams had met and flipped a coin to determine the playoff location, if needed. The Red Sox had won the toss and elected to receive. Ron Guidry was the starting pitcher for the Yankees, with a gaudy 24–3 record, the highest winning percentage ever for a 20-game winner. Mike Torrez, 16–12, took the mound against his old team. Both were going on three days' rest. The Sox were confident. "We were excited to play them at Fenway," says Lynn. "Even facing Guidry. We thought, 'We got them now.'"

This game would mark the zenith of the great Red Sox–Yankee rivalry that had defined the seventies for the two teams, the perfect juxtaposition of two sets of great players, personalities, and characters, who did not like each other or the other city's fans. There was nothing contrived or made-for-television; it was genuine and everybody felt it.

Torrez was sharp and pitched six shutout innings while the Red Sox scored in the second on a Yaz home run. In the sixth, the Sox appeared to have a chance to blow it open. Rice singled to score Burleson. Guidry then intentionally walked Fisk to pitch to the left-handed Lynn with two on, two out, trailing 2–0. Lynn hooked a line drive into the corner in right field that looked like a triple. But Piniella was playing four or five steps closer to the line because he thought Guidry was tired and Lynn might pull him more than usual. "He shouldn't have even been near there," says Lynn. Piniella made a great play, snagging the ball just before it hit the wall, saving two runs and, more importantly, keeping Guidry in the game.

In the Yankee seventh, Chris Chambliss and Roy White singled, only the third and fourth hits of the game for New York. With two outs, shortstop Bucky Dent, the number nine hitter in the order, hitting .140 over the previous 20 games, stepped in. Dent had hit four home runs all year and undoubtedly would have been removed for a pinch hitter if Billy Martin had still been manager, as was Martin's habit. After a first-pitch strike, Dent fouled a ball straight down off his left foot. While he was hobbling around, the next hitter, Rivers, noticed a crack in the bat and handed him a new one. It must have been a good one.

Ahead in the count 0–2, Torrez planned to throw inside, to back Dent off the plate, then come back with a slider away. "It wasn't a bad pitch," says Torrez. "It was a fastball inside, but it tailed a little bit back toward the plate. I didn't get it inside enough." Dent, who had a tendency to step in the bucket, got it right in his wheelhouse. He lofted the ball toward left field. Anywhere else, it would have been a routine fly; a can of corn. But this wasn't anywhere else, it was Fenway.

Between the sixth and seventh innings, the wind had shifted. Instead of blowing straight in, it had started blowing out to left. Fisk hadn't noticed. When the ball left Dent's bat, he initially felt relief—only two innings to go. Then he looked up and saw Yaz, the most experienced arbiter of good and bad flies in Green Monster history. Carlton watched helplessly with the rest of the team as Yaz drifted to the wall, paused, then put his head down and slumped his shoulders. The ball landed in the screen seven inches above the top of the fence.

But the game wasn't over. Dent had merely given the Yankees a one-run lead (along with acquiring a new middle name). Munson followed with an RBI double in the seventh and Jackson hit a home run in the eighth to put the Yankees up 5–2.

Symbolic of their season, the Red Sox didn't give up. With the shadows closing in on the park, the Sox battled back in the eighth. Yaz knocked in Remy with one out. Fisk followed him to the plate. Goose Gossage, the premier fireballing reliever of the era, got two quick strikes but couldn't finish him off. Fisk fouled off five two-strike pitches and then singled up the middle on the 11th pitch of the at bat. Lynn singled to score Yaz and make it 5–4 with one out and two on. But

Gossage then got Hobson on a fly to right and struck out Scott to end the threat.

In the ninth, still trailing 5–4, Burleson led off with a walk. Remy followed with a line drive to right field that Piniella lost in the sun. Piniella deked Burleson into thinking he was going to catch it, then made a quick stab of the ball when it hit the ground and bounced to his side. Had the ball gotten past Piniella, Burleson would have scored. Instead, he had to hold up at second. Rice flied to the warning track in right and Burleson tagged and moved to third. With runners on first and third with two outs in the ninth, Carlton watched from the on-deck circle as Gossage pitched to Yaz—power against power. This was the confrontation baseball fans lived for. The wind was still blowing out to left. Yaz took a mighty swing and popped the ball up toward third.

The next spring Carlton talked about the still painful memory: "I knew the season would be over as soon as Yastrzemski's pop-up came down. It seemed like the ball stayed up forever, like everything was cranked down into slow motion. I was trying to will the ball to stay up there and never come down . . . what a dumb thing to have run through your mind. Even the crowd roar sounded like a movie projector at the wrong speed when everything gets gravelly and warped. After the last out, I looked around and the crowd was stunned. Nobody moved. They looked at each other like, 'You mean it's over now. . . . It can't be over yet . . . oh, nuts.' It had only been going on for half a year, but it seemed like a crime for it to end."

Fenway Park fans stood and cheered the Red Sox as they walked off the field. Fisk and Remy lingered near the walkway to the clubhouse, not wanting to leave the season behind. Fisk still had his batting helmet on from the on-deck circle. "What I remember the most is the clubhouse after the game," said Burleson. "Not only how quiet it was, but looking at the bags we had packed to go on to Kansas City to start the playoffs. It was a sad sight to look over there at the luggage."

The 99 wins were the most by a Red Sox team since the 1946 team won 104, but, as Peter Gammons later wrote in *Sports Illustrated*, "The Red Sox, for all they had accomplished, were just another second-place team."

The painful memories would linger a lifetime. "Boston and New York were the two best teams in baseball that year, by far," says Torrez. "I would have loved to play the Dodgers [in the World Series].

There was no doubt in anyone's mind we would have beaten them easily."

"When you say '78 to me, all I see is the playoff game," says Lynn. "Sorry, I can't get that out of my head. It was very frustrating, even looking back on it now. We were so good."

They didn't know it, but forces would soon ensure that the great young Boston team would never recover and would be dismantled. This had been the last chance for one of baseball's memorable teams.

11 It Just Isn't the Same

FOR ALMOST A DECADE, Carlton Fisk and Thurman Munson had waged a private war fought in front of millions. It's difficult to pinpoint exactly when the rivalry between the two started. It just seemed to be the natural order of things: the leaders of two intensely rival teams, closely related by geography and history. The running down the baseline incident in 1971 was irritating to Munson, but he lived to be irritated, he thrived on it; he looked for little things to get mad at opponents about. Had Fisk just been a September call-up who faded the next year, the incident would have been quickly forgotten.

Sometime during the 1972 season—when Fisk began to take the national spotlight and All-Star votes—is when he really first inspired Munson's disdain. Munson had been the overwhelming choice as the best catcher in the league until Fisk showed up. He had been the only catcher in league history to be selected Rookie of the Year—until Fisk showed up. It drove Munson to distraction that fans and writers could even suggest that this interloper could possibly be better than he was.

By all accounts of teammates and journalists who covered the Yankees, Munson greatly resented the popularity of Carlton Fisk; each All-Star vote for Fisk seemed to Munson to be a personal affront, an unfathomable slap in his face. "It's Curt Gowdy on the Game of the Week always playing him up," Munson complained. "He used to be the Red Sox announcer, he loves them, and now he's on the national games and he's always talking about Fisk this and Fisk that. And you know what? Fisk is always getting hurt, and I'm always playing through injuries, and he's getting credit for things he might do if he was healthy. Gowdy has this thing for him." Munson proudly pointed to the fact that he had never been on the disabled list while Fisk was on the DL four times from 1972 through 1976.

"Maybe it's because Fisk is a big, tall, good-looking guy and I'm short, I'm pudgy, and I don't look good in a uniform," said Munson. They certainly did contrast in their appearance. Fisk was striking—tall, almost regal-postured, handsome, and always clean-shaven. Munson was squat, short-legged, constantly scowling, with three days' worth of stubble and a Fu Manchu. They both chewed tobacco but, somehow, Fisk's uniform was usually immaculate while Munson's was covered in tobacco juice. Even though Munson played in New York, he missed out on commercial deals, which made him furious when he watched as Fisk's chiseled features and stature garnered American Express and tobacco company commercials. In Munson's 1978 autobiography, he mentioned that he got a new commercial, and wrote, "Guess who did a TV commercial? I did . . . Eat your heart out, Fisk."

"For a while it was like I didn't even exist," Munson said in 1976. "He got all the publicity and most of the All-Star votes. I don't hold it against him personally, but he's never been as good a catcher as I am. If we were on the same team, I might even like him." Then he added, "But he'd have to play another position."

Fisk even made famous the very nickname that rightfully should have belonged to Munson. Certainly if either had the body that should have inspired its owner to be called Pudge, affectionately or otherwise, it was Thurman Munson. But Munson never got the go-to nickname. Writers and others halfheartedly called him Tugboat and Squatty Body, but neither caught on and he hated them both.

Teammates and writers soon realized how much Munson disliked Fisk and used it for laughter (theirs) and motivation (his). Gene Michael, who roomed with Munson for five years, used to tear out Fisk stories and pictures from magazines and put them in Munson's locker. Everyone in the clubhouse enjoyed watching the reaction. Munson never found out who the culprit was. "Finally, one day, they'd been piling up the stuff I'd put in it," Michael said. "He came running out of the locker and screamed, 'What the hell, do you guys think this is funny or something? This ain't funny anymore!' He was a very prideful guy. . . . Thurman always felt a little slighted."

Munson was supposedly so jealous of Carlton that he regularly checked the stats to make sure he was ahead of him in every category. An oft-told story was that Yankee public relations man Marty Appel once handed Munson a stat sheet (in some versions Munson read in the paper) that had Fisk leading the league in assists, six ahead of

Munson. Munson went out in the game that day and purposely dropped "about a half dozen balls" on third strikes and threw the batters out at first to edge Fisk for the assist title. Sabermagician Rob Neyer, in his book *Rob Neyer's Big Book of Baseball Legends*, debunks this myth. Neyer went through Retrosheet, checking Munson's defensive stats, and determined that the most assists Munson ever had in one game was four and the most to first base was two, once in 1971, before the rivalry, and the other in 1977, after Appel had left the team.

The truth becoming greatly exaggerated into legend is also apparent for the game in September 1971 in which Carlton allegedly showed Munson up by beating him down the first baseline. Later versions had Fisk receiving a throw to get Munson out and Peter Gammons, in *Beyond the Sixth Game*, even claimed that Fisk took the throw for a rare double play with the catcher covering first. According to play-by-play accounts in Baseball-reference.com, there were no groundouts hit by Munson during this period in which a play was made at first to the catcher. But whether or not these stories were completely accurate is only of secondary importance. It's the spirit that counts. As Winston Churchill wrote of the Arthurian Legend: "It is all true or it ought to be; and more and better besides."

Despite the media hype and embellishment, the rivalry between Fisk and Munson was real and it was spectacular. Sometimes Munson would talk to Fisk about things he saw in the papers he didn't like when Fisk came to bat (calling him by his last name). "Listen, Fisk, I saw what you said in the paper this morning and it's bullshit."

And they were so open and honest about it; no politically correct niceties. "We don't send each other Christmas cards, put it that way," Carlton told a reporter in 1977.

Another time, when asked by reporters after a spring game in which an air of belligerence was noted in the way they passed each other on the field, Carlton said charitably, "He's not one of my best friends, nor is he my worst of enemies."

"What does that mean?" they asked, not happy with the answer.

"It means I don't like him worth a damn," Carlton replied.

Once after Carlton had taken a challenging step toward the mound when a Yankee pitch sailed over his head, Munson told a reporter Fisk was fortunate he had gone no farther. "He would have had his butt kicked."

The rivalry was so great, so delicious, because it arrived at just the right time, when baseball's two signature franchises and their fans renewed their overt revulsion for one another. And here were two singular warriors, each of them—and their fans—absolutely convinced that they were the ones who deserved to win, vanquishing the Philistines from New York or Boston (pick one). It was a rivalry made, if not in heaven, certainly somewhere on the road between Mudville and Cooperstown; it was perfect for baseball fans. The fact that they were in their prime and played two such important positions, the same position of course, positions that allowed them three to five times a game to stand within arm's reach of each other—while one was holding a wooden club, mind you—and exchange glances and even whisper sweet nothings if so desired, made it all the more delightful. It was one of baseball's all-time great personal rivalries; at the perfect time and place. Had one played in, say, Seattle and the other Cleveland, it wouldn't have been the same.

Speaking of Munson in 2005, Carlton said, "He wore the Yankee pinstripes and he looked like a walrus. I wanted to be better than he was. . . . I wanted our team to be better than them. There was nothing that I would not do in that regard. . . . The teams and media fed off that." They brought out the best in each other.

Fisk made six appearances in the All-Star Game between 1971 and 1978 and Munson made seven. Fisk had more power, Munson hit for a better average. They were both great receivers who excelled at managing pitchers and calling games and had strong arms. Fisk had a better arm, but Munson had quicker feet and got rid of the ball faster. Munson won more Gold Gloves, but after an arm injury in 1974 made his throws sail into center field, the two he won in 1974 and 1975 (despite 22 and 23 errors, respectively) were more due to reputation. Munson frequently chatted up opposing batters and umpires. Fisk, all business, rarely did.

But their differences were relatively small, mere technicalities. In truth, probably the single most important factor that stirred the disinclination within each for the other was that deep in their hearts, they knew, without a doubt, that they were exactly alike. Both were driven and highly competitive—so competitive that they placed duty and winning above friendship. Both were somewhat difficult to get to know. They both were the type of player opponents loved to hate, and teammates loved to have on their team. Both were unusually athletic catchers; they hustled, they hit, they ran the bases hard, they never avoided conflict. They were proud, not at all slow to realize an insult; or hold a grudge. They both believed in a hard work ethic, for themselves and their teammates, and didn't shy away from saying what they believed. They were basically the same guy, just in different bodies and uniforms.

Over the years, with age, maturity, and the recognition of similar experiences in the bonds of the catching brotherhood, the relationship between the two became less militant. Not that they were ready to pick out curtains, but they developed almost a fondness based on mutual admiration; a respect given to a worthy foe, an unspoken appreciation for how much good the rivalry brought to their game. Around 1977, they began sharing a not-so-unpleasant word or two at the plate—an acknowledgment of how much their bodies hurt from the grind of catching—and, sometimes, even a joke or two. "We never had dinner or anything like that, but we'd joke together at the All-Star Games or during the regular season," Carlton said in 1980. "In 1977, I was coming off a knee injury and there was a play at the plate when he could have run me over, but he just came in standing up. Later I said something to him about how I had blocked the plate and he said something like, 'If your legs feel like mine do, I wouldn't try to hurt any other catcher's legs.' "

In a September 1977 game at Fenway, Carlton fouled a ball into the seats. Munson watched it and joked, "I'm not going into those stands."

Carlton replied, "That's a good decision. You go in there and you may never come back out."

August 2, 1979, Thurman Munson climbed into his Cessna Citation jet at the Akron/Canton airport with a flight instructor to practice takeoffs and landings. A family man, he had learned to fly for the express reason to be able to return home more often during the season to see his wife and children. He experienced trouble in the air and never made it back to the airport. The 32-year-old Yankee captain died in the crash. The baseball world was shocked to learn of the death of Thurman Munson. Word spread throughout locker rooms and sports pages across the country.

When asked for a comment, Carlton Fisk said, "People always said Boston–New York was Fisk vs. Munson and there was a personal rivalry. If we were, as people said, the worst of the best enemies, it was because we had the highest amount of respect for one another. We both thought for a while that we were the two best catchers in the league, and we tried to prove to one another that each of us was better than the other. I talked to him more than anyone else when we played them. We'd talk about catching, about how we hurt. . . . I'll really miss him."

After the accident, Linda Fisk sent a sincere handwritten letter to Diana Munson, Thurman's wife. She described the respect Carlton had for Thurman and explained that a real bond had developed between them. She said that after hearing of the accident, Carlton told her that he felt like he had lost family and "might as well have stayed in the hotel instead of playing when he heard of the crash—emotional pain can't be iced down."

In 1980 Carlton said, "Thurman was a part of my life, no question. That part is gone. That part of my career is gone too. It's over. It just isn't the same without him."

The 1979 season was the most frustrating of Carlton Fisk's career to that point. His right elbow had bothered him all winter. X-rays showed two calcium deposits embedded in the muscle that were felt to be scar tissue resulting from a tear incurred during the 1978 season that hadn't been allowed to heal properly; a tear most likely caused by playing every day while changing his throwing style to accommodate the broken ribs. He was told by doctors that surgery would be complicated and might not correct the problem.

Resting the arm over the winter hadn't helped. He slowly worked the arm in the spring, stretching and throwing lightly. It seemed to feel okay, but the first time he tried to snap a hard throw in a spring game, excruciating pain shot up the arm. The next day he could barely throw a ball thirty feet. After waiting in vain for it to improve, he was placed on the 15-day disabled list.

Meanwhile, the five-year contract was due to expire at the end of the 1980 season. Carlton reinforced what he had always told everyone: "I want to stay in Boston the rest of my career because I'm from New England." There was an understanding that the Red Sox front office would open contract talks to extend the deals to keep Fisk, Lynn, and Burleson in Boston. They had recently renegotiated the contracts of Rice and Eckersley to lock them up; it seemed to be the way of the future—sign your core players to long-term contracts so they won't leave as free agents. But attitudes in the Boston front office had changed harshly in regards to the whole money thing. After the bottomless-pockets approach failed to bring a pennant in 1978, they recoiled to the opposite extreme. Tiant was allowed to leave (to the hated Yankees no less) via free agency. The Red Sox did not pursue any free agents before the 1979 season. Things were suddenly very frugal around Boston. When confronted with the desire for a long-term deal for Lynn, Burleson, or Fisk, Haywood Sullivan, now firmly in control of the front office, responded, "Show me in writing where I said I would do that?"

As Carlton sat out exhibition games, complaining of elbow pain in the spring of 1979, Sullivan quipped to reporters, "His contract may be bothering him more than his elbow." Upon hearing of the comment, Carlton burst into Sullivan's office, slammed the door and offered to have it out. Sullivan apologized, claiming it was made half in jest, but the comment would come back to haunt him—and Red Sox fans.

Although the core of everyday starters remained essentially the same, the Sox were only a shadow of the team that had the second best record in baseball in 1978. In addition to the loss of Tiant, Sullivan had given away Bill Lee to Montreal for utility infielder Stan Papi—the final purge of the Buffalo Heads. The owners had failed to recognize the value of Tiant, which extended far beyond the field. "Losing Tiant hurt," says Torrez. "He was the heart of the team. We really missed him in the clubhouse. The team started changing that year. We stopped having as much fun. Guys were worrying about where they were going with free agency, things like that. The changes pulled the guys away from having fun."

Gary Allenson opened the season as the Red Sox' catcher. Fisk was activated May 22 but only saw duty as a pinch hitter and designated hitter. The arm would bother him all season. He didn't start a game at catcher until June 18, then reinjured his arm making a throw in mid-August. He finished the season catching only 35 games and DHing another 42, hitting 10 home runs and 42 RBIs. The Red Sox were close through July but then slowly slid back and finished in third place with a 91–69 record, 11 and a half behind the Orioles.

As Fisk worked out during the winter after the 1979 season, he had to wonder how much baseball his future held. Even though he was a career .284 hitter to that point, Red Sox management had put him in a position that if he didn't catch, he couldn't play. After picking up Bob Watson for the 1979 season, they signed Tony Perez to play first base and DH for 1980. Along with Yaz, those slots were taken. But Fisk couldn't catch with a sore arm.

The status of 32-year-old Carlton Fisk's right arm, and his baseball career, remained unknown as the team reported to Winter Haven, Florida, in 1980. He told everyone that it felt fine. He worked very slowly, on his own schedule. Meanwhile, nothing had been done on his contract. All along, Kapstein kept waiting—in vain—for the Red Sox front office to open discussions on Lynn, Burleson, and Fisk. Obviously the team was waiting on the verdict regarding Fisk's arm before deciding whether to offer a contract or cut him loose, but their plans for the other two remained a mystery as well. Burleson told a reporter he hadn't heard anything in weeks.

Fisk caught two innings in an intrasquad game and was scheduled for more when another work stoppage occurred. It was quickly resolved, but the team headed north without Fisk playing in a real game. After watching the Red Sox get pummeled by the Brewers the first two games of the 1980 season, by a total of 27–6, and watching the Brewers crowd the plate and belt opposite field home runs, Carlton decided he had to catch. "Somebody's got to go down," he said. "The Brewers can't be allowed to hang out over the plate like that." He told Zimmer, "To hell with it, I'm playing. I can't stand watching it." The next day he was behind the plate and the first Brewer batter mysteriously got drilled. The Sox won 4–1.

Carlton hit his first home run of the season April 17—an 11th-inning bomb off Tiger bullpen ace Aurelio Lopez into the screen in left field for a 5–4 win. The arm seemed to be holding up, almost as good as ever. He credited Texas Rangers manager Pat Corrales with helping him. Corrales, a former catcher who backed up Johnny Bench for years, watched Fisk throw before a game and sent word over to tell him to pull the ball straight back out of the glove, rather than the natural up and back motion. That eliminated the sweep of the elbow and took away strain. Fisk almost immediately began throwing well. "I don't know what would have happened if I'd continued to throw the way I'd always thrown," Fisk said a little later. "It's taken a great deal of the trauma, stress, and strain off the elbow. . . . I feel more comfortable now than I did at any time last year, and the doubts and fears that go with not knowing whether your next throw is your last one have disappeared."

In the first 43 games, the Red Sox were 1–11 when Carlton didn't catch, 20–11 when he did. He continued hitting well, staying over .310 most of the summer and made the All-Star team once again. While Fisk enjoyed a resurgent season, the team reeled. Several key players were injured and the pitching rotation suddenly consisted of Torrez and Eckersley and whoever else they could find. The Red Sox finished tied for fourth place, 19 games out. It was the first time in 13 years the team had finished lower than third. There was no depth. The penny-pinching ways of the front office had gutted the team.

And still, nothing had been considered as far as contracts for Lynn, Burleson, or Fisk. The sound of silence on the subject emanating from the Boston front office throughout the season was deafening. Haywood Sullivan told reporters that he wanted to know by the World Series if the three could be signed—if not, he would trade them rather than go into the 1981 option year. Lowball verbal offers were made to Lynn and Burleson in October, but by mid-December, Fisk still had not heard anything. Before long, everyone would be hearing about a contract— and the news would not be good for Red Sox fans.

12 Two Days Late

BY 1980 JERRY KAPSTEIN HAD BECOME THOROUGHLY loathed by baseball executives. Many general managers dumped his clients rather than endure the protracted, painful, and expensive negotiations he was certain to require. This strategy, while saving short-term cash, devastated teams and particularly killed off the great Cincinnati Reds and Oakland A's dynasties.

After assuming control of the Red Sox in late 1977, Haywood Sullivan had proven to be a tightwad with little appreciation for talent, player development, or the art of a deal. His purge of the Buffalo Heads, while no doubt encouraged by Zimmer, had resulted in dealing Jenkins, Carbo, Willoughby, Cleveland, and Lee for essentially nothing. Although he claimed to not have money for players, Sullivan would end up making a pretty good deal for himself through his ownership of the Red Sox: when Mrs. Yawkey died in 1992, her representative, John Harrington, bought out Sullivan's share of the team for a reported $33 million—not a bad return on an original $100,000 investment. In 1981 he was still trying to learn how to navigate the new world of free agency and high-priced talent.

Carlton Fisk had come back from his injury to have a good season in 1980, hitting .289 with 18 home runs and 62 RBIs. His arm seemed to be healthy, as strong as ever. In addition to being represented by Kapstein and certain to require a significant raise in salary to remain in line with what other All Star–caliber catchers were now making, he had given Sullivan and LeRoux other pains. When asked by reporters, he had questioned their qualifications as major league owners and questioned whether some of the wording in their financial arrangements would adversely affect players' contracts and, consequently, the quality of the team. He had gone on record complaining about the moves that cost the Red Sox valuable pitchers Jenkins, Lee, and Tiant at a time in which the team was loaded with offense, but lost the pennant due to lack of pitching. The chasm between Fisk and Sullivan had continued to grow after Sullivan's remarks in spring training about the sore elbow. There appeared to be genuine animosity between the two. Sullivan had reportedly rudely avoided Carlton and his wife, Linda, at a pre–All-Star Game party in 1980 and was noted by office staff to make disparaging remarks about the two.

As the deadline for new contracts rapidly approached, Fisk, inexplicably, had still not heard anything from the Red Sox. Nada. Zilch. There was a very good reason for this: they had a plan. They felt that since the contracts of the three players had been signed under the pre-1976 Basic Agreement, an option year was built into the contracts and they were eligible for salary arbitration. Sullivan feared they would take the team to arbitration, win huge bucks, and then still be able to walk the next year, leaving the Red Sox with nothing in return. He was determined to avoid that.

There was no doubt that they would cost real money. Lynn was coming off an injury-filled 1980 season, but had a monster year in 1979, hitting 39 home runs with a .333 batting average and was considered one of the top all-around players in baseball. The fiery Burleson was the heart of the infield, a three-time All-Star and a Gold Glove winner in 1979. In the fall, Sullivan had made inquiries to Kapstein regarding Lynn and Burleson (Kapstein later maintained that Sullivan never even mentioned Fisk) and determined that it would be impossible to re-sign them for any amount he was willing to pay. "We have to maintain some sanity here [regarding salaries]," Sullivan would explain to reporters later. With that in mind, he made a deal for Burleson, trading him to the Angels, along with Hobson, for Carney Lansford, Mark Clear, and Rick Miller in December. Then he shopped Lynn around but teams were frightened away by the contractual demands Kapstein was certain to make.

The deadline for offering major league contracts was, as it had been for years, December 20. On December 22, 1980, Haywood Sullivan's office mailed contracts to Carlton Fisk and Fred Lynn. The contract sent to Fisk was for the same $210,000 he was paid in 1980, an amount that in 1981 would have made him—an All-Star in all seven of the complete seasons he had played—the 17th highest paid catcher in the major leagues.

Union boss Marvin Miller promptly informed the Red Sox that he had filed a grievance seeking immediate free agent status for Lynn and Fisk. The Players Association contended that Fisk, Lynn, and Burleson, along with John Mayberry of Toronto, were unique among all current major leaguers in that they had signed contracts under the owners-players agreement that was in effect during the 1976 season and that those contracts had now expired, with no option year. This issue was open to interpretation, but since the contract was tendered late, it became a moot point—the players should now be free.

"I couldn't believe it [the contracts being mailed late]," says Lynn. "You're supposed to have your contract mailed to you December 20. Everybody knows that. Carlton's and mine got mailed December 22. I wasn't sure how that could happen. Clerical error? The next thing you know we were in New York and an arbitrator was going to declare us free agents. It was black-and-white, a no-brainer. Did they do it on purpose? I don't remember anybody getting fired over it. Was it a calculated way of getting rid of two guys? Who knows what they were thinking. Only they knew, and they're gone now."

New England was shocked. Headlines throughout the region screamed that the Sox could now lose both Lynn and Fisk. Fans and media questioned how this could have been allowed to happen; and how the Red Sox front office didn't see it coming—they had five years to be prepared. It was openly questioned why the team had not attempted to renegotiate the contracts of the three in 1979 when they did so for Rice and Eckersley. The whole mess could have been avoided.

But Sullivan held fast and told everyone he was right. By some convoluted reasoning, he felt that mailing the contracts late had voided the players' right to seek arbitration, but that they were still bound to the Red Sox for the option year. A hearing was scheduled in New York before an impartial arbitrator for January 23, 1981. At the heart of the matter was the need for the Red Sox to prove that the contracts signed in 1976 contained a valid sixth year as an option. If so, they could have the stars for one more year at their 1980 salaries. If the belated contracts violated the Basic Agreement, the players would become free agents. Although Sullivan continued his bluster in front of the media, a representative for the Players Association called the case "as cut and dried as we've grieved."

Sullivan continued to complain to the press that he was trying to reach a pre-hearing agreement on a new contract, but Kapstein and

Fisk weren't listening. Still, no formal offer had ever been made. On the eve of the January 23 hearing in New York, the Red Sox finally submitted an offer of three years and $1.5 million, an offer Kapstein summarily dismissed as inadequate. At the same time, Sullivan was able to reach an agreement with the Angels to trade Lynn, but he received only an aged Joe Rudi and sore-armed Frank Tanana in return.

At the hearing in New York in front of arbitrator Raymond Goetz, a University of Kansas law professor, Players Association lawyers riddled Sullivan's reasoning so badly that observers almost felt sorry for him. Following the hearing, Goetz returned to Kansas to study the matter for a few weeks before issuing his decision. Meanwhile, the two sides were free to resume bargaining. But there was little bargaining being done.

Whereas in 1976 the media and fans had been squarely united against the holdout players, in 1981 sentiments had shifted dramatically. Typical was the column in *The Boston Globe* by Peter Gammons' February 1 titled "Is It Greed . . . Or Poor Management." In it, Gammons wrote of the growing frustration with the state of owners. "Ownership tries to blame players. It tries to blame agents. It talks about 'greed' and Marvin Miller and 'disloyalty.' But greed, agents and the mad inflationary spiral are symptoms, not the disease. The disease is baseball management itself, megabucksters who want George Steinbrenner's fame and incompetents adept at saying 'yes.'"

When Burleson and Lynn were traded, fans were outraged, but some said good riddance, annoyed at the haggles over money. But losing Carlton Fisk was another matter. Almost uniformly, in the press, bars, and on the streets throughout New England, people questioned why the Red Sox would even consider letting a local icon of Fisk's stature go. If they could dump him, what was next? Selling the USS *Constitution* for scrap wood? Converting the Old South Church into a bed-and-breakfast?

The feeling intensified as the weeks went by and it began to appear the Sox would actually lose Fisk: "Carlton Fisk is one of us whether Haywood Sullivan and Buddy LeRoux understand it or not," Gammons wrote February 7. "The Red Sox are *the* regional sports franchise. Fisk isn't the same [as Burleson and Lynn] . . . he is the one-in-the-millions to fight his way through the cold and the odds. . . . This time it's Fisk and Fisk is one of us."

Red Sox broadcaster Ken Harrelson, even though the team was

partly responsible for his paycheck, chimed in against the owners, labeling Sullivan "almost the laughingstock of the American League," and said if "they didn't have the money to pay [Lynn, Burleson, and Fisk] they can't afford to own the ball club." He added, "Fisk is a symbol of Red Sox baseball and the way management is treating him is beyond me. They're operating out of weakness and desperation."

Sullivan and Kapstein talked in New York toward the end of January, then did not speak for almost two weeks. Sullivan continually voiced optimism and told reporters, "We do want him to play here." But an unnamed team source said, "The feelings [have gotten] so bad, I don't see them getting together."

Indeed. Although Fisk had always strongly stated that he wanted to remain in New England, his feelings were rapidly changing due to what he perceived as a lack of interest and a lack of respect from the Red Sox. Will McDonough reported in the *Globe* that Carlton had not forgotten the remark Sullivan made about his elbow in the spring of 1979 ("His contract may be bothering him more than his elbow") and had never forgotten how his integrity was questioned. McDonough doubted that even if the outcome of the case was in the Sox' favor that Fisk would stay beyond one more season now.

Kapstein, ever the astute agent with his finger on the financial pulse of baseball, planned all along to wait until the decision on free agency was made, then see where the money was. He continually parried the Red Sox' offers and requests for discussions. Arbitrator Goetz was expected to make his ruling in early February. Both the Players Association and the owners' Player Relations Committee sent their post-hearing briefs to Goetz in Lawrence, Kansas, via express mail. Goetz was then to study them over the weekend and announce his decision on Monday. All of New England held its breath.

Meanwhile, salaries around baseball continued the process of rapid expansion with no limits in sight. Dave Winfield played the free agent game and signed a 10-year, $23 million contract with the Yankees. Four-time All-Star catcher Darrell Porter, coming off a .249 season with 51 RBIs, signed with the Cardinals for $700,000 and, in a chilling note to anyone interested in a perennial All-Star catcher with a .284 lifetime average, Yankee catcher Rick Cerone, a .238 lifetime hitter who had hit more than .234 exactly once, was awarded $440,000 in arbitration. The price for even mediocrity was rising daily.

It became official February 12. Goetz released his 21-page decision, which stated that since the club had not sent out the contract by the December 20 deadline, Fisk was a free agent. That was the heart of the matter—the rest of the argument was just so much fluff. Goetz wrote that although Fisk's free agency was "indeed an unfortunate consequence for the Club in comparison to the minor inconvenience to him flowing from the belated contract tender, that is the inevitable effect of the condition to which the parties agreed" in their contract, a condition from which Goetz "is powerless to deviate." In layman's terms, Sullivan canceled the whole deal by not sending the contract in time—no quitsies or takebacks allowed.

Marvin Miller told reporters that his only surprise in the whole fiasco was the incompetence of the Red Sox front office. "Why anyone in his right mind, with any knowledge of proper labor relations . . . was all set to waste everybody's time and money on this case, which was so clear-cut, is beyond me. That would be almost as bad as looking at the agreement that says the minimum salary is $32,500 and saying, 'No it isn't.' All the rest of what happened was an attempt to confuse the arbitrator, and they couldn't do it successfully."

Sullivan had said in the hearing that the club had not sent out the contract by the 20th because his counsel told him that he didn't have to, that the wording of the August 1976 contracts made the option year of their agreements binding, whether they had a new contract or not. Apparently the owner of the Angels, when informed of this opinion, had initially concurred. "Then over that weekend, we learned that California had tendered Burleson an offer and the PRC [Player Relations Committee] told us we had nothing to lose by sending them out," Sullivan explained. "So we did on the 22nd, but we made no attempt to deceive anyone. We could have backdated it on our postal machines, but we did what we believe is right." He repeated his assertion that he could have "lost twice if I had sent the contracts out the 20th and they'd have gone to salary arbitration." In truth, Haywood Sullivan had been severely uninformed on the rules and contracts, had rolled the dice, and lost. At least the team got some players back for Lynn and Burleson, but they got nothing for Fisk.

Back in Boston, on February 12, Sullivan walked into the Fenway Park press room, where the 1981 press guide was being handed out and a horde of media members were munching on free food. Local Channel 4 television caught the whole amateurish announcement, from someone shouting "Shut up" to quiet the noisy room to the disheveled

Sullivan telling them, "I just found out five minutes ago that Fisk has been declared a free agent." He continued, "We went in with thoughts about what we thought was right and another process said we were not right." Then, trying to convince the mob that all was well, he added, "I think we'll sign him. We want to re-sign him very badly and Carlton and Jerry should know that by now. We want to work things out, we want him to stay, and I firmly believe that he wants to play here."

Then, Sullivan threw up his arms and said, "Reopen the bar."

When further pressed, Sullivan tried to explain why there had been no contact with Fisk regarding negotiations prior to the December 22 mailing. "His physical condition put it off for a long time, then there was the question about the change in the Basic Agreement and compensation, then the threat of a strike."

As Leigh Montville wrote, "Sullivan has answers to all the questions, but nobody is listening. The Red Sox haven't been lower in the public mind than they were yesterday for a long, long time."

Kapstein called every other team to gauge the interest level in Fisk. Carlton, as he had promised from the beginning, called the Red Sox as soon as he heard the decision. He informed the Red Sox that they would be treated like every other team. Fisk told reporters he was "happy with the decision, but not surprised. I went into this like I go into everything I do—to win."

Condemnation of Sullivan and the Red Sox front office was swift and brutal. Ray Fitzgerald wrote in the *Globe*, "In one off-season the Red Sox front office has scored a hat trick and won the Connie Mack Memorial Award for dumping highly-paid stars. In one fell swoop, the three most important players . . . have been, shall we say, removed. . . . Red Sox fans everywhere are still mystified over the front office blunder that allowed him [Fisk] to escape to free agency. The fact that a player who is arguably the best catcher in the 80-year history of the franchise got away for nothing is an embarrassment the front office will never live down." The opinion was echoed throughout New England.

Sullivan tried to portray his position, not as penny-pinching, but as a moral stand against outrageous salaries. "The insanity has to stop somewhere; here's a list of three players signed for over $13 million. And I'm stupid? Go to hell," he said a month later.

Kapstein made a counteroffer to the Red Sox on February 13, reportedly for five years and $2.5 million. The team did not seem interested at that price. Little was accomplished over the next month except for volleys through the media. On March 18, 1981, Carlton Fisk announced he had signed with the Chicago White Sox; his days as a member of the Boston Red Sox were over.

New England fans were devastated. Their winter of discontent was now complete. "The Fisk episode was the worst moment for Red Sox fans since the team sold Babe Ruth," South Hadley, Massachusetts, native, Yale professor, and future commissioner of baseball Bart Giamatti later said.

Fisk had always said that he would never leave Boston. Why would he? "Never once did I ever think I'd be playing elsewhere," he said in 1993. "The dream of most boys in New England was to play for the Red Sox or the Celtics. There were no other teams, no other dreams." But the dream, once so bright, had faded with the expectations and complications of money.

"It broke my heart to leave New England," he said in 2000. "To be able [to play for the Red Sox] was a dream come true. Then Mr. Yawkey died, two other guys became involved as owners and did things to players that hurt us."

Why had the team let him go so easily? Conspiracy theorists point to the fact that Haywood Sullivan's son, Marc, was a catcher lurking somewhere in the Red Sox system. Boston management had been soundly ridiculed when they had made Marc Sullivan a second round draft choice in 1979—most analysts considered him to be a much lower round talent. It was the first time a son had been drafted by a team that his father presided over. Marc Sullivan, a lifetime .222 hitter in the minor leagues, would be rushed to the majors a few years later, presented with a job, and proceed to hit .186 as a major leaguer.

Whether or not nepotism played a small role, all indications are that the bottom line was, first and foremost, the bottom line. Haywood Sullivan did not want to pay Carlton Fisk what he thought it would take to keep him in Boston. Everything else was superfluous.

There's no question that Fisk had wanted to stay in Boston. Team spirit, team pride—few men ever took more pride in wearing the uniform with "Boston" stitched across the chest than Carlton Ernest Fisk of Charlestown, New Hampshire. *There were no other teams, no other dreams.* What would it have taken for him to stay? A less astute, less aggressive agent? Certainly. A willingness to accept much less money than he was worth by market standards? Almost definitely. Should he have been expected to do that? To swallow his pride and take a one- or two-year deal for $300,000 or $400,000 when mediocre catchers were getting twice that?

But Carlton Fisk didn't leave Boston for money. He left for principle. He considered the late contract mailing to be a complete show of disrespect. It was the last in a series of slights from the Red Sox front office. He could have lived with a little less money to remain in Boston, but he could not bear the insults to his honor.

From 1971 through 1980 Carlton Fisk had been a part of one of the most celebrated, most revered, most written-about, most romanticized, most . . . heartbreaking teams in baseball history. They had experienced incredible highs and painful lows together. They were considered a team of destiny and also considered by some a team of chokers. They were beloved by their loyal fans like few teams ever have been. If not for the smallest of misfortunes, they easily could have added pennants in 1972, 1977, and 1978 to the one of 1975 and been considered a dynasty. The heart of that team through the glory years— Petrocelli, Burleson, Lynn, Rice, Evans, Yaz, Fisk, Lee, Tiant—would never be forgotten.

Like great Red Sox teams of previous decades, they had an overpoweringly offensive starting lineup but were doomed by a lack of bench support, lack of a few more good pitchers, and the fact that they were built specifically for Fenway Park. They were ultimately done in when their paucity of speed and defensive shortcomings were exposed on the road, particularly in big AstroTurfed stadiums and also by the damaged psyches of pitchers trying to throw with the Green Monster peering over their shoulder.

"When I look back on those Red Sox teams of the seventies, I feel that if we had one more pitcher we would have been a dominant team," said Bob Montgomery. "Just one more starting pitcher and the Red Sox would have been the team of the seventies."

The players, regardless of occasional disagreements, developed a closeness—athletic men in their youth fighting together for a common cause, in front of millions; an us-against-the-world type of feeling, a type of confidence and familiarity difficult to form in other areas of life. "We were pretty close for six years," says Fred Lynn. "Even today, all these years later, when we get together for a charity event or golf event or something, it's fun. It's like going back in a time machine. It's a bond we have. You never lose it. When guys are in their twenties;

you're on a team, you get a special bond that you don't form with other guys when you get older. It was great."

Now, all the promise of the 1975 season, the expected pennants, the dynasty, were only memories—it was the dynasty that never happened. More than anything that had occurred on the field, the contract debacle of 1981 soiled the legacy of the great team.

13 Chicago: The Dawn of a New Era

WHEN CARLTON FISK SIGNED with the White Sox on March 9, 1981, he told reporters a major part of his decision was the city and the potential of the club. "I mentioned to my parents a couple of years ago that if I ever was uprooted from New England, I'd like to go to the Midwest," he said. When asked about bad relations with Red Sox management, he didn't sidestep. "What it has come down to was a breach of contract. I was not tendered a timely contract on the last possible date that was to be honored." When asked if he was bitter, he replied, "I don't think I'm bitter. I have a lot of fond memories of playing there. I have a lot of friends and had a good rapport with the fans and media." He added, "It was my hope that I would end my career with my previous team."

During the free-agent period, the Red Sox appeared to believe that no other clubs would pursue Fisk—some even postulated that there had been an understanding that other owners wouldn't interfere by making him offers—and he would somehow return to them asking for forgiveness. The White Sox owners and general manager had confounded that belief by enthusiastically courting him. They had flown to La Jolla on February 20 to personally present their offer in Kapstein's California office. Part of their 10-hour meeting with Kapstein included a 90-minute conference call with Carlton and Linda in their Raymond, New Hampshire, home. Their efforts to personally travel to talk face-to-face with Kapstein paid off—Carlton was impressed with their desire. He felt wanted, a quaint sentimental emotion that had been lacking from Boston management for several years. Carlton defended his decision not to meet with the Red Sox to give them a chance to better the Chicago offer. "I was not going to horse auction myself around," he said bluntly. "The other teams made their offers in confidence and I wasn't about to run around asking if they could do better. I made no promises to do so. If they took a chance, they blew it."

When questioned about loyalty, his anger flared, "Loyalty is a two-way street. Not once in my time with Boston did I renege on anything I said I would do. I gave the best possible effort at all times. There is no way anyone should challenge my loyalty because I never compromised myself or my situation. In fact, I played a lot when others wouldn't, couldn't, or shouldn't." And if there was any doubt about his feelings about the Red Sox owners, he added, "Why didn't you ask me about Buddy [LeRoux]? When you see him, tell him I've got my hat on my head, not in my hand."

But regardless of statements to the press, it wasn't easy for Carlton Fisk to leave the Boston Red Sox. That had never been the plan. The way he was treated by Red Sox management and the feelings of being unwanted and forced out would never be forgotten. In 1993, Linda told a reporter, "That was very personal to him. Carlton was from New England and wanted to play for the Red Sox forever, but they took that away from him."

There were indeed hard feelings for the Boston management team. A year later, Fisk would wear a T-shirt that read "Haywood and Buddy Suck" every time he faced his old team.

The city of Chicago became Carlton Fisk's new place of employment. As a sports town, Chicago had experienced a long drought. Both the White Sox and the Cubs had been equally feeble throughout the seventies. Similarly the Bears, Blackhawks, and Bulls were all mediocre or worse. The city had not had a sports title team, or even a division winner, since the 1963 Bears.

The Chicago White Sox had been miserable for years. They hadn't won a World Series since 1917 and hadn't seen the postseason since a World Series appearance in 1959. Their most notable contribution to the baseball world in the 1970s was to wear outrageous uniforms that made their players look like either softball players or clowns. All too often the team played like both. They were otherwise noted for the infamous Disco Demolition Night in 1979, in which thousands of drunk young people became so enthused in their destruction of disco records that they proceeded to storm over the barriers and cavort all over the field in a general riot. They had so much fun that the field was demolished beyond repair and the White Sox were forced to forfeit the game. (Amazingly, no one saw that coming.)

Chronically cash-strapped owner Bill Veeck had tried everything to entice fans to the park—everything, that is, except getting a good team. All that appeared to change when Jerry Reinsdorf and Eddie Einhorn, leading a consortium of about 80 limited partners, bought the team for $19 million in early 1981, closing February 3. Reinsdorf was a 45-year-old native of Brooklyn. After obtaining a BA from George Washington University he had moved to Chicago, where he earned a law degree from Northwestern in 1960. A CPA and lawyer, he started his professional life as a tax attorney for the IRS, learning the rules so well that he left and made his initial fortune in real estate, taking maximum advantage of the tax code.

Ambitious, energetic, and supremely intelligent, Reinsdorf was a born deal maker. He hacked his way through the corporate world and hit it big when he sold his investment company, Balcor, to American Express for over $100 million and stayed on as chief executive officer. In his business dealings Reinsdorf had shown an especially acute acumen for the art of negotiation. He was both opportunistic and carnivorous.

Eddie Einhorn was one of the most colorful and flamboyant men in sports. A native of New Jersey and a classmate of Reinsdorf at Northwestern Law School, he had lived dangerously in the emerging world of television sports production and marketing with the TVS network he founded in 1961. Convinced of the future popularity of college basketball, he felt there would eventually be a market for it on television. It was an opinion shared by very few at the time. He began by broadcasting the early rounds of the NCAA tournament. He paid the NCAA $6,000 for the rights to the 1961 championship game with Ohio State and Cincinnati, but no station outside Ohio or Kentucky would run it. Undeterred, he plugged on, often losing money in the early years. In 1968, however, he hit pay dirt when he put together the first nationally televised regular season college basketball game, an affair between UCLA and Houston in the Astrodome. Game day arrived with UCLA ranked number one, riding a 47-game winning streak, and Houston ranked number two, undefeated since being beaten by UCLA in the 1967 semifinals—it was the original basketball Game of the Century. When Elvin Hayes and the Cougars beat the UCLA team of Lew Alcindor (later known as Kareem Abdul-Jabbar) in a 71–69 thriller, college basketball was changed forever. Einhorn sold TVS in 1973 and became a multimillionaire. He was producing *CBS Sports Spectacular* when Reinsdorf invited him to become co-owner of the White Sox.

The two split most managerial duties in Chicago with the exceptions of Reinsdorf doing all the contract negotiations and Einhorn using his marketing expertise. Although they both had degrees from Northwestern, they were still considered out-of-towners and, even worse, New Yorkers. There was some initial wariness and lack of acceptance in Chicagoland. An early Chicago television report referred to the new owners as a "skulking real estate mogul who grew up in Brooklyn and a television tycoon who still lives in New York." Welcome to the Windy City.

Reinsdorf and Einhorn were neophytes when it came to baseball management, but they were smart enough to hang on to some good help left over from the previous regime. General manager Roland Hemond was one of the shrewdest minds in the business. Hemond, who was universally respected for his class and character, had taken the general manager job for the White Sox near the end of a disastrous 1970 season in which the team lost 106 games and drew a mere 495,000 fans. He not only faced the task of trying to put respectable major league talent on the field for a team with very little money, but he had to battle the fact that Comiskey Park, the oldest in the majors, was in pitiful shape and sat in a bad neighborhood in which fans feared for their lives—the South Side of Chicago *was*, as Bad, Bad LeRoy Brown understood, the baddest part of the whole damn town.

But Hemond knew baseball and knew how to make deals. With very little to offer in the way of money or minor league talent, he soon pulled rabbits out of his baseball cap. The biggest coup was obtaining slugger Dick Allen, who put the White Sox in the pennant race for much of 1972 and won the MVP Award. Throughout the seventies, Hemond consistently did more with less than any general manager in baseball— keeping the team's head above water and maintaining fan interest. In 1977 he cobbled together a one-year, hard-hitting, fan-friendly team that came to be known as the South Side Hit Men. They won 90 games and finished third that year, but Hemond didn't have the resources to keep them together and the team slid back to their usual sad state.

In the other holdover, the White Sox had one of the game's best managers, but no one knew it yet. Tony La Russa had just finished his first full season as manager in 1980, leading a team of young pitchers and few good hitters to a 70–90 record; second to last in the American League West. La Russa had played briefly with the Kansas City A's in 1963, and later had very brief stops with the Braves and Cubs but spent most of his professional career as a minor league middle infielder. He played his last game in the majors in 1973, but hung on in the minors until 1977. After giving up his playing career, he was working toward a law degree at Florida State when Bill Veeck offered him a baseball job.

La Russa held various minor league managing and major league coaching positions the next two years within the White Sox organization. Meanwhile, the White Sox went through three managers. When Don Kessinger resigned after starting the 1979 season 46–60, Veeck hired La Russa. At 34 years old, La Russa was the youngest manager in the big leagues and the prevailing theory was that he was hired for one reason: because he came cheap.

La Russa was seen as the new breed. He was not a craggy-faced, tobacco-spitting, cliché-spewing old-timer. He spoke a language not usually heard in clubhouses and was more frequently spotted carrying a briefcase than a fungo bat. He initially faced brutal, daily criticism from the team's broadcasters Harry Caray and Jimmy Piersall. Early on, Hemond warned La Russa honestly that he had few friends, saying there were five good reasons everyone hoped he would fail: "You're young, you're handsome, you're smart, you're getting your law degree, you have a nice family. I don't think you're going to last very long." Now get out there and have fun.

The new owners wanted to quickly convince Chicago fans they intended to win and would spend money to do it. Advised of his new bosses' desires, Hemond was ecstatic at the convergence of opportunity and chance when Fisk officially became available a week and a half later. Hemond astutely realized they could not only improve the team, but make a statement—to the city and the organization. At his urging, the new owners pursued Fisk vigorously. "We couldn't believe it when we first heard that Fisk was available," said Einhorn in 2000. "We didn't want to get involved if we were only going to drive the price up for the Red Sox. But I had a good relationship with Kapstein from some other deals. He told me that we had a legitimate chance."

"That was a key component of our club for years to come," said Hemond in 2004, speaking of the Fisk signing. "It showed our fans that the new owners were very willing to go out and do the best they possibly could to bring a winner."

"The signing of Carlton Fisk changed the attitude of Chicago toward the White Sox," Reinsdorf added. "This team was the Rodney

Dangerfield of baseball. It got no respect. When a player of Carlton Fisk's caliber decided he was going to come to the White Sox, it sent a message to people that we were for real and really wanted to win and it was the dawn of a new era."

Excited White Sox fans stormed the ticket windows within days, convinced that good days were ahead for the team. "Carlton Fisk's signing really energized the White Sox fans," says Bob Verdi, who had written sports for the *Chicago Tribune* since 1967. "It was a declaration that the new owners meant business. It gave fans new hope."

"You knew he was a perennial All-Star and had played on some great teams," says Donn Pall, a young college pitcher in 1981 who had grown up in Chicago as a rabid White Sox fan. "To add a player like that to our team gave everybody confidence that things were definitely on the way up."

Fisk reported to the team in Sarasota, where they had already been practicing for a few weeks. He pulled into the parking lot of Payne Park and met with La Russa at 8 A.M. He signed autographs, posed for pictures, took some batting practice, threw a little, and ran sprints. Then he said hello to seemingly a hundred new people and spent the day trying to familiarize himself with his new teammates—the first such business he had been forced to do since joining the major leagues a decade earlier.

Mike Squires, a 29-year-old first baseman, had been with the White Sox since 1975. He had seen the lack of money continually keep the team from competing and knew what the new addition meant. "We players knew Jerry Reinsdorf wanted to be a winner. When he immediately went out and got Carlton that proved to us as established veterans that they were going to do what it took to have a good team. We knew we were going to have a chance to win right now. I was on the training table, lying down, the first time Carlton came into our clubhouse. He walked up to me with a grin, grabbed my leg and shook it and said, 'You can't make the club in the trainer's room.' That was my introduction to him. Right away the attitude changed on the team."

"I had been on the White Sox about five years when he came in," says speedy outfielder Chet Lemon. "I had played against him a lot through those years, so we knew about him and what kind of player he was. It was a huge thrill for all of us to be getting one of the top catchers in baseball. We'd had some good young players, but the problem with the White Sox had always been that we never kept any of our guys very long because of money. To add a guy like Carlton Fisk, we thought that was the beginning of building a strong team—things were going to be different. Talent was coming *to* the team now, instead of always leaving."

To fans, Carlton Fisk looked out of place in a Chicago uniform—he looked out of place in any uniform other than that of the Boston Red Sox. He later said, "The first few times I walked by a mirror in a White Sox uniform, I did a double take." Soon after signing, he had announced that he would wear the unusual number of 72. White Sox pitcher Ken Kravec already owned the 27 Fisk had worn in Boston. Rather than bargain for it, Fisk opted for the reversal of the number, saying that he wanted to "turn things around." He added that it was significant for the year he broke into the majors full time and the year his son Casey was born.

The White Sox team Carlton Fisk was joining was much different from the team he left. He would not be surrounded in the lineup by All-Stars Fred Lynn, Jim Rice, Carl Yastrzemski, and Dwight Evans. It would be Mike Squires, Chet Lemon, Jim Morrison, and Wayne Nordhagen. The fans were also different. The White Sox didn't draw nearly as well as the Red Sox. Boston staff members openly scoffed and questioned writers as to how they thought Fisk would like playing in front of 4,000 fans at Comiskey Park.

Einhorn and Reinsdorf continued to spend. Soon after getting Fisk, they purchased Greg Luzinski from the Phillies March 30. Again, they found a player with the three qualities they were looking for: he was an established star, he had played for a winning team, and he was available. "As of today, I think the rest of the American League West has to consider us seriously," Hemond, perhaps giddy from finally being able to throw some real money around, told the press. A power-hitting outfielder who had won a world championship with the Phillies in 1979, Luzinski had been one of the best hitters in the National League in the seventies. In nine seasons, the 30-year-old Luzinski had hit .281 with 223 home runs and 811 RBIs. Nicknamed the Bull, by 1980 he more resembled a bull elephant and was no longer fit for duty on defense in the National League. He was unhappy and coming off two straight bad seasons. But Hemond felt he could still hit and would be a valuable asset at designated hitter.

It was immediately apparent that the White Sox were a new team. "It seemed like a different atmosphere with the club," said La Russa in 2014, noting that the addition of a few good players can make all the difference. "Both Carlton and Greg were great teammates. They were leaders in drills on and off the field. They had terrific work ethics. Showing the proper way to do drills in spring training is very important. They didn't go through the motions, they did them correctly and that rubbed off on everyone else. You can't overestimate how the culture changed, how our work ethic improved when those two men joined the team . . . just for younger guys to watch how they went about their business, knowing they were established leaders who had won pennants. You could feel it. We knew we could be good now."

A new word was being thrown around Sarasota for the first time in years. The word was "contender."

Chicago writers and media could not help but be impressed with Carlton Fisk, the man as well as the player, when they met him. They hadn't seen the likes of him in years. "He just had a certain presence about him, in the clubhouse and on the field," says Bob Verdi. "John Wayne would be a pretty good comparison." Some were intimidated by his appearance of aloofness. "He didn't seek the spotlight for himself. He was never looking for cameras. But if you ever sat down with him, you got an honest, thoughtful answer. A lot of times he would pause and think about each answer. He didn't just hand out the same old answers and clichés. I found him to be extremely interesting. He was very perceptive."

"Carlton became a real leader on the field immediately," says Lemon. "He was always a very confident individual. He wasn't shy. He had all the qualities you look for in a leader. Another thing that I don't think I realized until later was that he was such a hard worker. It's really great for young players to be around a guy like that. It makes you understand that if you're going to be good in this game you have to work. That's the sort of guy you want in your organization. Also, he was always the kind of guy that you knew exactly how he felt when he was on the baseball field. He was very expressive in his play and the way he went about his business; you could feel the emotional intensity in his game. If he did something good, you knew it. If he was mad about something, he didn't hide it. You hated that about him if you were on the other team. Some guys are passive and just play. Some guys play with a lot of confidence. You know, if he does well, it's 'I just beat you.' If you do good, it's 'Okay, but I'll get you next time.'"

As if the script had been written for a cheesy movie, the White Sox played the Red Sox on opening day, April 10, 1981. In Boston. Carlton

Fisk arrived at Fenway Park, just as he had nine times before on opening day. This time, however, he had to find his way to the visiting team's clubhouse. It was eerily uncomfortable to look at the Fenway diamond from the visitor's dugout and to gaze across the infield and see former teammates. A crowd of 35,124, second largest for a Fenway opening day, was waiting. Outside, on Yawkey Way, a vendor was selling bumper stickers that read "Haywood and Buddy are Killing the Sox." Business was brisk.

WGN television broadcast the game back to Chicago, a rare appearance for the White Sox on the rival station. Before the game, Carlton was interviewed on the field by Jimmy Piersall. With the familiar sights of the Fenway outfield in the background, Carlton looked distinctly out of place wearing an untucked, solid dark-blue jersey with an open collar and a wide lapel with "Chicago" across the front. The uniform looked more like a dentist's smock or a pajama top than a major league baseball uniform. "We ran the full gamut of emotions in this particular move," he told Piersall. "We're happy, we're sad, we're a little disappointed. But, it's a challenge. There's nothing I like better in this world than a challenge."

Piersall asked, "Are you scared today?"

"No, I'm not scared. I've just got about 8,000 butterflies running around in my stomach. It's going to be strange."

It was strange for the Fenway faithful as well. As the teams lined up for introductions on the beautiful, sunny afternoon, there were initial boos when Carlton was introduced. He tipped his cap and stood there stoically. The boos were quickly drowned out by a crescendo of claps, cheers, and whistles, with many of the fans standing.

Dennis Eckersley started for the Red Sox. Carlton came to the plate in the top of the first inning, hitting third, with one out and a man on first. This time, there were only scattered boos as half the crowd stood and applauded. He worked the count and then tapped a curveball back to Eckersley for an easy out.

Eckersley blanked the White Sox on three hits and led 2–0 before walking the leadoff man in the eighth inning. After a single, Bob Stanley came in to replace Eckersley. Mike Squires sacrificed the runners to second and third. Carlton Fisk stepped in as the Fenway shadows reached halfway across the infield; two on, one out, down by two. On the first pitch, Fisk reached down for a sinker, catching it flush, and lined it to left. Before Harry Caray could say "Holy Cow," the ball cleared the Green Monster and banged into the screen—a three-run home run. As Carlton quickly ran around the bases with his familiar high-kneed gate, the crowd seemed ambivalent; a dramatic go-ahead home run by Fisk off a low sinker over the Green Monster—they had seen this before and knew they were supposed to cheer, but what now? They stood, mostly watching in silence. Carlton looked for Linda as he rounded the bases, wanting to give her a sign, but couldn't find her. He bunny-hopped the last two steps into the White Sox dugout where he was swarmed by his happy new teammates.

"That was special," says Lemon. "We knew he had some great years and so many memories in Boston. And the big crowd was there for the game. We were happy to win the game, of course, but it was really good to see him get to do that in his first game back also."

After the White Sox finished with a 5–3 victory, reporters from both cities crowded around Fisk in the visiting clubhouse. So many piled in that he was forced out of the clubhouse and into a side room normally used for baggage. There, he held an impromptu press conference while leaning on a trunk.

As nine-year-old Casey Fisk, wearing a White Sox cap that hung over his ears, helped his dad unbuckle his shin guards, he snorted, "What's the big deal anyway? It was only a three-run homer."

Reporters peppered Carlton with questions. He tried to downplay any animosity toward the Red Sox, but admitted it was a thrill. "You always fantasize that the game might turn out the way it turned out," he said. "But you never really think it's going to."

He said he was happy about the mostly positive reception from the fans of Boston, whom he would always hold in high regard. "If some are mad at me [for leaving as a free agent], they simply don't know the whole story and probably never will. It hasn't all been told yet." He later added to friendly reporters, "I felt like waving up to Haywood and Buddy's box and telling them that that one was for them, but even that might have given them some satisfaction."

In Chicago April 14, Fisk was introduced to a huge ovation from an adoring home–opening day record crowd of 51,560. With two outs in the fourth inning, the White Sox leading 3–0, Fisk hit a grand slam. The fans stood and roared until he emerged from the dugout for a curtain call. It was official—they loved him in his new city.

Fisk continued to give Chicago fans plenty of reasons to be happy that he now belonged to them. Three days later, with Boston at Comiskey, he faced Frank Tanana in the fifth inning of a scoreless game with a man on. With a 30-mile-per-hour wind blowing in, Fisk drove a pitch straight into the wind and powered it into the left field stands. The White Sox hung on to win the game 2–1. He hit four home runs in the first week. By the end of April, the White Sox were 11 and 5 and Fisk was hitting .351 with 14 RBIs. The way he played was as important as his results. "He brought an edge," says White Sox historian Mark Liptak, who sat through many games at Comiskey. "He cared. He was one of those guys that every team needs—if you lose the first two games of a three-game series to a bad team, he was going to explode. He would not put up with that stuff. He was not willing to accept losing and guys would feel the brunt of it. Fans could see that. More than anything else, you could tell that he cared. That's why Chicago fans fell in love with him so quickly."

The White Sox had a promising pitching staff, led by LaMarr Hoyt, Rich Dotson, and Britt Burns—all in their first few years in the majors. "We had some great young arms," says Lemon. "Some of the best arms in the American League, but they were young. It's always a challenge at first until you get experience, just a great arm doesn't always make you a winner. Carlton took charge of the pitching. He had everything to do with the success of the pitching over the next few years. To have a guy who can do that behind the plate is worth its weight in gold. Then you add the hitting, that was extra. Not many guys can do both."

Taking charge of a pitching staff had always been high on Carlton Fisk's to-do list. "It takes a while to find out what you should say to which pitchers," he said in May. "Some, you don't really have to say much at all. Some need to be kicked, some need to be kissed, if you know what I mean."

The young pitchers appreciated what he brought to the team. "I grew up in Cincinnati, I was a Reds fan," says Dotson, who was 16 in 1975. "I remember his home run. I didn't really appreciate it at the time, but it was okay since the Reds won the Series the next day. Then to be able to play with him was special. It was real important for the team to get a guy like that. He was competitive; he had been through it all in Boston. He immediately commanded our respect. I liked pitching to him. I learned a lot. As a catcher, he was like a pitching coach. Off the field, he was a good guy; reserved, kind of quiet, hard to get to know—he seemed aloof at first. You had to get to know him, sometimes you needed to prod him, but once you did, you realized he was a good guy."

In only his second full season, La Russa already had a presence in the clubhouse. He was quick-minded and decisive during games and there was little doubt about who was in control. A good communicator, he was popular with players—they knew exactly where they stood at all times—and he let them play without too many petty rules or restrictions. He didn't hesitate to yell when things weren't right, but backed his players against common enemies like umpires, opponents, and the media. Players respected the fact that he was always more than willing to take the blame for any failure, of his or his players. "I came up with Tony," says Dotson. "He was my manager in the minors. I had him for about nine years. He was easy to play for. Two things: you knew how much he wanted to win and you knew he always had your back."

As intense as he was intelligent, La Russa was known to toss post-game spreads after tough losses—and he took them all tough. He looked at every angle, used every advantage possible to beat the other guys. He was thoroughly prepared before each game, although sometimes in his early years, afraid of missing the slightest detail which would give his team an edge, he overprepared and overmanaged. But he was on his way to becoming a brilliant baseball strategist. In the first few years of his managerial career, he had sought out and took time to pick the brains and steal ideas from the best baseball minds in the game. Paul Richards, the legendary baseball innovator whose career dated back to the late 1920s, was the White Sox farm director in 1978 and 1979 and greatly influenced La Russa. Richards was a pitching and defense guy—he had molded the powerful Baltimore Orioles of the sixties based on these two foundations. Hemond also took La Russa with him to the 1979 World Series and he sat with other managers, soaking it all in, as they dissected the strategy.

By early June, the White Sox team was beginning to gel. They won four straight, putting their record at 31–22, only two and a half games out of first. But clouds had been forming over major league baseball all season—it was that pesky money problem again. Fans sadly watched as economics pushed the game off the field. Owners and the Players Association were—again—at odds, both vowing to hold to the bitter end in the struggle to the death. Unable to reach an acceptable agreement, the players walked out on June 12, 1981. It was the first time an

American sport had been interrupted by a strike in midseason and it would be the worst strike in baseball history to that point.

The major issue was free agency. Owners felt salaries were escalating much too rapidly due both to the premium being paid to free agents and the lucrative, long-term contracts being given to stars to prevent them from leaving. The average major league salary had risen from $51,000 in 1976 to $144,000 in 1980. Owners wanted compensation for losing a free agent. Players felt that any type of compensation or restriction on free agency would diminish their overall worth. Neither side was in a mood to bargain.

The players did not return until August 10—a full two-month layoff. Under the format agreed upon to stimulate interest, the first-half winners would play the second-half winners in a playoff to determine the overall winner of each division. This plan was most damaging to teams like the White Sox, who were close, but not in first at the time of the strike. "The strike really hurt us," says Squires. "It came at the worst possible time because we were just starting to come together. If we could have played one more week we would have taken first. I really think we had the team to win the division that year. The strike just cost us the chance." By the peculiarities of the schedule, the White Sox played their first 15 games after the strike on the road. The combination of the two-month layoff and the brutal schedule broke their momentum. They managed to stay close until a disastrous stretch at the beginning of September in which they lost 10 of 11, then the pitching went south and the team collapsed.

After the strike, Fisk struggled monstrously on the field. He had always been a slave to regimen, but during the layoff there had been no schedule; there was no way of knowing if it would last one day, one month, or longer. He lost weight and was in the worst shape of his playing career. He had been hitting near .300 when the players went out in June. After returning, his batting average slowly fell, then he barely hit .200 for September. The home runs stopped coming. The RBIs stopped coming. He had only two home runs and 16 RBIs in the final two months, and both home runs came in the same game. He blamed the weight lost during the strike for his power outage. "When I don't have a regularly scheduled exercise program, I don't burn as many calories and I'm not hungry. When I'm not hungry I don't eat. . . . I never thought [the strike] would go more than 10 days. . . . I went day to day thinking it would end at any time."

The White Sox crawled to a disappointing 9–19 record the last month. Still, they finished with an overall record of 54–52, the first winning season in Chicago since 1977. This was cause for some mild celebration and optimism. Chicago fans weren't as demanding as their Boston counterparts—they didn't need pennants to be happy, only .500 teams.

Meanwhile, the Fisk family was busy adjusting to the Midwest. Carlton and Linda maintained their property in New Hampshire, and their hearts would always remain there, but Chicago was now their home. They picked out an expansive house in Lockport, Illinois, about 35 miles southwest of Comiskey Park. It was located in a flat, cornfield area. "We wanted to be as far out in the country as possible," Carlton explained. "We tend to stick to ourselves, and we're country people." Never one to enjoy the busy streets of a city, Carlton preferred the simple pleasures and slower pace of rural life. The kids assimilated into their new surroundings, becoming active in local youth sports. Carlyn was now 11, Casey nine, and Courtney six. Like their father, they were all athletic and competitive. Carlton quickly fit in with his new teammates and found guys who had similar interests. "I got to know him pretty well," says Squires. "We lived maybe a half an hour apart. In the off-season we played golf quite a bit. We went out to dinner a few times. He was a great teammate. Away from the field he was a great guy."

"We had a lot of fun together, on and off the field," says backup catcher Marc Hill. Although Hill had previously been a starter in the major leagues, he readily accepted his role and became the type of anything-for-the-team, happy-to-be-here player every good team needs. He and Fisk became good friends. "I didn't mind being the backup to Carlton Fisk. He was the best catcher I knew. We got along great. And I could always beat him in golf, so that made me feel better."

Carlton also discovered a jewel in the White Sox clubhouse—Willie Thompson. A mountain of a man with a shiny bald head, the ageless Chicken Willie was the clubhouse manager and general team philosopher. He put out the best postgame spread in the business, laden with soul food, including his famous fried chicken. Always ready with a huge toothy smile and a laugh, he took care of the players' morale as well as their stomachs. He told everyone his goal was for the White Sox to win the pennant so he could buy a chicken stand. "Willie was absolutely the best," says Lemon. "He was invaluable. He was always happy. We all have days when we don't feel good, but I don't think I ever saw him not happy. He was always saying, 'You gotta get some more chicken in you if you want to get some hits.' He always brought a smile to your face. It was impossible not to feel good around him. He was part of the family." Once a White Sox player needed his ankle taped and the trainer was busy. Willie volunteered, grabbed a roll of tape in his big hands, and proceeded to wrap it so tightly that the poor player lost feeling in his toes and his entire foot swelled up and turned purple. Fearing that gangrene would set in at any moment, the player cut the tape off with scissors. Not about to be insulted by the lack of confidence in his taping skills, Willie huffed, "If you didn't want it done right you shouldn't have asked me."

In the off-season, Einhorn and his team of white-collared executives working out of suites in the John Hancock Center on North Michigan Avenue's Miracle Mile made a concerted effort to establish a new image, to let everyone know that they were serious about the baseball business. They upgraded Comiskey Park's sound system. The old scoreboard was stripped and replaced with a $5.1 million Diamond Vision and message board. Corporate partners were signed on. They widened both dugouts, established a weight room for players, and doubled the size of the clubhouse. They spent money to improve their farm system, adding teams and minor league coaches. Everything was going to be first-class. Unlike a certain team in the East, the White Sox management was trying to make money by spending money. And it appeared to be working. They were out to take over Chicago.

But it wouldn't be as easy as throwing a lot of cash around. Although the Cubs had been terrible for a decade, they had a solid fan base and a superstation, WGN, to blast their games far and wide. To compete with the Cubs' WGN television domination, the Sox added a 43-game free TV schedule. At the same time, believing that they should not entirely give away their product, Einhorn's pet project was to eventually remove the White Sox from free television and place them on a monthly cable subscription television program called SportsVision that also included the Bears and Blackhawks and was set to begin in limited fashion in 1982.

The team still had a lot to improve, in all areas. But Reinsdorf and Einhorn remained committed. They picked up guys who not only had talent, but also brought leadership to the clubhouse. They rented high-priced slugging left fielder Steve Kemp for a year, adding him to Fisk, Luzinski, and center fielder Ron LeFlore as making at least $600,000 a year. Thirty-five-year-old first baseman Tom Paciorek was signed from Seattle. Paciorek was not only a perennial .300 hitter but was also one of the funniest men in any clubhouse. They also spent money on veteran pitchers Dennis Lamp and Jerry Koosman.

Koosman, who would be 39 years old during the 1982 season, had been a hero of the Miracle Mets of 1969 and one of the toughest left-handers in the National League. He was closing in on 200 wins for his career. Koosman was a smart player with near-total recall for games and pitches he had made. He no longer possessed lightning in his arm, but was still able to get guys out consistently with his location and savvy. Having won at the highest level and universally respected, his presence in the clubhouse was immeasurable. He was an intense competitor who hated to lose but, like Paciorek, he had a great sense of humor and helped keep everyone loose. He seemed to instinctively know what to say, when to laugh, when to kick butt. Koosman became the heart of the clubhouse.

The opening day lineup for 1982 earned just under $4 million, or more than twice as much as La Russa's entire 1980 roster. In addition to the quality players added from trades and via free agency, the White Sox had a homegrown star in the making. Twenty-three-year-old right fielder Harold Baines, entering his third major league season, was becoming recognized as a great player. A famously clean-living, soft-spoken man, almost impossible to make mad, Baines had been picked by Bill Veeck number one in the entire draft in 1977. He was a great competitor and late-inning clutch hitter and became the most consistent member of the team. He had speed, range, a strong arm in the outfield, and one of the sweetest swings seen in Chicago since Billy Williams of the Cubs. In 1982 he broke out with 25 home runs and 105 RBIs.

With the team adding several talented pitchers from the minors, the staff began to look solid. La Russa, optimistic with the bevy of talent now in his coffers, boldly predicted a pennant in the spring. The team started hot, 8–0, and stayed near the top of the division through late July. A slide after the All-Star break, however, doomed the team's pennant hopes. Although they still didn't quite have the team to contend, the White Sox played good ball through the end of the season and finished in third place at 87–75, a marked improvement. It was the first time the franchise had back-to-back winning seasons since the 17 straight from 1951 to 1967.

Fisk led the American League in All-Star votes in 1982. He had a solid, if not spectacular, year, hitting .267 with 65 RBIs. Still able to run well for a catcher and turned loose on the base paths by La Russa, he stole a career-high 17 bases while being caught only twice.

Despite the obvious improvement in the team, Tony La Russa was still fighting for his professional life. He continued to be ripped mercilessly by Caray and Piersall. They second-guessed every move and never missed a chance to throw in an extra insult. Piersall, who also had a WMAQ-AM radio call-in show, was a loose cannon who frequently seemed angry at everyone and everything, regularly verbally assaulted the owners and players, and once referred to baseball wives as "horny broads" on the air. Piersall's favorite target, by far, was the White Sox manager. Piersall had a large following of fans who enjoyed his brand of journalism and he whipped them into a frenzy of vitriol against La Russa. They booed his every appearance on the field.

Once, in mid-1982, having had enough, La Russa and assistant coaches Jim Leyland and Art Kusnyer drove to the SportsVision studio to discuss their differences with Piersall in person. The debate soon got dangerously out of hand and La Russa and Piersall had to be physically separated.

The players supported La Russa and gave him protection when the media came after him. "It has been inconceivable to me and to the rest of the team that La Russa has had to bear the brunt of criticism to the point where his job reportedly is on the line," Fisk said after ending a slump with five RBIs on a pair of singles and a three-run home run to lead the White Sox to a 9–6 win over Boston. He placed the blame on himself for not performing up to standard.

After the team finally dropped out of contention in August, Einhorn indicated to the press that La Russa's job was in jeopardy and that it was up to Hemond as to when to pull the trigger. But Hemond had seen bad baseball in Chicago, and he knew this was not even close. He realized what he had in La Russa and knew that the team was actually coming along right on schedule. Better things were ahead.

14 Winning Ugly

THE WHITE SOX OWNERS CONTINUED TO SPEND, and after just two years they had assembled the puzzle pieces to make good on their promise of a pennant. The team's offense was impressive. In addition to Fisk, Luzinski, and Baines, the White Sox added twenty-five-year-old rookie Ron Kittle in 1983.

The 6-4, bespectacled Kittle was a peculiar sight in left field, but while he looked like a giraffe chasing butterflies trying to field his position, he soon showed that he could knock in many more runs than he allowed. The son of a steelworker in nearby Gary, Indiana, Kittle had been a low-level Dodger minor leaguer when a disastrous neck injury forced him out of baseball. Washed up as a professional at 20, he was back home working in the steel mill with his father, playing for a local semipro team when his long home runs caught the attention of the White Sox. His tryout, before a Royals–White Sox game at Comiskey Park in 1978, became the stuff of legend. He took a huge swing at the first pitch and missed completely. He then launched 12 balls over the fence, one of which left the stadium through the open arch in the lower deck. With players from both major league teams watching, he hit the last one on the roof. Owner Bill Veeck reportedly sent down orders that Kittle not be allowed to leave the park until he had signed. Kittle hit 40 home runs in the minors in 1981 and topped that with 50 in 1982. His easygoing personality, subtle sense of humor, lack of ego, and monster home runs quickly made him a favorite of the media, fans, and teammates.

When missed buses, fights with the manager, and finally a fly ball that hit him on the head led to the exit of talented-but-troubled center fielder Ron LeFlore, untried Rudy Law took over. Law was the product of another good trade by Hemond, who picked him up for two minor leaguers from the Dodgers. The book on Law at the time: great speed, suspect hitting, poor arm. The book would turn out to greatly underestimate his impact. Law would prove to be a terrific leadoff hitter, continually getting on base and distracting pitchers and would end up shattering the team stolen base record in 1983.

The big deal over the winter was the signing of pitcher Floyd Bannister from Seattle. The 27-year-old had led the AL in strikeouts in 1982 and was the most sought-after free agent of the off-season. Hemond enlisted Carlton Fisk and Tom Paciorek, who had played with Bannister in Seattle, to help convince him to come to Chicago. Those two, along with a contract for $4.5 million over five years, did the trick. Bannister had turned down several offers of more money elsewhere to sign with the White Sox. Fisk was present at the press conference announcing the signing. He said he had told Bannister the White Sox had a very good chance to contend in 1983 and that the owners seemed committed to keeping a good team on the field. He also advised him that Comiskey was a pitcher's park. Chicago fans were incredulous that their team was now a choice destination for high-priced talent.

The pitching rotation suddenly looked great. LaMarr Hoyt, 28, was a craftsman with incredible control who could stealthily vary the speed of his fastball by six to eight miles per hour and paint the edges of the strike zone. Obtained from the Yankees in the 1977 trade that sent shortstop Bucky Dent to the Yankees and a date with destiny, he had been 19–15 in 1982 and was the team's ace. Tough, fireballing Rich Dotson, 24 years old in 1983, had been a regular in the White Sox rotation since he was 21 and had won 32 games the previous three seasons. He had developed a masterful change-up and was poised for a breakout season. Veterans Koosman and Dennis Lamp, along with live-armed youngster Britt Burns, provided relief and spot starts.

In addition to the quality players the White Sox brought in, they went after good coaches. Reinsdorf challenged the time-honored notion of coaches merely being cronies and drinking buddies of the manager, and encouraged Hemond to get guys who knew what they were doing and could help the team. With that directive, Hemond compiled a unique assemblage of some great baseball minds.

Dave Duncan became La Russa's pitching coach in 1983. Duncan, a former catcher for the A's, Indians, and Orioles, had first met La Russa with the A's in the 1963 Florida Instructional League. Duncan was an ex-military type who had no problem telling people what he felt; he commanded respect, and got it. Duncan was one of only four ex-catcher pitching coaches in the major leagues at the time. As someone who used to try to hit, he had a better understanding of the batter's standpoint and this gave him an advantage, which he turned into his area of expertise—exploiting hitter tendencies. Duncan's pitchers loved him because he was always building them up; when he went to the mound, it was with a suggestion to correct mechanics and a word of encouragement, not just a morale-damaging threat. Also, as an ex-catcher, he firmly believed in the catcher's responsibility to call a good game—a belief that immediately made him Carlton Fisk's favorite pitching coach.

Duncan also ingratiated himself with Fisk with his inquisitive mind. "Dunc was always talking with us about hitters and pitchers," says Marc Hill. "We'd give each other situations, 'What would you do?' Learning what to do in different situations, how to get out of different problems. And not just in the clubhouse. We could be having lunch or in a bar and we'd be talking things over about baseball." Duncan possessed a rare ability to break down and explain problems. He would develop into one of the best pitching coaches in baseball, particularly renowned at reclamation projects, and become La Russa's right-hand man over the next three decades.

Charlie Lau had joined the team as hitting coach in 1982. Like Duncan, Lau was a former major league catcher, but he had experienced much less success as a player—a career .255 hitter as a backup with five teams over 11 major league seasons. After he finished playing, Lau became a hitting coach—and proceeded to revolutionize the way hitting was taught. Lau studied video when no one else did. He broke down the swings of successful hitters, frame by frame, in order to scientifically study why some players could do what he could not—hit major league pitching successfully and consistently. His philosophy evolved to: head on the ball at all times, weight on the back foot before striding with a weight shift, an inside path to the ball, hitting the ball where it was pitched, top to bottom swing with no upper cut and great post-contact extension, releasing the top hand if necessary to achieve the extension. When his prized pupil, George Brett, flirted with .400 deep into the 1980 season (he ended up at .390), Lau became the first rock star hitting coach and his philosophy influenced the way hitting was taught for the next 25 years. Fisk was already familiar with Lau's teachings, having studied under Lau disciple Walt Hriniak in Boston in the late seventies. White Sox players would gather around the re-spected bat-whisperer in the clubhouse and on the plane and listen to his discourses on situational hitting, moving runners over, scoring them with two outs, and hitting in general.

Added to those two coaches was Jim Leyland, the third base coach. Leyland had worked his way up the managerial ladder in the Tigers' system and was viewed as not only a great player's coach but a future managerial star. He had been hired by the White Sox in 1982 and would later leave them to manage the Pirates in 1986 and go on to amass 1,769 wins, three pennants, and a World Series title in 22 years as a manager with four teams. Other than Lau, who had been around for years, it was a staff of up-and-comers—as impressive a staff as has ever been put together.

With these pieces in place, La Russa, and White Sox fans, had good reason to be optimistic for the 1983 season. But they had no way of knowing just how good it would be.

The White Sox were 20–7 in spring training, the best record in base-ball. But spring training records are forgotten one day into the regular season and the White Sox started poorly, losing a three-game sweep in Texas. On paper the team felt they should hit. On paper, they knew they possessed the kind of defense that would keep La Russa up all hours—listening for things that go clank in the night. While the hit-ting did not produce, the defense came through as expected right from the start. They committed 34 errors in the first 26 games, including a 13–6 loss in Cleveland in which six different players made errors.

As the season passed into May, the White Sox continued to flop. The weak defense seemingly hurt the team every game and affected the psyche of the pitching staff. The bullpen had blown several games. Bannister, perhaps pressing to justify the enormous price tag to fans, was having trouble winning and Hoyt started 2–6. Luzinski and Fisk flailed unsuccessfully at the plate for most of the first two months, both hitting below .200. Luzinski endured a 3-for-53 slump. Fisk's defense was also suffering. He had seven passed balls by May 20, an enormous number for him. (Four times previously, he had four or fewer for an entire season.)

After fighting to get even at 12–12, the team stumbled again; by May 26 they were 16–24, seven games out. Amid media calls for La Russa's head, Hemond defended him to both the press and, in private meetings, to Reinsdorf and Einhorn. When the team lost six of seven a week later, however, it was openly questioned how much longer La Russa could last. The team had spent money on free agents, had good pitching and hitting on paper—they were supposed to win.

Luckily for the White Sox, no one else in the division was playing well; the AL West was being called the AL Waste. This prevented them from falling too far behind while they tried to find themselves. Confident of the talent in their midst, the veterans assured their younger teammates that they were only a few short winning streaks from being back in it. Also, in what many felt was the key to the team's eventual success, the players never saw La Russa panic from the pressure. Paranoia is contagious, but La Russa kept his cool and insisted to the players that they would pull out of it. This cool helped buy time to save La Russa's neck and the season for the team.

Carlton Fisk was 35 years old, well past the age when most catchers are through, or switch to another position—the age when a few months of a lousy batting average at the start of a season provokes whispers that maybe it's time to hang it up. Although he had been named to the All-Star team in 1981 and 1982, both seasons were below the standards he had set for himself over the previous decade. Before being axed after one too many rants early in the season, Jimmy Piersall had emphatically labeled Fisk as over-the-hill. While Carlton slumped pathetically the first part of the 1983 season, he made Piersall look like a prophet.

Compounding the frustration of Fisk's poor performance were the boos he began hearing in Comiskey. He felt unfairly singled out. Some of the boos directed at the highest paid players were due to leftover resentment from the 1981 strike, channeled by working-class fans caught in an endless recession. Fisk was a star and there were responsibilities and expectations that go with the money and status and the expectations weren't being met. Regardless of the cause, or whether they were deserved, the boos at home hurt.

In addition, Carlton had difficulty dealing with La Russa in the first half of the season. There was a series of angry confrontations, separated by tense silence. A major source of irritation for Fisk came in the form of an electronic device that would soon revolutionize the world, including baseball, provoking the enmity of all who relished the old days: the computer. La Russa, with his pitching coach Duncan, had been one of the first managers to embrace this new technology, and he continually explored ways to maximize its use. Every aspect of the game could be analyzed; individual players' tendencies in every possible situation could be instantly retrieved. The computer could tell him how well a batter hit a particular pitcher, how often he hit a particular pitch from a particular pitcher, things that in the past had been left up to players' intuition and experience, seat-of-the-pants stuff—the kind of stuff a man like Carlton Fisk relished.

Fisk had always taken pride in his knowledge of the game and his ability to read hitters and pitchers. He considered a well-called game one of the highest aspirations of a professional catcher. He was certain his well-honed instincts were better than any machine. He was not just sitting on his heels back there, throwing the ball back to the pitcher and occasionally throwing to second on a steal attempt, he was the quarterback, the general on the field. He had chafed when Darrell Johnson—a thinking catcher's catcher—had questioned his pitch selection in 1976. Now, with seven more years of experience, he sure as hell wasn't going to quietly step aside and let an ex–utility infielder with a briefcase full of computer printouts call his game for him. He was certain beyond a reasonable doubt that while the computer could tell past history, it could not take into account intangibles such as the crowd, game intensity, slumps, or hot streaks and how a given man on the mound was throwing a certain pitch on a given day; the feel of the game at hand—stuff a catcher could process faster than any microchipped meddler. Fisk smoldered with each challenge of his expertise.

Tony La Russa was not one to avoid confrontation on a subject he felt was hurting the team. When he had computer evidence to dispute what Fisk was doing, he presented it to him and he refused to back down. "If a manager hesitates to discuss a player's mistakes face-to-face, he won't have much credibility in the clubhouse," he said later in the season. "Pudge was letting his batting slump affect the way he caught a game. He allowed some hitters to be pitched to their strength in game situations and called sequences of pitches that didn't keep them off balance. A lot of what I told him sounded like I didn't have much respect for his ability, and nothing could be further from the truth. . . . Carlton Fisk has courage and a strong ego. That's why we're paying him big bucks. For the first time in his career, the fans were booing him and the manager was on his back. I didn't expect him to crawl into a shell. He came out fighting, the way a winner reacts to a challenge. If he's got something against me because of words we exchanged, that's part of a manager's job." Confronting his stubborn, respected, veteran catcher was one of the key tests in La Russa's early managerial career.

Fisk's average tumbled to .136 by May 2, straining his confidence in his ability and decision-making process. La Russa experimented with solutions such as allowing Marc Hill to catch Floyd Bannister after the $900,000-a-year left-hander went 0–5 with Fisk as his battery mate. He outright benched Fisk a few times and even pulled him for pinch hitters, things that hadn't happened since his rookie season.

Fisk angrily fought back. "I couldn't believe baseball has changed so much this year that I can't play it anymore," he said late in 1983, looking back at the difficult period. "I didn't appreciate the finger of blame being pointed at me because the staff wasn't pitching well. Trying to figure out how to help the pitchers affected the way I hit and that affected the way I caught, so it all ended up with me not playing the way I should. What I did before in the majors had always worked out. Suddenly, somebody's telling me that's not the right way and showing me computer printouts to let people know what hand they should wipe their nose with. I rebelled about that. They were attacking my roots."

On May 22, La Russa, still searching for solutions, made a lineup change that would prove fruitful. Seeking more power near the top of the lineup, reasoning that it would help to get a guy up to the plate more often who could end a game with one swing, he moved Fisk to second in the batting order. At the time, the number two slot was traditionally a place for pesky little second basemen with good bat control and little power, who took a lot of pitches and put the ball in play; or speedy slap-hitting outfielders who could get on base and make things happen. Fisk was hardly either—he was a big guy who lumbered up to the plate wearing an offensive lineman's number on his back. It was a radical idea for the time. "Carlton was struggling early in the season," La Russa said in 2014. "He had the talent, he was giving the effort, but it wasn't working and it was getting to him mentally. . . . I went to Charlie Lau and talked with him about it. . . . Sometimes a different look can help you mentally. . . . It was a nice change of pace for him because now Rudy Law gets on and Carlton starts taking a pitch or two to see if Rudy will steal a base. Then, maybe he hits a ground ball to the right side and Rudy gets to third or if he's in scoring position Carlton's going the opposite way and drives in a run." La Russa also knew he had enough power in the middle of the lineup with Luzinski, Baines, and Kittle to afford the move.

Fisk, who hadn't agreed with La Russa on much of anything else early in the 1983 season, initially did not appreciate the move. He had hit in the 3, 4, or 5 slot throughout his career. Still only hitting .179, he went 1–5 in an 11–3 win the first game in the number two spot. Over the next five games, he continued his batting slumber, then slowly some balls began to fall in. He hit in five of six games and suddenly was in the rarefied air of .200—a place he hadn't seen in months.

The team as a whole continued to underperform, however, and the noose was tightening around La Russa's neck. On the night of June 10, Einhorn, more impetuous than his methodical partner, talked to Reinsdorf on the phone to discuss the future of the team, particularly the managerial situation. The talk lasted until early in the morning. They agreed to wait until the All-Star Game to decide.

With so much tension, both internally and externally, a blowup was inevitable and it came between games of a June 12 doubleheader in Oakland. The White Sox had just experienced two demoralizing defeats by the A's—one in which they scored a single run in 15 innings and the next day when they let a late-inning lead evaporate. The entire team could not have been more down as they prepared for the Sunday doubleheader. Fisk was irritated when he found out La Russa had brought up catcher Joel Skinner from the minors without the courtesy of telling him. He was further irritated when Hill started the first game of the doubleheader and he was infuriated when he found out that Skinner would be starting the nightcap. Fisk immediately confronted La Russa on the field. The two stood behind the screen near second base, in the middle of warm-ups, and a screaming match ensued—red face to red face—in front of the whole team. Fisk made his point, then stalked off. "I went to the bullpen . . . and told myself, 'Forget him. Just go out and play,'" he said later. "Maybe that was all I needed to get the whole thing off my mind."

The White Sox won both games of the doubleheader, without Fisk, and most observers later looked back on the doubleheader as a turning point in the season. "Right after that we started playing consistently," says Squires. "It was a key moment for the team. That kind of lit the fire, I think. The move in the lineup really helped Pudge because he started seeing more fastballs in the number two slot. He could take pitches with Law on base and it started making a difference. Getting the air cleared with La Russa and then starting to hit better just changed everything."

The Sox got an additional spark when second baseman Julio Cruz was obtained from the Mariners in a trade for Tony Bernazard on June 13. Nicknamed Juice, Cruz had blazing speed and provided a real defensive presence up the middle. He could bunt, steal, and was unparalleled at turning double plays. He brought energy to the team and the effect was immediate. With Cruz and Rudy Law, old-timers were reminded of the Go-Go Sox of the late 1950s. La Russa began letting the two run almost at will.

Then suddenly, Carlton Fisk broke out. Beginning June 17, he had two or more hits in four of five games. Soon after he launched a home run barrage and went on one of the best hitting streaks of his career; over 38 games from June 17 to July 30, he hit .388 with 14 home runs and 41 RBIs. The team, riding on the back of their catcher, broke .500 for the first time in over a month on June 22. They continued to win and took first place July 18 when they beat Cleveland 5–3 as Fisk hit a home run, had four RBIs, and picked a runner off first for the final out.

There was a direct connection between the explosion of production from Fisk's bat, his newfound attitude, and the team's record. The whole team played better, but Fisk seemed to be the ignition. He didn't get up in the clubhouse and make pep talks, but everyone picked up the unspoken message he delivered with his play.

Teammates noticed and respected the fact that he had endured the frustration without making excuses and, though he had challenged La Russa, he hadn't tried to go behind his back and undermine his authority. He directly confronted La Russa instead of pleading his case to the press—perhaps a lesson learned in Boston. "La Russa and Carlton did butt heads, but it was never counterproductive," says Hill. "It never hurt the team. You'd see them go in the office, they might get loud, then they'd come out and the game that night would go pretty good. I think they both respected the other's talents."

While making important contributions on the field, the older players were invaluable in the clubhouse, setting a good tone for their teammates and helping to pull them together. "We had a great veteran presence on that team," says Hill. "You can't overestimate what an impact that made." Most of the veterans had postseason experience and embraced their roles as leaders. Koosman and Luzinski developed the habit of renting a suite at the hotel in every road city so the players would have a place to hang out. They would order up burgers, pizza, and beer and invite the whole team. The guys would talk baseball, eat, and rag on one another. Baseball, laughter, and insults filled the room until the early-morning hours. It was a great team builder, especially valuable in allowing the young players to learn the ropes in the big leagues, to feel accepted and have fun with their teammates, and to keep them out of trouble and focused on the road.

La Russa also held mandatory team parties on the road once a month. They would close the doors to the clubhouse after a game and bring in food and drinks. "All the guys would be there," says Marc Hill. "And you could say anything you wanted. We'd talk baseball and talk about things we should be doing. If there was a problem on the field, that was the time to bring it up. Everybody had to be there. Some guys would drink a beer or two, guys like Scott Fletcher and Vance Law, who didn't drink, we called them the milkshake drinkers, they would come and had fun too. Harold Baines, who wouldn't say anything if he had to, he would be there. We just all enjoyed being around each other. Those parties were great for keeping us together." It was 25 guys congregating at the same time, learning from mistakes, and enjoying one another's company—a rare atmosphere in major league baseball, a chemistry that is almost impossible to manufacture, but is born out of circumstance, unique personalities, and nourished by winning.

"We had the right blend of personalities," Ron Kittle later wrote. "You don't find that too often. Even most winners have some guys unwilling to give themselves up for the team, but as long as things go well, dissent gets swept under the rug. Nobody on the Sox started pointing fingers when we didn't get out of the gate fast enough." With so much laughter and ragging going on, "you couldn't sit around and brood in our clubhouse."

Fisk and Luzinski, as the unquestioned alpha males and elder statesmen by way of their experience and the backs of their baseball cards, were afforded a level in the clubhouse their status deserved. They were rarely the targets of the pranks and jokes. Fisk brought a businesslike approach that was appreciated. His locker area was usually quieter than the rest of the clubhouse. Dennis Lamp kept everyone in stitches with his talent for mimicking players, managers, and umpires. Paciorek, nicknamed "Wimpy" after the old Popeye cartoon character due to his voracious appetite for burgers, kept up a regular hilarious banter. He later bragged that he and Luzinski could outdrink any *team* in the league.

The pranks on the team, and there were many, were led by Marc (aka

Booter) Hill. His signature caper was the old shaving-cream-in-the-phone-earpiece trick: "Hey, there's a phone call for you in the clubhouse," the unwitting victim picks up the phone and holds it to his ear, and gets an earful of shaving cream. According to legend, he once got President Jimmy Carter who was visiting the clubhouse. "That's true," he confesses, noting that since the statute of limitations for pranking the leader of the free world has now run out he can come clean. "It was funny because he didn't realize that he had shaving cream in his ear and the Secret Service guys were dying trying to keep from laughing."

On the road, Hill prowled novelty shops and was especially enamored with little devices that could be stuck into the ends of cigarettes to make them explode. Whenever chain-smoking third base coach Jim Leyland would nervously come off the field between innings and head back down the tunnel for a quick smoke, the entire dugout would go quiet, waiting for the inevitable bang, followed by "Dammit, Booter!"

"We'd be rolling on the floor, laughing our guts out," wrote Kittle.

"We had a fun team," says Hill. "We were a very close-knit team. I was one of the pranksters. I'd get guys and then they'd get me back. A baseball season is long, 162 games; you have to stay loose. It was a great mix of young guys and old guys, not just for '83 but for several years. We had great veteran leadership, with Bull, Koozer, and Pudge. We laughed and had fun. Tony was in charge, but he let us do our thing. We were winning, so he didn't mind."

In 1982, Koosman, searching for something else to help bring the talent together, had approached La Russa about starting a kangaroo court. Luzinski and Koosman were the judges and Squires was the treasurer, responsible for tracking down guys to get the money from the fines. Offenders were fined for on-field and off-field gaffes. Harold Baines, who if he'd had any less emotion would have been comatose, once stole second base, executed a pop-up slide, and gave himself a little clap. "He got fined for showing too much emotion," says Squires.

Anyone was fair game. "We were allowed to wear shorts in the clubhouse," adds Squires. "Once Jerry Reinsdorf saw me and made a comment about my shorts." The comment was not nice and included some impolite words. "There were some people not connected with the club and they heard him. So I told him, 'That's gonna have to be a fine.'" Flush with victory, Reinsdorf agreed and magnanimously offered to match the pot. "I don't think he had any idea how much we had in there. I said, 'I really don't think you want to do that.' He said, 'No, I'll match it. How much is it?'" It ended up costing him about $1,500—the team used the money for a party when they finished the season on the road.

"I had more fun with the '83 White Sox than any other team I ever played for," said Jerry Koosman years later. "They were such a positive group. You'd go to the park every day and nobody had any bad things to say, there were no negative feelings around."

"I don't think any team's ever had more fun than we did in 1983," Ron Kittle concurred. No teammate would disagree.

Once the team got rolling, they were unstoppable. July 4, they were a mere two games over .500 and in third place. After taking over first July 18 they quickly put distance between themselves and the rest of the division. La Russa didn't grow complacent or cautious after they started winning—he poured on the pressure. As the season went on, he got more and more aggressive, charging ahead, using their speed on the base paths. He manipulated the 25-man roster like a master, using everyone in their roles. And, more importantly, the bench players accepted their roles.

"Everybody contributed in 1983," says Hill. "Guys did whatever the team needed." Carlton symbolized the team-first spirit as he embraced the number two slot in the order, taking pitches and advancing runners. For months during the summer, the catcher-manager relationship had been one conducted with silent reserve as each went about his job. It thawed somewhat with the joy of victory. Winning has a way of making everyone happy. And the White Sox were certainly happy as August turned into September and they continued to pull away.

Even though they were compiling the best second-half record in baseball, the White Sox and their faithful still felt a lack of respect. Several national writers said the team would be no better than fifth in the American League East. August 19, as the White Sox prepared to start a four-game series in Texas, Ranger manager Doug Rader told reporters the White Sox bubble was bound to break soon. "They're winning ugly," he said.

The White Sox took three of the four games and also took home a battle cry for the season. Soon "Winning Ugly" was plastered everywhere in Chicago. "Winning Ugly Isn't a Miracle on 35th Street" T-shirts did a brisk business. The players relished the label and it became their official motto.

The White Sox were 59–26 (.694) after the All-Star break; 46–15 from August 1 to the end of the season. By September they were 29 games over .500 and 17 in front. A few years earlier they had been near bankruptcy and rumored to be leaving Chicago; now they electrified the city. They broke the Cubs' city single-season attendance record while drawing 2.1 million (up from 1.5 in 1982). During the last two months, Comiskey Park rocked every night, packed with fans who were into the game and having a blast and the players fed off it. Organist Nancy Faust whipped the crowd into a frenzy with songs like "I'm a Believer" and the song she had pioneered in stadiums back in the seventies, "Na Na Hey Hey Kiss Him Good-bye," whenever an opposing pitcher trudged off the field after being knocked out. Comiskey Park was the place to be and everybody loved it.

Everything was clicking for the White Sox, hitting, speed, defense, power, and pitching. They were, and believed themselves to be, unbeatable. They won 17 consecutive games at home late in the season before finally losing the last week. Players couldn't wait to get to the field every day. "Every time we showed up at the park we expected to win the game," said Paciorek. "When we finally got beat [at Comiskey], we sat around the locker room afterwards saying, 'How did we lose that game?'"

"We were never out of a game," says Dotson. "It was one of those special years. We just hung in games. You knew it was a matter of time before somebody would do something and we would win."

"Every day we knew if it was in the last inning and it was tied or we were down by one, we just knew we were going to win," says Hill.

Throughout the hot days of summer, the White Sox catcher was the emotional leader on the field and seemed to be in the middle of every rally. After the blowup in Oakland, Fisk hit .331 with 70 RBIs in the remaining 90 games of the season. The old swagger and confidence was back, as if it had never left.

Clinching was a mere formality. September 17, their magic number down to one, the White Sox faced the lowly Mariners in Chicago. Jerry Koosman started and took a 3–1 lead into the ninth inning, but was relieved after a few scratch hits. Dennis Lamp then gave up two runs to tie it. With the fans on their feet screaming, the White Sox loaded the bases in the bottom of the ninth. Harold Baines poked a fly to mid-center field and Julio Cruz tagged and raced home, pouncing on home plate with both feet to touch off the celebration. The whole stadium, and packed bars around Chicago, erupted. Players rushed onto the field and pounded on each other as fireworks lit up the night.

Fans poured over the rails, a sight of euphoria not seen at Comiskey since Disco Demolition Night, but this time the fans were intoxicated on victory. "Pandemonium here at Comiskey Park," the announcer said on television as fans raced across the field, jumping and waving their hands in the air. Chicago was no longer a city of losers. The White Sox had ended a 24-year playoff drought for the city.

After so many close calls, Carlton Fisk had his second taste of victory champagne. "[It was a sense of] joy, but there was a sense of relief in that we had proven what it takes to win ball games," he said later.

The players filed into the clubhouse, which had been draped in plastic to protect clothes and equipment from the celebration that was sure to follow. Writers were soon struggling to write notes on their drenched pads. Broadcaster Ken Harrelson waded through the champagne-filled air to interview his "Pards." La Russa put in context what the championship meant after so many years of futility: "I think our city needs it. I know our ball club needs it."

Owners Einhorn and Reinsdorf, ecstatic over the results of their concerted efforts and spending, came in and were immediately drowned in bubbly showers. Reinsdorf said, "I've lived here 26 years. They had a defeatist attitude in Chicago. Now it's gone."

Einhorn added, "I don't want to hear anybody ever say again, 'They can't do it in Chicago.'"

Luzinski hugged the soaked Fisk and laughed as they wiped the stinging champagne out of their eyes. "They wrote us off early," he said. "We came back, buddy. The old guys."

The agony and disagreements of the first two months were forgotten. La Russa, like most of the White Sox players, realized the important role Fisk had played during the team's turnaround and fantastic second half. During the raucous clubhouse celebration, he gave Fisk a big hug and added, "You're the MVP."

The clubhouse party lasted long into the night. So long that the next day La Russa had to canvass the team for volunteers to play (he not only pieced together a team but they won 6–0). Before the game, White Sox players stood along the foul line and were introduced as the 1983 Western Division champions while fans cheered wildly. Mike Squires, who had the longest tenure with the team, and assistant general manager Dave Dombrowski climbed on the roof of the stadium and hoisted the division championship flag. "It was great to be up there raising the flag," says Squires. "Especially after all the years there. But it was really windy that day and I was working on maybe three or four hours' sleep because we had been celebrating all night. I was a little scared up there. Also, I was starting that day. They had to hold the game up because it took me a while to get down off the roof and onto the field."

White Sox fans, who had seen the arrival of Carlton Fisk as the first true sign that their team would now be taken seriously, loved him for delivering on the promise. He finished with his best season in five years: 26 home runs, 86 RBIs, and a batting average of .289. The home runs eclipsed the previous team record for home runs by a catcher, which had been 22. He finished third in the American League MVP voting.

The White Sox finished at 99–63 and won the division by a league-record 20 games. Along with the best record in baseball, they led the majors in runs while outscoring opponents 800–650. In addition to Fisk, the offense was powered by Luzinski's 32 home runs and 95 RBIs, Baines's 20 home runs and 99 RBIs, and Rookie of the Year Kittle's 35 home runs and 100 RBIs. Paciorek hit .307. Rudy Law stole 77 bases, Cruz 57.

LaMarr Hoyt won the Cy Young Award with a 24–10 record. Dotson went 22–7 and Bannister 16–10. Along with Britt Burns, the starting pitchers had been an incredible 42–5 after the All-Star break.

Whereas winning was new to the White Sox and their fans, their opponents in the playoffs, the Baltimore Orioles, were old hands at it. The Orioles (98–64 in 1983) had the best record in baseball over the past quarter century—winning more division titles and championship series than anyone else. They had been to the World Series as recently as 1979. Although the White Sox only had five players with playoff experience: Tom Paciorek (Dodgers in 1974), Luzinski (1980 Phillies), Koosman (1969, 1973 Mets), Dick Tidrow (1976–78 Yankees), and Fisk, they felt, to a man, that they were a better team than the Orioles. White Sox players appeared at a "White Sox Pride Day" pep rally for the team on Chicago's Loop before the playoffs. Luzinski told the cheering crowd, estimated at more than 10,000, "We'll be back this Friday to hang the American League pennant in Comiskey Park."

LaMarr Hoyt started the first game of the playoffs in Baltimore. Hoyt had not lost a game since July 23, reeling off 13 consecutive wins to end the season. The White Sox scored a run with two outs in the third inning when Rudy Law and Fisk singled and Paciorek followed with a hard grounder that bounced off the third baseman and rolled into short left field. They didn't know it at the time, but that would be their big offensive outburst for the series.

Hoyt was in charge the whole way. He threw 26 first-pitch strikes to the 31 batters he faced and strikes on 74 of his 98 pitches. He gave up no walks and threw a five-hitter. With two outs in the ninth and the White Sox clinging to a 2–0 lead (the other run had scored on a double play grounder), the Orioles got a double and league MVP Cal Ripken followed with a single to make it a one-run game. Eddie Murray stepped in with the tying run on base and Memorial Stadium rocking. Hoyt got Murray to ground out weakly to short on the first pitch and the White Sox won 2–1.

After the game, Fisk said of his potbellied, bearded pitcher: "He just did a big favor for everybody that doesn't work out, because they'll take a look at his body and go eat anything they want." Earlier in the season, Fisk had been talking to reporters when he spied a towel-clad Hoyt emerging from the shower. "You have to admit, LaMarr has a lot of stomach—I mean guts."

As a harbinger of things to come, the White Sox had one hit in 13 tries with men in scoring position in the first game. In the last three innings, they were given five walks, had two singles, a balk, a wild pitch, and two pitches that bounced behind the catcher—and still didn't score a run.

Mike Boddicker pitched a shutout for the Orioles the next day. Over and over he dropped curveballs in for third strikes, ringing up 14 strikeouts in all. Bannister couldn't match Boddicker's performance. The Orioles scored a run in the second on a Vance Law throwing error. They added a run in the fourth, then Gary Roenicke hit a two-run homer in the sixth. With the Orioles up 4–0 in the top of the ninth, the White Sox loaded the bases with two outs. The left-handed Cruz sliced a pitch into the left field corner that appeared to hit the foul line, potentially scoring three runs, but it was called foul. He then struck out looking to end the game.

The teams flew to Chicago with the best-of-five series knotted up a game apiece. All of the next three games, if needed, would be played in Chicago. The price of scalped tickets skyrocketed.

A crowd of 46,635 showed up on Friday, October 7, cheering madly from the first pitch. Rich Dotson started for the White Sox and gave up a three-run homer to Eddie Murray in the first inning. The crowd was deflated in an instant. The Orioles gradually added to the lead while White Sox hitters continued their futility. Then things turned ugly. Leading off the fourth, on a 3–0 count, Oriole starter Mike Flanagan hit Kittle on the left kneecap with a fastball. Kittle groveled in pain, then got up and went after Flanagan, but was restrained before he got to the mound. The dugouts emptied and a general jawing and shoving match ensued. Baines followed Kittle with a rocket to second that was turned into a 4-6-3 double play. Kittle's knee swelled severely by the next inning and he had to come out of the game. He would not play the rest of the series.

Dotson was considered the enforcer of the Chicago staff, the toughest guy, the one man who always protected his teammates. The next inning, with two outs and no one on, Dotson drilled Cal Ripken. Ripken trotted to first, then called to Dotson, "Is that all you got?" Dotson threw the next pitch way inside to Murray, who waved his bat threateningly. Dotson shouted something back and everybody came out on the field again. After order was restored and both benches and pitchers warned, Dotson walked Murray, then gave up a double to make it 6–1. The Orioles continued to pile on and won 11–1.

After the game, La Russa declared to reporters, "I'm here to tell you Ripken was not hit intentionally." It was a nice, polite sentiment, but a little confusing, since Dotson was on the other side of the clubhouse telling people that not only did he "hit Ripken on purpose," but he had "taken a poll" to find out which Oriole "would be the best to hit," since orders had "come down from the grapevine." Three White Sox had been hit to that point in the series and it was time to retaliate. The next day La Russa cleared up the confusion by calmly explaining to reporters that Dotson had been a little "worked up" and possibly misunderstood (and La Russa was also apparently shocked, shocked, that there was gambling going on in Casablanca).

The all-important fourth game was an epic battle. Every Chicago player knew that a win in this game would bring the unbeatable Hoyt back in front of a frenzied Comiskey mob with the pennant on the line for the finale. The two teams fought for three hours and 41 minutes in a steady driving wind. The White Sox got men on base in each of the 10 innings, but couldn't get a run. Afterward, Baltimore catcher Rick Dempsey said, "That was the toughest game I ever participated in. It was mentally draining, and physically, you couldn't make any mistakes."

Britt Burns plowed through the Oriole lineup, pitching superbly. Inning after inning, he shut them out. The White Sox continued to mount threats against Oriole starter Storm Davis, but pressure intensified as, on the brink of elimination, they could not push across a single run. The absence of Kittle, a man who could have broken the scoreless tie with one swing, was significant.

In the seventh inning, as *Chicago Tribune* writer Bob Logan put it, "One of the colossal nonrallies in baseball history broke out." Three singles and a balk resulted in exactly zero runs in the inning for Chicago. They led off with two singles, the first of which knocked out Davis. Infielder Jerry Dybzinski tried to bunt but catcher Rick Dempsey grabbed the short bunt and threw to third for an easy force-out. Cruz followed with a line single between third and short. Vance Law rounded third hard, but third base coach Jim Leyland saw the charging left fielder get to the sharply hit ball quickly and he threw up the stop sign. Dybzinski rounded second in full flight and found himself trapped when the throw from the outfield was cut off. As they ran Dybzinski back toward second, Law broke for home and was thrown out by yards—men on first and second and two outs instead of bases loaded, one out. The pitcher then balked. The next batter, Rudy Law, lined one to left where it was caught to end the inning.

La Russa made the fateful decision to let Burns take the hill for the 10th inning. After nine and a third innings and 149 pitches, Burns had done a brilliant job. However, on his 150th pitch, little used Oriole outfielder Tito Landrum, only in the game because the regular right fielder was hurt, Bucky Dented the ball into the left field seats. La Russa removed Burns and the Orioles got two more runs to pad the lead, though they would only need the one.

White Sox players were stunned—the season was over. The momentum from their incredible roll in September was finished. The clubhouse was silent. "It was really tough on all of us," says Hill. "We knew we had fought so hard. But we just didn't get the hits when we needed them. I don't think I've ever been in a dimmer clubhouse. Some guys went to other guys and encouraged them. Some guys snuck off to be alone. I went back in the tunnel and just sat there for a while. We knew we were meant to win it all. I can still see that ball [Landrum's hit] going out of the ballpark today. Just unbelievable."

After everyone had time to cool off, La Russa came in to talk to the team. He had to stop several times, choking up. He finally was able to get his message out: he was proud of the team and the season and the best team didn't win.

Using a mixture of strong pitching and big innings, the Orioles had outscored the White Sox 19–3 over the four games. Amazingly, both teams got the same number of hits: 28. Baltimore had been much more resourceful with their chances. The Orioles pitchers had refused to throw a fastball to the meat of the White Sox order—only teasing them with fastballs off the plate—they changed speeds and threw curves, in and out, and it worked to perfection. The White Sox had only four extra base hits, all doubles, and stranded 35 runners, 18 from the seventh inning on. Luzinski got a pop-fly double in his first at bat, then went 1-for-14. He struck out three times looking and popped up to the catcher twice in the final game. Fisk wasn't much better, going 3-for-17. Baines was 2-for-16. There were no RBIs between the three after 284 during the season.

The total collapse of the White Sox offense, so strong the second half of the season, was inexplicable. Some postulated that the team had lost its edge after clinching so early; unable to recapture their intensity. Going into the playoffs, the White Sox hadn't played a .500 team since late August. Perhaps the length of time not seeing good pitching and defense had caused them to grow stale. "I'm not going to say the pressure didn't affect us because that would be wrong," Fisk said after the playoffs ended. "Mostly it was outstanding Baltimore pitching that stopped us, but we certainly didn't hit the way we should have."

As Casey Stengel said: "Good pitching beats good hitting and vice versa."

Once more Carlton Fisk had been a member of a great team that fell just short. He didn't know it at the time, but it would be his last chance for postseason glory.

15 Pumping Iron

THE WHITE SOX' OFFICIAL SLOGAN for 1984 was "Let's Do It Again." The new owners had been in town only three years and the team had nearly reached the top. Boundless optimism permeated Chicago's South Side. Continuing the formula that had built the team up, Hemond spent big money to lock up Kittle, Cruz, Hoyt, and Dotson and they were able to add a future Hall of Fame pitcher when they picked up Tom Seaver as compensation for losing Dennis Lamp as a free agent. Seaver, who had 273 major league wins by that time, had inexplicably been left unprotected by the Mets in the compensation draft and Hemond alertly snapped him up.

Despite the confidence, an almost identical lineup from 1983, and the addition of Seaver to the young rotation of Hoyt, Dotson, and Bannister, the magic was clearly gone. The White Sox started slow, plagued by injuries, slumps, and weight problems. Although teasing with their talent, they couldn't ignite a streak. Fisk developed a mysterious pain in the abdomen the first game. The pain affected his swing, his throwing, and his mobility behind the plate. Although a definite cause could not be identified, it would bother him all season, eventually forcing him to the disabled list.

May 8, the White Sox took on the Milwaukee Brewers at Comiskey Park, a seemingly unremarkable game played by two teams fighting to stay above .500. Veteran pitcher Don Sutton started for the Brewers, rookie Bob Fallon for the White Sox. The game was a scoreless tie until the Brewers got a run in the seventh inning. The White Sox matched that in their half of the seventh. The Brewers took a 3–1 lead in the ninth, but the White Sox tied it once more with a two-out single to stay alive. The game went into extra innings and the teams continued to play; and play, and play. Runners reached scoring position six times in extra innings, only to be stranded.

As the clock moved past midnight, the home plate umpire noted that players were getting punchy. "Guys would look at the catcher and smile or hit him on the shin guards: 'You awake?' " he later said. The game was halted after 17 innings with the score tied 3–3 at 1:05 A.M. due to a league rule at the time preventing a new inning from starting after one. The two teams met before their regularly scheduled game the next day to finish up. The Brewers got a three-run home run in the top of the 21st inning, but the White Sox improbably came back with three of their own. And they played on. The game eventually took 25 innings. La Russa ran out of pitchers and sent word to the clubhouse for Tom Seaver, set to pitch in the day's regularly scheduled game, to come on in relief. Seaver finished the 25th inning and got the win when Harold Baines hit a home run in the bottom of the inning. In the following game, Seaver retired 14 of the first 16 batters, pitched into the ninth inning, and won that one also, achieving the rare feat of winning two games in one day without both of them being in relief. The game set a major league record for duration in time (eight hours and six minutes) and tied for the longest completed game (Brooklyn and the Boston Braves had played to a 1–1 tie in 26 innings in 1920). Carlton Fisk, 36 years old, caught all 25 innings, setting a record for the most innings caught in a single game.

A week later, on May 16, Fisk had another memorable day. Playing at Comiskey against the Royals, he doubled in the first inning. His second time up, he singled in a run. In the fourth inning, he hit a home run to give the White Sox a 6–4 lead. He led off the seventh, facing Royals relief ace Dan Quisenberry, and tripled, giving him the cycle. He was only the third White Sox player to ever hit for the cycle and the first to do it at Comiskey. Somewhat symbolic of the kind of season it would turn out to be, however, he got one more at bat, in the bottom of the ninth with the White Sox trailing 7–6, with one out and a runner on first. He hit into a 5-4-3 double play to end the game.

By the All-Star break the White Sox were starting to play well, having won seven straight and were in position to put together another run as they had in 1983. Fans, expecting more of the good times, continued to pack Comiskey, and would end up topping two million again. After the All-Star break the team immediately fell flat, however, losing six of seven. They went into a downward spiral and never recovered. They staggered to a disappointing fifth place, 14 games under .500, at 74–88. The promise of the 1983 season proved to be fleeting for the White Sox; a mere blip on the screen.

The sudden drop was disappointing, and incomprehensible. With the exception of Harold Baines, who had 29 home runs and 94 RBIs while hitting .304, every single player on the White Sox performed much worse in 1984 compared to 1983. Several players, like Luzinski and Paciorek, had been pushing the limits of their age, but one year should not have been expected to cause that big of a dip. The hitting slumps were contagious. The lack of support affected the pitchers, who were also much less effective than they had been the previous season.

Luzinski had trouble keeping his weight down and his average up. He ended with only 13 home runs and 58 RBIs while hitting .238. After the season, a free agent, he got no offers and gave up the game at the age of 34. Hoyt was also severely overweight and lost 11 of 15 by July. He ended up 13–18. Kittle experienced the first of a series of injuries that would hamper his career and prevent him from ever approaching the production of his rookie season. Although he hit 32 home runs, his average dropped to .215. Rudy Law slipped from .283 and 77 stolen bases to .251 and 29. Julio Cruz, fresh off a million-dollar contract, hit .222 with only 14 stolen bases. Dotson fell to 14–15 and Bannister had an ERA more than 1.50 higher than in 1983. Nagged by injuries, Fisk hit a career-low .231 with only 43 RBIs in 102 games. It was an epic team-wide funk.

"I remember later Tony [La Russa] saying that we went to spring training still thinking it was 1983," says Squires. "He wasn't as hard on us. I don't think we were as hungry as we had been in 1983. We definitely had a letdown. It's hard to stay hungry once you've had such great success as we had in 1983. Also we really missed Jerry Koosman. He had really been one of the leaders in the clubhouse. It was a completely different atmosphere without him."

The trade of Koosman, swapped to the Phillies in December for Ron Reed in a trade of 40-year-old pitchers, proved to be one of Hemond's worst. Koosman won 14 games for the Phillies while Reed went 0–6 for the White Sox. More important was the loss of Koosman's leadership and steadying influence over the team—traits that were not fully appreciated by management until he was gone. "Koos and Bull were great together," says Dotson. "The chemistry of the team changed so much by losing Koos."

"The atmosphere was definitely different in 1984," says Hill, "but also I think the competition got a lot better all of a sudden. You had the Royals with Willie Wilson, Brett, and Saberhagen and then the Twins came up with Hrbek, Puckett, and Viola. Before we could get straightened out we were looking at a 10-game deficit. That just kills you."

Carlton Fisk turned 37 in December of 1984. There were questions again—the inevitable questions, asked by management and the press: how much longer? Catching is the most demanding position in baseball. The foul tips off the body, the collisions with runners, the thousands of times squatting and standing up—eventually all catchers are defeated by the position. Few major league catchers had ever remained effective in all phases of the game after 33 or 34. Yogi Berra was predominantly an outfielder by 35. Johnny Bench was a first and third baseman by 33 and, born within a month of Carlton Fisk, had retired at the end of the 1983 season.

The bad year for Fisk in 1984 only increased the questions. He would be entering the final season of the five-year contract in 1985. The length of the contract had been a point of contention in his original signing, as the White Sox did not want to gamble that, at his age, he could be effective as a catcher for five complete seasons. That was looking like an accurate reservation by the winter of 1984. But the reports of his impending demise only provoked defiance as Fisk's pride blazed forth. Questions could not be prevented; the reaction to them could. He would not accept it. He would not go down looking. "I knew that I'd do everything in my power to get ready to play," he would say the next summer.

Fisk had started lifting weights seriously for the first time while rehabbing his knee in 1974. Liking the way he felt and feeling stronger at the end of the season, he kept it up. The lifting was not heavy by weightlifting standards and most of the leg work had been curls and extensions and later various Nautilus exercises. Not long after moving to Chicago, Carlton had met Phil Claussen, 28 years old in 1985, a chiropractor in nearby Oak Brook. They began working out together and became good friends. Claussen was more than just another guy at the gym. He was a world-class trainer who would later be strength and conditioning coach for the Chicago Cubs, the Bahaman Olympic team, and be inducted in the National Fitness Hall of Fame. Claussen was a svelte 250 pounds and had less fat on his body than he had hair on his head—and he was bald. In the mid-eighties, strength and conditioning were not the household words they are now. Claussen was ahead of his time.

Fisk had been checked by several doctors looking for the cause of the mysterious abdominal pain that plagued him throughout the 1984 season. He was tested for tumors, cancer, kidney stones, "just about everything short of pregnancy," he later said. Claussen ultimately determined that the problem was due to a severe strain of the external oblique muscle.

As soon as the 1984 season ended, Claussen developed a training regimen designed to get his friend back on the field. He replaced the Nautilus workout with free weights. Traditionally, baseball players had used running and stretching to keep their legs in shape. Claussen added weightlifting routines that were more commonly used by football players and bodybuilders, based on the theory that running and stretching were the same things a player did during a game and only increased the wearing down of muscles throughout a season, whereas intense heavy lifting actually built the muscles back up and complemented their movements. This type of regimen was not used on baseball players at the time—the prevailing thought for years had been that heavy weights would make players muscle-bound and reduce their mobility.

The cornerstone of Claussen's program was heavy squatting. During the winter of '84, Fisk began working out squatting 135 pounds. By the end of the off-season, he was working out with 315. Strengthening the legs with squats would turn out to play a major role in keeping them in the kind of shape needed to allow him to catch years longer than anyone expected. In addition, Claussen focused much of the training regimen on strengthening the abdominal area in order to rehab the muscular strain. He also changed Fisk's diet—salads, fish, chicken, rice, and pasta replaced salt, fats, and red meats. And the dip and chewing tobacco Carlton had used for years were now history.

They started in mid-October for two hours a day, four days a week, gradually increasing to four and five hours a day, six or seven days a week. Carlton would make the 45-minute drive from his home in Lockport to Yeager's Fitness Center in suburban Chicago every day of the week, except Sunday. Not a total Spartan, he treated himself to a day off for Christmas (but not Thanksgiving). Yeager's wasn't one of those trendy boutique fitness clubs populated by fat executives and housewives in spandex doing Jane Fonda step aerobics; it was a dimly lit, smelly place filled with stacks of metal plates and hard men doing serious reps. Carlton punished himself throughout the winter, his obsession with training becoming all-consuming. He was driven by the doubt others showed, both in his ability to play and his ability to take pain. His code had given him a singular work ethic. *If you're going to do something, do it right or don't do it at all.* He pushed the limits of exertion—then pushed beyond. There were days he worked out so hard he didn't know if he could make it home. "We had some take-no-prisoners approaches to sessions . . . testing my resolve to human endurance," Fisk later said. He did leg lifts with Claussen standing on his stomach, endless sit-ups with Claussen pounding on his belly with his fists. He did sets of exercises in which he jumped from a squat position onto a 36-inch-high table, landing in a squat position, over and over until his legs felt like Jell-O.

Linda Fisk, who had to endure her husband's absences during the season, now faced them during the off-season. It would have taxed a less dedicated wife. Carlton later said, "I'm proud of my wife. She put up with me. I was no fun to be around. I was brain dead most of the time. We went out a couple of times, but mostly I'd come home and she'd start talking to me and . . ." He would nod off.

This type of severe regimen had never been performed by a baseball player. They were in uncharted territory. Would it get rid of the pain he had felt in his stomach virtually the entire past season? Would the increased strength translate into better performance on the baseball field? They thought it would. They hoped it would. But it might not. Still, he plodded on. He had to resist a multitude of temptations: the temptation to give in to pain, to wonder if it was all worth it, to be satisfied, to settle for a little less of himself.

When the 1985 baseball season opened, Carlton Fisk was ready. He had increased his weight from 202 to 230. The abdominal pain had disappeared, along with any residual pudge. He hit a home run and four RBIs in the opener and was hitting .309 by the end of April. Home runs began jumping off his bat: eight in May, six in June, nine in July. The White Sox rebounded from the disappointing 1984 season and were in contention throughout the summer.

Fisk's relationship with La Russa continued to be tenuous at best. Both held firm opinions and were not shy about voicing those opinions, but La Russa remained ultimately in charge. Fisk had been unhappy during the winter when he read that La Russa had said he wasn't too bright for criticizing the trade of LaMarr Hoyt to San Diego. When questioned by reporters, Fisk said that he didn't think it was appropriate to mumble under his breath about losing his best pitcher. "I accept Carlton for the way he is," said La Russa. "He speaks his mind, which means sometimes I have to speak mine. We've always gone in the same direction, though sometimes we disagree as to how that should be done." (The trade would turn out to be a good one though, as it brought the White Sox Ozzie Guillen, Luis Salazar, and Tim Lollar, while Hoyt was soon found to have severe drug problems and was out of baseball within two years.)

Ozzie Guillen, a slick-fielding, motormouthed shortstop, moved into the starting lineup as a rookie. Guillen combined talent with a particular zest for life. He always had fun, never let teammates feel stale, and was a tremendous competitor. He was also afflicted with a severe case of verbal diarrhea. He talked when the pitcher was in mid-windup. He talked when he was fielding the ball. He talked after he threw to first. He . . . never . . . shut up. Once during a mound conference with the pitcher, catcher, and manager discussing the batter, Guillen joined the group and immediately accused Fisk of having an ugly face. He would say anything, anytime, seemingly without ever pausing to think about what came out of his mouth. Teammates were amazed that he could talk nonstop and still concentrate in the field, yet he quickly established himself as one of the premier defensive shortstops in the major leagues.

Tom Seaver would long remember his introduction to Guillen. In spring training everyone was talking about Seaver's approach to the 300-win milestone. He was warming up one day when a rookie ran up to him, spouted, "I'm going to make the last out of your 300th win and then I'm not going to give you the ball," then scurried off laughing maniacally. "Who the heck is that?" Seaver asked a teammate. "Oh, that's your shortstop," came the reply. "He probably *will* make your last out and he probably *won't* give you the ball." Guillen provided a needed spark for the White Sox, solidified the entire infield, and became the American League's Rookie of the Year for 1985.

Fisk and Seaver developed a terrific relationship on the field and in the clubhouse. They discussed pitching and situations and developed a rapport in which each instinctively knew what the other wanted to do in a given situation. Each recognized the talent in the other and loved picking the other's brain. Bright and articulate, Seaver was one of the most astute players in the game when it came to the art of pitching. Knowing that he no longer possessed the powerful hose that blew hitters away during the sixties and seventies, Seaver learned how to pace himself, how to put a little more on or take a little off his pitches, and he always seemed to hold back at least one or two of his best fastballs for key situations. He was unsurpassed in setting hitters up and then getting them out with a master's touch.

"He taught me a lot," Fisk said of Seaver. "An awareness that there are things other than physical talent important in this game. He knew his limitations."

Seaver was always thinking, preparing for each start four days in advance. He knew how to outsmart hitters and never lost confidence in his ability. One day, after watching him warm up before a start in the bullpen, pitching coach Dave Duncan told him with disgust, "Tom, you don't have shit."

Seaver answered, "Yeah, so what?" He pointed to the other dugout. "They don't know that. So what's the problem? By the time they find out, it'll be too late."

Out of uniform, Seaver and Fisk, similarly aged and built, were sometimes mistaken for each other by fans. "When they used to mistake Seaver for me and ask him for my autograph, Tom would scream, 'No f***ing way!'" Carlton said later. "That was great for my image."

Fisk and Seaver enjoyed each other's subtle forms of humor, such as the time in an airport when they put dark sunglasses on rookie outfielder Daryl Boston, who bore a striking resemblance to Stevie Wonder, and each grabbed an arm and walked him through the concourse. Everyone was convinced that it was the blind singer and no one noticed the two future Hall of Fame players escorting him.

"We haven't been particularly close," Fisk told a New York reporter in midseason when asked about their off-field association. "But I think our relationship is more of a situation where there is respect for one another for what we have both done and the years we have done it." Away from the field, old enough to prefer solitude, they went their separate ways. Seaver had always famously enjoyed his space. But in the clubhouse they shared a common bond of age, excellence, and experience. They also kidded each other, with gallows–locker room humor: "Why don't you retire and give some young kid a chance?"

Seaver got his 300th win in Yankee Stadium on August 4, with Carlton catching. It didn't come easy. With two outs in the eighth inning, Seaver was in trouble. Physically exhausted after throwing more than 130 pitches, he held a 4–1 lead but the Yankees had two on with slugger Dave Winfield at the plate. The 40-year-old pitcher looked to the dugout, expecting the hook. Fisk slowly walked to the mound.

"Tom, don't even think of someone else coming in here," Fisk said. "You are responsible for this. . . . This is yours, this is your time, your moment." Seaver then worked to Winfield and put him away by getting him to swing and miss at a 3–2 change-up (that Seaver later said he decided on in mid-windup) that Fisk had to dig out of the dirt. In the ninth inning, Seaver once again struggled. With two outs and a man on first, he gave up a walk and faced the dangerous Don Baylor. Dave Duncan, acting as manager after La Russa had been ejected earlier, and Fisk went out to the mound. Carlton slapped Seaver on the rear and walked back behind the plate. Baylor flied out on the first pitch and Seaver had his historic win.

After the game, Seaver told reporters about the ninth-inning conference: "Duncan said, 'It's up to you.' There was no way I was coming out. Not with Carlton standing there. He gave me a kick in the pants and said, 'Let's go get him.' . . . I was beat but if you're one out from 300, if you can't get up for an out, you'll never get up." Fortunately for Seaver, the final out went to the outfield and not to Ozzie Guillen. Fisk retrieved the ball and gave it to Seaver's daughter.

Another highlight for Fisk in 1985 came when he was involved in a unique 8-6-2-2 double play on August 2. With no outs in the seventh inning at Yankee Stadium, tied 3–3, Bobby Meacham of the Yankees was on second and Dale Berra on first when Rickey Henderson hit a shot to left center that center fielder Luis Salazar barely missed. Meacham was tagging up at second, with Berra sprinting a few feet behind him, when the ball fell. Meacham stumbled leaving second. Third base coach Gene Michael wanted to hold Meacham at third but, with Berra so close behind him, had no choice but to wave him home. Berra, running hard, ignored Michael throwing his arms up wildly and continued home also. The relay from Salazar to Guillen to Fisk beat Meacham by yards. After the two collided, Fisk lunged forward to tag Berra, who had stumbled himself rounding third—tagging two men out at the plate on one play.

Carlton had been in Chicago almost five years now. He and his family had settled into life in the Midwest, happier than he'd been the last few tension-filled years in Boston. "I'd been living in New England for 33 years," he said. "Moving was a major change for us. We had to decide if we wanted to make that commitment. The Midwest doesn't have New England's mountains, its forests, its lakes. We said, 'We'll never know until we try it.' We have, and now we love it. It's our home."

They enjoyed their life in suburban Lockport. Carlton found places to fish and golf and enjoyed his new teammates, but it was obvious in his comments that he still retained sentiment for New England. And part of that sentiment inspired him to pummel his old team. During his first five seasons with Chicago, he hit .355 (65-for-183) against the Red Sox with 18 home runs and 46 RBIs. "Who deserves to be haunted more by me than the Red Sox?" he said to a reporter after hitting two home runs in an early August series at Fenway. "I get excited about playing in Boston. I still run the emotional roller coaster when I come back. The excitement of being back at the old ballpark does conflict with the sadness of what it would have been like should they have allowed me to stay here. I'm not glad I left. I never wanted to leave."

As the 1985 season progressed, Carlton continued hitting home runs at a faster pace than ever before in his career. He had always been a good power threat, but his previous high in home runs had been 26 in 1973, 1977, and 1983. He passed that by the end of July and was leading the league in home runs. The American League record for home runs by a catcher was 32, set by Tiger Lance Parrish in 1982. The major league record was 40 by Roy Campanella in 1953 (Campanella had an additional home run as a pinch hitter and Bench hit 45 in 1970 but several came at other positions). Bench had been the only catcher to ever lead either league in home runs.

Fisk hit his 30th homer the first week of August. He was a marvel of old-age efficiency. Whereas now a player of that age producing big numbers would unfortunately raise the specter of medicinal enhancement, in 1985 that was still a few years away. Fisk's impressive results after the off-season strenuous lifting program were the talk of baseball. He continued the regimen throughout the season, something that was also unheard of at the time. The season was no fluke; it was a tribute to Fisk's tenacity and dedication. "In a lot of ways, this could be the most rewarding year I've ever had," he said late in the year. "It's rewarding to work as hard as I did to prepare myself and to be able to see the fruits of that work."

"I have to think the man was stung by what happened last year and felt he had something to prove," said La Russa. "There's a lot of pride in Carlton Fisk."

Fisk's slugging pace slowed somewhat after he strained a ligament in his left wrist in the All-Star Game but he finished with 37 home runs and 107 RBIs. The home runs tied the club record and almost doubled the previous record by a 37-year-old catcher (Ernie Lombardi with 19 in 1945).

Most of the core remained from the 1983 White Sox team. Baines hit .309 with 113 RBIs, Kittle had 26 home runs. Greg Walker, a reserve in 1983, was developing into a good hitter and had 24 home runs and 92 RBIs. Although Britt Burns won 18 games and Seaver 16, the pitching was too thin. Dotson had never recovered from injuries and Bannister slipped to 10–14. The White Sox were in first place from June 11 to June 20, then lost 10 of 11 and slid back. They went 50–41 the rest of the way, but it was only good enough for third place (85–77).

The White Sox were still a solid team—not good enough to win the pennant, but only a few key players away. After their second consecutive disappointing season, however, a drastic shift took place in the front office behavior of the White Sox. Reinsdorf seemed to become bitter over the inability to win a championship despite heavy spending. The team was good, but he wasn't satisfied with just good. The fact that several lucrative long-term contracts had been handed out to players who then became injured or ineffective stoked his discontent. Rather than continue with the program, he abandoned his spending on the Sox, becoming perhaps more interested in the Chicago Bulls basketball team, which he had bought in 1985 and who appeared to have more potential due to their emerging star Michael Jordan. Over the winter, for the first time in the Reinsdorf-Einhorn era, no major additions were made. There were a few trades of equivalently talented mediocre players, but they did not add a single free agent or major star. Radical changes were in store for the White Sox.

They decided to blow up the team. According to the *Sporting News*, Reinsdorf and Einhorn "solicited testimony from several persons" on how to solve the team's problems, but only broadcaster Ken Harrelson offered a "blueprint" to get them a pennant. On October 2, 1985, Harrelson, even though he had never held a management position at any level, moved from the television booth to take over for 15-year general manager Roland Hemond. Possessing the nickname "Hawk," which derived from the beaklike profile of his prodigious proboscis, Harrelson had always been a different sort of baseball man. He didn't just dress himself each day, he made fashion statements, famously sporting Nehru jackets and mod hairstyles in the sixties. He had parlayed a few good years as a player into mammoth contracts by pitting owners against each other and walked away from the game early, leaving a few more good years on the table. Unable to stay completely away from baseball, he became a broadcaster, first in Boston in 1975, then Chicago in 1981. With his folksy southern accent, cowboy hats, and pithy remarks he quickly became a fan favorite. He demonstrated a good baseball mind, with often brilliant, incisive commentary. But moving from the booth to the general manager's position, while not entirely unprecedented, was rarely a good idea. Harrelson had been on good terms with Carlton Fisk when the two were in Boston and he had been one of the few familiar faces near his age when he moved to Chicago. The good terms would soon be just a memory.

With his five-year deal up, coming off a huge season, Fisk expected a big payday. Only six other players in the major leagues had both 30 home runs and 100 RBIs in 1985 and they were all under contract for the next year. The timing appeared to be great. White Sox management did not seem overly eager to have Fisk back, however. They tried a sign-and-trade deal to send him to the Yankees for Don Baylor in December, but that fell through when Fisk and Baylor, both represented by Kapstein, let it be known that they would not waive their rights to agree to the trade as 10–5 men (players with 10 years of major league experience and five with the same club had the right to refuse a trade) and the baseball world was spared the sight of renowned Yankee-hater Carlton Fisk wearing pinstripes. That concluded, the White Sox seemed content to let Fisk test the free agent waters, strangely not acting particularly enthusiastic about retaining a catcher who hit 37 home runs. They let him know they would welcome him back if he was unable to make a deal elsewhere, however.

But there seemed to be curiously little interest in free agents all over baseball that winter. The other big-name free agents also felt a chill. Of the 35 free agents, only four changed teams, and those four were not wanted by their old teams. Most received no offers at all. Finally, with so many free agents still floating around, the Major League Player Relations Committee agreed to extend the deadline two hours and,

The two oldest Fisk boys, winter 1948–49. Calvin is on the left. The happy little guy on the right was already being called Pudgy.
COURTESY LEONA FISK

The Fisk family, circa 1950. Left to right: Leona (holding Conrad), Carlton, Calvin, Cecil, and Cedric. Voracious appetites and plenty of fresh food gave all the boys a healthy pudge. Hard farmwork soon turned it into muscle.
COURTESY LEONA FISK

Carlton, age 5, 1952. COURTESY LEONA FISK

The Charlestown High School undefeated State Champions, 1963. Carlton is in the center, number 20. Other starters include Jim Hogancamp, number 10, Carl McAlister, number 40, George Pebbles, number 42, and Roger Conant, number 32. Coach Silva is on a knee in front holding the plaque. COURTESY ROGER CONANT

Carlton holding high school
basketball hardware, 1963.
COURTESY ROGER CONANT

The reigning American
League Rookie of the Year,
spring training, 1973. NATIONAL
BASEBALL HALL OF FAME LIBRARY,
COOPERSTOWN, NEW YORK

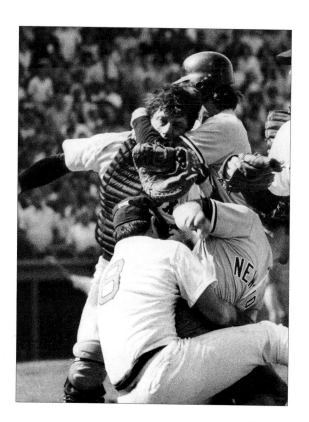

August 1, 1973, Fenway Park. Carlton is in the arms of Yankee Gene Michael. Carl Yastrzemski, number 8, grabs Thurman Munson. It was the official resumption of hostilities between the two teams. AP IMAGES

Carlton was all smiles early in 1974 as both he and the Red Sox were the class of the league. NATIONAL BASEBALL HALL OF FAME LIBRARY, COOPERSTOWN, NEW YORK

Carlton addresses the press inside the jubilant Red Sox clubhouse after sweeping Oakland in the 1975 Playoffs. Carlton hit .417 for the series. There would be more postseason heroics. NATIONAL BASEBALL HALL OF FAME LIBRARY, COOPERSTOWN, NEW YORK

The mask is already off and Carlton is looking up at the ball when he has a brief interlude with Cincinnati Reds batter Ed Armbrister in Game Three of the 1975 World Series. Was it interference? The call is still hotly debated. Umpire Larry Barnett watches. AP IMAGES

October 22, 1975, 12:34 AM. Carlton waves as his twelfth-inning, Game Six drive heads toward immortality. AP IMAGES

Carlton traded socks in 1981.
NATIONAL BASEBALL HALL OF FAME
LIBRARY, COOPERSTOWN, NEW YORK

By 1983, the White Sox were in the postseason. NATIONAL
BASEBALL HALL OF FAME LIBRARY, COOPERSTOWN, NEW YORK

After tagging Bobby Meacham, Carlton lunges to tag Dale Berra for the second out
of a rare double play at home plate at Yankee Stadium, August 2, 1985. AP IMAGES

The Fisk family poses in front of Otsego Lake in Cooperstown, New York, July 23, 2000. Carlton is holding his new Hall of Fame plaque. Left to right: Calvin, Cedric, June, Leona, Carlton, Cecil, Conrad, and Janet. CHARLESTOWN HISTORICAL SOCIETY

Carlton tours the outfield at Chicago's U.S. Cellular Field, May 22, 2008. He was honored by the White Sox in a ceremony before the game. AP IMAGES

after furious last-minute negotiations, Fisk and most of the others signed with their original teams. Carlton had wanted a three-year deal, but was forced to settle for two. He got a raise to $850,000, up from $550,000 in 1985. "My family is happy here," Carlton told reporters at the press conference. "That was worth a lot more than the few dollars more I might have gotten by going someplace else."

"We're delighted we worked it out," a smiling Reinsdorf told the press. "It was a long and difficult negotiation, but a great deal of integrity always remained. The differences were worked out basically because Carlton wanted to come back." As Reinsdorf smiled and talked about integrity, he knew a dirty little secret that would not come out for two years.

When Ken Harrelson took over the job as general manager he immediately made noise with brash proclamations and promises. He put out word around the majors that he was on the prowl for deals. He showed up for spring training games in uniform, with "Hawk 40" on the back, full of enthusiasm and hubris, talking about innovative changes. Unfortunately for the White Sox and their faithful followers, the zany ideas turned out to be mostly annoying and little else. He openly shopped Seaver, the best pitcher on the team, and would end up trading him to Boston June 29 for Steve Lyons. He brought in former reliever Moe Drabowsky to be a sort of second pitching coach, announcing that Drabowsky would be in charge of the bullpen while Duncan would be responsible only for the starters—an unprecedented move that just led to confusion. He gutted the minor league managerial staffs and reduced the number of scouts. Writers speculated that the death watch for La Russa had officially started.

Soon after taking over, Harrelson called Carlton Fisk and asked, "Can you play third base?" Fisk answered, "No, not at this point in my career." For reasons unknown, and without asking him, Harrelson was convinced that Fisk's catching days were over. When Fisk arrived in Florida, he learned that he was the new left fielder. The White Sox catching job was handed to 25-year-old Joel Skinner, who had been up briefly several times in the past few years. In six minor league seasons, the strong-armed Skinner had topped .270 in batting only once.

Fisk made no secret of the fact that he was not happy—with the move or with how it played out. "I just got up one morning and read that I was the left fielder," he said during the spring. "They say this is good for prolonging my career, but I've worked so hard on my conditioning that I never got tired catching. . . . How can I hit 37 homers?"

"I feel uncomfortable with it because I've spent 20 years perfecting a trade, and the majority of those years I have been an All-Star catcher," he explained. "For me to go from that level to where I may only be average may not be comfortable for me."

"You don't put an all-star catcher in left field," he said later. "It makes you feel as though you're not appreciated." He told Peter Gammons, "It's the New Englander in me that says, 'No one is going to tell me what's good for me or what I can't do.' That's like my father. You may be right, but until he says so, you're not. It was demeaning. I thought I'd earned something, and that job was being given to someone else." The forced move "was like having your heart torn out and shoved back on a platter right in your face."

He did not sugarcoat his feelings of insult that his job was given to someone who did not put in the same effort he did. "I hope Joel is ready to take the game seriously this year. That hasn't been the case in the past. He's never yet made the total commitment that a major leaguer has to make to be a winner. I've been disappointed Joel never asked many questions or sought my help in the past."

In addition to being forced to risk embarrassment out in the field, Carlton was giving up a shot at a number of all-time catching records. He had overcome obstacles, fought back from injuries that had claimed almost the equivalent of four seasons, and now the records were within reach—but only if he was behind the plate. During the spring Fisk was overheard saying, incredulously, to Harrelson, "You're ruining my career for Joel Skinner?"

Despite his misgivings, Fisk dutifully trotted out to left field, trying to learn an entirely new position after 15 major league seasons. He did not catch at all during spring training. Although he was a good athlete, it was a struggle. He had to learn all the nuances of outfield play: cutoffs, judging fly balls, game situations, reacting to bounces off the wall. He took hours of extra fly balls. All those years squatting had taken their toll on his legs; he could no longer sprint like he could when he was 20. He went through postgame aerobics and bicycle work four times a week to improve his agility, but it was obvious he would be one of the slowest outfielders in the game.

The season started with Carlton Fisk standing in the unfamiliar territory of left field, and watching. He had always loved the field leadership and constant action afforded by catching. To stand idly by and watch from a perch in left field 300 feet from the action was more than he could bear; it seemed so foreign. When he played left field in front of the Green Monster for the first time he told reporters, "I feel like I'm turning my back on an old friend."

The combination of the forced position change and the leftover feelings of having been insulted by the club, left to hang until the last hour before signing, made Fisk feel unwanted for the first time since moving from Boston. The honeymoon was over. It was a feeling that would only grow in the years to come.

By early May, the left field experiment was put to rest. The team was 7–18 and Skinner, while hitting .157, had thrown out only one of 12 base stealers. In Fisk's first game behind the plate on May 9, he threw out the first two men who tried to steal. He had been hitting .200 as a left fielder, but suddenly his bat seemed rejuvenated by the move, as well as his overall attitude. The White Sox won 10 of the next 13 games with Fisk behind the plate while he hit .308 with 12 RBIs. Moreover, the team ERA was 2.29 in that span, slightly more than half what it was before. Thereafter, Fisk was the regular catcher once again with only an occasional day of rest or as designated hitter. Skinner would be traded in July and play part-time for two other teams over the next five seasons, compiling a lifetime .228 batting average.

The Skinner experiment was part of a trend that would continue for a number of years in which the White Sox ran into trouble through their efforts to prematurely replace Carlton Fisk. In the 1985 draft the White Sox selected, with the fifth pick in the entire draft, a high school catcher from California named Kurt Brown, who would never make it past Triple A in seven minor league seasons. While it was not thought to be such a bad pick at the time, in seven years Carlton Fisk was still playing well in the major leagues, as was the man the White Sox passed over to select Brown—an Arizona State outfielder named Barry Bonds. They also passed up a pretty fair pitcher from USC named Randy Johnson in the same draft.

Although clearly happy about being back at his old position, Fisk was still upset with the circumstances. "I get a little worked up when I start talking about this all over again," he said when asked. "It's been claimed that I've been selfish about this whole thing, that I wanted to catch because I wanted to catch. Well, fine. I'm selfish then. I feel that after what I've done, what I've proven, I deserved to catch. . . . I get a little worked up when I start thinking about how I've been screwed around here." He alluded to a bonus for the previous year's All-Star Game that had not been paid as promised and the "contract business, which was a circus all winter. One thing after another."

After not making any moves to improve the talent over the winter, it was inevitable that the White Sox would perform poorly in 1986. Rather than address the true cause, they fired Tony La Russa after a 26–38 start and brought in Jim Fregosi to be the new manager. La Russa would soon be snapped up by the Oakland A's, and along with his pitching coach Duncan would lead them to the World Series in 1988, 1989, and 1990, then lead the St. Louis Cardinals to the Series in 2004, 2006, and 2011. He would retire with the third most managerial wins in baseball history, behind Connie Mack and John McGraw. Jerry Reinsdorf would later publicly declare that firing La Russa was the worst decision he made in baseball.

During this time, in something of foreshadowing if he was paying close attention, Carlton Fisk got to watch a guy who should have quit a lot sooner. The White Sox signed 41-year-old, 300-game-winning, Hall of Fame–bound pitcher Steve Carlton in August 1986 after he had been released by the Giants, who had signed him in July after he had been released by the Phillies. He had won only six of his last 19 decisions. In an ultimate episode of ignominy, Steve Carlton, who had famously given up talking to the press decades earlier, was forced to endure a humbling press conference in which he appeared to try to make nice with media members. He spoke of problems with his mechanics and the need to only correct a few minor things—assured that he still had a lot of baseball left. It was apparent, however, that he had nothing left and he was the last to know. He stayed with the White Sox through the end of the season and, after being let go, latched on with Cleveland and then Minnesota before finally giving up—a painful sight for fans who remembered his glory days.

The 1986 season ended as frustratingly as it started for Carlton Fisk. He contracted a severe viral illness in midseason. In addition to losing 30 pounds, he experienced night sweats and insomnia and it affected his visual perception. He was in and out of the lineup with the illness. He came back, obviously weak, and went 0-for-25. He spent most of the rest of the season battling to regain his strength. He was perilously close to the Mendoza Line before a late 11-for-33 stretch raised his average to .215 in August. Fregosi benched him temporarily, then the White Sox tried to trade him to Toronto, but the deal fell through when Carlton again refused to waive his rights to agree to the move.

The White Sox blundered through a miserable year as they went 72–90 and were last in the league in batting average, runs, and home runs. Carlton, bothered by the switch to the outfield and the late-season illness along with several nagging injuries, hit .221 with 14 home runs and 63 RBIs in 125 games. The 63 RBIs were still enough for second on the team to Baines's 88—illustrating the futility of the White Sox offense.

Carlton was not alone in his unhappiness in 1986. There were a lot of unhappy people in the clubhouse and press box. Harrelson resigned after the season, but the damage was done. The organization was a mess and it would take years to build the team back up to respectability.

16 Colluded Waters

AFTER ANOTHER GRUELING WINTER OF WORKOUTS, Carlton Fisk was once again healthy and listed as a catcher. But he soon discovered that he was no longer considered the starter. The White Sox catching job was given to 23-year-old rookie Ron Karkovice, a great-looking defensive talent who had been the White Sox' first round draft choice out of high school in 1982. Karkovice had spent three years at AA, and had hit .282 with 20 home runs in 1986. He had been brought up to Chicago in August of 1986 and played fairly well while subbing for the ailing Fisk. Manager Jim Fregosi continually assured the press that he had faith in Fisk but at the same time offered what seemed to be thinly veiled insults, such as saying that he hoped to get him 400 at bats (only 400 for the man who was second on the team in RBIs the previous season?) at various positions such as first base, outfield, designated hitter, and catcher. Catcher was conspicuously listed last.

Karkovice got off to a horrendous start. Almost every day was an o-fer at the plate. Once, when Karkovice was given a day off, he was sitting in the bullpen that was on the field, down the foul line, when Fisk hit a foul fly ball. While chasing it, the Seattle outfielder ran into Karkovice, resulting in an interference call and Fisk was ruled out. A teammate quipped, "Karkovice even makes outs when he doesn't play." In mid-May, with Karkovice hitting .078 with four hits and 20 strikeouts in 51 at bats, Fisk was reinstated as the regular catcher. Previously struggling himself to stay above .220, Fisk began hitting well after returning to his spot and soon launched an 11-game streak in which he hit .396 (19-for-48) with five home runs and 16 RBIs.

Along with battling the frustration of being in a different position each day as the team continued to lose, Fisk became annoyed at management, which he felt was trying to save money rather than win.

Baines and Guillen were proven stars. Homegrown first baseman Greg Walker was a solid hitter and rookie Bobby Thigpen emerged as the ace of the bullpen but, once again, the team had made no moves to improve obvious trouble spots. Whereas the White Sox had always had a good mix of young players and veterans, suddenly, overnight, Carlton Fisk was one of the few veterans left. There was also a series of petty rules put in place by new general manager Larry Himes. Although Himes would eventually engineer the building of a playoff caliber team in the early 1990s, he had a talent for rubbing people the wrong way. Himes fined at least three players for not wearing socks with their dress clothes in the clubhouse in 1987. In July, he banned beer from the clubhouse and team flights, a move that was, not surprisingly, very unpopular. As the team elder, Fisk made his feelings known. "Let's face it," he told reporters, "pizza and a Sprite after games just don't get it." Part of the ritual of baseball Carlton had always loved was sitting in the clubhouse with teammates and discussing the game over a beer. Now they seemed to be encouraged to exit and go their separate ways as soon as the game was finished.

A few weeks later, Himes took as literal a comment by Fisk claiming to keep a cooler of beer in his locker. In a move that would be comical if it wasn't so absurd—Captain Queeg searching for missing strawberries while the USS *Caine* founders—Himes alerted Comiskey Park security to detain Fisk at the gate and search him for beer. "I wish I'd known that [ahead of time]," Carlton told reporters. "I would have brought papaya juice in so they could all have some. If he really thought I'd try to do something like that, it shows he doesn't know me."

Soon, Carlton Fisk was given another very good reason to distrust and dislike management. There had been questions all along about why he hadn't been rewarded after his big year of 1985; why no major league team wanted a catcher who hit 37 home runs. In 1984, 16 of the 26 major league teams had signed free agents from other teams. In 1985, with the exception of a couple of players that the former teams made clear were not wanted, that number dropped to zero. In fact, only one of the 29 available free agents received a bona fide offer from another club before his former team announced it did not intend to re-sign him. Thinking that the sudden, total loss of interest by every single team was highly suspicious, the Players Association filed a class-action grievance, claiming that owners were guilty of collusion to restrict the free agent market. Once again, Carlton Fisk was at the center of a controversy that would be decided by the grievance arbitration process.

The basis of the case was that the owners had violated Article 18 of the Collective Bargaining Agreement, which read: "The utilization or non-utilization of rights under [the free agency provision] is an individual matter to be determined solely by each Player and each Club for his or its own benefit. Players shall not act in concert with other Players and Clubs shall not act in concert with other Clubs." This clause had been added at the request of management during the 1976 CBA negotiations. Owners still remembered the episode in 1966 in which Sandy Koufax and Don Drysdale jointly held up the Dodgers. The two superstar pitchers told Dodger management that neither would sign unless the demands of both were met. Owners wanted to make sure something like that never happened again. The union responded with a counterproposal: that wording be added to prevent owners from acting in concert also. Myopically not foreseeing a situation in which they would want to, the owners easily agreed.

As free agency drove salaries out of control during the ensuing decade, owners realized they had a problem, and a major part of that problem was the fact that they couldn't control themselves. On October 22, 1985, during the World Series, baseball commissioner Peter Ueberroth addressed owners in St. Louis at the headquarters of Anheuser-Busch and, lecturing them on the financial folly that had been affecting their profits, said, "If I sat each one of you down in front of a red button and a black button and I said, 'Push the red button and you'd win the World Series but lose $10 million. Push the black button and you would have a $4 million profit and you'd finish in the middle.' You are so damned dumb. Most of you would push the red button." He challenged them to look in the mirror and figure out what was wrong with that logic. "You are smart businessmen. You all agree we have a problem. Go solve it."

A few weeks later at a meeting of general managers, Ueberroth told them, "It's not smart to sign long-term contracts. They force clubs to want to make similar signings. Don't be dumb. We have a five-year agreement with labor." The owners apparently got the message.

The key word of Article 18 was "concert." The lawyers who drew up the agreement had specifically selected the word over several other possibilities. According to common-law definition, "acting in concert" is defined as working toward a common goal, whether or not pursuant to an express agreement. How much direct vocalization was given to the plan will never be known, as the involved refused to talk, but there can be no question that the common goal was achieved: free agency was stopped dead in its tracks. Veteran Chicago sportswriter Jerome Holtzman later wrote that of the prominent free agents that year, "Only Fisk got as much as a nibble from another team. George Steinbrenner of the Yankees admitted he made an offer for Fisk but it was withdrawn after he got a call from White Sox chairman Jerry Reinsdorf." For the first time, amazingly, all owners had acted together without a solitary renegade running off to stack his own team. It was great. But, unfortunately for them, it was also expressly forbidden by the contract they had signed.

Arbitrator Thomas Roberts conducted 32 days of hearings that were scheduled over almost a year and reviewed evidence that filled 5,674 transcript pages. The owners' counsel testified to Roberts that each team had made a totally independent and rational decision to forgo free agents. Apparently feeling that he did not believe their argument, halfway through the hearing the owners pulled a Saturday Night Massacre and fired Roberts. He was reinstated to finish the process after a grievance was filed by the Players Association (owners later successfully fired him after the case was concluded). In September of 1987, Roberts issued his ruling: owners had been guilty of collusion— they had worked together on an understanding not to pursue the free agents of other clubs, thereby forcing the players to re-sign with their original clubs at a much lower rate than they would have if true free market forces had been in effect. Roberts would later assess fines of $10.5 million, which would be spread among the free agents of 1985.

After acrimonious negotiations, Fisk signed a one-year contract with the White Sox in December 1987 for $700,000. Even though he had placed highly among major league catchers with 23 home runs and 71 RBIs, he was forced to take a pay cut from the $875,000 he had made in 1987. Both he and the White Sox added nonfinancial demands to the deal: the White Sox wanted his assurance he'd take an active leadership role with the young pitching staff (a role he'd taken his entire career) and Carlton wanted a guarantee he'd go to camp as the starting catcher (a luxury he had not enjoyed the previous two years).

In January 1988, in the conclusion of the collusion ruling, Roberts stated that seven players, most prominently Kirk Gibson and Carlton Fisk, were free to test the waters as pseudo–free agents—they could hear offers from other teams without relinquishing their current contracts until March 1. Gibson left the Tigers and signed with the Dodgers for three years and $4.5 million and would lead them to the World Series championship that fall. Fisk did not have as much luck. Several teams mentioned that they wouldn't waste their time because they didn't think he would seriously consider moving at this point in his career. A few other teams showed mild interest but, scared by Kapstein's $1.2 million asking price, did not submit serious bids. The Kansas City Royals were the only team to negotiate with Kapstein, but they would not even match the $700,000 for the 40-year-old catcher, no matter what his hitting numbers had been in 1987.

The final chapter of the collusion fiasco came in 1990 with a $280 million award (added on top of the previous fine), which was to cover collusion from the years of 1985 to 1987. The money was given to the Players Association in one lump for appropriate distribution to affected players. Appropriate distribution turned out to be an elusive premise, however. Unable to come up with a better plan to divvy up the loot, the Players Association mailed questionnaires to all players and asked them to submit their claims. Not surprisingly, 800 players responded with claims that totaled more than $1 billion. Some players asked for an elaborate pyramiding amount that compounded each year over five years. Some players who were never free agents claimed that the overall market had been held down and, thus, they deserved compensation. One ex-player, Babe Dahlgren, requested compensation for allegedly being colluded against back in the 1940s. Some of the more egregious claims resulted in cases that went all the way to the Supreme Court, dragging out through 2001. The final payments were not made until 2005—20 years after the original collusion.

The 1988 season was another in a seemingly endless line of rebuilding years for the Chicago White Sox. They were a bad team. Only Fisk, Baines, Walker, and Guillen were left from the Harrelson regime of just two years earlier. The roster was filled with young—and cheap—players. Fisk was becoming a stranger, years older than his teammates except for 39-year-old pitcher Jerry Reuss, who had been added in the off-season. The starting rotation averaged 24.8 years old. After 31-year-old journeyman outfielder Gary Redus was traded in July, Fisk and Reuss were the only players on the team over 30.

Regardless, Fisk continued to defy time and doggedly plugged along on the field. And he let everyone know he preferred catching. He explained his ability to keep going at the demanding position saying, "When you play this game, you have to be of a singular mind and purpose."

Carlton Fisk was indeed of a singular mind and purpose. He continued his fanatical workout regimen. To save on time driving to the gym, he built a state-of-the-art weight room in his home in Lockport. Racks of weights, a couple of mats, and lifting benches filled the glassed-in, solarium-like room in the back of the house where he worked out most days. He continued to drive to Yeager's twice a week during the winter to work with Claussen. His off-season routine included four days a week of three-hour workouts and two days of 90 minutes. He concentrated on his legs three days and upper body two; the rest was aerobic work. "The commitment to being the best you can be doesn't have an easy way out," he told a visiting reporter. "I remember talking to Carl Yastrzemski. Yaz had one of the greatest seasons ever [in 1967] after working out with a trainer who beat the hell out of him. I asked Yaz why he never went back to the guy again afterward, and his face was pained when he answered me: 'Too hard. I didn't want to go through it again.' That always stuck with me. Success has no shortcuts, only a high price of pain and humiliation."

Because of Fisk's devotion to the workouts, his legs were in better shape than they had ever been. During the season he lifted three or four nights a week in the clubhouse weight room—after catching nine innings—sometimes not finishing his workout until 1 or 2 A.M. He was on a first-name basis with the custodial and security people in every American League stadium. "I wonder why I'm doing it," Carlton said. "But most of the time, it's a 'work equals reward' kind of thought process." He put in the work and got the reward. The regimen allowed him to continue to outperform much younger men. He won the Silver Slugger Award as the best-hitting American League catcher in 1988 with a .277 average and 19 home runs at the age of 41.

Jeff Torborg was named White Sox manager for 1989. Animated, full of emotion and enthusiasm, Torborg was popular with his players. A former catcher himself, Torborg appreciated what Carlton Fisk provided to the team: "You can't measure what he means. It's one of those intangibles, especially for a young pitching staff. He controls the pitchers, he gives them confidence. . . . When he puts down a sign, they believe."

Reliever Donn Pall had revered Fisk while growing up in Chicago. Now Pall was in the position every kid dreams of: a teammate of his idol. "When I came up to the White Sox [1988] and first pitched to him, I was a little bit nervous," he says. "He was one of the guys I had admired and looked up to. I was almost afraid to go up to him at first. But I thoroughly enjoyed playing with him. He was just a great guy to have on your team. He was a great catcher to throw to. He was such a smart guy. He knew all the hitters and their tendencies. For a pitcher, it was like having a cheat sheet when he was back there. He just knew what to do. And he would let you know what he wanted. My first game, I hadn't really met him yet, I had just been called up. I was facing Jose Canseco. Fisk called for a fastball on the inside corner—he liked you to throw hard inside. I guess my pitch drifted a bit too far over the plate and Canseco drilled it into the upper deck, luckily foul by a few feet. After the game, Fisk grabbed me in the clubhouse and said, 'When I want the fastball inside, I want it *in here.*' He pounded me in the chest a few times. 'In here.' And he pounded me in the chest again, really hard. What do you say to that? 'Yes sir.' But he knew what he wanted and how to get guys out. That's why they called him the Commander. He ran the show.

"Another game I'll never forget," continues Pall, "Robin Yount was the batter, one of the best hitters in the league. Fisk calls for a fastball inside. My best pitch was a split finger/forkball, my fastball wasn't that great, maybe 85 tops. So he puts down a one and motions inside. I throw it, strike one. I'm thinking, 'I set him up, now come back with the forkball.' And Fisk puts down one, inside again. I think, 'Jeez, back to back?' But I do what he says and throw it, strike two. Now I'm thinking, 'Okay, now I've really got him set up for the off-speed stuff.' And Fisk comes back again, fastball, inside. I thought, 'No way.' So I shook him off. It was always a little unnerving to shake him off but there was no way I was going to throw Yount three straight fastballs. And Fisk just looks at me through the mask and nodded, 'Yes.' I had never had a catcher shake off my shake-off before, but what are you going to do? So I threw the pitch he wanted and it broke Yount's bat for an easy out. And I looked back at home plate and Fisk is just standing there with his hands on his hips looking at me, like 'I told you.'"

"He helped [my career] tremendously," said Jack McDowell, who was the fifth pick in the 1987 draft out of Stanford. McDowell won 59 games in three seasons for the White Sox from 1991 to 1993 and also won the

Cy Young Award in 1993. "I really only had about one and a half pitches when I started. I had a fastball and was developing the split finger pitch. I would have gotten killed without a catcher like him. He taught me how to use my fastball. There were games when I'd throw twenty, twenty-five fastballs in a row. Carlton, though, was moving them around . . . in and out, up and down and I was able to succeed. The way he prepared, the class he had, the way he played the game . . . you can't get better than him."

Fisk didn't force his views on other players or act like the clubhouse know-it-all. During games, he made sure he got what he wanted from the pitcher and he was always available afterward. Some players took advantage of his knowledge and some didn't. He developed a bond with the pitchers who sought his help, like McDowell, Bobby Thigpen, Greg Hibbard, and Pall. Hibbard said he "followed every order and suggestion" from Fisk without question.

"He was always great to talk to—he was more than willing to talk to guys and discuss baseball and how to pitch to certain guys," says Pall. "He knew so much baseball, it was like having an extra pitching coach on the team. We all had so much respect for him."

The moribund offense of the White Sox showed a marked improvement in 1989, which Fisk attributed to the tutelage of Walt Hriniak, who joined the team as hitting coach. Fisk enjoyed the reunion with the native of New England who had worked with him in Boston. They spent hours together in the bowels of stadiums throughout the American League, in batting cages, doing drills, hitting, talking. Hriniak understood the art of hitting, as did his mentor Charlie Lau. Hriniak was instrumental at this stage in helping Carlton make the adjustments that every aging hitter must make if he is to continue being effective; learning ways to compensate for the inevitable drop in bat speed, not trying to pull the ball too much, taking what the pitcher gives. Fisk also adjusted his technique to include removing his top hand at the end of the swing to get more extension. He later called Hriniak the single most important person in his baseball life.

Although the White Sox hit better and were 37–36 after the All-Star break, they were still a woeful team overall. They had suffered through three straight dreadful seasons of 77, 71, and 69 wins from 1987 to 1989. Despite the team's poor performance, Fisk continued to show up every day and play hard. In 1989 he led all major league catchers in RBIs with 68 and was second in batting average (.293). And during the 1988 and 1989 seasons, the ERA of the Chicago staff was 0.90 lower when Fisk caught than it was with anyone else behind the plate. At 42 years old, he was not only playing, he was considered to be the best all-around catcher in the American League according to a *Sports Illustrated* poll of coaches and managers taken in 1989. "It isn't just his longevity that makes Fisk great," said Torborg in agreement. "He's still the best in the league right now."

Frustrations mounted, however, as the team traded Harold Baines, their most consistent player for a decade, to the Rangers for pitcher Wilson Alvarez and a skinny outfield prospect named Sammy Sosa. A general malaise had settled over the White Sox organization. The Cubs had taken over Chicago. In addition to the mystique of Wrigley Field, an endearing historical pathos, and more colorful players, they had the marketing power of the Tribune Company, which had added the Cubs to their family in 1981. That family included the WGN television superstation and the city's largest newspaper. Einhorn's experiment with pay-per-view baseball had been a disaster in the pocketbook, but even more importantly in the battle for the hearts of Chicagoland fans. Chicago did not have the cable infrastructure at the time and bad Cub teams garnered many more fans with their ubiquitous presence on free television. Harry Caray, who had been a popular presence in the White Sox broadcasting booth from 1971 to 1982, had recognized the folly of pay-per-view and had jumped to the Cubs in 1983 and become a baseball broadcasting icon. "They [White Sox] wanted to sign me again, but with SportsVision, the White Sox are the best-kept secret in Chicago," Caray said late in 1983. "If their games were on free TV, they'd own the town now and be a byword across the nation. . . . They were talking about reaching 50,000 homes on pay TV instead of the 22 million people who watch the Cubs on WGN."

After winning the West and drawing a record 2.13 million fans in 1983, the White Sox were the toast of Chicago. They drew more than two million again in 1984, even though they had slipped to only 74 wins. Then the Cubs won their division in 1984, the Bears had a great team in 1985, and the Bulls of Michael Jordan took over the city. The White Sox were once again bottom-feeders in the Windy City. Comiskey Park, built in 1910, was the oldest in the majors and had the worst sight lines—it was no nostalgic jewel like Wrigley or Fenway. Reinsdorf and Einhorn began clamoring for a new stadium. They threatened to move the team to St. Petersburg unless the Illinois state legislature passed a generous financial aid package and, although they got the deal they wanted, the protracted public debate caused more damage to their image. Fisk was irritated that the timetable for the team now seemed to be geared toward opening the new park; they were wasting his last few years.

17 Respect the Game

CARLTON FISK WAS A LION IN WINTER. The fierce pride and passion for playing the game of baseball the right way had never wavered. He continued to work as hard, or harder, off the field than he ever had. As he said in a Nike commercial while walking away from a dark, sweaty weight room, "I didn't have to do this to stay competitive before. But hey, I'm not 40 anymore."

May 22, 1990, the White Sox were in Yankee Stadium, facing the Yankees and their 22-year-old rookie center fielder Deion Sanders. Neon Deion (aka Prime Time) was one of the first players to arrive in the majors already carrying his own personal brand. A two-time All-American football player at Florida State, Sanders had been the fifth player taken in the 1989 NFL draft and signed a four-year, $4 million contract with the Atlanta Falcons. He had also convinced the New York Yankees to pay him $100,000 to play baseball as a hobby.

While possessing blazing speed (his 4.2 time in the 40 at the NFL combine was the second fastest in history behind Bo Jackson), Sanders was far from a finished product on the baseball field. In 1989, Sanders had admitted to journalist Pat Jordan that he didn't even like baseball. "I'm only using it as leverage for football. . . . Baseball is boring to me because I'm not dominating in it."

Sanders gave new meaning to the term showboat. He wore shades indoors and enough gold around his neck to sink a Spanish galleon. He referred to himself in the third person, by his self-given nickname, as in "Prime Time wakes up every morning and says to the mirror, 'Mirror, mirror on the wall, who's the flashiest, best-dressed of them all?' And every morning the mirror says, 'You, Prime Time.'" Everything about him, from the way he wore his pants to the way he stepped into the batter's box screamed, "Look at me." When Sanders spotted a television camera and turned on his smile, Con Edison customers throughout the Northeast experienced a power drain.

Seeking a rapid return on his investment and, as always, loving to create a buzz, George Steinbrenner had rushed Sanders to the big leagues, bypassing the traditional training process that took place in the minors. After flopping early in the 1990 season, Sanders had been sent down to AAA and had only recently been recalled, but he didn't let a lack of experience or results take away from his style. He entered the White Sox game with a cool .100 batting average and more media coverage than most All-Stars.

Playing in his 24th major league game, Sanders led off the bottom of the first for the Yankees and, as was becoming his custom, drew a dollar sign in the dirt with his bat before stepping into the box. Peering through his mask behind the plate, Carlton Fisk, playing in his 2,172nd major league game (in his fourth decade), watched and thought, "This guy is driving me crazy already."

In the third inning, with one out and a man on third, Sanders hit a high pop-up toward the shortstop. He took a couple of steps, stopped and watched the ball, then turned and headed for the dugout. Fisk exploded, "Run the f***ing ball out, you piece of shit!" Sanders continued into the dugout without looking back.

The next time Sanders came up, Fisk pierced him with a steely stare as he approached the plate, but Sanders avoided eye contact. Instead, he drew his dollar sign in the dirt again—the very dirt Carlton Fisk and Thurman Munson had fought so desperately over during the seventies. Fisk felt the presence of Yankee Stadium ghosts. Sanders mumbled something inaudible with his head down. "What did you say?" Fisk demanded.

"Hey, man, the days of slavery are over," Sanders replied. Fisk walked in front of the plate, face-to-face with Sanders, and started yelling. Perhaps only because they felt they were supposed to, confused teammates trotted in from both dugouts and bullpens. There was no pushing or shoving as in most baseball fights, only standing around, trying to figure out what the heck was going on. The umpire quickly wedged himself between Fisk and Sanders and order was restored.

After the game, Sanders dismissed the incident when questioned by the press, saying only, "We just said we loved each other. The whole thing was nothing."

Fisk declined comment until the next night, then explained that he told Sanders, "There's a right way and a wrong way to play this game." He thought a moment, reminded of the epic battles he had waged against pinstriped sonsabitches over the years, then added, "It's the Yankee pride and the Yankee pinstripes involved here. Some of those guys have got to be turning over in their graves. . . . I play for the other team, but that offends me.

"There's no racial issue involved. It's professional etiquette. There's something special about Yankee Stadium, and that's why I didn't talk about it [last] night. I might have said something I'd be sorry for. I'm either old, or old and sentimental. Either way, I know what's right and what's wrong."

Fisk was infuriated that Sanders had tried to make race an issue in the incident, unjustly accusing him of hating a man's color when what he really hated was his attitude. Fisk told Sanders, "I don't care whether you are black or blue or pink or red. . . . If you don't start playing this game right, I'm going to kick your butt right here."

Sanders continued to downplay the incident to reporters, adding, "I'll tell you what, he couldn't say on TV what he said to me." It was reported that an unnamed Yankee coach confirmed that Fisk's version of the incident was accurate.

White Sox teammates found themselves laughing when they learned the details. "We didn't know what was going on at first," says Donn Pall. "We were out in the bullpen and suddenly Fisk was standing up in Sanders's face yelling. But afterwards, everybody on the team was thrilled he did what he did. Everybody knew Fisk was all about playing the game the right way, doing things right and respecting the game. We knew exactly where Fisk was coming from. You know, it's kind of funny. Of all the guys in the league, Sanders picked the wrong one to hotdog in front of."

The episode continued to get play in the media for weeks. It touched a nerve because of the contrast between the two players: Fisk's obvious devotion to the game and his reputation for hard work versus Sanders's baseless hubris. Sanders proceeded to hit .158 for the Yankees in 1990 and bolted the team in August when they refused his in-season demand for $2 million, leaving to join the Falcons. "Me! Me! Me! I! I! I! His selfishness offends me," Carlton said.

"It happened because I was offended," Fisk told a reporter in August. "I've never even done that to a teammate. I've talked to them, but have never yelled and screamed. Why would I get upset because a guy in a Yankee uniform is pimping around the field like he does? I don't know. I guess I had enough. There are certain 'stripes' you must earn before you can go about the way you put your mustard on. Sure, I'm an old dinosaur from way back, but I've put a lot of my life and a lot of my time into being who I am, what I do and how well I do it."

In 2005, reflecting on the incident, Fisk said, "The most storied and important part of my career was playing against the Yankees. As miserable as it was sometimes, I just cherished that confrontation because that's what you play for. This guy shows up and he's in a Yankees uniform. . . . He used to piss me off so bad because he was not a baseball player and he tried to bring his shtick into the area of baseball. I thought baseball was more hallowed than that. . . . After the game I was talking to Bo Jackson [his White Sox teammate who also played in the NFL], 'I came so close to kicking his ass.' And Bo said, 'You'd have pushed him into the cheap seats, he's pretty light in the ass.'"

L'affaire Sanders grew in stature with time. It cemented Carlton Fisk's place with a new generation of fans. Doing nothing more than adhering to the code by which he had lived his whole life, he had become the game's moral compass, the standard-bearer for old-school values. Reflecting on the episode, one sportswriter said Fisk should be nominated for baseball's man of the year award. Fisk was, as stated in *Baseball Digest*, "caretaker of the game's virtues." Other major leaguers and former players applauded his actions. There was a ring of nostalgia and truth in his words. He was taking a stand against all that people hated about the modern game, saying what needed to be said, what a lot of other people wanted to say, or hoped someone else would say. Writers started coming to him more frequently for his opinions.

Although he had fought hard during negotiations for his contracts, Fisk had never renegotiated in mid-contract for better terms, as became common practice for a lot of athletes. To him, a deal was a deal; a handshake meant something. After a good 1990 season, he was asked by reporters if he would renegotiate as salaries continued to escalate. His two-year deal, in which the second year would pay him $1.25 million, was already obsolete, eclipsed by exploding salaries. That winter, catchers Darren Daulton of the Phillies and Lance Parrish of the Angels had vaulted past him, signing for $2.25 million each. Don Slaught, a backup catcher for the Pirates, signed for $1 million. Fisk negated the thought. "Renegotiation doesn't show me much about a person's character," he said matter-of-factly.

He spoke of the discipline involved in the pursuit of excellence and lamented that he didn't see that dedication in young players; their prime motivation seemed only to be paid as the best, not to perform or be recognized as the best. "What I really believe is probably an indictment of today's young kids. . . . They're always looking for shortcuts. . . . Families aren't as strict as when I was growing up. When I was a kid, it was 'shovel the driveway, mow the lawn, hoe the garden, and then go over to grandpa's house and do the same damned thing.' Now, though, the kids use a riding mower and a snowblower. And instead of walking or riding a bicycle, they have motorcycles or Camaro IROCs. Sure, all parents want a less stressful existence for their kid—they don't want any 'holes' in the kid's path. But if you eliminate those holes, then how will that kid know how to get out of trouble when he gets into it?"

He added another time, "A lot of young people's attitudes within the game today reflect people's attitudes within society. It's a little scary, when the country as a whole is creeping further and further away from the history that made this country what it was. . . . Some of that same attitude prevails in baseball. There's no sense of the game."

Carlton Fisk summed up his philosophy when he said, "The commitment to being the best doesn't have an easy way out."

Sure, he came off sounding like a curmudgeon or someone writing posters for a high school football team's locker room, but who could argue with Carlton Fisk when he spoke of discipline and dedication. Here was a man, older than most beer-league softball players, who spent his nights squatting over and over for two to three hours, flagging down 90-mile-per-hour fastballs, and then climbing the stairs to the weight room and sweating for another hour or more after everyone else had gone home.

While the actuarial tables said he should have been finished as a catcher sometime in the early eighties, Carlton continued to play year after year at the same high level he had established for himself. Each year baseball people expected to see him suddenly begin acting his age, but each year—other than a few ruined by injuries—he continued to act as though he had found the fountain of youth. He had. For Carlton Fisk the fountain of youth was in the sweaty weight room.

Manager Torborg talked about his dedication: "I never knew how hard he worked until I got here last year. There'd be nights I'd sit in my office until maybe 1 A.M., brooding after we lost, and then, thinking everyone else had gone home, I'd start to leave. But here would come Carlton soaking with sweat after working out in the weight room. What discipline."

Eddie Einhorn recalled a night in which he was ready to leave late after a game and remembered he had left something. Hearing a noise in the deserted clubhouse, he investigated and found Carlton Fisk. "No one else was around. The clubhouse was empty. Everyone had gone home. But there was Pudge, sweating like the game had just ended."

Discipline and self-sacrifice. He had taken better care of his body than the average ballplayer throughout his career, and now that restraint helped out as well. He had never smoked, even when, early in his career, over half of all baseball players smoked, many between innings. He had never been a big drinker. "It was a badge of courage to go drinking, then come in the next day and play the game in the bag," Fisk said. "I couldn't do it."

Because of the discipline and self-sacrifice, he now began to seriously challenge the boundaries of age and performance. The blown-out knee, broken right arm, two broken hands, countless torn muscles and ligaments, had all been overcome. Once thought of as brittle, Carlton Fisk had become an iron man in his old age. Until 1985, no catcher in major league history had ever caught 100 games in a season after the age of 36. Carlton did that, along with Bob Boone of the Royals, and kept going. He would finish with four seasons of catching at least 100 games *after* he turned 36. With his 100th stolen base in 1985, he had become the only catcher to ever hit more than 100 home runs while stealing 100 bases. In 1987, he had become the oldest catcher in history to hit 20 home runs in a season.

In 1987 he hit his 300th home run, becoming only the third catcher (after Yogi Berra and Johnny Bench) to have 300 home runs, 1,000 runs scored, and 1,000 RBIs. When he caught his 1,807th game in August, 1988, he broke the American League record for most games as a catcher, which had been held by Rick Ferrell, who caught for the Brown, Red Sox, and Senators from 1929–1947. In 1989, he passed Yogi Berra for most American League home runs by a catcher with 307. After the game, when a reporter asked him who sent the champagne he was drinking in the clubhouse to celebrate, he smiled and said, "It wasn't Larry," referring to general manager Larry Himes and the 1987 alcohol ban.

On August 9, 1990, Carlton hit his 327th home run as a catcher to tie Johnny Bench for the most in baseball history. He broke the record August 17. He had also become the all-time leader for home runs as a White Sox.

In 1991, he would become the oldest position player used in an All-Star Game. When he singled in the sixth inning, he was the oldest player to ever get a hit in the All-Star Game, 19 years after his hit in the 1972 game.

Carlton Fisk and Ozzie Guillen were appointed co-captains for the 1990 season, the first captains for the White Sox since 1930. Carlton had been the unofficial captain, the face of the franchise and acknowledged leader for years. "Just being around a guy like that makes a difference," said the motormouthed Guillen, with whom Carlton developed a close relationship built on respect for one another's talent and desire. "It's his attitude, his presence."

Playing in the final season in eighty-year-old Comiskey Park, the White Sox made it a season to remember. Consensus picks to finish in the basement, they won five of their first six games and never slowed down. They were 28–16 by the end of May and were baseball's biggest surprise, bearing no resemblance to the 92-loss team of the previous year.

Larry Himes had pulled off some great drafts in the late 1980s, as well as adding promising minor leaguers in trades. That talent had been developed in the minors and was now arriving in Chicago. Sweet-swinging third baseman Robin Ventura, starting pitchers Jack McDowell and Greg Hibbard, bullpen ace Bobby Thigpen, and center fielder Lance Johnson, all 26 or younger, were now impact players. In addition, monstrous slugger Frank Thomas was called up August 2 and immediately began the type of hard hitting that would carry him to the Hall of Fame, batting .330 for the rest of the season. The White Sox average age was 27.7, the youngest in the majors, and the number was considerably lower if you dropped the 42-year-old catcher from the equation.

Suddenly—unexpectedly—baseball was fun again on Chicago's South Side. White Sox tickets were once again the hottest tickets in town. After barely drawing one million in 1989, attendance topped 1.8 million for 1990, the third highest in team history. The incurably optimistic Torborg had the team playing above their heads, believing in themselves and playing the right way. The bullpen was fantastic all year, led by Thigpen's major league record 57 saves. The team ERA of the young staff, under Fisk's experienced direction, was 3.61, the second lowest in the league. Without much power, or hitting in general for that matter (Ivan Calderon led the team with 74 RBIs and Fisk's 18 home runs and .285 batting average were both team highs), the White Sox stayed in contention. "Everybody did their job," says Pall. "We found ways to win games."

It became known as the year of doing the little things; clutch hits, solid defense, and taking advantage of opportunities. They won one game on a wild pitch; another time Kittle was hit in the leg with a throw while on the base path, allowing the winning run to score. Fisk was hit in the back by a curveball with the bases loaded to force in the winning run in another. In July, the Yankees' Andy Hawkins threw a no-hitter at the White Sox but lost 4–0 when consecutive outfield errors in the eighth gave them four unearned runs. They were a threat to suicide squeeze at any time, with anyone at the plate. They played great fundamentals and didn't beat themselves. They never believed they were out of a game.

The exuberant young White Sox showed what Torborg referred to as "quiet character" and were close enough, and pesky enough, that they were able to get under the skin of opponents and ignite a war of words—something they hadn't been able to do in years. In a late June series in Oakland, the White Sox combined great pitching and timely hitting to sweep the two-time defending league champs. Jack McDowell, showing no signs of being intimidated by the bulging biceps of the A's Bash Brothers, and perhaps with a little encouragement from his catcher to work hard inside, plunked both Jose Canseco and Mark McGwire. After giving up the go-ahead run in the 10th inning of the series finale, Oakland's three-time 20-game-winning pitcher Dave Stewart took exception to some of the catcalls coming from the jubilant White Sox dugout (they may have been showing character but they definitely weren't quiet). Stewart demonstratively invited one and all to kiss his posterior region. They, of course, declined. After the game, Stewart lashed out in the media, saying Jack McDowell was a busher who belonged in AA and calling Steve Lyons a "borderline jerk" who should be selling insurance instead of playing major league baseball. He then added the immortal line: "There aren't any guys over there who could hold my jock as far as I'm concerned, except Carlton Fisk, Kittle, and Calderon, maybe."

Stewart's comments, as could be expected, delighted the White Sox players—it's great to be noticed. When asked by reporters whether they could indeed hold Stewart's jock, Guillen replied, "I don't care, I'm just here to be rich." Kittle added, "It's in my locker," and pointed to a jockstrap, with "Stewart, #34" written on the waistband, hanging from a hook supporting a steel weighted ball. One day later the White Sox moved into first place for the first time since 1985. In August when the A's visited Chicago, the White Sox beat Stewart 11–1 in front of a packed, electrified crowd and after Sosa put the game away with an emphatic rocket to the upper deck, jockstraps rained down on the field, hurled by jubilant fans.

The surprising Sox were 48–30 at the All-Star break and continued to battle the A's for first. The 1990 White Sox played well throughout the season and shocked the baseball world by finishing with 94 wins, third most in baseball. Unfortunately, the A's were just too strong and won 103, taking the division. Chicago missed the playoffs. "That was just a terrific year," says Pall. "Nobody had expected anything out of us at all. It would have been a great way to send the old park out by making the playoffs, but there was no wild card back then." The team became one of the all-time favorites and helped launch a new generation of White Sox fans.

The White Sox closed out the year by participating in the last game ever at historic Comiskey Park. Celebrities and politicians were everywhere, even in the clubhouse and trainer's room. Players couldn't help but get a feeling of awe and reverence when they considered the players the tunnels and dugouts had held over the years. Comiskey Park had been the site of the first All-Star Game, memorable World Series, including the Black Sox scandal, and for years had been the home of the annual Negro League All-Star Game, where the best talent never seen in major league games competed. It was a relic of baseball history, but its best days were clearly behind it. The game had passed it by. While many fans became sentimental at the closing, sentiment never interfered with progress—the game would continue without the old park, and never look back.

18 Escorted Out

CONTRACT NEGOTIATIONS BETWEEN CARLTON FISK and the Chicago White Sox had been difficult for a number of years. After the 1991 season they became personal and vicious. Even though Fisk had hit 18 home runs with 74 RBIs in 1991 (the third most home runs and fourth most RBIs of any catcher in major league baseball), the White Sox declined to pick up the $2.3 million option year of his previous contract. To make matters worse, he learned the news from the media; no one in the front office thought it important to tell him. The team offered him only $500,000 to come back for 1992. "Pudge has two options," new general manager Ron Schueler told reporters, "he can uproot his family and go elsewhere or he can suck up his pride and prove us wrong by having a great year." *Suck up his pride*? Not exactly words of respect for the man who had been the face of the franchise for a decade. Schueler loosed a further volley that pierced the heart of his catcher when he complained that Jeff Torborg (who left to manage the Mets in 1992) had let Carlton arrive late on game days and added that Carlton was not setting an example for younger players. The insult became even greater when the White Sox gave 31-year-old Dan Pasqua—an outfielder/first baseman with mediocre defensive skills who had never played in more than 134 games or driven in more than 66 RBIs in a season and had a career .244 batting average—a three-year, $6 million deal. After a month of nasty public exchanges, Fisk signed an incentive-laden contract for $1 million for 1992, taking a pay cut of more than half of his previous year's salary.

It was the continuation of a frustrating pattern of what Fisk viewed as insults and disrespect from the White Sox front office dating back to 1985 when Reinsdorf lost all credibility after the collusion episode. After consistently performing better than peers at his position, each

time Carlton's contract ran out he was forced to undergo painful negotiations for a new one, all while dodging invectives and personal af-
fronts from the other side. Standard operating procedure by the club
included an initial lowball offer, followed by stonewalling, the release
of a few well-placed, not-so-thinly-veiled insults, references to his age,
and how hard he was to deal with, and then leaving him hanging until
the last possible moment to sign. White Sox general managers came and
went, but one constant remained: when it was time for negotiations,
they all took their orders from the top.

Carlton Fisk had remained popular with White Sox fans. His mere
presence in one of the goofy White Sox uniforms had always been reassuring. Often in the previous half-decade, he had been one of the
few reasons for fans to go to the park. No matter how bad the teams
were, fans knew they always had at least one serious All-Star candidate, and later, one certain Hall of Fame candidate. He had been the
rare free agent buy—the guy who delivered for the money as promised. He had established the team's new era, kept them in contention,
and stayed in town. Astute Chicago aficionados realized this and
adored him.

The continuing contract struggles became a public relations black
eye for the White Sox. Fan Jim FitzGerald wrote to the *Chicago Tribune*,
summarizing the feelings: "The White Sox are the team of the hardworking people of Chicago's South Side. Carlton Fisk is the tenacious
embodiment of the South Side's resolute work ethic. I am writing to
express my extreme disappointment—indeed anger—at the Sox having all but lost this tremendous asset. I am all the more angered
because as the Sox slap Fisk in the face with a ridiculously low contract
offer with one hand, they raise my ticket prices with the other."

Reinsdorf's position was difficult to defend. Carlton Fisk was never
overpaid when compared to catchers of similar performance at the
time—often he was drastically underpaid by market standards. He
continued to throw out about the same percentage of stolen base attempts as he had in the 1970s (around 35 percent), and did not have a
drastic increase in errors or passed balls. In the late 1980s and early
1990s, the White Sox pitching staff ERA was almost a full run lower
when Carlton caught compared to when someone else did. He continued to hit well, with seasons of 23, 19, and 18 home runs and batting
averages of .277, .293, and .285. He won the Silver Slugger Award (given
to the best offensive player at each position) for the American League

three times in the eighties, the last in 1988 at the age of 41. He was named to the All-Star team as late as 1991 (his 11th). Reinsdorf was certainly getting his money's worth with each Carlton Fisk contract as far as performance on the field was concerned.

Off the field, there could be few complaints either. Sure he could be a pain in the ass to managers or general managers with his honest comments sometimes, but he was hardly disruptive and his influence on teammates was entirely positive. His example of hard work and preparation set a standard for young players. Even when the teams were routinely out of contention by the All-Star break in the late eighties, he never gave up and mailed in his game late in the season. He was viewed as a good citizen; he was never in any kind of trouble. He also did things around town that didn't get noticed because he didn't seem to care if anyone knew, like when he anonymously bought 700 tickets in 1991 and had the White Sox distribute them to 14 senior citizens' homes in the Chicago area.

The acrimony couldn't be blamed on Jerry Kapstein and his overly aggressive negotiating tactics either. In 1989, Kapstein had gone over to the other side by marrying the daughter of Padres owner Joan Kroc and joining the team's management office. Fisk negotiated his own contract in 1990, then hired agent Jack Sands, who was much less combative than Kapstein.

Some questioned why Reinsdorf didn't just make a token gesture and sign Fisk without all the anger and gnashing of teeth. Didn't Pudge deserve a little something for giving the franchise legitimacy? Wasn't that worth a little bit of goodwill? But Reinsdorf had never been one to allow emotion to interfere with fiscal responsibility.

While Reinsdorf could be glib, or even funny, on occasion, and was well on his way to becoming the most successful sports owner in Chicago history this side of Papa Bear Halas, when it came to business he was distinctly cold-blooded. There is no denying his business acumen—by 2011 *Forbes* magazine would estimate that his original $19 million investment in the White Sox had become worth $526 million. And there is no doubt that Reinsdorf wanted to win; but he wanted to win on his terms. During the eighties he became very close to Brewer's owner and future baseball commissioner Bud Selig, earned the respect of his peers, and was one of the most powerful owners in the game. He was a leader in owners' meetings and became known as a very anti-union, anti-labor hard-liner when dealing with both the Major League Baseball and NBA Players Associations. With his ever-present cigar and dark-rimmed glasses, he was cool, rational, and never seemed to care about his image. He was particularly immune to public criticism. He clearly understood his position of power, both with the team and within professional sports. He was referred to by *Time* as a "cheapskate" when discussing professional owners, and *Newsweek* would later label him as "one of the hardest heads in the 1994 baseball strike." As a skilled negotiator, Reinsdorf recognized Carlton Fisk's one crucial weakness in his contractual aspirations: he was a dedicated family man who had a settled suburban life with teenagers happily involved in a myriad of activities and, thus, had no desire to change locations at this point in his life. Reinsdorf not only recognized this weakness, he mercilessly exploited it, knowing that Fisk would always return—willing to give up money to remain in his situation—and continue playing baseball in Chicago. Carlton recognized this also, but was powerless to combat it. "Jerry was playing mind games with me," he said in 1993. "He could do it because he knew I didn't want to leave, because there was no great market for me."

But while Reinsdorf was able to save a few hundred thousand dollars or more with each contract (mere chump change when considering his total worth and the amount he laid out for other players), his loss in these deals was immeasurable. "Reinsdorf's claim that this is a baseball decision is an insult," wrote Martin Lolich in the *Chicago Tribune*. "Carlton Fisk is a proven performer whose leadership on this young club is invaluable. He is extremely popular with fans and not only fills seats, but sells merchandise."

"If I had been the owner of the White Sox, I would have called the world's biggest press conference last winter to announce that I was overpaying Carlton Fisk and bringing him back," said pitcher Charlie Hough. "I'd have figured I'd get my money back in publicity and attention. I can understand Carlton's bitterness in Chicago. He's a dedicated person, so why does he have to battle for a contract every season? He should have been treated more like the way Texas has treated Nolan Ryan in recent years." Ryan, 11 months older than Fisk, had struggled to stay healthy and effective for several years. But where Ryan was lionized by his club, given large contracts, special privileges, allowed to work at his own pace (allowed to almost never travel with the team for road trips), treasured, and marveled over by the press and the entire state of Texas, Fisk was portrayed as the grouchy relative who just won't leave when the welcome has long been over.

There would be more indignities. When Fisk showed up in camp in 1992, he learned that new manager Gene Lamont was committed to starting Ron Karkovice at catcher. Karkovice, now 29 years old, emerged as a solid starter once the season began. Fisk was hobbled by a bone spur in his foot, which led to Achilles tendinitis and plantar fasciitis—making him feel as though someone were kicking him in the heel with a steel-toed boot each time he tried to run. It would bother him for months. He was limited to 62 games, and hit only three home runs with 21 RBIs.

After showing improvement the previous two years under Torborg (two second place finishes) the White Sox regressed in 1992. When healthy, Carlton Fisk was openly at odds over playing time with Lamont. He didn't attempt to sugarcoat any criticism for the continued attempts to give his position away to unproven young players. No one had given him anything when he came up—he'd had to wait his turn, prove himself through years in the minors, then take advantage of his opportunity, grab it in an iron vise as tight as his old man's handshake, and refuse to let go. Now they were giving his job to guys who couldn't hit .200. The absurdity of it was an insult to his well-honed code.

"I have always believed in myself, even when no one else did," Carlton Fisk had told a reporter in 1989, when asked about retirement. "I just hope that when the time comes, I will be able to recognize it myself without being told." That's the wish of every good athlete, but it's never easy to know when the time has come.

They are always the last to know—the preeminent players in every sport fail to recognize when their transcendent talents have faded beyond that needed to compete with younger players. It is a sad spectacle, repeated often: the proud, once great player, trying to hang on, insisting he can still do it, while his batting average, win-loss percentage, shooting percentage, or rushing average plummets. They never want to stop playing the game they love; the only job they have known in their adult lives, the source of unabashed admiration and adulation. They were once able to do something better than almost anyone else—not an easy thing to give up. No one wants to walk away. They want to hang on to their youth, to put off the next stage of life.

There is also the secret fear; the fear of the unknown; the fear that nothing will ever be able to replace the camaraderie, the competition, and the highs of triumphs; that nothing will ever be as meaningful; and the fear of what comes next? "I'm afraid to leave the game because I'm afraid there's nothing out there for me," Carlton admitted to a writer in 1993. "I have no burning desire to do anything else. Baseball has been so much of my life. Will anything else be that rewarding?"

But time goes on and it is inevitable that at some point the old guys must yield the field. The very thing that drove them to be great—the pride and competitiveness—betrays them in the end. Professional sports teams must win, they can spend only so much time in nostalgic goodwill playing time. The aged players must go, one way or another. Few great players can accept the ultimate fate in time. The ones who don't are subjected to cruel injustice, humiliation, and hard feelings.

Carlton Fisk refused to give up after his miserable season of 1992. He continued to say he could play and help the team. "I'd like to quit when I'm no value to the team," he said. "When I decide I'm no value. Just because I no longer play like a Hall of Famer doesn't mean I have no value. I can still contribute. For years, the organization has presented obstacles to me. It motivated me to overcome them. The last few years, that's been deflating. Why do I have to prove this again?" But the White Sox didn't seem to have a desire to see if he could prove anything again. He was very low on their priority list. If he was wanted back at all, it was only at a very discounted price.

Carlton was eligible for arbitration but the White Sox did not make an offer before the deadline. By forgoing any offer, they made him a free agent, knowing there was little interest around the majors. That move allowed them to cut his salary by more than 20 percent. "It's strictly a procedural matter," said Schueler after announcing that Fisk had become a free agent at midnight the day before because he wasn't offered a 1993 contract. "We have every intention of signing Fisk to a new contract. But it just didn't get done by the deadline." *Didn't get done by the deadline?* Those words sounded hauntingly familiar.

The fight for a deal turned public and nasty. New agent Jack Sands negotiated on Fisk's behalf but was unable to get an acceptable deal until March 3, after Reinsdorf had publicly called Fisk "selfish," a "baby," a "prima donna," and a "spoiled child" and had issued a deadline saying, "The time has come to put an end to this silliness." He never claimed to be misquoted. In a further insult, the take-it-or-leave-it agreement was for a minor league contract and the Sox failed to invite him to spring training. An observer could conclude that, although very subtle, Reinsdorf and the White Sox were trying to give Fisk a hint of some sort.

Team management later claimed that they made the minor league offer so they could leave Fisk off the wintertime roster (with a guarantee to be back on the roster in spring training). This would have allowed them to protect a younger player, a practice that was fairly common at the time. Other aging players had agreed to such an arrangement. Fisk refused, further incurring Reinsdorf's antagonism.

The claim from the White Sox front office that it wasn't personal, it was just business, rankled Fisk. "You can say this is just business, but—it's not business. It's me . . . that's me you're talking about. I've taken this game personally for a long, long time. You say I can't do this, can't do that, that's personal."

It was indeed personal. By this time, their battles over contracts and verbal skirmishes in the media had led to an intense, personal animosity between Carlton Fisk and Jerry Reinsdorf. Fisk made no secret about it. He told reporters that Reinsdorf couldn't define the word "loyalty," and "when it comes to me, Jerry doesn't negotiate."

In April 1993, the Public Broadcasting Service documentary series *Frontline* aired a special on baseball titled "The Trouble with Baseball." While presenting viewpoints from both owners and players, the show focused predominantly on Jerry Reinsdorf and Carlton Fisk. Both players and management were enjoying ever-increasing revenue and were playing every angle possible to make even more. Reinsdorf had recently used a sweetheart deal from St. Petersburg and the threat of moving the team as leverage to force the state of Illinois to finance a new $150 million stadium in which the team played rent free. In spite of the cash that seemed to be flowing freely, owners were claiming that their revenue was ebbing, but payrolls were still rising. Owners were in the process of fortifying their ramparts in negotiations over a new Collective Bargaining Agreement, a process that would result in the worst work stoppage in baseball history—the catastrophic strike of 1994, which ended the season and wiped out the World Series.

On the show, Reinsdorf said, "Signing Carlton at that time [1981] was incredibly important. . . . When Fisk became a free agent, none of our fans thought we could sign a premier player like that. We were able to pull that off and it immediately created credibility." The admiration and appreciation had not lasted, however. "How many years can you overpay him?" Reinsdorf said when asked about the lowball offer for 1993. "He was entitled to have a year when he got paid more than he produced but not two years. I had promised Pudge he would be on the White Sox' opening day roster. People usually take me at my word. But he didn't." Perhaps Carlton had stopped taking him at his word after the 1985 collusion episode?

As the 1993 season approached, it became obvious that if this was to be Carlton Fisk's final year, there would be no happy ending; he would not get tear-filled, mushy good-byes, attaboys, and thanks-for-the-memories. Those celebrations were reserved for the players who played the owners' game as they wanted—who gracefully walked out the door when they held it open. Carlton would not do that. Hell, he wouldn't even go out the door when they put a boot in his back and shoved. He had no doubt that he could still contribute and resented any suggestion otherwise. Years earlier there had been talk of some position with the White Sox front office after he retired. There was no mention of that now from either side.

Fisk looked good on the field at the start of the 1993 season. He was playing about every other day and had five hits in his first five games. Then, without explanation or apparent reason, his playing time drastically dropped. He went two weeks with only three at bats and was banished to the bullpen. He was 45 years old. He sat and waited. He would haul his stiff body to warm up a young pitcher, then sit back down.

He needed to catch in 25 games to break Bob Boone's record for most major league games caught, 2,225. Some saw Carlton Fisk as pursuing the white whale of this record and others questioned whether the record was even important. But it was obviously important to Fisk. It *was* his white whale. It was a source of great pride for having battled all the injuries; a final nod to his work ethic—a prize for everything he had endured over the years, a validation of his determination, to do it better and longer than anyone else. Former teammates understood the meaning. "It has nothing to do with Pudge's age but, rather, with his ability to play through injuries," said Rick Burleson about the record. "The irony about Pudge's longevity is that it's probably *because* of an injury. The horrible knee injury he had in 1974. I remember how ghastly that one was—Pudge on the ground and his leg sticking out at some weird angle. He had to undergo an intensive rehab program just to survive."

He was the oldest position player in the majors by four years. And signs of the years were everywhere. No other player had to hold fan mail or menus at arm's length because he was too stubborn to admit defeat and get reading glasses. "I was stretching before a game early this year in Boston," he said. "I see this guy with all-gray hair, and glasses. I didn't know who he was. I figured he was some old-timer, some sportswriter around Fenway Park who I just didn't remember. Then he came over and started talking to me. It was Bill Lee."

Writers frequently pointed out the fact that Carlton was three years younger than the Twins' Tom Kelly, who had been a coach or manager for 15 years. He was only one year younger than the president of the United States. During a one-week rehab assignment to Sarasota after an injury in 1992, Carlton was prepared to hit when he peered out at the pitcher, 25-year-old Steve Renko III, whose father had pitched for Boston in 1979 and 1980. "He stepped in the batter's box and looked at me," says Renko. "Then he called time and stepped out and said something to the umpire and kind of smiled, then got back in. After the inning I asked the umpire what he had said and he said, 'I used to catch that kid's dad. Now that really makes me feel old.'"

Teammate Steve Lyons liked to joke that Pudge was so old, they didn't even have history when he went to school because no history had happened yet. But the real joke was the fact that there not only was history, but Carlton had lived through it. The commencement speaker at Carlton's high school graduation had spoken of the effectiveness of the American secondary education system despite the recent criticism due to the Russians taking the lead in space with their high-flying Sputnik. Carlton's brother had fought in Vietnam. Carlton had broken into the league five presidents ago, when Watergate, leisure suits, Jimmy Carter, and *Saturday Night Live* were still unheard of. He could remember filling his gas tank for five bucks—and getting change. He had walked off the job, while making $12,000 a year, so these modern guys could have their multiyear, million-dollar contracts. He came from a time and had seen a history his teammates could scarcely comprehend.

He had little in common with his current teammates, two of whom were younger than his oldest daughter. It was like trying to hang out at the mall with your kid's high school friends—no matter what, there is always a gap, in interests, language, activity level, and pursuits. He was much closer in age to the coaches and reporters, but natural gaps of other kinds prevented friendships there as well. Following the 1992 departure of Charlie Hough, who was only 10 days younger, he had no close friends on the team. He rarely palled around with anyone. His clubhouse banter consisted mostly of exchanging insults with George Bell or working out with Frank Thomas and Bo Jackson. His dressing cubicle was back in the farthest corner of the spacious clubhouse—next to the trainer's room and weight room. He seemed to camp on the fringe by choice. While younger teammates played Ping-Pong, watched television, talked on the phone, and listened to loud music before games, he sat by himself, going through pregame rituals developed over 20 years.

He continued to talk baseball with his teammates, especially the ones who sought him out. "He's still giving advice," said McDowell in June. "He has a lot to offer." But the atmosphere of the clubhouse had evolved over his career—more corporate and serious, yet more immature. He was disappointed in the lack of preparation by younger teammates and the lack of camaraderie he had come to love in his years in baseball. He commented to friends and reporters that when he was 25 he couldn't wait to get to the clubhouse before a game and hated to leave it after a game. Now, he couldn't understand why so many current players treated baseball as a 9-to-5 job and left as quickly as possible. He frequently found himself alone in the clubhouse half an hour after the game ended. Gone were the pranks he enjoyed watching—of Luis Tiant, Tommy Harper, and Carl Yastrzemski as they ripped each other's clothes to shreds, doused one another with ice-cold buckets of water, and nailed each other's shoes to the floor; or Tom Paciorek, Marc Hill, and Jerry Koosman cracking up the White Sox locker room. Players still had fun, but the jokes were different. While his current teammates clipped in their earrings and dressed up to hit the nightclubs after a game, Fisk grabbed his weight belt and trudged up to the weight room to work out.

It was difficult not to get depressed at times. "I remember fun," he said to a reporter in May. "I'm not having any this season, but I remember it." But, despite his apparent gloom, he continually reminded everyone that he still wanted to play somewhere in 1994.

As the season wore on, the media seemed anxious to usher him out the door. Every time he was mentioned in the paper, the words "Future Hall of Famer" seemed to precede his name, as if the active career was over. His legacy and enshrinement were a given, it was only a matter of when. They saw his insistence on continuing to play as a Quixotic quest to defeat time. "I have a lot of respect for Carlton and I hope he doesn't embarrass himself by going for an extra brass ring," said California manager Buck Rodgers, voicing what many people felt. "I hate to see a Hall of Famer lower his standards."

Writers venturing back to talk to Fisk were occasionally welcomed with wit, sarcasm, and honest opinions as well as nostalgia for better days. Other times they were chased away with a surly glare. White Sox officials intimated that Carlton had become an irascible character who was more trouble than he was worth and some in the media picked up the refrain. He became noticeably more cautious around writers, often avoiding interviews with those he didn't know and trust. He felt betrayed by several writers who were granted access and then painted him in an unfavorable light—portraying him as a crusty, bitter grouch who more properly belonged across Lakeshore Drive at the Field Museum with the other Jurassic-era collections of bones rather than at Comiskey Park. He was particularly upset about a feature article for *Sporting News* by Dave Nightingale that turned out to be titled "The Prince of Pathos" and a Pat Jordan article for *Men's Journal* called "Conversations, with the Dinosaur." Pathos? Dinosaur? What were they trying to say?

"I wrote an article about him for *Sports Illustrated* in 1993," says Leigh Montville, who had covered Carlton for *The Boston Globe* going back to his rookie season. "At first he didn't want to do it. He was really pissed at Pat Jordan over his article. They'd had some drinks and Carlton made some comments that Jordan put in the article. He was mad about that. After a while, he agreed to talk to me, though."

Montville found Fisk disappointed that age, and not performance, seemed to be defining his worth. He felt betrayed by the front office. "I've given my loyalty to this team and the team has not responded in kind," he said. "One of the things that has always been right about this game is that if you played a long time, on the way out you had valet parking. You're not supposed to wind up in Remote Lot F with the transporter bus. That's where I am. It's not right."

Fisk gave hints that bad blood would persist. "I don't want any ceremony when I set the record. I don't want anything. . . . I don't want the big kiss, some shallow attempt at reconciliation. I don't want things to be that cynical, everything written off by saying, 'Let's smooth it over.' Because it's not smoothed over." Along with the bitterness for the White Sox he had not forgotten the insults from the Red Sox. He told Montville that he didn't want to wear either cap to the Hall of Fame. He felt like a man without a country and asked if there was any rule against being pictured "as a civilian with a Nike swoosh across the front of my hat?"

"I don't know where I am right now," he added. "The whole situation just fractures my self-image. My wife wants me to forget about it, to retire at the end of the year and come home. I don't know."

But Carlton resolutely refused to quit, as he said elsewhere. "They've tried to write me off, kill me off, and they haven't done it yet."

It hurt that after enduring the countless White Sox rebuilding seasons for almost a decade—toiling and watching as management refused to assemble a remotely competitive team—now that the talent had arrived and the team started winning, he was not wanted. Others noticed. "There's definitely something wrong here," said McDowell. "He's definitely getting the short end of the stick."

Gene Lamont, a former catcher for the Tigers who hit .233 in 87 games over five years in the early 1970s, was trying to build a winner in Chicago based on the talented young players who had come up the past few years. It's difficult for a new manager to inherit a past-his-prime superstar; difficult to keep him happy while still trying to move the team forward. Whereas Jeff Torborg had treated everyone with respect and molded a family-type atmosphere within the team, the straight-shooting Lamont was not known for diplomacy and had public disputes with other veterans, such as George Bell and Bo Jackson. One of Lamont's first acts had been to ban players' kids from the clubhouse. One of the next was to relieve Fisk of his captain's title. There was no doubt that he had little affection for Carlton Fisk and Fisk made no pretense that the feeling was anything but mutual. In one episode, Fisk was left alone on the field arguing balls and strikes with an umpire and got thrown out. "He must have been out there two or three minutes," Pall said later, "and during that time, Gene never came out of the dugout. I mean managers always come out to defend their players and Gene didn't do that. I lost some respect for him that day and I'm sure the other guys did as well."

The relationship between Lamont and Fisk deteriorated to the point that they rarely spoke. Fisk was forbidden to work with the younger catchers or to contribute much to pregame team meetings. "Hey, I caught a long time and I'm pretty friggin' good at what I do," Fisk said. "I've been there before, so I know. Yet they told me to stay away from the younger catchers because I do things differently. Before a game, the pitchers and catchers go over the opposition with our coaches. They told me not to get involved because my answers are too long."

Regardless of the feelings of White Sox management, Carlton Fisk was still respected, both in his own clubhouse and around the league. Young players from other teams, who had cheered him when they were growing up, sent clubhouse attendants over with requests for auto-graphed balls. "It's a shame he can't go out in style," the Angels' Gary Disarcina told reporters in June after a White Sox game in Anaheim. Disarcina, 25 years old, had grown up in Malden, Massachusetts, idol-izing Fisk as a youngster. "He's a classy guy and to go out on such a bitter note is not appropriate for a player of his stature. . . . You don't like to see this."

When the team visited Seattle, a sign hung from the upper deck: "Pudge deserves better." After the game Carlton joked that he had been scared when he left the bullpen and climbed all the way to the upper deck to put up the sign. Boston general manager Lou Gorman was making plans to honor Carlton before a game when the White Sox came to Boston in mid-August. But it began to look like he might not make it until then.

Fisk brooded; management's opinion became self-fulfilling. The less he played, the worse he played. He had always prepared him-self to play, now it was difficult coming to the park each day not knowing when or even if he would play at all. "I always thought I would wear out," he told a reporter. "But now it looks as if they want me to rust out."

By June Fisk was hitting .167 and had failed to throw out the last 22 would-be stealers. There was an embarrassing appearance June 14 in which he gave up four stolen bases and a passed ball during a two-inning stretch in a 7–3 loss. "I'm not sure Fisk had really lost it by then," says Pall, who along with his teammates appreciated everything Carlton contributed to the team even when he wasn't happy about his playing time. "It's tough to play sparingly and stay sharp anytime, but especially at that age. It's hard to get comfortable. You press because you don't know when you'll play again. Nobody can be expected to do well playing under those circumstances."

Rumors of Carlton Fisk's impending demise with the team were as thick as the summer Chicago air. The White Sox had signed 32-year-old catcher Mike LaValliere in April and assigned him to Class A Sarasota. LaValliere was a likable, good defensive catcher who had been a key player for the Pirates' division-winning teams of the early nineties. He had been hurt and released by the Pirates in April. Now healthy, he was hitting .300 at Sarasota. When Karkovice had to be put on the disabled list June 21 because of a shoulder injury, the White Sox called up, not only LaValliere, but also catcher Rick Wrona from AA Nashville. Four catchers in town, one on the 15-day disabled list—the simple math didn't look good. And Lamont refused to give the job to Fisk with Karkovice out, announcing that Fisk and the left-handed hitting LaValliere would platoon.

On June 22 the White Sox held a Carlton Fisk Night ceremony before the game. Fisk had caught in 2,225 games and was scheduled to start that night. Former White Sox teammate Tom Paciorek was the master of ceremonies. The large crowd stood and cheered as Carlton walked out. Banners proclaiming "We Love You" and "Congratulations Pudge" waved proudly. The highlight of the ceremony came when Bo Jackson drove a motorcycle onto the field and presented it to Carlton. Jackson had gone to teammates asking if they would donate $500 each for the surprise gift. Carlton sat on the motorcycle and waved to the crowd while teammates clapped. His mother and father stood behind him smiling, while Linda dabbed at her eyes and stood beside the three kids, including 21-year-old Casey, who bore an eerie resemblance to Carlton Fisk circa 1972. Carlton took the microphone and called it one of the most satisfying nights of his career. "I don't know if it has sunk in yet. To have this happen tonight is beyond words. But it didn't happen by accident. I worked hard."

He spoke for almost 15 minutes, thanking everyone who helped him throughout his career; however, he made no mention of either Lamont or Reinsdorf. He nodded to his teammates and said, "I love these guys like my sons and brothers." He called out to Karkovice, noting that he "has handled his role with more patience than I ever could have. . . . He's come into his own. He's the number one guy. . . . He deserves your support."

After thanking the fans for their "encouragement and enthusiastic appreciation," just in case the owners were listening, he concluded with, "I hope this is not the end. This is not the destination but part of the journey." He walked down the line, getting tearful hugs from each family member.

He then squatted behind home plate and when he caught the first pitch from Alex Fernandez, the record was official. He stood and tossed the ball toward the dugout amid more applause. He played eight innings and went 0-for-2 with a sacrifice in a 3–2 win over the Rangers. A remnant of another time and place in Carlton's career, Larry Barnett, was the home plate umpire.

"It doesn't happen like falling out of a tree," Fisk told reporters afterward. "It takes endurance and perseverance. I've been lucky. I can't say I've been liked by everybody but I'm always prepared to play the game and I think I'm respected as a professional. . . . Most important, I played to win."

After the White Sox players demonstrated their admiration and affection with postgame congratulations while showering him with a beer bath, Fisk was noted to show more emotion than had been seen in a long time. The clubhouse was closed for a players-only party. For one night, the age difference didn't matter. "We stayed in the clubhouse until the next morning," says Pall. Late in the evening, some of the players went out on the field and started running around and sliding into bases, à la *Bull Durham*. The party lasted so long that a lot of the players stayed and slept in the clubhouse.

The next day, Carlton and Linda Fisk paid for a plane to fly over Fenway Park trailing a sign that said, "It all started here. Thanks, Boston fans. Pudge Fisk." Linda told a reporter, "It was something we wanted to do very much. Boston is home for us. We'll never forget growing up in New England and having Carlton's dream of playing for the Red Sox come true. He wanted to give them a little something back."

Boston fans had always given Carlton something back. They had never forgotten. "The last time I saw him in a game was at Fenway, in 1992 or 1993," says Katy Shaw Gould, who grew up three houses down from the Fisk house in Charlestown. "He was with the White Sox and it was late in his career. My husband and I had ordered tickets ahead of time, but when we got there, he had been injured and wasn't playing. We were sitting way out in right field, couldn't see anything. Late in the game, between innings, the crowd suddenly started cheering. We couldn't tell what was going on at first, but somebody was walking across the field, heading from the White Sox dugout toward the bullpen. I knew it was Carlton. My husband said, 'How can you tell?' He was so far away. But I said, 'I've seen that walk since I was a kid. I know that walk.' But the whole stadium cheered him just for walking out to the bullpen between innings to warm some pitcher up. I get chills just thinking about it."

With the White Sox in first place by two and a half games, they flew to Cleveland for a three-game series. The morning of June 28, Carlton got a phone call in his hotel room from general manager Ron Schueler—he was wanted in Schueler's 13th-floor hotel suite. "He thought I was calling him to talk about his role on the team in general," said Schueler, who had taken a dawn flight from Chicago to deliver the news. "I don't think he expected it. He still thought he was going to be here all season." The White Sox were letting Carlton Fisk go. He wasn't offered the dignity-saving option of voluntarily retiring—perhaps because they felt he wouldn't take that option—he was merely given his outright release. His baseball career was over. Schueler stated that Carlton was not shocked, but rather met the news with "disappointment and disbelief." He added that there were no tears, no angry exchanges, no obscenities; just 15 minutes of career-ending discussion. Fisk was replaced on the roster by rookie pitcher Rodney Bolton.

Carlton packed and checked out of the hotel quickly and was unavailable to the press before the game. Rather than hold a press conference to announce the exit of their most notable player, the White Sox sent faxes to the local media. Apparently they chose the start of the road trip to make the move to avoid the embarrassment of boos at Comiskey—to let fans digest it, and hopefully forget it, before the team came home.

"I know a bunch of fans out there and some people will be upset with me—but my job here is to win," Ron Schueler told reporters. "Maybe we were a little bit unfair. He didn't get an opportunity to play on a daily basis, where probably the throwing would have been improved and the catching would have been improved. But right now I just felt this is the move I had to make. . . . Obviously this hurts. Obviously it was a very tough decision. But with the direction I want to go with this ball club, Carlton wasn't a part of it."

Schueler said that in preparation for the decision, he had talked to most of the teams around the major leagues to see if anyone was interested in trading for Fisk but found no takers. He had also called Fisk's agent, and asked if he might be interested in retiring and was told, "Absolutely not. He thinks he can still play."

Reinsdorf emphasized that the decision was Schueler's, but that he and Lamont concurred. The owner said, "It is not fair to Gene Lamont and to our fans to carry somebody who can't possibly help the ball club."

"I agreed with the decision," said Lamont. "Ron asked me my opinion on strictly a baseball basis, and I told him. It was the right decision." Fisk was hitting .189 with one home run and four RBIs at the time. The White Sox front office, aware that a pennant was within reach of the team, did not want a 45-year-old catcher taking up a roster spot.

The move, and how it was carried out, did not sit well with Fisk's teammates, who were visibly upset in the locker room. "We were all shocked when he was released," says Pall. "We had heard rumors that something like that might happen, but to do it like that? I think it was just a poor decision on the part of the Sox to wait until we were in Cleveland before releasing him. Why have him get on the plane and fly all the way out there if you're just going to release him?"

"I'm upset about it," said rookie Jeff Schwarz, who added that Carlton Fisk was his idol growing up. "I feel like I've known him since I was five. You can tell by the mood in this room, not many people are happy."

Ozzie Guillen, never at a loss for words or afraid to voice his opinion, told reporters that night, "When you make too much money today, they'll get rid of you."

Second baseman Joey Cora put two pieces of masking tape on the back of his batting helmet and wrote "Thanks-72." Frank Thomas taped "72" above his own number on his helmet. Other teammates wrote "72" on the brims of their caps in indelible ink in a silent tribute. Reinsdorf was reported to be furious when he saw the caps. Also mad that the team was not performing as well as he expected, even though they were in first place, he threatened to make more moves: "All I know is that this is the biggest bunch of underachievers I've ever seen. I'm looking into what's wrong here and what can be done about it."

Carlton made a surprise appearance at Cleveland Stadium during the game that night, showing up in street clothes. "He went to the game that night," says Pall. "It was weird seeing him there, knowing he wasn't on the club anymore. It was kind of awkward but he talked to us. He was laughing. He hung around in the stands down the line near the bullpen during the game. He was joking and yelled at us, like, 'You guys suck,' and stuff, just having a good time. Then he went and sat in the outfield next to the guy who beat the drum; you know they always had that guy at Cleveland Stadium with the drum. He said that guy had always bugged him when he played. He bought the guy a beer."

After the game, Fisk avoided the media and returned to Chicago, alone. Once, late in his career when asked what he would miss most when he stopped playing, he said, "I'll miss the clubhouse atmosphere, the one-on-one confrontations, the bases loaded with no outs in the seventh inning, the extra hitting in the cage with Walter [Hriniak] and the rest of the guys. Once you're out of the game I don't think you'll ever find anything that can replace the game for the demands and relationships it makes." He later added, "I miss being at the ballpark. I miss being there on a warm summer's evening with the smells of hot dogs and brats filling the air . . . and the excitement, just the energy, overflowing at the ballparks. And you feel so good, and you feel so alive, and your mind and body are so sharp. I miss singing the National Anthem . . . standing at home plate before a home game. I miss singing the seventh inning stretch, but what I miss most, I miss that very very good feeling that you know, that you're part of something special." After 27 years of professional baseball, Carlton Fisk would never be part of that special something at the ballpark again.

The next day, agent Sands told reporters that Fisk had taken his phone out of service to have some privacy. They were waiting to hear from other teams. "He does not want to go somewhere else just to hang on. He wants to play. He wants to contribute. . . . He doesn't need the money. . . . He just loves the game."

Any club could have claimed him off waivers. According to his contract, the White Sox were on the hook for the vast majority of his $650,000 salary. The cost to a new club would have been no more than $60,000. They had a week to claim him. No one did.

When the White Sox made the playoffs at the end of the season, there was one more humiliation. Carlton showed up for the first playoff game of 1993 at Comiskey Park. Donn Pall, who had been traded late in the year, went to the clubhouse with him before the game. "We went by the clubhouse, we wanted to see our former teammates and wish them well," says Pall. The security guards, the regular ones who had been there all season, turned the two ex–White Sox players away. "I think they said it was a Major League Baseball rule or something." The guard acted embarrassed, shifted his weight from one foot to another, looked down and mumbled that he felt really bad about it, that he was just following orders. To not allow the former captain of the team to go in and wish everybody luck? "I stayed and watched the game because I had tickets, but Carlton didn't have a ticket, he had to leave the premises. I can't remember, but I think they may have escorted him out. I have never seen him more upset than he was then. I can understand him being bitter about that for a long time."

"He had no tickets and no credentials," David Schaeffer, director of park operations, told reporters when asked about the incident. "I just can't let Carlton stay around." *No credentials?* How about 2,499 major league games played, 376 home runs (214 for the White Sox, more than any player in team history)? What more credentials did he need?

"I even called the clubhouse beforehand," Carlton said in 1997. "And the guys encouraged me to come on down. But when I got to the door, I was turned away. Not welcome."

"I was shocked, absolutely crushed."

It was an unbelievably shortsighted move by the team, a petty remnant of hard feelings from contract haggles, and a poor way of treating one of the best players in team history. Did they not know he would be coming? Instead of giving him an invitation, maybe asking him to throw out the first pitch or at least allowing him to sit in an executive's box, they had him tossed out like an intruder. Carlton Fisk's White Sox days officially ended there in the parking lot, locked out of the game, unable to even watch from the bleachers. He drove home. He was an ex–Major League Baseball player.

19 Living Without the Game

"Behind all the years of practice and all the hours of glory awaits that inexorable terror of living without the game."

BILL BRADLEY, *LIFE ON THE RUN*, 1976

UNFORTUNATELY FOR CARLTON FISK, the last half of his career had been spent during the zenith of hatred between players and owners. Had he been able to hang on a little longer, his exit from the game would have undoubtedly been much less traumatic. After owners and players watched the game nearly slip into an abyss after the 1994 strike wiped out the World Series, they realized that there was much more money to be made for everyone if they could work together. An era of collegiality resulted and, at the same time, organized baseball realized that a vast untapped treasure lay in the nostalgic feelings of fans for the aging and former superstars of the game. The players were once again pushed to the forefront and celebrated. It became customary for retiring icons to be feted at every stop through the league; with sappy victory laps and maudlin ceremonies in which the schmaltz was laid on so thick, fans could cut it and put it on their bratwursts. How much better would Carlton Fisk's departure have been if teams and fans could have celebrated his 24-year career, dedication, and historic home run, rather than having him unceremoniously booted out of a lousy hotel room in Cleveland?

The first few years away from the game are the hardest. Initially, there is the adjustment to the time, never available before; lots and lots of time. Whereas life was once ruled by strict schedules—arrival at the park, batting practice, meetings, bus departure for the airport—now there is nothing but unorganized, free time. Then there is the ego-deflating experience of giving up the prestige of being something special, of being one of the best baseball players in the land. There is an emptiness after leaving the game, especially for the great players. There is also resentment; resentment to the game they loved, the game to which they gave so much, the game that dumped them so callously. The bitterness only increases when picking up the sports page or watching the television and seeing less-talented and less-driven people still playing—still making money—when they are no longer wanted. Also, it's tough to give up the support system, the family of teammates, coaches, trainers, clubhouse guys; the camaraderie and sense of common purpose of the locker room. Most disappointing is the realization that, unbelievably, the game of baseball goes on. Some players hang around in broadcasting or coaching—anything to stay close to the action. Some guys go cold turkey and make a clean break. Carlton Fisk was one of the latter.

He went into seclusion in the months following his forced retirement. He was rarely seen and gave no interviews. CBS television contacted him about being an analyst for the playoffs the first October, but he declined. He spent a lot of time learning to ride the Harley-Davidson his teammates had given him. "He's doing great," said Bo Jackson, who claimed to be his personal riding instructor. "He has 1,000 miles on it already."

Carlton Fisk dealt with what John Updike called "The little death that awaits all athletes." He busied himself getting used to his new life. He now had a chance to spend time with his family—and to reflect on what he had missed due to the requirements of Major League Baseball. Family was important to Carlton and Linda Fisk. They had always made special efforts to guard the family's time. During his playing career, Carlton had taken a pass on a lot of fun with the guys, family had always come first. "I think because the family is such a self-sufficient entity to me, I've never had a lot of what I consider close friends," he said in 1990. "Baseball makes a lot of friendly associations, but it's too uncertain, too transient for friendships."

Carlton had shared his accomplishments with the family. The kids had been present for most of his milestones. Casey had memorably welcomed him at home plate with a hug after he broke Johnny Bench's record for career home runs by a catcher. In 1992, when asked what his proudest achievement was, Carlton answered, "To have a wife and kids who still call me 'Dad' and love me and kiss me when I'm going and kiss me when I'm coming, no matter how big those teenaged muscleheads seem to think they are."

It had been difficult balancing family life while being on the road for half of the six-month season and while spending so much time working out to be able to maintain his performance level into his forties, but Carlton had made an effort. "When he was home, he was home," said Casey in 2014. "It was about the kids and it was about my mom."

There were plenty of Wiffle ball games in the yard and basketball games in the driveway—cherished memories, but sometimes Carlton felt regret that it hadn't been enough. "I had to give up things," Carlton said in 1993. "I was consumed by the game to a fault. I didn't want to take my wife out to eat, or mow the lawn, because it would distract me from the mental approach to the game."

He admitted that although he loved baseball, "I will never forgive the game for what I lost with my children. My oldest daughter is 23 and I hardly ever spent any time with her. I feel I've missed a closeness that can never be regained."

The kids shared their father's love of sports and athletic ability. Oldest daughter Carlyn became the most accomplished. She was also noted to have inherited the "Fisk walk," which sometimes caused trouble. "When I was a freshman [in high school] there were about five girls who wanted to beat me up just because they thought it was 'too cool' the way I walked," she told a reporter while in college. "People say I have a definite walk. My friends know it's inherited. Plus, I don't smile a lot just like my father doesn't. So by walking that way and not smiling people who don't know me think I think I'm really something. . . . In college, people are more grown up. Anyway, if I have this walk, I'm proud to have it." She was a five feet, seven inches record-setting volleyball star at the University of Illinois-Chicago, known for her hard work on the court and in the weight room as well as her killer competitive attitude and would later be elected to the school's Hall of Fame.

Fisk's younger daughter was the only one still at home when he retired. "Courtney is the only one of my children I was able to watch grow up," he said later. She helped Lockport High win the state championship in volleyball. "I'd yell 'Hey Grumpy!' and embarrass her half to death."

He tried to remain close to the kids as they left and established their lives. "The special moments now that the kids are grown up, whether it be my girls or my son, when they see me, they hug me and they kiss me, and I do the same to them. I missed a lot of them growing up, so I revel in the time we have now."

Casey was a senior baseball player at Illinois State University. Carlton volunteered to help the team for the 1994 season. More demonstrative emotionally and less demanding than his own father, Carlton had maintained a close relationship with his son. Casey had sometimes traveled with Carlton and served as batboy when he was able. When Casey was in high school, they had often worked out together. Now, for the first time, Carlton watched his son play baseball regularly. Casey spoke to a reporter of growing up with a baseball-playing dad: "In the past, when I had free time during the summer, he was working. And in the winter, I was in school and busy. It's a nice change to have him here. He hasn't seen me play hardly at all before this year."

"I see Casey more as a man," said Carlton. "Until this point, he's always been my baby boy. I still want to hug him and kiss him. . . . He's really grown up and I missed that process."

Carlton offered tips to all the players and helped study the opposing pitchers and catchers. Teammates enjoyed the former major league star's presence. "I was in awe when he got here," one player told a reporter. "He's so down-to-earth. He's gone from making millions to riding 10 hours on the bus with us to Omaha. He has put himself back in the minors. And he's taught us so much about the game."

It's difficult to try to play the same sport as a parent who was a legend. It's even more difficult when that parent is present in the dugout, regardless of his attitude. Although he enjoyed the presence of his father, it was stressful for Casey, especially since he switched from first base to catcher for the season, using one of his dad's old mitts. He got off to a 5-for-54 start at the plate. "I've tried to help the team," said Carlton in mid-season, "but for one player in particular I might have been a burden. In fact, I'm afraid I've been a pretty heavy burden and I wanted to be anything but. I hope he doesn't think I'm here in a judgmental capacity. Sometimes my heart aches for him. I hope he's not trying to play well to impress me. No matter what transpires on the field, my love for him is unconditional." Carlton was not a taskmaster. He was noted to frequently hug his son when they met on the field. Casey soon righted himself and hit .338 the rest of the season, was named Missouri Valley Conference Player of the Week once and made the conference All-Tournament team.

After graduating with a degree in exercise science and playing one year of independent minor league baseball, Casey became a physical trainer, eventually becoming owner of the Grand Rapids–based Fisk Performance Training. Working with athletes who have college or professional aspirations, particularly baseball, he puts to use many of the lessons he learned from his father.

It had long been speculated that Carlton Fisk would enter some sort of baseball job after his playing days were finished. With his commanding presence and knowledge of the game, it seemed a natural fit. But the jobs never materialized. There were offers. He didn't seem interested. He'd had enough of baseball executives and entitled young players and felt no desire to affiliate with either. Besides, he had tired of the endless hours on the road most baseball positions entailed. In 1994, after Haywood Sullivan had sold out his interest in the Red Sox, new general manager Dan Duquette reached out to him and offered a position as a roving instructor. Fisk declined. In January of 1997, White Sox general manager Ron Schueler wrote to Fisk, inquiring if he would like to help the team's catchers during spring training. "I recently got a return letter, and the answer is no," Schueler told reporters. "Pudge mentioned he still doesn't feel comfortable with the situation." The man who forced Carlton to give up the game as a player then added, "I don't know if I'm part of the reason or not."

When contacted, Carlton said, "Names aren't important. Before I left there, they wanted me to stay away from their prospects. Now they want me to coach them. I'm not ready yet. I was bitter for a while. I've tried to bury it." He had been wronged and insulted, by both teams. Carlton Fisk was not one to hypocritically pretend that nothing had happened. The bitterness he felt would take time to dissolve; a lot of time.

Other than the one-season gig as a volunteer with his son's college team, there was no involvement with baseball. His old manager Tony La Russa invited him to visit the Cardinals dugout in St. Louis in 1996. Carlton enjoyed being back around the smells, the atmosphere, and the give-and-take of a major league team. "It felt good, to be talking baseball with baseball people again," he said later. "Tony kind of felt me out about whether I'd be interested in getting back into the flow. But one thing I missed playing all those years was my kids, and they're not kids anymore. Two of them will get married this summer. That's another reason why it's not time. Maybe after that." But the time would never come.

When his old friend and teammate Ozzie Guillen managed the

White Sox from 2004 to 2011, he asked Carlton to help several times but the answer was always the same.

"I'm disappointed he's not involved in baseball," says Chicago sportswriter Bob Verdi. "Actually shocked. He was so knowledgeable of the game as a player. He could have been a great manager."

Then again, times and players had changed. He undoubtedly would have been frustrated with modern athletes who didn't share his dedication. A former teammate says, "Pudge wouldn't be able to manage nowadays. He'd get in a fight every day with the way guys are now, with their attitudes. He wouldn't be able to put up with it."

Another asks, "Can you imagine someone not putting out for Pudge? I don't know how he'd be able to take it, knowing how much he demanded from himself. He would just be so frustrated all the time because I don't think anybody would put into it what he did. I think he probably realized that and that's why he didn't take any of the offers."

Eventually old wounds began to heal as both the Red Sox and White Sox reached out to celebrate Carlton Fisk's accomplishments. But the process was as slow as one of Pudge's trudges to the mound—full of deliberation and emotion. Carlton settled with the Red Sox first. The transgressions of the team's management were further in the past and all the guilty parties were gone. In early September 1997, he was inducted into the Red Sox Hall of Fame. He enjoyed a triumphant return to the field at Fenway Park, basking in the cheers of Boston fans once more.

The White Sox honored him by retiring number 72 in a special ceremony a few weeks later. "Carlton Fisk certainly ranks as one of the greatest players to wear a Chicago White Sox uniform," said Jerry Reinsdorf when the occasion was announced. "He is very deserving of this honor and the special event will give the club and the Sox fans one more chance to thank him for all the tremendous memories." Four years after he was booted from Comiskey Park because he didn't have a ticket to a playoff game, Carlton stood in the infield as his number was retired. He got hugs from former teammates Ozzie Guillen and Robin Ventura and handshakes and backslaps all around. He visited with McDowell, Kittle, and Pall. It was reported that he had asked the White Sox to keep the tribute simple and without gifts. And he got his wish.

In his brief address to the crowd, he said, "All fairy tales have scary parts and uncomfortable parts and thanks to today, this fairy tale has a happy ending." In a mass interview with reporters in front of the dugout afterward, he thanked the fans for bringing about the reunion. "I think every situation demands a little time away. We've had a little time away and today is an appreciation and recognition."

It was a nice gesture from the team, but anyone who felt the event would fully repair the damage did not know Carlton Fisk very well. It was reported that he had declined to participate in any attempts to promote the event and he had communicated with the club only through the use of a fax machine. While Fisk was honored on the field, Reinsdorf watched from his private box. The two did not speak. The situation would demand more time.

In September 2000, the Red Sox retired Carlton's number 27, hanging it on the right field facade alongside those of Bobby Doerr, Joe Cronin, Carl Yastrzemski, and Ted Williams and making him the rare player to have the honor from two teams. "Carlton Fisk may tell you that growing up in New Hampshire he dreamed of playing for the Red Sox, I'm here to tell you that growing up in Massachusetts, I dreamed of being Carlton Fisk," Red Sox general manager Dan Duquette, a former catcher at Amherst College who had been 17 years old in 1975, told the crowd. "He's a big old handsome, stubborn, methodical, fiery, Yankee New Englander who accomplished all those dreams. And, along the way, he fulfilled our dreams, too."

"He played the game the right way," Yastrzemski told the crowd. Yaz then presented Carlton with a framed number 27 Red Sox jersey as the packed house stood and applauded. Carlton thanked Red Sox CEO John Harrington, who "opened the doors of communication to me after all these years," and Dan Duquette for "accepting me back and allowing me to be a part of this organization." He concluded telling the crowd, "I thank you for allowing me to come home." He then threw out the first pitch for the game—to surprise catcher Luis Tiant.

In 2005, the left field foul pole at Fenway Park was officially named "Fisk's Pole." After stadium renovations, the part of the original pole that had been hit by the famous drive now hangs on display inside the Fenway Hall of Fame.

Of course, the greatest honor for any baseball player is election to the National Baseball Hall of Fame. For Carlton, it seemed to be a mere formality, but he narrowly missed the first year he was eligible, in 1999.

It was a tough year, as Robin Yount, George Brett, and Nolan Ryan—all certain first-ballot guys, were in the mix. Although senior members of the Baseball Writers' Association of America could vote for up to 10 candidates each year, the most ever elected in one year was four and three players had gone into the Hall the same year only five times. There had never been as many as three first-time candidates elected in the same year. Johnny Bench had been the only catcher elected on the first try. Carlton fell 43 votes short of the required 373.

Carlton and his fans were much more optimistic the next year. The day of the Hall of Fame vote in 2000, the Fisk house in Charlestown was a busy place. Family, friends, and former teammates filed in and out. Leona Fisk put out a big stack of her famous cinnamon rolls. When the official call came in, David Conant was notified and he rang the Episcopal Church bell again, just as he had on that late October night 25 years earlier.

The happy new member of the Hall appeared on *Good Morning America* and said, "I don't know if it has really sunk in. It puts me in the same fraternity with guys you only dream of playing like . . . when you think about Joe DiMaggio, Ted Williams—can you imagine? Small-town boy from New Hampshire, it's hard to believe that I'm where I am." The Hall of Fame ring represented validation for his hard work and also the appreciation he felt that had been lacking from the Red Sox and White Sox in his later years with both teams.

The question of which cap he would wear into the Hall of Fame became an issue. At the time, players who had been on multiple teams were given the option. (The decision is now made by the Hall of Fame.) In 1990, when asked about it by Peter Gammons, Carlton had said, "It would have to be the White Sox. . . . I will have played more games for Chicago. And this is where my kids grew up." But feelings had changed as his career crawled to an end. He announced in January 2000 that he would wear a Red Sox cap. "I would like to say that this always has been my favorite hat and I will be wearing this hat probably the rest of my career. I think I've known for a long time. It's not like a lightbulb came on or I had a vision. I think this has always been a part of me." Jerry Reinsdorf, when contacted, declined to comment. A White Sox spokesperson said the organization was "disappointed" in the decision but wished him well.

Carlton was careful to make sure the fans of Chicago understood his position. "The strained relationship has absolutely nothing to do with the people of Chicago, or the fans who have supported me. The community has been so nice, so receptive. The strained relationship is with nobody other than the White Sox. The fans should not feel as though that strained relationship affects my relationship with them."

A large group made the trip from Charlestown to Cooperstown for Carlton's induction in July of 2000, most of them wearing Red Sox jerseys with "27" on the back. The entire Fisk family was there, along with former teammates, coaches, and friends. Sister Janet was in charge of the accommodations for the Fisk clan and rented out an entire bed-and-breakfast.

Carlton Fisk entered the Baseball Hall of Fame along with Tony Perez and Sparky Anderson on July 23, 2000. Reds broadcaster Marty Brennaman was inducted into the broadcasting wing, making it a mini-reunion of the '75 Series. Fisk was introduced by Commissioner Bud Selig, who read the Hall of Fame plaque: "A commanding figure behind the plate for a record 24 seasons. He caught more games, 2,226, and hit more home runs, 351, than any catcher before him. His gritty resolve and competitive fire earned him the respect of teammates and opposing players alike. A staunch training regimen extended his durability, and enhanced his productivity—as evidenced by a record 72 home runs after age 40. His dramatic home run to win Game 6 of the 1975 World Series, is truly one of baseball's most unforgettable moments."

Carlton stood at the podium and addressed the crowd of 25,000 in the sweltering heat. He talked of his life in baseball and paid tribute to all those who helped him. He gave a speech that seemed proportionately as long as his career, 37 minutes, well beyond the recommended length. He thanked everyone: high school coach Ralph Silva, each minor league manager, a sergeant and lieutenant from the Vermont Army Reserve unit, Curt Flood, Andy Messersmith, and Dave McNally for their pioneering efforts to help all players, Marvin Miller, the surgeons who operated on his knee, Phil Claussen, Tony La Russa, and Dave Duncan, his Red Sox and White Sox teammates, Charlie Lau and Walt Hriniak, Willie Thompson (the clubhouse man in Chicago), the generation of catchers in the seventies, Johnny Bench and Thurman Munson, umpires in general, and finally, his family. He concluded with, "This wouldn't happen if it wasn't for the most special person in my life. Linda, that's you. I've known her since I was 17 years old. She's been there all these years. Ups and downs and good times and the bad times. She's my friend, my lover, and the mother of my children, and I love you. Thank you."

With his induction into the Hall of Fame, there was no question that Carlton Fisk had finally impressed his father. "Dad was as proud as punch," says Calvin Fisk. "He just glowed that whole weekend."

During Carlton's acceptance speech, he had some special words for his father and hinted at the complicated relationship between the two, a source of motivation and also frustration. "I always wanted you to be proud of me, Dad. Sometimes, just because you could have done better doesn't mean you've done badly." He paused. "Through the years you always made sure that people knew that I was your son and I'm proud of that. But this weekend, guess what, you're Carlton's dad."

Carlton enjoyed becoming part of the special family of Hall of Famers. Each year the vast majority of living members return to Cooperstown for induction weekend. They are put up at the swanky Otesaga Resort on the banks of the beautiful Otsego Lake, a few blocks' walk through tree-lined streets from the Hall of Fame. They participate in a parade down Main Street, an annual Hall of Fame Golf Classic at the Leatherstocking Golf Club next to the resort, and otherwise revel in being members of the community of baseball greats. Each year, Sunday night after the induction, there's a special dinner at the resort. It's only Hall of Famers—a very exclusive dining group. For years, one table consisted of Tom Seaver, Bob Gibson, Don Sutton, Sandy Koufax, Rollie Fingers, and Steve Carlton. When Fisk was inducted, Seaver insisted that he join them. This is a table of the preeminent men who dedicated their professional careers to preventing batters from reaching base. Carlton was the only nonpitcher deemed worthy; accepted due to his efforts at calling the good game. Seaver said, "That's as good as it gets. Everybody has the understanding of the pitching. Everybody understood it. Everybody knows what it was about. We don't talk too much about pitching. We talk about wine and other things."

Carlton participates with the Hall in other ways. The bat he used to hit the Game Six home run (after years of being on display in his den) is currently on loan to the museum for an exhibit. He was part of the Expansion Era Committee, along with Jerry Reinsdorf, which unanimously selected Tony La Russa for the Hall of Fame in 2014. He contributed a chapter on his life and baseball career to a Hall of Fame book released in 2014.

———

Carlton Fisk never lost his willingness to confront wrongs when he saw them. And he didn't mind stepping on toes when he felt something needed to be corrected. When the Red Sox inducted Carlton into their Hall of Fame in 1997, the original plaque stated that he was a native of Vermont. He insisted that the plaque be recast (at a cost of $3,000 to the Red Sox) to reflect that he was raised in New Hampshire. In 1999, Carlton was chosen to be honorary captain for the American League All-Star team. Not surprisingly, he took the job more seriously than most and even fired a shot at a wayward player. Juan Gonzalez, one of the league's leading sluggers, refused his selection and planned to skip the game, claiming that he was tired and needed rest. "I think he's totally out of line," the honorary captain told reporters. "I know some players prefer three days off. Well, you can rest when you're dead, I think. This is a great honor."

Like a lot of players from previous decades, Carlton irately watched as ridiculously pumped-up sluggers ravaged the record book in the 1990s and beyond until baseball started mandatory steroid testing. While some of the older players diplomatically refused to call out the guilty parties—even as they seethed privately—Carlton made no attempt to hide his feelings on the subject. He spoke honestly when steroid-implicated players tried to pawn off lame denials and excuses, reminiscent of the headline from his rookie year: "Many Have Thought . . . Only Fisk Has Spoken." "I worked hard in the gym to look like I did and feel like I felt," he said in 2010. "But when you have some of these obscene numbers being put up by people who shouldn't even be there . . . you know what's going on. . . . The people it should have been most obvious to are the people who covered it up by not addressing it. . . . [It was] a federal offense for a long time. . . . The people who did it . . . they were breaking the law to start with. It doesn't have to be a baseball law. They knew what they were doing and the reason they were doing it."

He blasted Mark McGwire, Roger Clemens, and Barry Bonds and called McGwire's claim that steroids didn't help him hit home runs, that he only took them to feel better after injuries, "a crock." "There's a reason they call it performance-enhancing drugs. That's what it does. . . . Try having your knees operated on and catching for 30 years. Do you think you feel good when you go out there? [McGwire] had to stand around and play first base. So excuuuuuse me."

After a dozen years, Carlton's view of White Sox management

began to soften. In 2005 it was announced that the team would honor Carlton with a statue to be placed on the left field main concourse at U.S. Cellular Field (Comiskey's name since 2003). Carlton told reporters he was humbled and honored to receive such recognition. "It has been really special. I don't know if I deserve all this but it is nice to be on the receiving end."

When Jerry Reinsdorf was asked about their relationship, he said, "If I hadn't been reading in the newspapers that Carlton Fisk and I didn't get along, I wouldn't know it. We have never had a cross word with each other. And I have seen him periodically over the years. We have always been cordial to each other. As far as I know, there are no problems."

"This is the most spectacular and significant recognition that I've probably ever had in my whole life," Carlton said after he and Linda unveiled the statue. "I wanted to play forever. Now I'm going to stand here forever." His son and two daughters, along with four grandchildren and his parents, were present at the ceremony. "My mom and dad were there when I started out in Boston in '69. They were here when I came to Chicago in '81 and when we won here in '83 and when I retired in '93. They're here today. My dad is 92 and my mom 86."

He thanked Reinsdorf and former general manager Roland Hemond. Reinsdorf offered nice words: "Acquiring Carlton Fisk changed the White Sox organization. People did not expect us to sign him. We'd been losers for most of the last 20 years. Fisk started our change."

Carlton acknowledged that he and Reinsdorf had their troubles. "There were some bumps in the road, but a lot of water's gone over the dam. Jerry's involvement today is very special. This could not have happened without him."

In May 2008, it was announced that Carlton Fisk had accepted a new position as "White Sox ambassador." In a statement, Reinsdorf said, "It's a pleasure to have him back in the ballpark. . . . Tonight is about our fans and the White Sox welcoming Pudge back to Chicago. . . . We believe that you never leave the White Sox family." In a pregame ceremony, former teammates Kittle, Jackson, and Fisk (all three wearing amply filled out White Sox "72" jerseys) entered the ballpark on motorcycles through the center field entrance.

Acting in a similar role for the Red Sox, greeting fans as part of the Legends Series at Fenway, Carlton embraced the duties, making appearances on behalf of both teams. As one watches him rehash war stories for groups of fans, his enthusiasm belying the fact that he is telling the same story for the ten-thousandth time ("... and as I was in the on-deck circle, I felt that something good was going to happen, and I turned to Fred Lynn and said . . ."), it becomes apparent that Carlton Fisk has finally made his peace, with the game of baseball and his former teams.

20 Orchids

CULTIVATING AND COLLECTING ORCHIDS is one of the oldest and most popular plant-growing hobbies. With more than 30,000 species and 200,000 hybrids, no plant family is more diverse. The amazing difference in sizes, shapes, and growing habits and their unique ability to produce hybrids between species result in an endless appeal for enthusiasts. As stated on the Web site for the American Orchid Society, "Trying to own one orchid is like trying to eat one peanut." Carlton Fisk was bitten by the orchid bug in the eighties and never recovered. It became his passion.

Question: orchids?

What in the name of Thurman Munson was one of the toughest baseball players who ever grappled in the dirt around home plate doing playing with flowers? But Carlton Fisk had the DNA of generations of New England farmers coursing through his veins and loved putting his hands in the dirt. Raising orchids fit his personality perfectly. It's not something just anyone can do—you don't simply throw out some seeds and hose them down whenever you think of it. Growing orchids takes a methodical approach, preparation, and precision; patience, accountability, and determination. They require the proper amount of air, light, pH, nutrients, sun, and water. They need to be regularly checked for weather changes, signs of fungus or insects, and to have dead or dry leaves removed. They need repotting every few years and repotting itself is a skill. There's a challenge in growing them successfully, keeping them alive for years, cross-breeding, and developing a new hybrid (called a grex). It's a demanding, satisfying hobby. It's the type of hobby in which *success has no shortcuts*. They require time and energy, but if you can get them to bloom—no small task and, in the best of circumstances only once or twice a year—they are as beautiful as a well-struck ball sailing over a fence. It's a *work equals reward* kind of thought process. It requires a *singular mind and purpose*.

"My pride and joy," Carlton told Peter Gammons while showing off his orchids during an interview for *Sports Illustrated* in 1990. "A lot of nights during the season, by the time I've finished my lifting and driven home from the park, it's 2 A.M. Everyone's asleep, and I want to unwind for an hour or two, so I come out here. Orchids take meticulous care. The attention they require would drive most people crazy, but that relaxes me. And the beauty of the flower itself awes me."

He had a large room dedicated to them at his house, initially sharing space with his weight room, but eventually expanding to several long tables with a sprinkler system (they have to be carefully misted) and lighting with metal-shaded lamps where he obsessed over each plant. "They're so delicate," he told another writer. "They let you know if they're not happy. If I don't give them the attention they demand, I feel bad."

He threw his intellectual powers into the subject, learning about the different kinds and their care. Whereas most sports fans can't tell their *Ascocentrum* from a hole in the ground, Carlton can tell at a glance a *Phalaenopsis* from an *Angraecum sesquipedale* and explain their differences as easily as he could tell you whether Reggie Jackson liked a fastball or a curve and where. The genus and species names flow easily off his tongue. He can offer discourses on the name and care of each type of orchid.

A trip to Hausermann's massive orchid complex on Addison Road in North Chicago got his blood flowing as much as walking to home plate in the ninth inning of a tie game. On Carlton Fisk Day in 1993, the White Sox had made a $25,000 donation to the Chicago Botanic Garden for a Carlton Fisk Orchid Tree exhibit. Carlton and Linda became active in orchid societies, known to all the major orchid dealers in the region. Carlton learned how to crossbreed the plants to create new hybrids—a time-consuming, goal-driven process. There are now hybrids listed in the International Orchid Register under the names Linda Fisk and Carlton Fisk (genus *Rhyncholaeliocattleya*).

While some former players are never satisfied in retirement, constantly on the prowl for their next fix of action—on the racetrack, in the casinos, making money—Carlton Fisk found his action in the delicate, multicolored plant. He went all in. By 2010 he had 40 different varieties and more than 300 orchids in total.

———

Carlton had still been a young man of 45 when he left baseball. While all players who retired soon after he broke into the majors found it necessary to find a second career just to pay the bills, the guys who retired after the 1990s did not. He had never lived extravagantly. He hadn't wasted his money on frivolous expenses or hokey investment schemes. He had been frugal in his early years by necessity and in his later years by personal belief. He had made enough money in baseball that there was no need of a second career. His baseball pension, thanks to the efforts of the Players Association during his career, topped out at $180,000 a year—decent walking-around money.

In the initial years after baseball, he still had some lingering sponsorship deals and he made good money whenever he wanted at speaking engagements. Due to the explosion of interest in former players and memorabilia, there was also easy money to be made at card shows and signing events. This was especially true after he was able to add "HOF" at the end of his signature. He could make $40,000 for signing 800 items during a single day, such as at the annual Hall of Fame induction event. (Willie Mays, by comparison, was able to pull down $75,000.)

But Carlton found himself doing fewer of these as the years went by. Some ex-players, while they may not need the money, feel the need to be productive or have the challenge of a second career, the validation of doing something worthwhile; a new purpose, a new passion, a new mission. Carlton Fisk never felt that way. There were no second careers for him. Money held no particular appeal in itself; he had enough.

He stayed in shape. He didn't keep up the murderous routine of his playing days, but he was active. He hunted and played a lot of golf, for fun and in charity tournaments (occasionally joking to writers that he tried to wave golf balls back into the fairway but they didn't obey). He belonged to two golf clubs and got together with his brother Calvin, who lived three hours away in Indianapolis, for a round of golf whenever possible.

He walked his daughters down the aisle at their weddings, then spent years playing with his grandchildren, which eventually numbered 10. Though he and Linda were both from New Hampshire, they remained in the Midwest—it was home, where the kids had grown up and gone to high school. In 2002, he and Linda paid $650,000 for a large house in nearby New Lenox, Illinois, at the end of a private, wooded cul-de-sac. They also maintained a house in Bradenton,

Florida—splitting the year between sunshine and the Midwest. Their three-bedroom, 8,000-square-foot home in Bradenton, which includes a pool, was purchased for $800,000.

He lived a quiet life with Linda as their marriage entered its fourth decade. Although they had married young and baseball marriages are notoriously difficult, theirs endured. "Linda always tried to be protective of Carlton and his time," says one longtime friend. "She wasn't rude or anything but just tried to keep people from taking too much of his time, trying to make the marriage work."

Throughout his career Carlton only allowed people to know what he wanted them to know; now he allowed even less. He rarely gave interviews unless it was part of a promotion paid for by a team or a sponsor. He almost never contributed to books or articles. Numerous books were written about the historic seasons and games he played in, including Game Six and the 1978 playoff game. Writers would round up as many players as possible to interview. Carlton always refused. Numerous authors attempted to get him to contribute to an authorized biography or an as-told-to autobiography. Some players with far fewer accomplishments have published multiple autobiographies. Carlton never had any. He wasn't interested. He preferred his privacy.

He made some personal appearances and attended a few major league functions, but was otherwise rarely seen or heard from. Some in the media considered him to be reclusive, the J. D. Salinger of the diamond. "I never thought he was a recluse," says Bob Verdi. "I saw him at a few events over the years after he retired, golf outings and charity events. He was great with people, relaxed, having fun. He didn't act like he was above mixing with the public. If he has kept out of the spotlight, it's because he just wants peace and quiet. He was more of a private person."

He had often commented that he didn't think fans should worship players other than to admire what they accomplished on the ball field. He did not particularly enjoy the celebrity game. He could be gracious and friendly to fans or very rude to autograph seekers who interrupted a conversation or dinner. "In his early years with the Red Sox, you would see Pudge standing and signing autographs all the time," says Jim Hogancamp. "He would stand there until no one was left. But he changed over the years. It bothered him when people were rude. I can remember driving out of Fenway Park with him once. People were banging on the car, demanding his autograph. Not asking, demanding." It was totally foreign to his small-town upbringing, a time of leaving cars and doors unlocked, of people respecting other people. "I can't imagine people disrespecting someone like that. I don't know how he stood it."

Carlton had given back to his communities throughout his career. He had served as the membership chairman for the New Hampshire Easter Seals Society during the seventies while living in Raymond. "It was unreal, the amount of time he put in," said society president Larry Gannon in 2000. "He became a spokesperson for us, he went to events, and he made regular visits to our school."

In retirement, he and Linda stayed active in charity work. In 2007 they started the Fisk and Friends Celebrity Classic in Sarasota to benefit Suncoast Charities for Children, which helps special-needs children. The event includes breakfast and a chance to meet and golf with celebrity athletes. In the past it has included former athletes Jenkins, Kaline, Weaver, Francona, Havlicek, McCarver, Fregosi, Feller, Unitas, Nitschke, Blanda, Brock, Bench, Evans, and Rice. It is now in its seventh year. On a promotional video, Carlton explains that the cause hits home because he and Linda have a grandchild with Down Syndrome. "The appeal here is what we're doing for the children. It's a chance to make a definite impact for children and to make a difference in the community."

They also became involved with the Cancer Support Center in Illinois. Both Carlton and Linda serve as honorary board members and participate in fund-raisers. Carlton also requests that the $40 fee for autographs through the mail be sent with a check made out to the Cancer Support Center.

After Carlton was elected to the Hall of Fame, the town of Charlestown hosted "Pudge Fisk Day" to celebrate its most famous citizen. The town dedicated a state plaque by the old high school (now a junior high after the school was swallowed up by consolidation into Fall Mountain Regional High School), honoring Charlestown as the "Hometown of Carlton E. 'Pudge' Fisk." Roger Conant proudly points out, "It's one of the only one of those green official state markers for an athlete."

Jim Hogancamp was the chairman of the committee for Carlton Fisk Day. "Somebody came from Chicago and they wanted to make a statue for him in Charlestown," says Hogancamp. "And the Fisks said, 'Not over our dead bodies.' They were very proud of Pudge, but they didn't want anyone to elevate any of their kids over the others. They were proud of all of their kids."

That weekend the members of the 1963 championship basketball team all got together for the first time in years. "Afterward everybody met at my house," says Conant. "We had a helluva time, just like we'd been back in high school. Just relaxing and having fun. Later Calvin said Pudge told him that was the most relaxing time he'd spent in years. He'd gotten to where he couldn't go anywhere without people bothering him, wanting stuff, you know, autographs."

Carlton remained popular in Charlestown. Many former teammates and classmates had followed his career and compiled scrapbooks of his exploits. But he was seen infrequently over the years and reporters occasionally remarked that this didn't sit well with some of the citizens. As the town's most famous son, they would have liked him to acknowledge them more. The town's people would have loved him. But he didn't seem to want that. "Everybody here thinks he could be a big hero if he came around a little more often," says a former friend. "They would love him to be a big hero."

He did make a few formal appearances in town. He appeared for Old Home Day in 1995, riding in the parade on a tractor. He hosted a Carlton Fisk Little League tournament in Charlestown in 2000 to help raise money for the Little League program. He attended all the games for three days, watching in the stands with his parents, greeted each player personally, and gave his old coach, Ralph Silva, one of the best weekends of his life.

But he was uncomfortable being treated as a celebrity by people he had known all his life. He was also uncomfortable with unknown people who acted like old friends just because they wanted something. It was always annoying to sign something as a favor and then see it turn up on eBay. He is in town quite a bit, just with no fanfare. He frequently makes side trips to Charlestown when he is in Boston or Cooperstown, arriving to visit his mother and family. "When Pudge comes back to Charlestown, his arrival is not announced," says Hogancamp. "Even his siblings don't know a lot of times. If people find out, then he can't even talk to his mother without people wanting him for something. He can't go out anywhere and not be bothered."

Carlton Fisk never won any nice guy awards. As far as anyone knows, he never tried out for one. He was who he was—a complicated man.

He stands as a man who played the game of baseball as hard as possible for as long as possible, without regard for what opponents felt about him. He blended admirable old-school values with the modern athletic pursuit of money and never had cause to question the marriage of the two. Few baseball players ever worked as hard or were as dedicated, to both the game and his team. The mission always came first.

He was a man of immense pride and principle who lived by a strict code and expected the same from others; and was often disappointed when they failed. A large part of his success and an even larger part of the conflicts he experienced over his career could be directly traced to his code. Push him and he was just proud and stubborn enough to push back. Push him hard and you better be prepared for a fight. He sometimes chose principle over friendship and never bent his code to conform or for personal advancement. Where other athletes covered their tracks with platitudes and clichés, he spoke from the heart, sometimes when perhaps a platitude or cliché may have been more appropriate. He could be blunt, brutally so, and if the truth hurt, then so be it.

His legacy was found in the way he played the game in the major leagues in four decades. Styles, economics, and attitudes changed, but he never did. For an entire generation, he will always be pictured, standing on the mound with his chin thrust out, hands on his hips, his mask on top of his head with a look of disgust on his face; or standing in a swirl of dust, the ball in his glove, ready to fight an intruding runner; or, most of all, hopping down the first baseline, waving at the ball, waving at the one moment that embodied the dream of every boy who ever picked up a bat.

There will always be the Game Six Home Run; when Carlton Ernest Fisk transcended the sport. It remains one of the most famous and enduring images in American sports history. Strictly in a baseball sense, it was not quite as monumental as Bobby Thomson's home run, or Bill Mazeroski's, but it was better than any other. Joe Carter and Kirk Gibson had their World Series moments, but neither was in an elimination game—if they had struck out, their teams would have had another chance the next day. Also, the timing was special. Thomson and Mazeroski came before television, and viewers, had really matured; Carter and Gibson after. With Fisk's home run and the camera shot, there was an emotion that had never been seen before.

Even after 40 years, every interviewer and every glad-handing fan always, eventually, gets around to the Game Six Home Run. Did he ever get tired of hearing about it from strangers? How many times can you say thank you? How many times can you act impressed at someone's memory, enjoy the moment, repeat the same stock answers to the same question? "People think that's the only hit I got in my whole life," he told a reporter in 2004. True, it could be irritating. But also that was like saying people think the only thing Leonardo da Vinci painted was the *Mona Lisa*—some things are so extraordinarily special that all other deeds in a career pale.

In 1993, Dan Shaughnessy wrote in *The Boston Globe*: "How many times have we seen the video clip? A hundred? A couple hundred? Maybe more? Provincially speaking, it's right up there with Neil Armstrong walking on the moon, the Beatles' first appearance on the *Ed Sullivan Show* and John F. Kennedy exhorting, 'Ask not what your country . . .'"

The movie *Good Will Hunting*, released 22 years after the famous home run, brought Fisk a crossover appeal to a new generation. In 1997, before Bennifer, before the *Bourne* series, before one fought the Germans in Europe while the other patrolled the skies over Pearl Harbor, Matt Damon and Ben Affleck were two buddies, friends since their childhood in Boston, who were shopping around a movie script written by Damon about a troubled young genius living in Boston.

In a key scene, a psychologist played by Robin Williams explains to Damon's character the exact moment he knew his wife was the one: "October 21, 1975."

Damon is amazed. "You know the . . . date?"

Williams: "'Cause it was Game Six of the World Series. Biggest game in Red Sox History."

Williams explains that he and his friends had slept out all night and gotten tickets to Game Six. He goes through the scene of the last inning: "Bottom of the twelfth, in stepped Carlton Fisk, Ole Pudge." Interspersed with Williams's description is the actual game footage. "He clocks it. . . . It's a high fly ball down the left field line! Fisk, he's waving at the ball like a madman. Get over. Get over . . . 35,000 fans, they charged the field."

Damon: "Did you rush the field?"

Williams: "No, I didn't rush the . . . field, I wasn't there."

Damon: "What?"

Williams: "No, I was in a bar talking to my future wife."

Damon (incredulously): "You missed Pudge Fisk's home run to have a drink with some . . . lady you never even met?"

Williams: "You should have seen her, she was a stunner."

Damon: "I don't care if Helen of Troy walks in, that's Game Six."

Williams: ". . . I just slid my ticket across the table and said, 'Sorry guys, I gotta see about a girl.'"

Damon wanted a Boston sporting event for the character to have missed in order to meet his future wife that would evoke the maximum amount of primal emotion in his audience. He could have picked one of the many Bruins or Celtics championship moments: a Larry Bird–led rally or Havlicek steals the ball! But it was really a no-brainer. No other game could have matched Game Six in the hearts and minds of fans. Fisk had been Damon's hero when he was growing up—he even had a Red Sox uniform with number 27 on the back. No other game would have worked.

The scene concludes with Damon finally nodding thoughtfully, then adding, "Woulda been nice to catch that game, though."

"I didn't know Pudge was gonna hit a homer," answers Williams.

While the scene created the emotion Damon wanted, a large part of the audience left the movie thinking, "He missed Game Six for a girl? What an idiot!"

In 1998, *TV Guide* named the Game Six home run the greatest moment in the history of sports television. "A generation later, Fisk's home run remains the ultimate moment in television sports," it stated, "not for its drama (the Red Sox lost the seventh game), but because of its sheer beauty—an American dream come true."

In 2011, MLB Network named it the top game of the past 50 years. Bob Costas said, "It had such a dramatic ending in a classic setting like Fenway Park. . . . There were so many ins and outs within the game itself, so many potential turning points, so many nuances. . . . It was actually a significant game in television history, too, because of the rating it got and the way it was produced and directed. It had everything."

Fisk appreciated the importance of the home run and his place in history. He once told writer Roger Angell, "I leave the room whenever it's coming up [on TV]. I'm trying to keep something private, just in my head."

"It's not very often that a person has a moment like that in his lifetime," he said in 1988. "I was in the right place at the right time and produced the right result. I can't forget it and don't want to, just as baseball doesn't want to."

In a video for MLB.com in 2011, he said, "[It was an] unbelievable feeling. Why is this my moment in the universe? Sometimes I think if you're put in a certain situation, no matter who you are . . . that there's going to be a moment that's going to challenge you and it's going to be yours . . . if you're up to that challenge and I just felt that the man upstairs said, 'This is your moment. Stay fair.' And there it was. The only way it could have been any better was if it was the seventh game."

On the evening of October 30, 2013, Carlton Fisk returned to Fenway Park to throw out the first pitch for Game Six of the World Series. It was the first Series Game Six at Fenway since that magical night in 1975. Fisk had been designated to throw out the first pitch in Game Sixes in the 2004 and 2007 World Series, but the Red Sox had foiled the plans by winning before a sixth game was necessary.

Carlton emerged from the Red Sox dugout with Luis Tiant and they walked to the mound together, waving to fans. The public address announcer told the crowd, "Welcome the two men who started and ended the last Game Six of a World Series played at Fenway Park." Carlton pulled a fake beard out of his pocket and attached it (looking like the current Red Sox players with their trademark lucky beards). The two then threw out dual first pitches.

The grainy video of the famous home run played on the scoreboard. Carlton watched and thought, "Who is that young guy?"

Forty years ago. Where did the time go? Think back to how the game was before that moment: struggling in popularity, great players making $100,000 to $200,000 a year, great tickets—box seats by the rail—not only available to regular people, but available for six bucks, players frequently spending long careers with the same team. Everything changed. Some of the changes were for the better, some for the worse. The game was different as Carlton Fisk walked to the plate that night; *Ole Pudge*, representing not only the Red Sox, but all of New England—the region from which he so proudly hailed, the region he could never imagine leaving, for any reason. Life was different as he hit the long fly down the line that would change his life and the game. As he hopped, hoped, waved for it to stay fair, everything seemed simple. There was only one question at the time: If it stays fair . . .

Acknowledgments

Credit for the genesis of this book must go entirely to my editor, Rob Kirkpatrick. It was Rob who recognized the untapped potential in Carlton Fisk's story and the fact that it had never before been put to paper. This is our third book together and, as usual, Rob was great to work with. I have never been tempted to shake off one of his shake-offs. Rob's assistant, Jennifer Letwack, worked tirelessly to help keep me on the straight path and meet deadlines. Thanks once again to my agent, John Talbot, for his faith and help in keeping me pointed forward and always seeking that next book project.

Mark Liptak is a lifelong White Sox fan, one of the foremost White Sox historians alive, and a first-rate journalist. He has chronicled the history of the White Sox with a voluminous list of first-person interviews with players which he has posted online (great reading for anyone interested in the White Sox or baseball in general). He was incredibly generous with his time and opinions, as well as the offer of the use of the content from his interviews.

One of the challenges in writing about baseball history is the ability to contact former players. Thanks to Texas Tech professor and writer Jorge Iber for getting me in touch with a former Red Sox player and to sportswriter Lew Freedman for providing me with some White Sox numbers.

I would like to thank Roger Conant and George Pebbles for taking their time to meet with me and walk me through the scrapbooks of their high school days. Roger's father, in addition to being a renowned bell-ringer, compiled one of the most complete scrapbooks of Carlton Fisk's career and it has now passed to Roger's hands. Together, the totally inclusive collections helped me separate fact from myth regarding Carlton's high school heroics. Thanks also to Roger for the use of the pictures and to George for saving the old Charlestown High School scorebooks from oblivion when the school was swallowed up by consolidation. I enjoyed listening to their stories of the good old days.

Jim Hogancamp retains the organizational genius of a point guard and the head for numbers of an accountant. He not only knows everyone but has their phone number and e-mail in his head for ready recall. His help was invaluable in getting me in touch with former high school classmates and family.

Thanks to Joyce Higgins and the Charlestown Historical Society. This is a gem (located in a classic building under the old gym) which contains every historical artifact from the area dating back to the early 1700s—and Joyce knows exactly where each one is located. Thanks for the time and help in understanding the rich history of the area.

Thanks to Ernie Piacopolos of the Red Sox Web site Fenway Nation for advising me on just how much Carlton Fisk is still revered by the folks of New England.

As always, any work of nonfiction is indebted to those who volunteer their memories. I was very lucky when it came to finding those who witnessed Carlton Fisk's childhood, college years, and professional career. Thanks to Don Aase, Nick Anderson, Jeff Banister, Larry Barnett, Bobby Bolin, Tom Burgmeier, Bill Campbell, Roger Conant, Ray Culp, Rich Dotson, William Estey, Calvin Fisk, Leona Fisk, Lew Freedman, Mike Garman, Julie Hartley, Gene Hauserman, Glenn Herzig, Tom Herzig, Joyce Higgins, Marc Hill, Jim Hogancamp, Buddy Hunter, Ferguson Jenkins, Eddie Kasko, John Kennedy, Chet Lemon, Mark Liptak, Fred Lynn, Carl McAlister, Janet Fisk Miller, Leigh Montville, Donn Pall, Mike Paxson, George Pebbles, Gary Peters, Rico Petrocelli, Walter Piletz, James Powers, Charles Prediger, Joe Rahal, Steve Renko III, Mark Russell, Katie Gould Shaw, Ken Silva, Rac Slider, Mike Squires, Ken Tatum, Mike Torrez, Bob Verdi, Poody Walsh, Brad Weeks, and Jim Wright.

Leigh Montville has long been my literary idol. I consider him to be one of the greatest sports chroniclers and wordsmiths of our time. I use his books *The Big Bam* and *Ted Williams* as my textbooks to study how to write a good baseball biography. So it was a great thrill when he called me in answer to my letter and spent time discussing his early days on the baseball beat in Boston, which coincided with Carlton Fisk's early days there.

It is always a special treat to talk to former professional players and

I appreciate all of them for their time and honesty. A few warrant further mention. Rico Petrocelli was the heart of the Red Sox for many years. I had previously talked to Rico and his on-air partner Ed Randall on their Sirius/XM Saturday morning baseball nostalgia radio show about my other books (they have a blast together each week). I was very happy when Rico readily agreed to share his memories with me for this book.

When I was a teenager, I wanted to be Fred Lynn. We were both left-handed and both played outfield; unfortunately the comparisons went no further. My attempts to imitate his swashbuckling plays usually did not end well. I was thrilled when he answered my inquiry and agreed to talk to me. He was very generous with his time as he talked and reminisced about their great teams and it was a pleasure to talk to him. He has vaulted near the top of my all-time nice-guy list.

Donn Pall and Marc Hill were very helpful in fielding multiple phone calls for memories and fact-checking of their White Sox days. Chet Lemon is possibly the nicest, most enjoyable ex-major league player I have ever talked to. He seemed to genuinely enjoy discussing his playing days and baseball in general. It was somewhat sad to finally end the call.

Thanks to Tyler Munn at the Bartholomew County Public Library. His help, particularly in procuring rare and out-of-print books and newspapers via inter-library loan, was invaluable.

Thanks to my wife and family and to my office staff for their patience and assistance. Time spent with kids is precious once they leave, and I was very happy my son was able to take a break from medical school to spend a weekend with his dad on a research trip to Cooperstown and New Hampshire. His knowledge of new things like cell phones that take pictures proved valuable to a technophobic geezer.

Special thanks to Calvin Fisk and Janet Fisk Miller for their time and for fielding several additional fact-checking phone calls. Calvin is in many ways the consummate big brother. He maintained a near-complete collection of boxscores from his brother's major league career and is perhaps the proudest brother of a Hall-of-Famer in America. Also, thanks to Janet for walking me around their farm and introducing me to their mother.

I enjoy meeting new and interesting people during the research with every book, but it was especially a treat to get to meet and talk to Leona Fisk. She was incredibly helpful and it was impossible not to feel honored just to be in her presence. The ladies at the Charlestown Historical Society told me that everyone in town loved Lee Fisk, but that was a gross understatement. She is a very, very special lady and mere words cannot do justice to all she has accomplished. When she mentioned that she hadn't had time to keep up with the bumper crop of blueberries and blackberries this year (she is only 97), I offered to help and so me and my son found ourselves in the backyard, picking berries and listening to stories from a baseball Hall of Fame member's childhood. I can think of worse ways for a father and son to spend time together.

Appendix

CARLTON FISK'S MAJOR LEAGUE CAREER STATISTICS

Yr	Team	G	AB	R	H	2B	3B	HR	RBI	BB	SO	SF	HBP	AVG
1969	Red Sox	2	5	0	0	0	0	0	0	0	2	0	0	.000
1971	Red Sox	14	48	7	15	2	1	2	6	1	10	0	0	.313
1972	Red Sox	131	457	74	134	28	9	22	61	52	83	0	4	.293
1973	Red Sox	135	508	65	125	21	0	26	71	37	99	2	10	.246
1974	Red Sox	52	187	36	56	12	1	11	26	24	23	1	2	.299
1975	Red Sox	79	263	47	87	14	4	10	52	27	32	2	2	.331
1976	Red Sox	134	487	76	124	17	5	17	58	56	71	5	6	.255
1977	Red Sox	152	536	106	169	26	3	26	102	75	85	10	9	.315
1978	Red Sox	157	571	94	162	39	5	20	88	71	83	6	7	.284
1979	Red Sox	91	320	49	87	23	2	10	42	10	38	3	6	.272
1980	Red Sox	131	478	73	138	25	3	18	62	36	62	3	13	.289
1981	Red Sox	96	338	44	89	12	0	7	45	38	37	5	12	.263
1982	White Sox	135	476	66	127	17	3	14	65	46	60	4	6	.267
1983	White Sox	138	488	85	141	26	4	26	86	46	88	3	6	.289
1984	White Sox	102	359	54	83	20	1	21	43	26	60	4	5	.231
1985	White Sox	153	543	85	129	23	1	37	107	52	81	6	17	.238
1986	White Sox	125	457	42	101	11	0	14	63	22	92	6	6	.221
1987	White Sox	135	454	68	116	22	1	23	71	39	72	6	8	.256
1988	White Sox	76	253	37	70	8	1	19	50	37	40	2	5	.277
1989	White Sox	103	375	47	110	25	2	13	68	36	60	5	3	.293
1990	White Sox	137	452	65	129	21	0	18	65	61	73	1	7	.285
1991	White Sox	134	460	42	111	25	0	18	74	32	86	2	7	.241
1992	White Sox	62	188	12	43	4	1	3	21	23	38	2	1	.229
1993	White Sox	25	53	2	10	0	0	1	4	2	11	1	1	.189
Career		**G**	**AB**	**R**	**H**	**2B**	**3B**	**HR**	**RBI**	**BB**	**SO**	**SF**	**HBP**	**AVG**
24 Years		2,499	8,756	1,276	2,356	421	47	376	1,330	849	1,386	79	143	.269

Notes

All quotes are from personal interviews unless otherwise noted.

1: The New England Fisks

4 *In order to fully understand:* Personal interviews with Roger Conant, Ken Silva, Calvin Fisk, Janet Fisk, Leona Fisk, Jim Hogancamp, Walter Piletz, Katy Shaw Gould, George Pebbles, Brad Weeks, Glenn Herzig, Tom Herzig, Carl McAllister, Roger Conant. Also, the Charlestown Historical Society, U.S. Census.

4 *"The New England farmer":* David McCullough, *John Adams* (New York: Simon & Schuster, 2001).

8 *"In these parts":* Peter Gammons, "Sharp as Ever," *Sports Illustrated*, February 26, 1990.

9 *"We had chores":* Phil Rogers, "Fisk's Body of Work," *Chicago Tribune*, July 21, 2000.

9 *Once Carlton complained:* Vin Sylvia, "From Charlestown to Cooperstown," *New Hampshire Sunday News*, July 16, 2000.

10 *"Hey, you're Carlton's":* John Schulian, "New Hampshire Farm Boy Is Every Bit His Father's Son," *Chicago Sun-Times*, July 14, 1982.

11 *"With him you":* Ibid.

11 *"It was a motivating":* Peter Gammons, "Sharp as Ever," *Sports Illustrated*, February 26, 1990.

2: The Forts

15 *"[The Charlestown Forts] will send":* *Daily Eagle* (Claremont, NH), June 5, 1965.

18 *"How lucky can":* Bob Hookway, "A Legend Earns His Due," *Valley News* (West Lebanon, NH), November 19, 2005.

19 *"I love what":* Ibid.

19 *There was a lot:* Carlton Fisk, "The Simple Life" (50th Anniversary—New Hampshire), *Sports Illustrated*, April 26, 2004.

22 *"They sat behind":* Bob Hookway, "A Legend Earns His Due," *Valley News* (West Lebanon, NH), November 19, 2005.

23 *Using the sportswriter lingo:* Ruel N. Colby, "The Sports Galley," *Concord Monitor*, February 17, 1965.

24 *"This must be me":* John Feinstein, *Play Ball: The Life and Troubled Times of Major League Baseball* (New York: Villard, 1993).

24 *"With Pudgy Fisk":* Charlie Spencer, "Charlestown Wins Twin State Title," *Claremont Eagle Times*, March 24, 1963.

24 *"Carlton just had":* Gary Harrington, "Where Carlton Fisk Grew Up, They Called Him 'Pudge,'" *Keene Sentinel*, March 18, 2004.

24 *"Who is that . . .":* Tom Simon. "Carlton Fisk," in *The Green Mountain Boys of Summer: Vermonters in the Major Leagues, 1882–1993* (Shelburne, VT: New England Press, 2000).

25 *"I was 2 for 6":* Phil Rogers, "Fisk's Body of Work," *Chicago Tribune*, July 21, 2000.

26 *"Compliments from my father":* Pat Jordan, "Conversations with the Dinosaur," *Men's Journal*, March 1993.

26 *"Maybe I should have":* Vin Sylvia, "From Charlestown to Cooperstown," *New Hampshire Sunday News*, July 16, 2000.

26 *"I thought what":* Peter Gammons, "Sharp as Ever," *Sports Illustrated*, February 26, 1990.

29 *"In the spring of '65":* Gary Harrington, "Where Carlton Fisk Grew Up, They Called Him 'Pudge,'" *Keene Sentinel*, March 18, 2004.

31 *"It went about":* "Tim Ryan Recalls Fisk Homer at Cooperstown," *The Day* (New London, Connecticut), November 21, 1972.

31 *"How far did":* *Claremont Times,* date unknown (clipping in Charlestown Historical Society).

3: Joe College

32 *The University of New Hampshire was not:* "University of New Hampshire in the 1960s," Thomas Dart, 2013, www.bibiofaction.com; interviews with Calvin Fisk, Joe Rahal, William Estey, and Jeff Bannister.

35 *"a terrific kid":* Vin Sylvia, "From Celtics Dreams, to Red Sox Reality," *New Hampshire Sunday News*, July 23, 2000.

36 *"After the URI loss":* Ibid.

37 *"I was only 17":* Carlton Fisk in National Baseball Hall of Fame and Museum, *The Hall: A Celebration of Baseball's Greats* (New York: Little, Brown, 2014).

37 *"I hadn't learned":* Vin Sylvia, "From Celtics Dreams, to Red Sox Reality," *New Hampshire Sunday News*, July 23, 2000.

39 *"He had a good swing":* Zander Hollander and Phyllis Hollander, eds., *The Masked Marvels: Baseball's Great Catchers* (New York: Random House, 1982).

39 *"To tell the truth":* Peter Gammons, *Beyond the Sixth Game* (Boston: Houghton Mifflin, 1985).

40 *At the time:* Gary Harrington, "Bob Wilber Was Often Found with Fisk by His Side," *Keene Sentinel*, March 19, 2004.

4: Waterloo, Pittsfield, Pawtucket, and Louisville

41 *It was a tight situation:* Carlton Fisk with Lou Sabin, "Carlton Fisk: Big Man Behind the Plate," *Boy's Life,* September 1973.

42 *"I don't know if":* Phil Rogers, "Fisk's Body of Work," *Chicago Tribune,* July 21, 2000.

44 *One extremely hot:* Carlton Fisk in National Baseball Hall of Fame and Museum, *The Hall: A Celebration of Baseball's Greats;* Carlton Fisk Hall of Fame induction speech, July 23, 2000.

47 *"He was also slow":* Bill Lee and Dick Lally, *The Wrong Stuff* (New York: Viking, 1984).

48 *Ralph Silva later told:* Gary Harrington, "Where Carlton Fisk Grew Up, They Called Him 'Pudge,' " *Keene Sentinel,* March 18, 2004.

49 Sox *manager Dick Williams:* Larry Claflin, "Bosox Find a Mitt Pearl in Youngster Pudge Fisk," *Sporting News,* July 29, 1972.

49 *One day as he:* Clif Keane, "Carlton Fisk: He's a Take-Charge Guy, and, at 25, Sox Leader," *Boston Globe,* April 1, 1973.

49 *"One of the most":* Sporting News, March 15, 1969.

49 *Personnel director Dick O'Connell:* Sporting News, March 29, 1969.

51 *"I found out why":* Peter Gammons, *Beyond the Sixth Game.*

51 *"The reserves interrupted":* Carlton Fisk in National Baseball Hall of Fame and Museum, *The Hall: A Celebration of Baseball's Greats.*

52 *He was the subject:* "Catcher in the 'Nam: Fisk Eyes Baseball Career," *Tropic Lightning News,* September 1, 1969.

52 *"We'd spend a lot":* Gary Harrington, "Bob Wilber Was Often Found with Fisk by His Side," *Keene Sentinel,* March 19, 2004.

52 *One of the base:* "Little Leaguer Gets Big League Advice," *Pocono Record,* July 10, 1969.

53 *"I didn't feel like":* Carlton Fisk in National Baseball Hall of Fame and Museum, *The Hall: A Celebration of Baseball's Greats.*

55 *"have to go out":* Bill Liston, "The Challenge That Inspired Carlton Fisk," *Baseball Digest,* March 1973.

56 *"I got a lot of":* Pat Putnam, "New Dealer for the Red Sox," *Sporting News,* April 1, 1974.

56 *"I always worked hard":* Peter Gammons, "Fisk Takes Risk and Wins," *Sporting News,* June 14, 1980.

56 *"Pudge and I":* "Fisk Is Latest in Lengthy Line of Colonels' Classy Catchers," Ron Coons, *Sporting News,* May 29, 1971.

57 *"He broke the job":* Bill Liston, "The Challenge That Inspired Carlton Fisk," *Baseball Digest,* March 1973.

60 *In the winter:* Lee Maidrand, *Times Reporter* (Springfield, VT), 1971.

60 *"He just walked":* Gary Harrington, "Carlton Fisk Once Called Keene Home," *Keene Sentinel,* July 17, 2000.

63 *"He told me":* Lee Maidrand, *Times-Reporter* (Springfield, VT), 1971.

5: Boston

64   *"When I got to"*: Mark Liptak, "Gary Peters Interview," 2006, www.baseball
      -almanac.

65   *"Carl Yastrzemski is for"*: Jim Bouton, *Ball Four* (New York: World, 1970).

66   *"The only question"*: Vito Stellino, ed., *1972 Baseball Guidebook*, Maco Publish-
      ing, 1972.

66   *Smith responded, telling:* Vito Stellino, ed., *Sports All Stars 1972: Baseball*, Maco
      Publishing, 1972.

70   *Late in the game:* Allen Lewis, "Carlton Fisk: Diplomat with a Giant Heart,"
      Knight Rider Newspapers, in *Lakeland Ledger,* April 18, 1981; Carlton Fisk
      Hall of Fame Induction Speech, July 23, 2000; John Feinstein, *Play Ball: The
      Life and Troubled Times of Major League Baseball;* interview with Gary Peters.

6: Rookie of the Year

73   *"I've always liked him"*: Dave O'Hara, "Carlton Fisk Showing Improvement as
      Red Sox Rap Cardinals 2–0," AP in *The Telegraph*, March 16, 1972.

76   *Smith did not endear:* Bill Lee, *The Wrong Stuff.*

77   *"Finally, Some Good News"*: "Finally, Some Good News—Baseball Starts To-
      morrow," UPI in *Montreal Gazette*, April 14, 1972.

77   *Fisk was down:* Bill Liston, "The Challenge That Inspired Carlton Fisk," *Base-
      ball Digest*, March 1973.

79   *"Fisk took charge"*: Bill Lee, *The Wrong Stuff.*

82   *"In spring training"*: Harold Kaese, "Here's Hoping Fisk Beats Jinx," *Boston
      Globe*, August 6, 1972.

82   *Perhaps feeling a little:* Larry Keith, "A Sleeper to Boston Is a Sound Catch,"
      Sports Illustrated, September 11, 1972.

82   *"To tell the truth"*: "Fisk, .312 at bat (2d in AL) Unhappy at Work Behind Plate,"
      Evening Boston Globe, August 1, 1972.

83–89 *After finishing with . . . "By the time"*: Bill Liston, "The Challenge That Inspired
      Carlton Fisk," *Baseball Digest*, March 1973; Ray Fitzgerald, "The Fisk Furor:
      Rookie Charges Yaz, Smith Fail to Hustle," *Boston Globe*, August 9, 1972; "Fisk
      Says He Was Misquoted," AP in *Miami News*, August 9, 1972; Carl Yastrzemski
      with Gerald Eskanazi, *Yaz: Baseball, the Wall, and Me* (New York: Doubleday,
      1990); Larry Claflin, "Reggie Buttons His Lip, Lets Bat Do the Talking," *Sporting
      News*, September 2, 1972; Harold Kaese, "Many Have Thought . . . Only Fisk
      Has Spoken," *Boston Globe*, August 9, 1972; *Sporting News*, May 6, 1972; Larry
      Keith, "A Sleeper to Boston Is a Sound Catch," *Sports Illustrated*, September 11,
      1972; Bill Lee, *The Wrong Stuff.*

89   *"Carlton would make him"*: Bill Lee, *The Wrong Stuff.*

89   *"When are you going"*: Tom Keegan, "Duck Tales: Ex-MLB pitcher, KU Coach
      Marty Pattin Recalls His Playing Days," www2.kusports.com, June 28, 2011.

93   *Tom Yawkey, so excited:* Carl Yastrzemski with Gerald Eskanazi, *Yaz: Baseball, the Wall, and Me.*

94   *"You could look at":* Ibid.

95   *"he probably will receive":* Larry Claflin, "Fisk Should Climb to $30,000 Level," *Sporting News,* November 25, 1972.

7: New England Grit

96   *"I'm very pleased":* "Carlton Fisk and Sonny Siebert Ink Bosox Pacts for '73 Season," AP in *Lewistown* (Maine) *Daily Sun,* March 1, 1973.

96   *Sports Illustrated described:* Melvin Maddocks, "The New England Grit of Mr. Fisk," *Sports Illustrated,* July 30, 1973.

97   *"He [Fisk] and Frank":* Peter Gammons, "Homebody Fisk Roars Down Recovery Road," *Sporting News,* December 8, 1973.

97   *"I know a lot":* Ibid.

97   *"Tell him [Fisk] that people":* Peter Gammons, "Without Fisk Red Sox Could Be Dead Sox," *Sporting News,* July 13, 1974.

98   *"The idea is to":* Peter Gammons, "Fisk's Clutch Bat Bosox' Key Weapon," *Sporting News,* October 25, 1975.

98   *"Our pitchers have to":* Bill Liston, "The Challenge That Inspired Carlton Fisk," *Baseball Digest,* March 1973.

98   *"If you could":* Peter Gammons, "Without Fisk, Red Sox Could Be Dead Sox," *Sporting News,* July 13, 1974.

99   *"I realize that I":* Clif Keane, "Carlton Fisk: He's a Take-Charge Guy, and, at 25, Sox Leader," *Boston Globe,* April 1, 1973.

99   *"You do the catching":* *Sporting News,* August 18, 1973.

99   *"If I can get":* Melvin Maddocks, "The New England Grit of Mr. Fisk," *Sports Illustrated,* July 30, 1973.

100   *"Too many guys":* Ibid.

101   *" 'Some guys have to' ":* Ibid.

101–103 *On August 1, the Red Sox . . . "You know how":* Peter Gammons, "Carlton Fisk, Thurman Munson Fight in Red Sox' Win," *Boston Globe,* August 2, 1973; Peter Gammons, "Fisk vs. Munson: A True War," ESPN.com, July 23, 2000; Marty Appel, *Munson: The Life and Death of a Yankee Captain* (New York: Doubleday, 2009); Mike Vaccaro, *Emperors and Idiots* (New York: Doubleday, 2005).

105   *"Until maybe a":* Peter Gammons, "Homebody Fisk Roars Down Recovery Road," *Sporting News,* December 8, 1973.

105   *"He is gone and":* Peter Gammons, "Red Sox' Unity U. Presents Another Spirited Debate," *Sporting News,* November 24, 1973.

105   *"It only shows":* Ibid.

106   *"Some things were taken":* Peter Gammons, "Homebody Fisk Roars Down Recovery Road," *Sporting News,* December 8, 1973.

106 *"When he [Smith] was traded"*: Peter Gammons, "Red Sox' Unity U. Presents Another Spirited Debate," *Sporting News*, November 24, 1973.

106 *"It's true there's"*: "Carlton Fisk's Mother Pinch Hits Against Jackson," UPI in *Star-News*, November 8, 1973.

106 *"What does a pipe fitter"*: Jack Sands and Peter Gammons, *Coming Apart at the Seams: How Baseball Owners, Players and Television Executives Have Led Our National Pastime to the Brink of Disaster* (New York: Macmillan, 1993).

107 *"I hope you die"*: Peter Gammons, *Beyond the Sixth Game*.

108 *"It's ridiculous"*: Peter Gammons, "Without Fisk Red Sox Could Be Dead Sox," *Sporting News*, July 13, 1974.

109 *"Cheer up Pudge"*: Interview with Leigh Montville.

109 *"We did have our . . . friendship"*: Bill Lee, *The Wrong Stuff*.

111 *"The Red Sox just said"*: Ray Fitzgerald, "Bosox to Fisk: Thanks for Memories," *Sporting News*, April 4, 1981.

111 *"They could have"*: Peter Gammons, *Beyond the Sixth Game*.

8: The Best Game Ever

113 *"Everybody in America"*: Mark Newman, "Network Anoints '75 Series Epic as Top Game," MLB.com, May 19, 2011.

114 *"Before I got down"*: Peter Gammons, "Fisk Injury Curse Casts Pall over Bosox Camp," *Sporting News*, March 29, 1975.

116 *"It's just like"*: *Sporting News*, July 12, 1975.

116 *"This town doesn't deserve"*: Ibid.

117 *"I have no ill"*: Ron Fimrite, "It Was Like Old Times," *Sports Illustrated*, July 7, 1975.

119 *"We were fortunate"*: Peter Golenbock, *Fenway: An Unexpurgated History of the Boston Red Sox* (New York: Putnam, 1992).

120 *"That really meant a lot"*: Peter Gammons, "Fisk's Clutch Bat Bosox' Key Weapon," *Sporting News*, October 25, 1975.

122 *"They really came"*: *Boston Globe*, October 6, 1975.

123 *"Very good"*: Leigh Montville, "Red Sox Win the Pennant," *Boston Globe*, October 8, 1975.

123 *"I hate this stuff"*: Ray Fitzgerald, "Yes, They Did It Their Way," *Boston Globe*, October 8, 1975.

124 *"The American League Champion"*: Ibid.

125 *"You gotta understand"*: Lowell Reidenbaugh, "Balk-Call Crisis Brings Out Best in Red Sox Ace Tiant," *Sporting News*, October 25, 1975.

129 *"the angriest losing"*: Ray Fitzgerald, "Fisk the Ultimate Series Hero," *Sporting News*, October 25, 1980.

129 *"You saw the play"*: Peter Gammons, "A Call They'll Never Forget," *Boston Globe*, October 15, 1975.

129 *"It's a damn shame"*: Ron Fimrite, "Stormy Days for the Series," *Sports Illustrated*, October 27, 1975.

130 *"We should have had"*: Wells Twombly, "Ump's Call Will Live in History," *Sporting News*, November 1, 1975.

130 *"Baseball owes it"*: Ron Fimrite, "Stormy Days for the Series," *Sports Illustrated*, October 27, 1975.

130 *"Next year they'll:"* Peter Gammons, "A Call They'll Never Forget," *Boston Globe*, October 15, 1975.

130 *"Bleep the umpires"*: Ibid.

130 *"I would have"*: Bill Lee, *The Wrong Stuff.*

130 *"The Series is now"*: Mark Frost, *Game Six* (New York: Hyperion, 2009).

130 *"It was obviously interference"*: Lowell Reidenbaugh, "Hot Dispute Marks Vital Play in Reds' Triumph," *Sporting News*, November 1, 1975.

130 *"I ruled that"*: Ron Fimrite, "Stormy Days for the Series," *Sports Illustrated*, October 27, 1975.

131 *"The batter has"*: Ibid.

131 *"The ball bounced high"*: Lowell Reidenbaugh, "Hot Dispute Marks Vital Play in Reds' Triumph," *Sporting News*, November 1, 1975.

132 *"if I had"*: Clif Keane, "Umpire Barnett Sees Replay," *Boston Globe*, October 16, 1975.

132 *"Call Was bad"*: Ray Fitzgerald, "Call Was Bad . . . So Was Throw," *Boston Globe*, October 16, 1975.

132 *"I'm a Red Sox fan"*: "Kissinger Ducks Umpire Issue," AP in *Boston Globe*, October 16, 1975.

133 *"Tell me, when's"*: Russell Schneider, "Barnett Now Calls Series Hassle Good Break," *Sporting News*, April 17, 1976.

134 *"I wish the"*: Ron Fimrite, "Stormy Days for the Series," *Sports Illustrated*, October 27, 1975.

134 *"Let him go after"*: Ibid.

137 *"The patient was"*: Ray Fitzgerald, "The Best Game Ever!," *Boston Globe*, October 22, 1975.

138 "This is the . . .": "The Fisk Home Run," MLB.com video, January 10, 2011.

140 *Watching in the NBC truck:* Steven Marcus, "Louis Gerard, Cameraman Who Captured Iconic Series Moment, Dies," Newsday.com, February 22, 2013; Matt Crossman, "The Rat That Changed TV: Behind the Scenes During Carlton Fisk's Iconic Homer," www.sportingnews.com, April 19, 2012.

140 *"They didn't even know"*: Alan Schwarz, "Ideas & Trends; A Shot Seen 'Round the World," *New York Times*, October 15, 2000.

141 *As Gerard was leaving:* Matt Crossman, "The Rat That Changed TV: Behind the Scenes During Carlton Fisk's Iconic Homer," www.sportingnews.com, April 19, 2012.

141 *It became the camera shot:* Steven Marcus, "Louis Gerard, Cameraman Who Captured Iconic Series Moment, Dies," Newsday.com, February 22, 2013.

141 *"I've always wanted":* "Fisk Was Nearly Out of Focus on Homer," *Los Angeles Times*, May 10, 1987.

141 *"Though I never":* Steven Marcus, "Louis Gerard, Cameraman Who Captured Iconic Series Moment Dies," Newsday.com, February 22, 2013.

142 *"I don't think I've ever":* Ron Fimrite, "Everything Came Up Reds," *Sports Illustrated*, November 3, 1975.

142 *In Charlestown, New Hampshire:* Interview with Roger Conant.

143 *"The sixth game":* Ron Fimrite, "Everything Came Up Reds," *Sports Illustrated*, November 3, 1975.

143 *"Yes I'm drained":* Ibid.

144 *"I don't know":* Ibid.

144 *"If there was":* Shirley Povich, "12 Glorious Days in October '75," *Sporting News*, October 25, 1980.

144 *In late October:* " 'Fisk for Governor' Cry Hometown Fans," UPI in *Sarasota Herald-Tribune*, October 30, 1975.

9: The Holdout Three

146 *"got caught in the":* Carl Yastrzemski and Gerald Eskanazi, *Yaz: Baseball, the Wall, and Me.*

148 *"I do not talk":* Jack Sands and Peter Gammons, *Coming Apart at the Seams: How Baseball Owners, Players and Television Executives Have Led Our National Pastime to the Brink of Disaster.*

148 *"No one knows more":* Peter Gammons, *Beyond the Sixth Game.*

149 *"Most owners will be":* Larry Keith, "He's Baseball's Not-So-Secret Agent," *Sports Illustrated*, June 28, 1976.

150 *"I fully expect to sign":* "Carlton Fisk Inks Sox' Renewal Paper," AP in *The Telegraph* (Alton, IL), March 10, 1976.

152 *"It changed the club":* Carl Yastrzemski and Gerald Eskanazi, *Yaz: Baseball, the Wall, and Me.*

153 *"The label 'mercenary' ":* George Vass, "Will Mercenaries Ruin the Game?," *Baseball Digest*, September 1976.

153 *"[They] became a good":* Larry Keith, "What's the Pox on the Sox?," *Sports Illustrated*, August 23, 1976.

154 *"As a catcher":* Ibid.

154 *"I would never":* "Fisk Move Stunned Bosox Management," UPI in *Reading Eagle*, March 10, 1981.

154 *"My teammates would":* Larry Keith, "What's the Pox on the Sox?," *Sports Illustrated*, August 23, 1976.

154 *"When the three":* Carl Yastrzemski and Gerald Eskanazi, *Yaz: Baseball, the Wall, and Me.*

154 *"It seemed to take"*: Bill Lee, *The Wrong Stuff*.

155 *A Boston radio station*: Dan Epstein, *Stars and Strikes: Baseball and America in the Bicentennial Summer of '76* (New York: St. Martin's, 2014); Peter Gammons, *Beyond the Sixth Game*.

156 *"I used to take"*: "Yankees vs. Red Sox Forum" video, www.theforumchannel.tv, February 2005.

156 *"I'd be warming up"*: Ibid.

158 *"I wanted to make"*: Paul Doyle, "Lee vs. Nettles: Time Hasn't Healed Sore Feelings," *Hartford Courant*, May 20, 2002.

158 *"Goodbye Fenway, Goodbye"*: Peter Gammons, *Beyond the Sixth Game*.

159 *"I don't want"*: Peter Gammons, "Sharp as Ever," *Sports Illustrated*, February 26, 1990.

159 *"He's been second-guessing"*: Peter Gammons, *Beyond the Sixth Game*.

159 *"Right now my family"*: Ibid.

160 *"It was simply"*: *Sporting News*, July 3, 1976.

160 *"a lot is going"*: Peter Gammons, *Beyond the Sixth Game*.

160 *"It was like a"*: Carl Yastrzemski and Gerald Eskanazi, *Yaz: Baseball, the Wall, and Me*.

160 *"Coming to Boston"*: Larry Keith, "What's the Pox on the Sox?," *Sports Illustrated*, August 23, 1976.

160 *"I can't win"*: Peter Gammons, *Beyond the Sixth Game*.

161 *"We cannot blame everything"*: AP in *Spartansburg Herald*, July 20, 1976.

161 *"There are a lot"*: Larry Whiteside, "Unsigned Red Sox Players Hastened Darrell's Demise," *Sporting News*, August 7, 1976.

161 *"I guess it had"*: Frank Corkin, "What's Really Wrong with Bosox?," *Morning Record* (Meriden, CT), July 27, 1976.

161 *"How tragic that"*: Ibid.

162 *"the easiest guy"*: Carlton Fisk Hall of Fame Induction speech, July 23, 2000.

162 *"Baseball, because it demands"*: Larry Keith, "What's the Pox on the Sox?," *Sports Illustrated*, August 23, 1976.

163 *"[They] won a lot"*: Ibid.

163 *"a heckuva backup"*: "American League's Top Catchers: Thurman Munson vs. Carlton Fisk: It's an old Rivalry," Newsday Services, July 27, 1977.

164 *"teeth of second basemen"*: Herb Crehan, *Red Sox Heroes of Yesteryear* (Boston: Rounder Books, 2005).

164 *"Going into each"*: Larry Keith, "Suddenly They're Up in Arms in Boston," *Sports Illustrated*, July 3, 1978.

165 *"Let's see the"*: Richard Bradley, *The Greatest Game: The Yankees, the Red Sox and the Playoff of '78* (New York: Free Press, 2008).

167 *"If nuclear war"*: Peter Gammons, "There's a Rub in the Hub," *Sports Illustrated*, November 14, 1977.

10: The Massacre

169 *"One thing I can't"*: Chaz Scoggins, "Fisk Instills Confidence in Sox Pitchers," *Lewiston Daily Sun*, June 5, 1980.

171 *"Bear down. You've"*: Larry Whiteside, "'Bosox' Trio of Hill Beauts," *Sporting News*, September 3, 1977.

172 *"Fisk stood by me"*: Bill Lee, *The Wrong Stuff*.

173 *"someone is sticking"*: Peter Gammons, "The Boston Massacre," *Sports Illustrated*, September 18, 1978.

174 *Bill Lee later told*: William Nack, "Playing Hurt—The Doctors' Dilemma," *Sports Illustrated*, June 11, 1979.

174 *"I looked into"*: Ibid.

174 *"Pure Connecticut River granite"*: Bill Lee, *The Wrong Stuff*.

174 *"I wasn't about"*: William Nack, "Playing Hurt—The Doctors' Dilemma," *Sports Illustrated*, June 11, 1979.

174 *Fisk later told*: Peter Gammons, *Beyond the Sixth Game*.

175 *"This is the first"*: Peter Gammons, "The Boston Massacre," *Sports Illustrated*, September 18, 1978.

176 *"How can a team"*: Ibid.

176 *"Why do the Red Sox"*: Richard Bradley, *The Greatest Game: The Yankees, the Red Sox and the Playoff of '78*.

176 *"It was different"*: Carl Yastrzemski and Gerald Eskanazi, *Yaz: Baseball, the Wall, and Me*.

180 *"I knew the season"*: AU: TK

180 *"What I remember the most"*: Herb Crehan, *Red Sox Heroes of Yesteryear*.

180 *"The Red Sox, for"*: Peter Gammons, "October 2, 1978," *Sports Illustrated*, July 19, 1993.

11: It Just Isn't the Same

182 *"It's Curt Gowdy"*: Marty Appel, *Munson: The Life and Death of a Yankee Captain*.

183 *"Maybe it's because"*: *Sporting News*, August 20, 1977.

183 *In Munson's 1978*: Thurman Munson and Marty Appel, *Thurman Munson: An Autobiography* (New York: Coward, McCann & Geoghegan, 1979).

183 *"For a while it"*: Larry Keith, "He's a Dish Only Behind the Plate," *Sports Illustrated*, September 13, 1976.

183 *Gene Michael, who roomed*: Mike Vaccaro, *Emperors and Idiots*.

184 *As Winston Churchill wrote*: Winston Churchill, *A History of the English Speaking Peoples, vol. 1: The Birth of Britain* (London: Cassell, 1956).

184 *"Listen, Fisk, I"*: Marty Appel, *Munson: The Life and Death of a Yankee Captain*.

184 *"We don't send each"*: "American Leagues' Top Catchers: Thurman Munson vs. Carlton Fisk: It's an Old Rivalry," Newsday Services, July 27, 1977.

184 *"He's not one"*: Ibid.

184 *"He would have had"*: Ibid.

185 *"He wore the Yankee"*: "Yankees vs. Red Sox Forum" video, www.theforumchannel
.tv, February 2005.

186 *"We never had dinner"*: George Vecsey, "Fisk Returns; Bosox Win," *New York Times*, May 14, 1980.

186 *"I'm not going"*: Milton Richman, "Sports Parade," UPI in *Bryan Times* (Bryan, OH), September 20, 1977.

186 *"People always said"*: "Fisk Mourns Munson Loss," AP in *Kentucky New Era* (Hopkinsville, KY), August 3, 1979.

187 *Linda Fisk sent*: Marty Appel, *Munson: The Life and Death of a Yankee Captain*.

187 *"Thurman was a part"*: Larry Pantages, "Boston's Fisk Misses Rivalry with Munson," *Akron Beacon Journal*, September 14, 1980.

187 *"I want to stay"*: George Vecsey, "Fisk Returns; Bosox Win," *New York Times*, May 14, 1980.

188 *"His contract may"*: Peter Gammons, "Fisk Takes Risk and Wins," *Sporting News*, June 14, 1980.

189 *"Somebody's got to"*: Ibid.

189 *"I don't know"*: Ibid.

12: Two Days Late

192 *"We have to maintain"*: Peter Gammons, "No Other Teams Showing Interest," *Boston Globe*, February 13, 1981.

193 *"as cut and dried"*: Peter Gammons, "Red Sox 'Looked Other Way' on Lynn and Fisk in 1978," *Sporting News*, January 24, 1981.

194 *"Is It Greed"*: Peter Gammons, "Is it Greed . . . or Poor Management," *Boston Globe*, February 1, 1981.

194 *"Carlton Fisk is one"*: Peter Gammons, "Goodbye, Carlton? His Loss Would Really Hit Home," *Boston Globe*, February 7, 1981.

195 *"almost the laughing stock"*: "Hawk Blasts Sullivan," *Boston Globe*, February 7, 1981.

195 *"We do want"*: "Fisk, Sox Awaiting Decision Next Week," *Boston Globe*, February 3, 1981.

195 *"The feelings [have gotten]"*: "Bosox on Verge of Losing Fisk," AP in *Reading Eagle*, January 26, 1981.

195 *Will McDonough reported*: Will McDonough, "Fisk Can't Forget Sullivan's Remark," *Boston Globe*, February 5, 1981.

195 *It became official*: Roger Abrams, *Legal Bases: Baseball and the Law* (Philadelphia: Temple University Press, 1998).

196 *Marvin Miller told*: Peter Gammons, "Fisk Is Free—And Sox to Make Bid," *Boston Globe*, February 13, 1981.

196 *Sullivan had said*: Ibid.

197 *"I just found out"*: Ibid.

197 *"Reopen the bar"*: Peter Gammons, *Beyond the Sixth Game*.

197 *"His physical condition"*: Peter Gammons, "No Other Teams Showing Interest," *Boston Globe*, February 13, 1981.

197 *"Sullivan has answers"*: Leigh Montville, "The Team Fades into History," *Boston Globe*, February 13, 1981.

197 *"happy with the decision"*: Peter Gammons, "No Other Teams Showing Interest," *Boston Globe*, February 13, 1981.

197 *"In one off-season"*: Ray Fitzgerald, "Bosox to Fisk: Thanks for Memories," *Sporting News*, April 4, 1981.

197 *"The insanity has"*: Steve Wulf, "What—Me Worry?," *Sports Illustrated*, May 11, 1981.

198 *"The Fisk episode"*: Peter Gammons, "Sharp as Ever," *Sports Illustrated*, February 26, 1990.

198 *"Never once did"*: "The Trouble with Baseball," *Frontline*, Public Broadcasting Service, April 6, 1993.

198 *"It broke my heart"*: Phil Rogers, "Fisk's Body of Work," *Chicago Tribune*, July 21, 2000.

199 *"When I look back"*: Herb Crehan, *Red Sox Heroes of Yesteryear*.

13: Chicago: The Dawn of a New Era

201 *When Carlton Fisk*: "Carlton Fisk Changing the Color of His Sox," AP in *Palm Beach Post*, March 10, 1981.

201 *"I was not"*: "Fisk Raps Bosox Brass," UPI in *The Telegraph* (Alton, IL), March 20, 1981.

202 *"Loyalty is a two-way"*: Ibid.

202 *"That was very"*: Nick Carfardo, "Fisk Airs His Message: No Hard Feelings Boston," *Boston Globe*, June 24, 1993.

204 *"skulking real estate mogul"*: "Chicago White Sox, with New Owners, Prepare for New Season," The Classic Sports. Uploaded on YouTube September 16, 2010.

205 *"You're young"*: Buzz Bissinger, *Three Nights in August: Strategy, Heartbreak, and Joy Inside the Mind of a Manager* (Boston: Houghton Mifflin, 2005).

205 *"We couldn't believe"*: Phil Rogers, "Fisk's Body of Work," *Chicago Tribune*, July 21, 2000.

205 *"That was a key"*: *Winning Ugly: Twenty Years Later*, video produced by Jeff Einhorn, 2004.

205 *"The signing of"*: Ibid.

207 *"The first few times"*: Jeff Lenihan, "Carlton Fisk: He's a Durable Wonder Behind the Plate," *Baseball Digest*, December 1990.

207 *Soon after signing*: "Fisk Raps Bosox Brass," UPI in *The Telegraph* (Alton, IL), March 20, 1981.

207 *"As of today"*: "New Look White Sox Purchase Luzinski," AP in *Ocala Star-Banner*, March 31, 1981.

207 *"It seemed like"*: Mark Liptak, "La Russa 1979 Promotion to Sox Manager a Surprise to Future Hall of Famer," www.chicagobaseballmuseum.com, February 17, 2014.

209 *"We ran the"*: "1981 04 10 White Sox at Red Sox," WGN-TV broadcast, April 10, 1981. Classic MLB on youtube.com, uploaded December 14, 2013.

210 *"What's the big"*: Will McDonough, "Carlton Fisk Bashes Red Sox in His Return," *Boston Globe*, April 11, 1981.

210 *"You always fantasize"*: "White Sox' Facelift Paying Dividends," *Sporting News*, May 16, 1981.

210 *"If some are"*: Will McDonough, "Carlton Fisk Bashes Red Sox in His Return," *Boston Globe*, April 11, 1981.

210 *"I felt like waving"*: Peter Gammons, *Beyond the Sixth Game.*

211 *"It takes a while"*: "White Sox' Facelift Paying Dividends," *Sporting News*, May 16, 1981.

213 *"When I don't have"*: *Sporting News*, October 17, 1981.

214 *"We wanted to"*: Peter Gammons, "Sharp as Ever," *Sports Illustrated*, February 26, 1990.

215 *"If you didn't"*: Ron Kittle with Bob Logan, *Ron Kittle's Tales from the White Sox Dugout* (Champaign, IL: Sports Publishing, 2005).

217 *"It has been inconceivable"*: "Fisk Defends His Boss with Word and Action," UPI in *Deseret News* (Salt Lake City, UT), July 31, 1982.

14: Winning Ugly

223 *"If a manager"*: Bob Logan, *Miracle on 35th Street: Winnin' Ugly with the 1983 White Sox.*

224 *"Carlton was struggling"*: Mark Liptak, "La Russa 1979 Promotion to Sox Manager a Surprise to Future Hall of Famer," www.chicagobaseballmuseum.com, February 17, 2014.

224 *"I couldn't believe"*: Bob Logan, *Miracle on 35th street.*

225 *"I went to the"*: Ibid.

227 *"We had the right"*: Ron Kittle with Bob Logan, *Ron Kittle's Tales from the White Sox Dugout.*

228 *"We'd be rolling"*: Ibid.

229 *"I had more fun"*: Mark Liptak, "Jerry Koosman interview," whitesoxinteractive .com.

229 *"I don't think"*: Ron Kittle with Bob Logan, *Ron Kittle's Tales from the White Sox Dugout.*

229 *"They're winning ugly"*: Ibid.

230 *"Every time we"*: Mark Liptak, "Tom Paciorek Interview," whitesoxinteractive .com.

231 *"[It was a sense of] joy:"* *Winning Ugly: Twenty Years Later,* video produced by Jeff Einhorn, 2004.

231 *"I think"*: Ibid.

231 *"I've lived"*: Ibid.

231 *"They wrote"*: Ibid.

231 *"You're the MVP"*: Bob Logan, *Miracle on 35th Street.*

232 *"We'll be back"*: Ibid.

233 *"He just did"*: Ibid.

233 *Earlier in the season:* Ron Kittle with Bob Logan, *Ron Kittle's Tales from the White Sox Dugout.*

234 *"I'm here to tell you"*: Frank DeFord, "Knocking Their Sox Off," *Sports Illustrated,* October 17, 1983.

234 *"hit Ripken on purpose"*: Ibid.

234 *"worked up"*: Ibid.

234 *"That was the toughest"*: Ibid.

235 *"One of the colossal"*: Bob Logan, *Miracle on 35th Street.*

236 *"I'm not going"*: Ibid.

15: Pumping Iron

240 *"I knew that"*: Ross Newhan, "Carlton Fisk Has Nothing to Hide: After Suffering a Dismal Summer of '84, the 37-Year-Old White Sox Catcher Is Having a Delightful '85 and Thinks His Best Years May Still Be Ahead of Him," *Los Angeles Times,* September 23, 1985.

241 *"just about everything"*: Ibid.

242 *"We had some take-no-prisoners"*: Carlton Fisk Hall of Fame Induction speech, July 23, 2000.

243 *"I accept Carlton"*: Ross Newhan, "Carlton Fisk Has Nothing to Hide: After Suffering a Dismal Summer of '84, the 37-Year-Old White Sox Catcher Is Having a Delightful '85 and Thinks His Best Years May Still Be Ahead of Him," *Los Angeles Times,* September 23, 1985.

243 *"I'm going to make"*: *Sporting News,* July 23, 1990.

244 *"He taught me"*: Pat Jordan, "Conversations with the Dinosaur," *Men's Journal,* 1993.

244 *"Tom, you don't"*: Pat Jordan, "The Constant Gardener," *Sports on Earth,* December 12, 2013.

244 *"When they used to"*: Pat Jordan, "Conversations with the Dinosaur," *Men's Journal,* 1993.

244 *"We haven't been"*: Phil Pepe, "Behind Every Great Pitcher Is a Great Pitcher," New York *Daily News,* August 4, 1985.

245 *"Tom, don't even"*: John Feinstein, *Play Ball: The Life and Troubled Times of Major League Baseball.*

245 *"Duncan said, 'It's' "*: "Tom Seaver Notches Win No. 300," AP in *Lewiston Daily Sun,* August 5, 1985.

246 *"I'd been living"*: "Fisk Sets His Goal: Five More Seasons," *Sporting News*, March 26, 1984.

246 *"Who deserves to be"*: Debbi Wrobleski, "Fisk's Presence Still Felt in New England," *The Telegraph* (Alton, IL), August 9, 1985.

246 *"In a lot of ways"*: Ross Newhan, "Carlton Fisk Has Nothing to Hide: After Suffering a Dismal Summer of '84, the 37-Year-Old White Sox Catcher Is Having a Delightful '85 and Thinks His Best Years May Still Be Ahead of Him," *Los Angeles Times*, September 23, 1985.

247 *"I have to think"*: Ibid.

247 *"solicited testimony from"*: Joe Goddard, "Harrelson Handed Front Office Keys," *Sporting News*, October 14, 1985.

249 *"My family is happy"*: Late Deadline Helps Fisk Get Whale of Deal," AP in *Boca Raton News*, January 10, 1986.

249 *"We're delighted we"*: "Baseball Teams 'Beat the Clock,'" AP in *The Dispatch* (Lexington, NC), January 9, 1986.

249 *"Can you play"*: Peter Gammons, "Sharp as Ever," *Sports Illustrated*, February 26, 1990.

250 *"I feel uncomfortable"*: Mike Kiley, "Pudge Won't Budge," *Chicago Tribune*, January 10, 1986.

250 *"You don't put"*: Al Hamnick, "Dinosaur Roars at Hot Dogs," Knight Ridder in *Spokesman-Review* (Spokane, WA), August 17, 1990.

250 *"It's the New Englander"*: Peter Gammons, "Sharp as Ever," *Sports Illustrated*, February 26, 1990.

250 *"was like having"*: *Sporting News*, July 31, 1989.

250 *"I hope Joel"*: Mike Kiley, "Pudge Won't Budge," *Chicago Tribune*, January 10, 1986.

250 *"You're ruining my"*: Peter Gammons, "Baseball," *Sports Illustrated*, April 14, 1986.

251 *"I feel like"*: *Sporting News*, May 5, 1986.

251 *"I get a little"*: Bob Verdi, "Fisk's Just Glad to Be Back Home," *Chicago Tribune*, May 23, 1986.

16: Colluded Waters

254 *"Karkovice even makes"*: Craig Ewing, "World Traveler Eager to Be Major Hit Orlando's Karkovice Out to Make Chicago Return Address," *Orlando Sentinel*, March 23, 1988.

255 *"Let's face it"*: "They Said It," *Sports Illustrated*, July 27, 1987.

255 *"I wish I'd"*: *Sporting News*, August 3, 1987.

256 *"The utilization or"*: Roger Abrams, *Legal Bases: Baseball and the Law*.

256 *"If I sat each"*: Jerome Holtzman, *The Commissioners: Baseball's Midlife Crisis* (New York: Total Sports, 1998).

256 *"It's not smart"*: John Helyar, *Lords of the Realm: The Real History of Baseball* (New York: Villard, 1994).

257 *"Only Fisk got"*: Jerome Holtzman, *The Commissioners: Baseball's Midlife Crisis.*

259 *"When you play"*: Ronald Schachter, "Fisk Still Prefers Catching," *Christian Science Monitor* in *Lewiston Daily Sun*, August 4, 1988.

259 *"The commitment to being"*: Peter Gammons, "Sharp as Ever," *Sports Illustrated,* February 26, 1990.

259 *"You can't measure what he"*: Dave Van Dyck, "Receiver with Believers," *Sporting News*, June 19, 1989.

261 *"followed every order"*: Dave Nightingale, "The Prince of Pathos," *Sporting News,* May 17, 1993.

262 *"It isn't just"*: Peter Gammons, "Sharp as Ever," *Sports Illustrated*, February 26, 1990.

262 *"They [White Sox] wanted to"*: Bob Logan, *Miracle on 35th Street.*

17: Respect the Game

264 *"I'm only using it"*: Pat Jordan, "The Two Faces of Prime Time," *Special Reports*, 1989.

264 *"Prime Time wakes up"*: Ibid.

265 *"This guy is"*: *Joe Morgan Show*, August 26, 2011; John Kass, "When it Comes to Heart, Truth Hurts Sanders," *Chicago Tribune*, January 30, 2011.

265 *"we just said"*: "Yanks Win After Heated Exchange," AP in *Spokesman-Review* (Spokane, WA), May 23, 1990.

266 *"There's a right way"*: Joe Donnelly, "Fisk's Outburst at Sanders Was One for Yankee Pride," *Los Angeles Times*, May 24, 1990.

266 *"I don't care whether"*: *Joe Morgan Show*, August 26, 2011.

266 *"I'll tell you what"*: Alan Solomon, "Fisk Berates Deion's Play," *Chicago Tribune,* May 24, 1990.

266 *"Me! Me! Me!"*: Pat Jordan, "Conversations with the Dinosaur," *Men's Journal,* 1993.

266 *"It happened because"*: Al Hamnick, "Dinosaur Roars at Hot Dogs," Knight Ridder in *Spokesman-Review* (Spokane, WA), August 17, 1990.

267 *"The most storied"*: "Yankees vs. Red Sox Forum" video, www.theforumchannel .tv, February 2005.

267 *"reflecting on the"*: Ron Rapoport, "Fisk Tells Sanders to Show Respect," *Los Angeles Daily News*, May 27, 1990.

267 *"caretaker of the game's"*: Jeff Lenihan, "Carlton Fisk: He's a Durable Wonder Behind the Plate," *Baseball Digest*, December 1990.

267 *"Renegotiation doesn't show"*: "Low-Paid Fisk Decries Crybabies," AP in *Spokesman-Review* (Spokane, WA), March 5, 1991.

268 *"What I really believe"*: Dave Nightingale, "Boone and Fisk: They Were Built to Last," *Sporting News*, May 22, 1989.

268 *"A lot of young"*: *Sporting News*, March 16, 1992.

268 *"The commitment to being"*: Art Spander, "Fisk's Fondest Wish: 'Extra 10 Years to Play,'" *Sporting News*, September 3, 1990.

268 *"I never knew"*: Dave Nightingale, "The Prince of Pathos," *Sporting News*, May 17, 1993.

269 *"No one else"*: Phil Rogers, "Fisk's Body of Work," *Chicago Tribune*, July 21, 2000.

269 *"It was a badge"*: Pat Jordan, "Conversations with the Dinosaur," *Men's Journal*, 1993.

269 *"After the game"*: Peter Gammons, "Inside Baseball," *Sports Illustrated*, July 3, 1989.

270 *"Just being around"*: Jeff Lenihan, "Carlton Fisk: He's a Durable Wonder Behind the Plate," *Baseball Digest*, December 1990.

271 *After the game*: Alan Solomon, "Sox' Bench 'Jocks' Can't Forget Stewart," *Chicago Tribune*, June 26, 1990.

272 *"I don't care"*: Ibid.

18: Escorted Out

273 *"Pudge has two options"*: *Sporting News*, November 18, 1991.

274 *"The White Sox are"*: Letter, *Chicago Tribune*, November 20, 1991.

276 *"cheapskate"*: Joel Stein, "The One and Only," *Time*, June 22, 1998.

276 *"one of the hardest"*: "Hoop Dreams," *Newsweek*, March 20, 1995.

276 *"Jerry was playing"*: Dave Nightingale, "The Prince of Pathos," *Sporting News*, May 17, 1993.

276 *"Reinsdorf's claim that"*: Martin Lolich, "Comiskey's Draw," *Chicago Tribune*, November 20, 1991.

276 *"If I had been"*: Dave Nightingale, "The Prince of Pathos," *Sporting News*, May 17, 1993.

277 *"I have always believed"*: John Brockmann, "Fisk Endures Through Good and Bad," *Sarasota Herald-Tribune*, March 31, 1989.

278 *"I'm afraid to"*: Pat Jordan, "Conversations with the Dinosaur," *Men's Journal*, 1993.

278 *"I'd like to quit"*: Ibid.

278 *"It's strictly a procedural"*: Jerome Holtzman, "Fisk a Former White Sox—For Time Being," *Chicago Tribune*, December 19, 1992.

278 *Reinsdorf had publicly called*: *Sporting News*, March 15, 1993.

279 *"You can say this"*: Leigh Montville, "Bitter Ending," *Sports Illustrated*, May 31, 1993.

279 *He told reporters*: Dave Nightingale, "The Prince of Pathos," *Sporting News*, May 17, 1993.

279 *In April 1993*: "The Trouble with Baseball," *Frontline*, Public Broadcasting Service, April 6, 1993.

280 *"It has nothing to do"*: Dave Nightingale, "The Prince of Pathos," *Sporting News*, May 17, 1993.

281 *"I was stretching"*: Leigh Montville, "Bitter Ending," *Sports Illustrated*, May 31, 1993.

282 *"He's still giving"*: Mike DiGiovanna, "Fisk Finds Twilight Is Chilly: As Catcher, 45, Nears End of Career, Acrimony Taints Relation with White Sox," *Los Angeles Times*, June 22, 1993.

282   *"I remember fun"*: Dave Nightingale, "The Prince of Pathos," *Sporting News*, May 17, 1993.

283   *"I have a lot"*: Ibid.

283–284 *"I've given my loyalty"* ... *"The whole situation"*: Leigh Montville, "Bitter Ending," *Sports Illustrated*, May 31, 1993.

284   *"They've tried to"*: Mike DiGiovanna, "Fisk Finds Twilight Is Chilly: As Catcher, 45, Nears End of Career, Acrimony Taints Relation with White Sox," *Los Angeles Times*, June 22, 1993.

284   *"There's definitely something"*: Leigh Montville, "Bitter Ending," *Sports Illustrated*, May 31, 1993.

284   *"He must have been"*: Mark Liptak, Donn Pall interview, whitesoxinteractive.com.

285   *"It's a shame"*: Mike DiGiovanna, "Fisk Finds Twilight Is Chilly: As Catcher, 45, Nears End of Career, Acrimony Taints Relation with White Sox," *Los Angeles Times*, June 22, 1993.

285   *"I always thought"*: AU: TK

286   *the White Sox held*: "Carlton Fisk Addresses Crowd at 1993 Tribute," June 22, 1993, YouTube, uploaded by the Classic Sports, accessed June 8, 2014.

287   *"It doesn't happen"*: Joe Mooshil, "Chicago's Fisk Catches 2,226th Game," AP in *Gadsden Times*, June 23, 1993.

287   *"It all started"*: Nick Cafardo, "Fisk Airs His Message: No Hard Feelings Boston," *Boston Globe*, June 24, 1993.

288   *"He thought I"*: Joey Reaves, "It's All Over, but Fisk Didn't Expect It," *Chicago Tribune*, June 29, 1993.

288   *Schueler stated that*: "White Sox Release Fisk," AP in *Toledo Blade*, June 29, 1993.

288   *"I know a bunch"*: Ibid.

289   *"Absolutely not"*: Joey Reaves, "It's All Over, but Fisk Didn't Expect It," *Chicago Tribune*, June 29, 1993.

289   *"It is not fair"*: "White Sox Release Fisk," AP in *Toledo Blade*, June 29, 1993.

289   *"I agreed with"*: Joey Reaves, "It's All Over, but Fisk Didn't Expect It," *Chicago Tribune*, June 29, 1993.

289   *"I'm upset about"*: Ibid.

289   *"When you make too"*: "White Sox Release Fisk," AP in *Toledo Blade*, June 29, 1993.

289   *"All I know"*: "Trouble in Chicago," AP in *The Day* (New London, CT), July 4, 1993.

290   *"I'll miss the clubhouse"*: Paul Ladewski, "Carlton Fisk, Inside Interview," *Inside Sports*, August 1992.

290   *"I miss being"*: Carlton Fisk Hall of Fame Induction speech, July 23, 2000.

290   *"He does not want"*: Joey Reaves, "Fisk Waits, Wonders at Home," *Chicago Tribune*, June 30, 1993.

291 *"He had no tickets"*: "Caught on the fly" *Sporting News*, October 18, 1993.

291 *"I even called the clubhouse"*: Bob Verdi, "Pudge Just Needs a Nudge," *Chicago Tribune*, February 1, 1997.

291 *"I was shocked"*: "Peace Reigns as Fisk, White Sox Play Catchup" AP in *Spokesman-Review* (Spokane, WA), September 15, 1997.

19: Living Without the Game

293 *"He's doing great"*: Joey Reaves and Alan Solomon, "In the Final Excruciating Months of His Career, Almost . . ." *Chicago Tribune*, October 3, 1993.

293 *"The little death"*: John Updike, "Kid Bids Hub Fans Adieu," in *Assorted Prose* (New York: Alfred A. Knopf, 1965).

293 *"I think because"*: Peter Gammons, "Sharp as Ever," *Sports Illustrated*, February 26, 1990.

293 *"To have a wife"*: Paul Ladewski, "Carlton Fisk, Inside Interview," *Inside Sports*, August 1992.

294 *"When he was"*: *Red Sox Report: The Carlton Fisk Story*, video by Red Sox Productions, www.redsox.com, May 8, 2014.

294 *"I had to give"*: Pat Jordan, "Conversations with the Dinosaur," *Men's Journal*, 1993.

294 *"I will never forgive"*: Bill Vogrin, "After 22 Springs Apart, Baseball Brings Carlton Fisk and Son Together," Associated Press, April 23, 1994.

294 *"When I was a"*: Gary Reinmuth, "She's Following in Dad's Footsteps," *Chicago Tribune*, October 27, 1991.

294 *"Courtney is the only"*: Phil Rogers, "Fisk Rides Emotional Wave," *Chicago Tribune*, July 24, 2000.

294 *"The special moments now"*: Steven Rosenbloom, "Carlton Fisk," *Chicago Tribune*, July 21, 2004.

295 *"In the past"*: Bill Vogrin, "After 22 Springs Apart, Baseball Brings Carlton Fisk and Son Together," Associated Press, April 23, 1994.

295 *"I see Casey"*: Ibid.

295 *"I was in awe"*: Ibid.

295 *"I've tried to"*: Ibid.

296 *"I recently got"*: Bob Verdi, "Pudge Just Needs a Nudge," *Chicago Tribune*, February 1, 1997.

296 *"Names aren't important"*: Ibid.

296 *"It felt good"*: Ibid.

297 *"Carlton Fisk certainly"*: "White Sox to Honor Fisk," AP in *Today's News-Herald* (Lake Havasu, AZ), August 15, 1997.

297 *"All fairy tales"*: "Peace Reigns as Fisk, White Sox Play Catchup," AP in *Spokesman-Review* (Spokane, WA), September 15, 1997.

298 *"Carlton Fisk may tell"*: Jimmy Golen, "Red Sox Retire Fisk's Number 27," AP in *Gadsden* (Alabama) *Times*, September 5, 2000.

299 *"I don't know if"*: "Carlton Fisk, Hall of Famer," AP in *Cape Cod Times* (Hyannis, MA), January 25, 2000.

299 *"It would have to"*: "Sharp as Ever," Peter Gammons, *Sports Illustrated*, February 26, 1990.

299 *"I would like"*: *Chicago Tribune*, January 15, 2000.

299 *"The strained relationship"*: Phil Rogers, "Scars Lone Smudge for Pudge," *Chicago Tribune*, January 12, 2000.

301 *"That's as good"*: Fay Vincent, *It's What's Inside the Lines That Counts* (New York: Simon & Schuster, 2010).

302 *"I think he's totally"*: Ron Kroichick, "Fired-Up Fisk Tees Off on Absent Gonzalez," *San Francisco Chronicle*, July 13, 1999.

302 *"I worked hard"*: Fred Mitchell, "Carlton Fisk Blasts Mark McGwire," *Chicago Tribune*, January 20, 2010.

303 *"It has been really"*: Fred Mitchell, "Fisk Awaits Reinsdorf's Call," *Chicago Tribune*, June 26, 2005.

303 *"If I hadn't been"*: Ibid.

303 *"This is the most"*: Bill Jauss, "Statuesque—On, Off Field," *Chicago Tribune*, August 8, 2005.

20: Orchids

306 *"My pride and"*: Peter Gammons, "Sharp as Ever," *Sports Illustrated*, February 26, 1990.

309 *"It was unreal"*: Vin Sylvia, "From Celtics Dreams, to Red Sox Reality," *New Hampshire Sunday News*, July 23, 2000.

312 *"People think that's"*: Steven Rosenbloom, "Carlton Fisk," *Chicago Tribune*, July 21, 2004.

312 *How many times:* Dan Shaughnessy, *Boston Globe,* June 29, 1993.

312 *In a key scene:* Good Will Hunting, directed by Gus Van Sant, Miramax Films, 1997.

313 *"A generation later"*: "Special Collector's Edition," *TV Guide,* July 11–17, 1998.

313 *"It had such"*: Mark Newman, "Network Anoints '75 Series Epic as Top Game," MLB.com, May 19, 2011.

313 *"I leave the room"*: Tom Verducci, "The Passion of Roger Angell," *Sports Illustrated*, July 21, 2014.

313 *"It's not very"*: Ronald Schachter, "Fisk Still Prefers Catching," *Christian Science Monitor* in *Lewiston Daily Sun,* August 4, 1988.

314 *"[It was an] unbelievable"*: "The Fisk Home Run," MLB.com video, January 10, 2011.

314 *"Who is that"*: Anthony Gulizia, "Carlton Fisk Never Grows Tired of Watching His Game 6 Moment," *Boston Globe,* October 31, 2013.

Bibliography

Abrams, Roger. *Legal Bases: Baseball and the Law*. Philadelphia: Temple University Press, 1998.

Appel, Marty. *Munson: The Life and Death of a Yankee Captain*. New York: Doubleday, 2009.

Bissinger, Buzz. *Three Nights in August: Strategy, Heartbreak, and Joy Inside the Mind of a Manager*. Boston: Houghton Mifflin, 2005.

Bouton, Jim. *Ball Four*. New York: World, 1970.

Bradley, Richard. *The Greatest Game: The Yankees, the Red Sox and the Playoff of '78*. New York: Free Press, 2008.

Crehan, Herb. *Red Sox Heroes of Yesteryear*. Boston: Rounder Books, 2005.

Epstein, Dan. *Stars and Strikes: Baseball and America in the Bicentennial Summer of '76*. New York: St. Martin's, 2014.

Feinstein, John. *Play Ball: The Life and Troubled Times of Major League Baseball*. New York: Villard, 1993.

Frost, Mark. *Game Six*. New York: Hyperion, 2009.

Gammons, Peter. *Beyond the Sixth Game*. Boston: Houghton Mifflin, 1985.

Golenbock, Peter. *Fenway: An Unexpurgated History of the Boston Red Sox*. New York: Putnam, 1992.

Gutlon, Jerry. *It Was Never About the Babe*. New York: Skyhorse, 2009.

Helyar, John. *Lords of the Realm: The Real History of Baseball*. New York: Villard, 1994.

Hollander, Zander, and Phyllis Hollander, eds. *The Masked Marvels: Baseball's Great Catchers*. New York: Random House, 1982.

Holtzman, Jerome. *The Commissioners: Baseball's Midlife Crisis*. New York: Total Sports, 1998.

Jordan, Pat. *The Best Sports Writing of Pat Jordan*. New York: Persea, 2008.

Kittle, Ron, with Bob Logan. *Ron Kittle's Tales from the White Sox Dugout*. Champaign, IL: Sports Publishing, 2005.

La Russa, Tony, with Rick Hummel. *One Last Strike*. New York: William Morrow, 2012.

Lee, Bill, and Dick Lally. *The Wrong Stuff*. New York: Viking, 1984.

Logan, Bob. *Miracle on 35th Street: Winnin' Ugly with the 1983 White Sox.*

Munson, Thurman, and Marty Appel. *Thurman Munson: An Autobiography.* New York: Coward, McCann & Geoghegan, 1979.

National Baseball Hall of Fame and Museum. *The Hall: A Celebration of Baseball's Greats.* Hachette Digital, 2014.

Neyer, Rob. *Rob Neyer's Big Book of Baseball Blunders.* New York: Fireside, 2006.

———. *Rob Neyer's Big Book of Baseball Legends.* New York: Simon & Schuster, 2008.

Pepe, Phil. *Talkin' Baseball: An Oral History of Baseball in the 1970s.* New York: Ballantine, 1998.

Robbins, Mike, ed. *The Yankees vs. Red Sox Reader.* New York: Carroll & Graf, 2005.

SABR. The Impossible Dream

Sands, Jack, and Peter Gammons. *Coming Apart at the Seams: How Baseball Owners, Players and Television Executives Have Led Our National Pastime to the Brink of Disaster.* New York: Macmillan, 1993.

Shaughnessy, Dan. *The Curse of the Bambino.* New York: Dutton, 1990.

Shropshire, Mike. *The Last Real Season.* New York: Grand Central, 2008.

Simon, Tom. *The Green Mountain Boys of Summer: Vermonters in the Major Leagues, 1882–1993.* Shelburne, VT: New England Press, 2000.

Tiant, Luis, and Joe Fitzgerald. *El Tiante: The Luis Tiant Story.* New York: Doubleday, 1976.

Vaccaro, Mike. *Emperors and Idiots.* New York: Doubleday, 2005.

Vincent, Fay. *It's What's Inside the Lines That Counts.* New York: Simon & Schuster, 2010.

Yastrzemski, Carl, with Gerald Eskanazi. *Yaz: Baseball, the Wall, and Me.* New York: Doubleday, 1990.

Index